DIVERSITY

The Invention
of a Concept

PETER WOOD

Encounter Books
San Francisco, California

First edition published in 2003 by Encounter Books, an activity of Encounter for Culture and Education, Inc., a nonprofit tax exempt corporation.

Encounter Books website address: www.encounterbooks.com

Manufactured in the United States and printed on acid-free paper.

The paper used in this publication meets the minimum requirements of ANSI/NISO Z39.48-1992 (R 1997)(*Permanence of Paper*).

Library of Congress Cataloging-in-Publication Data

Wood, Peter.
   Diversity : the invention of a concept / Peter Wood.
     p. cm.
   Includes bibliographical references and index.
   ISBN 1-893554-62-7 (alk. paper)
   1. Pluralism (Social sciences)—United States.   2. Multiculturalism—United States.   3. United States—Ethnic relations.   4. United States—Race relations.   5. Minorities—United States.   6. Group identity—United States.   I. Title.

E184.A1 W715 2002
305.8'00973—dc21

2002029992

10 9 8 7 6 5 4 3 2 1

In memory of my parents,

Isabel R. Wood, 1919–1996
and
Walter P. Wood, 1915–1997

CONTENTS

ILLUSTRATIONS

PREFACE

Diversity is a large idea in the way that Wyoming is a large state: it is a big part of everyone's map of America, but there is not much there.

Of course, on closer inspection the comparison falters. Wyoming has Casper, Rock Springs, Thunder Basin National Grassland, Cheyenne, I-80, Bighorn National Forest, Devils Tower, lots of fossils and, its crowning glory, Yellowstone National Park. Diversity has . . . well, what does diversity have? Mainly, diversity has lots of admirers.

If an idea can be said to be important simply because of the number of people who uphold it, diversity is indeed an important idea; many millions of Americans regard it so. They are, I think, mistaken. In this book I argue that it is time to retire diversity from the small company of concepts that guide our thinking about who we are as a people and how we might best reconcile our differences.

I do not mean to diminish the idea of diversity unduly. It has genuine imaginative appeal, and the millions who extol it are not merely deluded. Rather, they are moved by its promise of providing a way of looking at the world anew and a way of escaping tired old prejudices. Diversity bids us to be tolerant, open-minded, helpful and fair; and many respond to this call in good faith. But diversity offers doubtful directions to these worthy destinations.

The concept of diversity in its contemporary social and political sense is fairly new. It was admitted to the union, so to speak, by one man, Justice Lewis Powell, in June 1978, in his stand-alone opinion in the Supreme Court case *Regents of the University of California v. Bakke*. In that case, Justice Powell asserted that the goal of "attaining a diverse

1

student body" provided a "constitutionally permissible" reason to allow racial preferences in admissions to a medical school. In Powell's view, the goal of achieving diversity overrode the Fourteenth Amendment's guarantee of equal protection under the law.

The discontents and longings that diversity gives voice to, however, are older, and the story continues long past Powell's eccentric legal whim. Diversity as we know it has been shaped by an odd history of opportunism, idealism, miscalculation, shrewd maneuver, deception, self-deception, truth-telling and deceit. To present this story in an entirely straightforward way would be, in some ways, to falsify it. Diversity entered our lives more by half-recognized allusions, pinpricks of implication and evocative symbols than by a clear sequence of events. I have written its biography accordingly, and its intellectual geography as well.

Wyoming fits four-square into our map of the country, but if we merely speed across it on I-80 in a hurry to get to Utah, it is likely to remain to us essentially a blank—familiar in outline but not understood in its specificity. To see it rightly we must take its inner dimensions. Diversity too has its dry washes full of fossils, its eerie basalt towers of infernal design, and its azure depths of scalding springs.

In the pages ahead, I provide the reader with a geologist's crack hammer and a few other tools—rock pick, pry bar and chisel as needed—to get beneath the surface of diversity.

ONE

DIVERSITY IN AMERICA

Loose Threads

In his *Letter from Birmingham Jail*, April 16, 1963, Dr. Martin Luther King Jr. offered a striking image of human unity. He wrote:

> Injustice anywhere is a threat to justice everywhere. We are caught in an inescapable network of mutuality, tied in a *single garment of destiny.* Whatever affects one directly, affects all indirectly.

King had used the phrase "single garment of destiny" before, as early as a 1961 commencement speech at Lincoln University, and he would use it again in many more speeches and sermons. Sometimes he varied the surrounding language:

> We are caught in an inescapable network of mutuality, tied in a single garment of destiny. All life is interrelated.
> (Nobel Peace Prize lecture, Oslo, Norway, December 11, 1964)

> We are tied together—white and black Americans—in a single garment of destiny. There cannot be a separate black or white path to power.
> (Address at the University of Pittsburgh, November 2, 1966)

> You must recognize in the final analysis you are all tied together in a single garment of destiny, caught in an inescapable network of mutuality.
> (Sermon at Washington National Cathedral, Palm Sunday, 1968)

And sometimes he was oddly misquoted:

> You must recognize in the final analysis you are all tied together in a single *garnet* of destiny.
> (Quoted in *The Cathedral School*, January 18, 2002, supposedly transcribing the text of a sermon at St. John the Divine Cathedral, May 17, 1965; emphasis added)

> Quoting Martin Luther King Jr.—"We are woven into a seamless garment of destiny"—Clinton called for Americans to make the country "one America."
> (Report in CNN/Time on President Clinton's speech in Little Rock, Arkansas, commemorating the Little Rock Nine, September 25, 1977)

But King wore the garment of destiny so often in his speeches that there could be little doubt that it was to him among his most important turns of phrase.

I don't know where Dr. King originally found this metaphor with its biblical echoes (e.g. "for he has clothed me with the garments of salvation," Isaiah 62:10; Joseph's "coat of many colors," Genesis 37:3) or if he came to it first while composing his 1961 commencement speech. Perhaps King's deep interest in Gandhi, who had made much of boycotting British textiles and spinning his own cloth, is also woven into the image. In any case, by dint of repetition the "single garment of destiny" became a figure woven into King's own legacy. It is probably quoted in his honor in thousands of sermons and speeches each year.

The "single garment of destiny" in which we are all tied or bound is a slightly strange image. King's language ("network," "tied together") suggests that we are all part of the *fabric* of this garment, but the garment itself is vague. What is this unity of which we are all part? Society? Humanity? And who wears the garment?

Granted, we ought not to make too much of a metaphor, which serves its purpose if it lights up one good idea. And King's metaphor does that splendidly: he puts us in mind of the myriad connections that make us one people.

King's emphasis on our connectedness and underlying unity is self-evidently *opposed* to what we now call "diversity." This presents a problem for those who today would honor King's memory but discard most of his message. For proponents of *diversity*, King's "single garment of destiny" is a musty old wrap, but too well known simply to throw away. For some, the solution has been to reinterpret it by emphasizing the separateness of the threads rather than the forceful interweave.

This thread-finding has become an increasingly common conceit. In January 2002, Rohit Ananth, a seventh grader from Park Forest Middle School in central Pennsylvania, won a Martin Luther King Day essay contest on the theme "A Single Garment of Destiny." Young Mr. Ananth opined, "It is unrealistic to think that our country is like a perfectly woven garment. There are many loose threads." These loose threads, presumably, are the people not fully woven into the fabric of American life: individualists, outcasts, whole groups that go their separate ways, the excluded and the self-excluded.

But once we deny Dr. King's basic premise—that we are all part of "an inescapable network of mutuality"—the whole garment unravels. In fact, Americans in the last quarter-century have turned that unraveling into a new social ideal. This is what we call *diversity*, a word that I will italicize when it refers to the contemporary set of beliefs, as distinct from its older meanings. *Diversity* bids us to think of America not as a single garment, but as divided up into separate groups— on the basis of race, ethnicity or sex, for starters—some of which have historically enjoyed privileges that have been denied the others.

Diversity, though, is more than a propensity to dwell on the separate threads that make up the social fabric. It is above all a political doctrine asserting that *some* social categories deserve compensatory privileges in light of the prejudicial ways in which members of these categories have been treated in the past and the disadvantages they continue to face. *Diversity* sees itself as a tool for knocking down the door to exclusive enclaves—colleges, workplaces, churches, organizations of all sorts—of the favored groups. A university that admits more minority students, a company that hires more minority workers, and a museum that shows more works by minority artists can each be said to have taken the first step toward *diversity*.

Many more steps follow. *Diversity* is not merely a reformulation of the idea of equal access to social goods; it is also an attempt to redefine the goods themselves. The ideal of diversity is that once individuals of diverse backgrounds are brought together, a transformation will take place in people's attitudes—primarily within the members of the formerly exclusive group, who will discover the richness of the newcomers' cultural backgrounds. Diversity will breed tolerance and respect, and, because it increases the pool of skills, will enhance the effectiveness of work groups and contribute to economic prosperity. In the more extended flights of the diversiphile's imagination, *diversity* creates good will and social betterment in every direction. The African-American manager, the gay white secretary and the Latino consultant learn from each other's distinctive cultural experience and become better workers, better citizens, better persons.

Diversity in this cascade of meanings is deeply appealing to many Americans, but not all. Those who resist the dream of *diversity* see it instead as a rubric for racial and ethnic quotas in college admissions and on the job; for acts of petty and not so petty discrimination; and for a system of ethnic favoritism that undercuts the principle of rewarding demonstrated merit and ability. *Diversity,* to its critics, calls to mind cultural elites who promulgate convoluted reasons why discrimination is wrong, except when *they* do it.

Diversity is only a few decades old, but diversity (without the italics) is nothing new. Let us start with the older meaning. America was made up of diverse peoples even before the first Europeans (and soon after, the first Africans) arrived. People who thought seriously about the New World and about the North American colonies that became the United States were already thinking about diversity centuries ago. In his first letter back to Spain in January 1493, Christopher Columbus carefully described the people he encountered in the Caribbean, who he said were not "slow or stupid," and whom he hoped to "conciliate" to Christianity and the Spanish Crown. His hopes in this regard, as in so much else, were dashed by the rapacity of the Spanish conquerors, but Columbus's legacy is far more complex than either the old schoolroom story of simple "discovery" or its up-to-date replacement, a story of nothing but genocide.

Dr. Diego Alvarez Chanca, the physician who accompanied Columbus on his second voyage, has left us a letter in which he describes the joy of some Native Americans rescued by Columbus from their cannibalistic captors. Columbus had arrived in the New World to find not one people, but myriads of peoples, many in perpetual war with each other. One of his first tasks was to come to some practical understanding of this diversity of native peoples. That concern has echoed through hundreds of years of Spanish, French, English and Russian colonial relations with Native Americans and echoes still in the independent states that arose from European colonization.

The diversity *among* native peoples posed intellectual as well as practical problems that generations of historians, theologians, philosophers, linguists and eventually anthropologists wrestled with, as they also confronted the problem of the diversity *between* Europeans and Native Americans as a whole. As early as the 1550s, some Europeans were offering profound arguments in favor of an encompassing concept of our common humanity. At that time, Bartolomé de Las Casas, a Dominican priest, wrote his passionate and learned book *In Defense of the Indians* as a plea to the Catholic Church to intervene against the enslavement and brutalizing of Native Americans.

Diversity in this older sense of relations between culturally disparate groups is a major aspect of the history of all New World nations. Their patterns of resistance to and accommodation of cultural diversity differed, and the United States can be understood as a particular answer to the problems posed by cultural multiplicity. By the time of the American Revolution, we not only claimed but also *felt* a sense of unity as a people, but we also divided ourselves by region, state, race and religion. The many-ness, the diversity of America, was not somehow overlooked or invisible to the founders. They saw it clearly, took steps to keep it from overwhelming the unity they hoped would thrive, and persisted in worrying whether those steps would be sufficient.

Negro slavery loomed as perhaps their greatest worry, for as certain as many of the founders were that slavery was wrong, they also saw the difficulty of successfully assimilating African-Americans, who had been deprived of education, as free and equal citizens. Benjamin Franklin in the last few years of his life served as the president of the Pennsylvania Abolition Society, penning calls both for the end of slavery and for public assistance to "emancipated black people." Franklin's last public act at age eighty-three was to compose and sign a petition dated February 3, 1790, to the U.S. Congress citing its constitutional duty of "promoting the welfare and securing the blessings of liberty to the people of the United States" as grounds for abolishing the enslavement of "fellow-creatures of the African race."

The Constitution set up an unstable compromise on the issue, allowing slavery to stand in the states that permitted it and, for purposes of taxes and apportionment of seats in the House of Representatives, counting the population of the states as "the whole number of free persons, including those bound to service for a term of years, and excluding Indians not taxed, three-fifths of all other persons." The Constitutional Convention also set a date, 1808, when the federal government would be empowered to end the importation of slaves, which in fact it did. In December 1787, James Wilson, a Pennsylvania delegate to the Constitutional Convention, expressed the hope of many that this provision would lay "the foundation for banishing slavery out of this country."

The temporizing of the founders on slavery, however, is rightly understood as part of a larger history of diversity. They were engaged with a real question of how much real diversity a free nation could contain without pulling itself apart, and diversity in that sense has remained central to the definition of American society, through the early republic, the Civil War, emancipation, the great waves of immigration, and on up through the Civil Rights struggle and King's telling metaphor. Diversity—called appropriately by diverse names—has always been on our minds.

But diversity is not *diversity*. The new movement is something different, and in some ways a repudiation of the older attempts to find a oneness in our many-ness. *Diversity* in its new form tends to elevate many-ness for its own sake. But I do not aim in this book to oversimplify a complex social and cultural movement. The new *diversity* has its vision of unity too, and many separate threads of its own.

But let's not take just a thread-by-thread view. *Diversity* is big. It's everywhere. Schoolchildren are taught to celebrate it; high courts weigh and scrutinize it; corporate personnel offices assiduously seek it out; unions that once feared it now robustly champion it; artists offer searching introspections of diversity in their own lives; museums exhibit it; restaurants serve it; churches worship it; and tourists vacation in it. *Diversity* is enunciated in the dolls we buy for our children (the American Girl collection), the fashions teenagers buy for themselves (think of the "United Colors of Benetton" ads, featuring lots of contrasting flesh tones), and in the admissions brochures of the colleges and universities those teens hope to attend. *Diversity* plays its part in every electoral campaign for every candidate and in the sales pitches for a great many products. The pursuit of *diversity* is held to be both practically good and personally redemptive; and *diversity* is depicted in popular entertainment as both fun and—there is no better word for it—virtuous.

Marvelous Wonders

Now largely forgotten, Henry Davenport Northrop was a popular writer of the 1880s and 1890s who catered to the taste for the eye-opening spectacle of human variety. He was the IMAX theater of his day, with heavily illustrated books such as *Marvelous Wonders of the Whole World* (1886). But it would be difficult to find a writer less suited to the temper of *our* times. The title alone of his 1891 volume, *Indian Horrors or Massacres by the Red Men, Being a Thrilling Narrative of Bloody Wars with Merciless and Revengeful Savages . . .* , shows Northrop to be a man who dealt in sensationalized stereotypes, a stirrer-up of the fantasies that fuel discrimination and ethnic strife. Northrop represents a part of cultural history that most Americans today notice only with a shudder.

Yet Northrop may still have some important things to teach us. His world was one that abounded in surprises. Diversity for him was not the thin gruel of attempting to accentuate slight differences among people who, in every important respect, are similar. His diversity was rather a feast of differences, from his delight at watching native Hawaiians surf, to his mischievous pleasure in describing the African Wagogo as "great thieves and extortioners" whose enlarged earlobes "fall as low as the shoulders." Northrop's dislikes and enthusiasms were unfiltered; ours, by contrast, are timid and self-conscious. Respectful, eager to understand, fearful of offending, our basic stance toward human difference is that we must admire it.

Must we really?

Northrop is also surprisingly ahead of us in his sense of the ironic complexity of the exchanges between cultures. *Indian Horrors or Massacres by the Red Men* lives up to its ghastly title, but doesn't hesitate along the way to mention how the name of the great Delaware chief Tammany (actually *Tammanend*), who sold the site of Philadelphia to the English in 1682, became a Philadelphia May Day festival, and in time the Tammany societies and Tammany halls of American towns.

Northrop observes, "The old relic of Indian greatness has degenerated onto an organization for political purposes."

Interspersed with his account of raids and killings, Northrop quietly retells other stories of Indians cheated and betrayed. Some of the stories come with a history of retellings that make clear that Northrop is the heir not just to a tradition of anti-Indian lore, but also to a countertradition of recognizing the bonds of common humanity. He repeats Benjamin Franklin's recounting of a story that Franklin had received in turn from Conrad Weiser, about Cassanatego, an Onondaga Indian who shrewdly told him how the fur traders colluded to cheat the Indians, and more:

> If a white man, in traveling through our country, enters one of our wigwams, we all treat him as I do you—dry him if he is wet; warm him if he is cold; give him meat and drink that he may allay his thirst and hunger; and we spread soft furs for him to sleep on.
>
> But if I go into a white man's house in Albany and ask him for meat and drink, they say, "Get out, you Indian dog!"

In telling this story, the author—no matter what other tales he tells—has taken hold of a corner of Martin Luther King's "single garment of destiny."

Diversity As Counterprinciple

For Northrop, Indians were both victims and perpetrators of injustice. While I think we can still acknowledge this as a realistic assessment, the pieties of our age push us strongly toward seeing only the victimization. We remember General Custer's depredations on the Sioux culminating in his defeat at Little Big Horn in 1876, but not the Outbreak of 1862, in which the Sioux in Minnesota massacred some seven hundred innocents.

The new perspective of *diversity* is not just about emphasizing groups at the expense of the whole; it is also about treating groups as having saved up a right to special privileges in proportion to how much their purported ancestors were victimized in the past. This quid-pro-quo view has become a quasi principle that aims to encompass American life. It is invoked by its advocates, for example, as a reason why the federal government should set aside a certain percentage of federal contracts for minority-owned businesses, and why the federal courts should *not* apply the Equal Protection Clause of the Fourteenth Amendment to racial and ethnic preferences in college admissions.

But it is more than a matter of government mandates. The *diversity* principle is also a *belief* that the portion of our individual identities that derives from our ancestry is the most important part, and a *feeling* that group identity is somehow more substantial and powerful than either our individuality or our common humanity. *Diversity* combines these elements of law, belief and intuition to claim both cold legal authority and warm personal allegiance.

Few principles spread so widely and so deeply through a society. In America, the only principles of similar scope are those on which the nation was founded. Indeed, to find any ideas of comparable sweep in American society, we have to go back to such antique concepts as the notion that all men are created *equal,* and that one of the fundamental human endowments is *liberty.* These ideas, like the idea of *diversity* today, were understood not as narrow technical or merely legal doctrines, but as basic claims about the right ways for humans to behave toward one another.

Equality was certainly meant to entail equality before the law, but it also voiced the American sense of personal equality. We did not regard—and mostly we still don't—other people as *better* than us just because they were richer or descended from more illustrious ancestors. Equality, like *diversity,* was an idea that could be translated into law, but was simultaneously part of everyday experience.

As with equality, so with *liberty.* Our basic liberties are enunciated in the Bill of Rights and, in this sense, they have clear legal form. But the principle of liberty goes much further than the law can or should imagine. One of the basic stories of American life is the recognition by individual men and women that they are responsible for themselves and must choose exactly who they want to be. Many of our key national stories, whether grounded in fact or created as literature, deal with this choice. The treason of Benedict Arnold and the attempted usurpation of Aaron Burr, no less than George Washington's decision to risk everything on the Revolution, are stories about the nature of liberty; but so too are *Huckleberry Finn, The Great Gatsby* and *On the Road.* We Americans make ourselves by our own choices large and small, these stories tell us, and we are therefore ultimately responsible for what we become.

Liberty can, of course, be ironed and starched into a formal caricature of itself, but Americans have generally embodied the *spirit* of liberty, not just its outward form. We are people who like to defy conventions—or at least show we can defy the old rules before submitting to an updated version of them that we have made our own. We have done this over and over in popular music, from nineteenth-century folk songs through rock-and-roll, and we have done it as well in dance, sports and movies. Singers from Robert Johnson to Snoop Doggy Dog, dancers from George Primrose (of soft-shoe fame) to Twyla Tharp, and sports figures from John Heisman (whose proposal to add the forward pass to football was adopted in 1906) to the snowboarding champs at the Salt Lake City Winter Olympics have created new rules by defying the old ones. The American love of change is rooted in our love of liberty, for we don't feel free unless we have actually freed ourselves from something. As a nation, we may live in a perpetual adolescence of finding fault with the previous generation, but that is by no means a heavy doom or too large a price to pay to ensure a deeper cultural continuity. For each generation that finds its parents' conventions stultifying, dull or phony discovers its own sense of liberty.

Like the principles of equality and liberty, *diversity* is gigantic in its ambition. The size of that ambition will perhaps best be judged by the end of this book, but let us at the outset hear what one friend of *diversity* has to say about its scope. Charles Vert Willie is a Harvard professor of sociology who was once a classmate of Martin Luther King Jr.'s at Morehouse College. In 1987—a breakout year for the *diversity* creed—Professor Willie explained his view of diversity to a reporter from the *Christian Science Monitor*:

> "If we want our laws to be beneficial to all, we have to make sure that the lawmaking structures are diversified," he stresses. "Diversity is our source of security. It was our source of security when the Constitution was formed, and it will continue to be our source of security today."

This is a peculiar assertion. The diversity of the colonies and their inhabitants was indeed on the minds of the delegates of the Constitutional Convention from May 25 to September 17, 1787, and it was an issue in the subsequent public debate over the ratification of the draft Constitution—but diversity was seen almost entirely as a source of difficulty and *in*security. The question for the founders was whether they could create a stable and good government despite the many differences separating the states and dividing the broader population. Madison's view of diversity—which he called "faction"—can be fairly gauged by his comment in *The Federalist* No. 10:

> A zeal for different opinions concerning religion, concerning Government and many other points, as well of speculation as of practice; an attachment to different leaders ambitiously contending for pre-eminence and power; or to persons of other descriptions whose fortunes have been interesting to the human passions, have in turn divided mankind into parties, inflamed them with mutual animosity, and rendered them much more disposed to vex and oppress each other, than to co-operate for their common good.

The most that Madison could say in favor of diversity was that if the republic were sufficiently large and the "variety of parties" sufficiently great, the chances of "one party being able to outnumber and oppress the rest" would be diminished. A well-designed republic might have the capacity to thwart the naturally destructive tendency of diversity.

Professor Willie does not stop with the idea that "diversity is our source of security." He adds: "to the extent that gender and race are important social variables in our society, these ought to be represented ... and ought to be prescribed by law." And he says he would legislate that "the members of our decision-making groups must consist of unlike kind, and the unlike kind should represent major social categories that are significant at the period when such persons are being selected."

Professor Willie's vision of *diversity* as a basis of governing the United States would, in other words, replace our freedom to elect leaders of our own choosing with quotas of people chosen to represent whatever "unlike kinds" *someone* has decided are "significant." Diversity thus trumps liberty. And as "social categories" under this principle of diversity would command representation, Professor Willie's principle of *diversity* trumps individual equality as well.

But even this does not capture the full scope of this vision of *diversity* for Professor Willie. He adds, "Indeed, I would classify diversity as the source of our salvation."

Diversity—our supposed source of security, grounds for radical transformation in the ways we elect and appoint our decision makers, and source of salvation—*diversity* in this vision is truly gigantic in its ambition. And like the genuine constitutional principles of liberty and equality, it proposes to organize a whole society and, in so doing, to make that society better. But unlike equality and liberty, the principle of *diversity* is not announced in the Declaration of Independence. In fact, it is not discernible anywhere in the founding documents of the United States. Nor was it a stowaway idea, like the right to privacy, that some later interpreters located in the "penumbra" of the Constitution, even though it was not mentioned as such. "Diversity" is not cited in the Declaration of Independence, the Constitution or the Bill of Rights; not covered by some synonymous term; not even remotely implied.

Madison and the other founders were, however, on the alert against the dangers of factions. *Diversity* might well be understood as an attempt to reverse the founders' efforts to check the growth and power of factions in American society. *Diversity,* in effect, enshrines certain kinds of factionalism as a universal good, just like liberty and equality. Well, no, not *just* like liberty and equality—better. *Diversity* raised to the level of counterconstitutional principle promises to free people from the pseudo-liberty of individualism and to restore to them the primacy of their *group* identities; and *diversity* raised to the summit of "critical thinking" insists that traditional notions of equality are a sham. Real equality, according to diversicrats, consists of parity among groups, and to achieve it, social goods must be measured out in ethnic quotas, purveyed by group preferences, or otherwise filtered according to the will of social factions.

The Declaration of *Inter*-dependence?

The absence of *diversity* as a positive principle in our founding documents and the likelihood that it would have been seen as a rationalization of factionalism are not necessarily arguments against it. Perhaps the advocates of *diversity* have discovered a flaw in our constitutional arrangements that they can now help us rectify. Perhaps we are a more far-seeing and enlightened people than those who came before us.

After all, diversity advocates tirelessly remind us, the framers of the Constitution made room for slavery. Why should we listen to *those* dead white males?

But if we are prepared to consider *diversity* on its merits, we should understand the stakes. *Diversity* is not about fine-tuning American society or replacing some worn-out parts; and it is not about adding some new features that weren't available in the earlier model. *Diversity* isn't a way of tweaking equality and liberty to achieve *more* equality or *greater* liberty. It is, rather, a brand new thing, a principle that aims at no less than transforming American society through and through.

We do not, of course, usually talk about *diversity* as such a revolutionary idea. No one has proposed a *"diversity* amendment" to the U.S. Constitution. Even the strongest advocates of *diversity* do not generally argue that it is time to scrap the Declaration of Independence, or that *diversity* should be explicitly acknowledged as trumping equality and liberty. (I have, however, come across a plea from a worshipper at the shrine of *diversity*, a "diversity consultant" named Bryant Rollins, for a new national "visionary statement" in the form of a "Declaration of *Inter*dependence.")

So is the rise and widespread acceptance of *diversity* as a principle really a challenge to the constitutional order in the United States? And if it is, why does it seem so uncontroversial to so many?

The answer to both questions lies in whether we see the constitutional order of our society primarily as the set of legal doctrines through which we govern ourselves or as the set of cultural assumptions that underlie the legal order. I believe that the cultural assumptions are more fundamental and what we call the constitutional order sooner or later is adjusted to reflect what we really think about ourselves as a people and as a society.

Our constitution, in this view, is more than our Constitution. The actual document adopted in 1788 and subsequently amended twenty-seven times compels our deepest respect, but it is not everything. Long before it was written, the mostly English colonists in what was to become the United States had worked out a view of what they understood to be the liberties of free men and had developed a clear sense of social equality. In drafting the Declaration of Independence, Jefferson drew on particular formulations of these ideas that he had read

in Locke and various Enlightenment thinkers, but he was not pro-
pounding strange and foreign ideas for his colleagues and countrymen. Rather, he was giving eloquent form to views that were already
widely held by American colonists.

In this sense, cultural change can precede legal change, as it frequently has, and a constitutional order emerges from the widespread
acceptance of a new fundamental principle. So the real question is
whether *diversity* amounts to such a fundamental challenge.

In the chapters that follow, I aim to show that in one area of American life after another, the principle of *diversity* represents an attempt
to alter the root cultural assumptions on which American society is
based. Even if the *diversity* movement fails to achieve a new constitutional order in the United States, it already has achieved a substantial
record of increased social discord and cultural decline. The *diversity*
movement has contributed significantly to falling educational performance and lower academic standards (e.g. attacks on the SAT as a
tool for identifying high school students who have the aptitude to
succeed in college); undermined love of country (by elevating racial
separatism); trivialized art (by emphasizing the social identity of the
artist, e.g. Toni Morrison); and made certain forms of racialism
respectable again. This is not to say that diversity is always and everywhere detrimental to our legal, social, moral and personal well-being.
To many, it is an attractive idea and, in the right circumstances, can
be enlivening and uplifting. But that could also be said of Turner Movie
Classics, and we are not tempted to turn our key legal judgments and
the tenor of cultural life over to the custody of cable television.

Whatever its virtues, *diversity* is a challenge to higher virtues and
greater goods. We jeopardize liberty and equality by our friendship
with this new principle. It is an unruly guest in our house, and the
time may have come to call a cab and send it home.

Bias

Writing a book about the history of the *diversity* movement presented
some unusual challenges. *Diversity* is an idea without a clear intellectual context. Its background is murky, and the language in which its
proponents speak is often misleading.

Thus, to see diversity clearly we must always look more than once. Sometimes, within what looks like arrant prejudice, such as in Henry Davenport Northrop's accounts of *Indian Horrors*, lurks a hint of real diversity. And sometimes the opposite is true: what proclaims itself as diversity turns out to be little more than prejudice. This book is concerned with both kinds of diversity: the real (and natural) diversity of our social life, and the movement that has appropriated the name of diversity, not to achieve a better kind of national unity, but to give license to ethnic privilege and other forms of separatism.

This separatist, privileging *diversity* is simultaneously a concept, a political orientation and a personal taste. It is, if not literally everywhere in contemporary American society, nearly so. We need, however, a name for its proponents. Sometimes these advocates of *diversity* are spoken of as "the multicultural Left" or simply "multiculturalists," but these terms cover only part of the story. Diversilogues trade in the ideology of *diversity;* diversidacts teach it; diversicrats regulate it. Each of these words has its place in the story, but for the sake of having one term for the whole tribe, I will write of "diversiphiles" when I mean to speak generally of those who elevate the ideal of *diversity* above the ideal of national unity. Diversiphiles are a dominant voice in many precincts of American culture.

I write as an opponent of the *diversity* movement as a whole, but one whose opposition is rooted in disappointment. The concept of diversity draws on some profoundly important human realities that, call them what we will, ought to be central to any enlightened and humane view of humanity. But diversity in this sense is mangled, compromised and ultimately destroyed by *diversity* in the sense that has prevailed in the *diversity* movement.

America's *real* diversity sometimes seems on the verge of disappearance, while a phony, impostor *diversity*—made up of spurious claims to separate cultural identities, fashion statements and fantasy vacations—has taken its place.

A Million Pillows

In 1996, Susan Jacobsen and Larry Marcus founded a store in Delmar, New York, to sell handmade goods from artisans around the world.

Taking their inspiration from "their idea that 'all of our lives are woven together in a garment of destiny,'" they named their store "Destiny Threads." There one can choose among kimono-silk quilts, mudcloths, wool sweaters, tapestry handbags, baskets made from pine needles, sweetgrass, paper, reeds, roots or telephone wire, and "about a million" pillows.

Ms. Jacobsen and Mr. Marcus have, I think, named their store aptly. Destiny Threads implies a kind of reduction of Dr. King's "single garment of destiny" to its myriad filaments of silk, wool, pine needles, sweetgrass, reeds, roots and telephone wire. This is an image not of the magnificence of the whole, but of the smaller pleasures, the textures and the particularities of the parts.

Diversity is far more than a political movement or a demand for social privileges; it is also the sort of cultural principle that shapes personal tastes. Destiny Threads caters to a longing many Americans have found in themselves for an authentic touch of cultural otherness. A century or so ago, when Northrop wrote *Indian Horrors,* Americans had a lively sense that cultural difference might be hedged with mortal dangers. In midcentury, Dr. King summoned Americans to overcome their sense of mutual estrangement. Today we have a million pillows.

TWO

IMAGINED DIVERSITY

On visiting the Aru Islands southwest of New Guinea in March 1857, Alfred Russel Wallace encountered some diversity:

> At early morn before the sun has risen, we hear a loud cry of "Wawk—wawk—wawk, wok—wok—wok," which resounds through the forest, changing its direction continually. This is the great Bird of Paradise going to seek its breakfast. Others soon follow his example; lorries and parroquets cry shrilly; cockatoos scream; king-hunters croak and bark; and the various smaller birds chirp and whistle their morning song.

When I recently came across Wallace's description of the cacophony of bird calls at sunrise on the Aru Islands, it brought to mind the Aviary on Pittsburgh's Northside. When I was growing up in Pittsburgh in the 1960s, the Aviary was one of my favorite places. The Northside was then a faded, rather seedy part of town, but it had the Buhl Planetarium, where I went for Saturday morning science classes, and a few blocks from the Planetarium was the Aviary, which at the time was like a giant, igloo-shaped greenhouse. Inside, a walkway took one at treetop level through a microcosmic rainforest. Turtles basked on logs in the artificial creek thirty feet below, next to long-legged birds persistently wading in search of nonexistent fish, while in the diffuse light of a perpetual dawn, other birds flitted about or, unseen, made raucous cries from the trees.

In the Aviary, birds from the Amazon mingled with birds from Queensland and the Congo. Species whose ancestors last met when *Tyrannosaurus rex* still was king now found themselves part of the bird equivalent of Mr. Rogers' Neighborhood. (The real Mr. Rogers' neighborhood was across town at the WQED studio.)

Years later, by the time I was finishing college, Pittsburgh's Northside had been gentrified and the Aviary expensively renovated. The new, much larger Aviary featured exhibits of birds in simulations of their natural habitats. One could now stand in front of a window and watch fourteen cockatoos sit on an authentic dead Australian tree, patiently serving their life sentences. The Aviary was still a special place filled with shrill cries and strange whistles, but its enchantments were now fugitive. It had become self-consciously educational.

Yet on reflection, despite my pleasant days in the Pittsburgh Aviary, I've never really heard anything like Wallace's birds of paradise wawk-wawk-wawking at the break of day. Wallace was a witness to natural (I am tempted to say *real*) diversity; I was only a visitor to a menagerie, to the dreamlike diversity of someone who planned a world free of predators, where the northeast monsoon never blows and birdseed or fresh fruit magically appears twice daily. It was no more real than the coral reef at the New England Aquarium near where I live now—a similarly charmed instant of eternity as long as the pumps are turned on and the divers feed the sharks.

Tenuous Diversity

In the last two decades, American society has gone to great trouble to create aviary- or aquarium-like imitations of cultural *diversity*. Our college campuses are perhaps the best examples of these simulacra, designed to look as real as possible.

College campuses, however, face an almost impossible task, since the diversity they attempt to conjure is itself a rather tenuous phenomenon. The truth is, much of the diversity of which we speak in America exists nowhere but in our minds. We have been encouraged to imagine people to be much more different from ourselves and from each other than they actually are. We take real but small differences and magnify them into chasms. We conjure other differences out of thin air. In school we learn about the self-enclosed worlds of peoples in other places and times—Samoans, Egyptians, the Akan Kingdoms of Ghana, the Plains Indians—and vainly imagine that the differences between a black middle-class family and a white middle-class family living on the same street in a suburban American neighborhood are likewise a profound cultural divide. We are drunk with the idea that every difference of ethnic custom, every foreign or regional accent, every traditional recipe and every in-group attitude betokens a distinct worldview.

In all these ways, we invent an image of diversity that bears little resemblance to the facts of American life. The United States does indeed contain some enclaves—communities of recent immigrants, Native Americans committed to maintaining a distinct heritage, insular groups such as the Amish—that stand somewhat aside from the mainstream culture, but it is easy to exaggerate even these differences. In a deep sense, America has one culture. We have a single currency of ideas and values, just as we do of money. Even recent immigrants and communities of Native Americans and religious dissenters share far more of this currency than may appear at a casual glance.

It is human nature for the members of a tribe to be more alert to its internal disputes than to its shared premises. The visitor from abroad—the twenty-five-year-old Tocqueville touring seventeen states in 1831–1832, Dickens on an Ohio steamboat in 1842, or some modern traveler such as Jonathan Raban wandering the country from Guntersville, Alabama, to Seattle—is more apt to be impressed with the commonalities. The America that is plainspoken, ambitious, at once pious and profane, proud of achievement, skeptical of privilege, and egalitarian through and through impresses most strangers. Whether it is to admire our energy or to sneer at our busyness, the visitor has no doubt that we are essentially one culture. In fact, it worries some of them. They fear that a society as rich and powerful as the United States will simply impose its culture on the rest of the world.

I don't intend to give much space here to Euro-snobs, Rolex-wearing Latin American revolutionaries and antiglobalist crybabies, but I acknowledge that they do see something clearly that our home-grown diversiphiles and multiculturalists altogether miss. America is indeed one culture, not a "salad bowl" of distinct peoples. The diversiphile vision, with its endlessly repeated refrain that America is "not a melting pot," is really a form of nostalgia for the days before the melting was complete. Now that the old ethnic groups have taken firm hold in the common enterprise and common values of America and the barriers to new groups have been torn down, we have the curious phenomenon of an ideological movement that asserts that our continuing differences are gigantic.

But diversiphiles betray themselves at every turn by showing they are worried that the preciously thin evidence of cultural differences among us might melt away like a scrim of snow on an April morning. They worry, for example, about public schools teaching English by rapid immersion to those students who speak a foreign language at home, instead of corralling these children into "bilingual education" classes. The immersion method obviously works. Immigrants in the past learned this way and we now have the irrefutable facts of what happened in California when a ballot initiative (Prop. 227) in June 1998 forced an end to long-term bilingual education. In the California school districts that implemented the change, students' scores on standardized tests (the "Stanford 9") jumped dramatically upward in 1999 and 2000. In August 2000, California released data showing that the percentage of students classified as speaking "limited English" and scoring above the 50th percentile on the test rose from 25 percent in 1999 to 32 percent in 2000. According to an account in the *New York Times,*

> the average reading score of a student classified as limited in English increased 9 percentage points over the last two years, to the 28th percentile from the 19th percentile in national rankings, according to the state. In mathematics, the increase in the average score for the same students was 14 points, to the 41st percentile from the 27th.

But in the city of San Jose, which defied the new law, test scores for Latino students continued to languish.

A thoughtfully administered form of English immersion is without question the most effective way to teach children in American schools. But the diversiphiles shudder at the prospect of this success and pour their energy into stopping it. Why? They worry *not* that mainstreaming will fail to work and will hamper the educational progress of children, but that it *will* work—and thus threaten what they view as the preservation of separate cultures. Its willingness to impose inferior education on immigrant students is a powerful indication of the insecurity at the heart of *diversity.*

Diversiphiles offer a make-believe account of American life as filled with a robust *diversity* of cultural traditions. But the political behavior of diversiphiles shows their grasp of the reality: the traditions they say are so robust are in fact so evanescent that we are urged to do all we possibly can to perpetuate them. Hence the diversiphiles give us a contradictory vision of *diversity* as something that is, on one hand, deeply rooted and ineradicable, and on the other, frail and endangered. It is simultaneously the durable diversity of rock-steady ethnic heritage and the imperiled *diversity* of a fragile ethnic ecosystem.

The diversiphiles' paradox is, from an anthropological point of view, easy to resolve. The actual diversity in American society is real but superficial. It is the sort of diversity that exists mainly because people say and believe it exists, not because it arises from profound and fundamental differences. Diversity in this sense is largely (but not entirely) an illusion. It is cobbled together from other illusions, the most significant of which is racial diversity. Americans believe in the existence of race and that belief continues to have dramatic consequences, no matter that "race" is, scientifically speaking, a nullity. (That is, races are social conventions, not biological realities.) The language of race gives Americans a way of talking about and emphasizing some social differences and repressing or ignoring others. And the language of *diversity* provides a new and somewhat surprising way to recategorize "race." We live, perhaps as most cultures live, in illusions that enwrap other illusions.

Two Diversities

Among the many meanings of diversity, let's for the moment distinguish two: the actual racial and ethnic condition of America, which I will call *diversity I*, and the diversiphile ideal of how American society should recognize and respond to its racial and ethnic composition, which I will call *diversity II*. In principle, it ought to be easy to distinguish between these two meanings. One refers to the facts, the other to hopes or wishes. *Diversity I* is the sort of thing that we might expect could be counted, or at least approximated, with wide agreement. We know with reasonable certainty, for example, that about 13 percent of the U.S. population considers itself of African descent. We can and do argue with one another over the significance of this fact, but the fact itself is not seriously in dispute.

Diversity II, by contrast, is an ideal. It expresses a vision of society in which people divide themselves into separate groups, each with profound traditions of its own, but held together by mutual esteem, respect and tolerance. It would be futile, however, to look for general agreement about the exact details of this ideal. Many Americans do not share it, and even among those that do profess a favorable view of it, opinions vary as to what precisely a truly *diverse* society should be. *Diversity II* supporters do, however, often translate their ideal into numerical "goals" for particular situations—and they do so by invoking *diversity I*. So, for example, we hear that because 13 percent of Americans are of African descent, 13 percent of T.V. anchormen should be of African descent. The basic political program of *diversity II* advocates (the diversiphiles) is to create a society in which the real diversity of society at large is *proportionally* represented in schools, colleges, the workplace, government, the arts, and all other positively valued social contexts. Thus *diversity II*, the ideal, depends—at least in principle—on *diversity I*, the facts.

Yet the distinction between these two basic meanings of *diversity* is not always easy to maintain. While Americans generally accept the idea that we are a diverse people, we are highly uncertain about whether and how to identify the parts. On closer inspection, categories such as black, white, Asian and Hispanic break down. We continue to use them as labels, but are increasingly aware how much they distort reality.

The label "Asian," for example, lumps together the immigrant hotel manager from Gujarat State in Western India, the Japanese-American business executive, and the Khmer-American fisherman. The label combines into one category people who speak completely unrelated languages: Gujarati, for example, is an Indo-European language descended from Sanskrit; Japanese has so far defied linguistic classification but seems to have some distant connection to Altaic languages; and Mon-Khmer is an Austronesian language. The "Asian" label likewise mixes people who adhere to unrelated religions: Hinduism in Gujarat, Confucian-inflected Shinto in Japan, and Theravada Buddhism in Cambodia. And the label further makes a spurious unity out of people who take their cultural and historical bearings from completely unrelated traditions. Western India, Japan and Cambodia were never joined in a single empire, never shared a single culture, and never even experienced similar forms of colonialism or Western contact. The life experiences of a Gujarat-American, a Japanese-American and a Cambodian-American have only one significant commonality: not that they are Asian, but that they are American. The term "Asian," of course, lumps together far more than Gujaratis, Japanese and Khmers; it encompasses hundreds of cultures, some related, some not.

Nor is "Asian" the only one of these familiar labels to fall apart under inspection. The term "Hispanic" notoriously plays similar tricks, jamming into one category people of disparate origins and outlooks. "Hispanics" of my acquaintance include a distinctly Anglophilic Andean professor, a Jewish Brazilian who works in banking, an Argentine poet, an aspiring screen writer whose parentage is part Puerto Rican and part French-Canadian, an Azorian janitor, a lawyer and school superintendent born in Cuba who is a dedicated opponent of bilingual education, and another Castro refugee who went crazy and lives on the streets of Boston, perpetually firing a make-believe gun at tourists. The term "Hispanic" clearly doesn't describe common social background; it doesn't designate a common language; and it doesn't, for that matter, describe gross physical appearance. Some "Hispanics" look like Europeans; some show Native-American ancestry; some have African features.

Such group identities may seem real enough to politicians trolling for votes and marketers looking for regularities in consumer behavior, but in fact they are shadowy formulations and deeply at odds with our cultural imperative to treat individuals as individuals, regardless of their ethnic backgrounds. And increasingly, Americans seem to see themselves not as *members* of a single *group*, but as *participants* in several *cultures*.

This shift was reflected in the rejiggering of group identifiers in the 2000 U.S. Census. By mixing racial and ethnic categories and an all-purpose Latino designation, the census offered 126 ways to label our social identities. The idea was to recognize the Tiger Woods phenomenon. In 1997, when the golfer was asked by Oprah Winfrey how he classified himself, Mr. Woods replied that as a teenager he invented the word "Cablinasian"—CAucasian-BLack-INdian-ASIAN—in recognition of his father's mixed Caucasian, Black and Indian ancestry, and his mother's Thai heritage. Despite pressure from many African-Americans, who would prefer that Woods adhere exclusively to an "African-American" identity, he continues to refuse to pigeonhole himself in a single racial category. A growing number of other Americans seemingly feel the same way about their own identities.

The profusion of categories in the 2000 Census gave people the scope to claim such multiple ethnic identifications, which would seem to be a blow against *diversity II.* The diversicrat hope of creating discrete blocks of people based on specific and exclusive identity claims and distinct cultural resentments would be derailed if large numbers of the target populations were to opt out of the categories. And indeed some identity groups, such as the NAACP and the Japanese Citizens League, opposed the Census provision to allow individuals to check off multiple ethnic boxes. But the new system was, at least in intent, more of an effort to save the *diversity* doctrine by adjusting the categories than a step toward their abolition.

One of the people who designed the new categories was Roderick Harrison, a senior fellow at the Joint Center for Political and Economic Studies in Washington, D.C. Harrison explained to a reporter: "From a social and historical point of view, we do have these different people who have gone through exclusion and oppression that our nation is still trying to rectify." In short, Harrison acted on standard-issue diversiphile clichés. And explaining the provision that allows individuals to select multiple racial identities, Harrison added: "This isn't an academic exercise. The question was intended for those who have serious commitments to multiracial identity." Thus the U.S. Census was altered to lend assistance to a political movement whose avowed purpose is to replace the common American identity with a collection of disparate group identities. To guard against people like Tiger Woods defining themselves out of the system, the Office of Management and Budget propounded a rule that anyone who checked the "white" box and also another box would be "allocated to the minority race."

The results of the Census, however, offer further evidence of the growing shift from viewing identity as a matter of *membership* in a group to viewing it as a form of *participation* in a culture. The U.S. population was less a salad bowl and more a melting pot than the diversiphiles expected. About 4 percent of Americans claimed a multiracial background. This percentage may sound small, and surely it is but a fraction of the multiracial reality in America, but the 4 percent should be considered in comparison: the number of professed "multiracials," for example, is only a little less than a third the number of professed African-Americans. That is a substantial rejection by ordinary people of the *diversity II* grid of mutually exclusive categories.

It is interesting, too, that the self-designation of "mixed race" is found not just in the states where it is most conspicuous, such as Hawaii and California, but across the country. In Columbus, Ohio, for example, 18,800 people identified themselves in 2000 as having more than one race, and 21 Columbus residents "identified themselves as being of five races." One reporter wondered whether the 2000 Census might be the start of a historical trend leading to an idea of race as "more someone's description of his mood than his identity."

After considering the shallowness of conventional categories such as "Asian" and "Hispanic" and seeing the growing popular trend toward acknowledging mixed heritages, we ought to wonder whether the conception of America as a constellation of ethnic groups is really valid. Certainly many Americans regard their ethnic heritage as an important part of their identities, but that sense of attachment is one thing, and the claim that America is best understood in terms of the fortunes and rivalries of ethnic groups is something else.

Thus *diversity I*—diversity in the sense of actual racial and ethnic variety—is more elusive than the definition at first suggests. And its murkiness is compounded by the strong tendency of the *diversity II* movement to conflate facts with its ideals. *Diversity II* advocates, for example, routinely describe the United States as rapidly becoming "minority majority," by which they mean that the population comprising members of minority groups will soon be larger than the population of nonminority whites. Although this claim has a genuine demographic basis, *diversity II* advocates typically employ it in a highly misleading fashion. They imply that the members of the coming "minority majority" will look upon access to American colleges and universities, jobs and elected offices in exactly the fashion the *diversity II* advocates themselves do: as spoils to be divided in proportion to the demographic size and political strength of the groups.

The political tactic of *diversity II* advocates, in other words, is to convert the mere numbers of *diversity I* into organized groups committed to *diversity II* ideology, and to that end they practice the old political trick of pretending that what they hope will happen already has. Indeed, ethnic interest groups that claim to speak for whole categories of people do exist and have achieved considerable power in some states. The so-called "Hispanic Caucus" in California, for example, seems to have garnered the power in that state's legislature to force Hispanic quotas on the University of California system. The university administrators, who had little will to resist anyway, seem to be capitulating to the demand. Still, we should take care to recognize that *dividing* Americans into supposed ethnic categories does not guarantee that Americans will *act as members* of those categories.

In this sense, the "minority majority" is a political fiction. It can be conjured up as a demographic artifact by taking note of the growth in the Hispanic population through a high birthrate and high immigration, and then adding the Hispanics to the other "minority" populations in the United States. But whether the great variety of people swept into this demographic artifact will act in the fashion hoped for and predicted by the *diversity II* movement remains to be seen.

Real Diversity

I would like to linger a moment on the distinction between diversity as something real in the world, and the *diversity* that we sometimes manufacture as a substitute for the real thing. Those who advocate *diversity* as an ideal often go to great lengths to invent and impose counterfeit varieties, partly because they have lost sight of the important differences between real and artificial diversity.

The new category of sexual nonconformists, "gay-lesbian-bisexual-transgendered" (often abbreviated GLBT, sometimes LGBT), for example, corresponds to nothing in the real world. It merely groups together some of many sexual orientations and appetites that have been subject to disapproval within our culture. Why these four and not others? There is no obvious answer, but the supracategory GLBT is now common on college campuses, while as yet there is no call for sympathetic recognition of, say, necrophiles.

The gulf between the real diversity of the world and the artificial and often imaginary diversity of our social experiments is very large. Real diversity can be thrilling, not least because it can sometimes be deadly. Herman Melville, who jumped ship in the Marquesan Islands and sojourned some weeks among the tattooed, cannibalistic Typee people, encountered real diversity. But the child from the suburbs who, in venturing off to college, encounters people in his dorm sporting fake Polynesian tattoos has not yet met real diversity at all.

Real diversity is often profoundly provocative. To encounter people who are fundamentally unlike yourself is fundamentally unsettling. When Western missionaries fanned out across the Pacific in the early decades of the nineteenth century, some went mad after only a few days or weeks spent alone among people who viewed the world on utterly different terms than anything the missionaries ever knew. For example, in 1791 the missionary William Harris, having spent only four days on Tahuata in the Marquesan Islands, was rescued by British sailors who found him hiding in the hills, "in a most pitiable plight, and like one out of his senses," according to the captain of the ship.

Of course, the missionaries recruited by the London Missionary Society and its American counterparts were not venturing into these foreign cultures because they were enamored with the idea of diversity; rather, what we call diversity was to them an occupational hazard. They hoped to win converts, not to enrich their own experience of human difference.

Our orientation to such cultural diversity has changed radically and in a remarkably brief period. Consider Joseph Conrad's short novel *Heart of Darkness,* published a century ago (1902). Conrad offers a dark vision of a civilized Western man in deep confrontation with another culture, and Conrad's character Kurtz, like the missionary William Harris, is driven mad by the experience. Kurtz, an exemplar of a civilized European, goes far upriver (usually taken to be the Congo), where he descends into murderous savagery. Dying, Kurtz achieves an instant of clarity, "that supreme moment of complete knowledge," in which he cries out, "The horror! The horror!"

One might say that whatever else this complex story is about, it does *not* advance the idea that we can achieve happier and more fulfilled lives by plunging into cultural exchange and exploration of our links to other peoples. *Heart of Darkness* is quite plainly framed by the idea that the cultural otherness of the Congo is a dangerous thing, and powerful enough to unhinge a strong and cultivated man like Kurtz. Generations of readers have had no trouble penetrating this far up Conrad's river.

But contemporary American higher education is an odd place— as odd in its way as the old Aviary in Pittsburgh—and *Heart of Darkness* has now been turned on its head and made into a tool, of sorts, for promoting the *diversity* worldview. We have good testimony on this: David Denby, a critic for the *New Yorker,* took a leave in 1994–1995 to retake Columbia University's "Literature Humanities" and "Contemporary Civilization" courses, which he had taken many years before. One of his first reports on the experience, "Jungle Fever," was an account of Professor James Shapiro teaching *Heart of Darkness* to a class consisting mostly of freshmen. Professor Shapiro began the class discussion of the story by asking, "Who here comes from a savage race?" He was intent, seemingly, on making sure that his students distanced themselves at the outset from Conrad's ethnocentric assumptions about the indigenous peoples of central Africa, and he aimed to provoke as well a recognition in the students of their own seed of Kurtzian darkness.

Denby provides not only a vivid portrait of the class but also a useful brush-up on the strong aspersions cast on Conrad's novella by, among others, Chinua Achebe and Edward Said. Achebe, the celebrated Nigerian novelist best known for *Things Fall Apart,* attacks *Heart of Darkness* as "a story in which the very humanity of black people is called into question." He sees Conrad as essentially vindicating Western superiority. Said, by contrast, professes to love *Heart of Darkness,* but nonetheless attacks Conrad as a captive of the colonial mindset. He indicts the story as "an organic part of the 'scramble for Africa,'"—the late-nineteenth-century race among European powers to establish their own spheres of control on the continent. It is not clear whether the students in Professor Shapiro's class have actually read Achebe's and Said's comments, but they have clearly somehow absorbed their spirit.

Most of the students in the class focus on *Heart of Darkness* as an indictment of Western imperialism. King Leopold's rape of the Congo was, by any measure, a nasty episode, and Conrad has indeed provided an indelible portrait of it. Professor Shapiro's students are also alert to the idea that the darkness in Mr. Kurtz may be a darkness in Western civilization itself. Certainly Kurtz's civilized life does not prevent him from committing—and enjoying, as Conrad implies—acts of gross cruelty.

But read in this way, the story is reduced to a kind of warning against prejudice. If only Kurtz had escaped from his pernicious stereotyping of the natives—or perhaps, if only Conrad had made that escape—things would have turned out well. Kurtz could have learned to enjoy the polyrhythms of central African music and to play the *mbira*, and his indigenous friends could have gained a useful intermediary to the Belgian state.

Denby defends Conrad's artistic vision, but finds his own understanding sharpened by Achebe's and Said's challenges, because they "jarred" him into recognizing the political intent of Professor Shapiro's reading of the story. Shapiro concludes the class discussion by reassuring the students that although the world is dark, "We ourselves have the ability now to recognize, and even to fix and change our society, just as literature reflects, embodies, and serves as an agent of change."

By Denby's account, Professor Shapiro is no ideologue, and many of his students clearly come to wrestle with this important book. Still, the class reads *Heart of Darkness* under the diffuse illumination of *diversity*, and in that light the story of a morally disastrous temptation to identify with the primitive "other" disappears behind the story of a world corrupted by colonialism. And, thus, *Heart of Darkness* becomes one more demonstration of the need to achieve open-mindedness in the face of cultural diversity. The possibility that Kurtz may perhaps have been a little too open-minded just disappears. Kurtz, after all, met his downfall not out of hatred for the culture of the Congolese, but through some kind of infatuation with them.

Of course, cultural contact *can* be mind-opening in constructive ways. For the few missionaries driven mad, there were dozens who came to admire profoundly the people they lived with and who became expert linguists and ethnographers intent on creating an enduring record of the fast-changing cultures they had come to love. And for every murderous Kurtz stranded upriver, there were hundreds of native people who bravely ventured downriver to discover the new intercultural world created in the ferment of the coastal cities.

New England once was—and in some ways, still is—such a place. The opening pages of *Moby Dick* give a glimpse of the city of New Bedford as the crossroads of the nations. Today, New England's universities have some of that international flavor. Ideally, a university on the New England littoral would be a place where those thirsty for knowledge from every corner of the world, from great capitols to upriver hamlets, would seek their passage to higher education.

That I take to be a dream of diversity worth dreaming, for surely we have much to learn from each other when we meet as equals united by the common pursuit of knowledge. Real diversity in some extreme forms—such as going to live among the Typee or, like John Walker Lindh, joining the Taliban, might not be good for you, but real diversity within certain bounds most certainly is. But what are those bounds? And how does a university, or any other institution, achieve real diversity?

Justifiable Exclusions?

In the last few decades, American higher education has done a poor job in answering these questions. In most cases, it has not been for lack of good will. If anything, we have wanted diversity too much, and in the process of reaching for it, have knocked it over.

A real diversity on campus *could* come from rigorously eliminating any form of linguistic, ethnic, national, sexual or religious favoritism—indeed, any favoritism based on social identity. For very practical reasons, that extreme is impossible, and for ethical reasons, it is undesirable. On the practical side, who, for example, would teach in a university with no common language?

The ethical side is more complicated. It *is* sometimes justifiable to exclude students from a university or to review their entrance according to stricter criteria depending on their nationality or their religious commitments. Universities do not labor under some obligation to educate the youth of hostile powers in fields that might endanger our national security. We ought not to welcome into nuclear engineering programs Iraqi students sent to America on Saddam Hussein scholarships. Nor do universities have a presumptive obligation to admit students who profess beliefs that are fundamentally at odds with the ethical foundations of liberal education. *Jihadists* should be kept out.

The ethics of exclusion on the basis of social identity also involve the question of whether single-sex colleges, tribal colleges and historically black colleges are legitimate. Each of these types of college practices an absolute or a relative policy of exclusion, and could not exist without that policy. Are the ethical imperatives against discrimination and in favor of real diversity *within* every college campus so great that we should abolish this other kind of diversity *among* colleges?

Eliminating barriers may not always produce the diversity some think is ideal. A real diversity produced by building a community that is an aristocracy of talent could end up with disproportionately large numbers of people in one social category and few in another. And therein lies the temptation: to domesticate cultural diversity, to arrange it to suit our tastes and our political and social convictions. *Diversity* offers a vision in which different ways of life, different customs, different outlooks will be celebrated side by side—but according to certain softly stated proportions in the number of celebrants.

Two More Diversities

The vision of the university (and the larger society) governed by a doctrine that each "group" will receive its due proportion of the good things that everybody wants has an undeniable appeal to a large number of Americans. Its appeal is based in part on the conviction that America really is composed of separate groups all competing for access to the same resources. It is, in a certain light, an enchanting vision—for it assigns each of us a kind of primordial identity, so that we are born with a rightful claim on our portion of the world. In almost the same light, however, it is also a very disenchanting vision, since it means we are born into a world where other groups are always trying to muscle in for a larger share and we will have to join with our "own" kind to defend our portion.

To see the world in this way is perhaps to be primed for the advantages of concocted *diversity*. Lest there be a struggle in which the stronger groups ruthlessly dominate and despoil the weaker, wouldn't we be better off with a government bureaucracy that ensures that each group gets only its own portion? If we accept the premise that American society is a battleground of competing ethnic groups (and some groups defined on other *diversity* criteria, such as handicap or sexual preference), the idea of a certain kind of *diversity* enforced from above seems far more palatable.

I cannot ponder that idyllic vision for long, however, without coming back to my memory of those long-legged birds futilely stalking the shallows for nonexistent fish in the Pittsburgh Aviary—and the fourteen cockatoos forever sitting on the same dead tree. The concocted *diversity* of contemporary campus life has precisely that element of charmed artificiality, a deadness and inertia beneath whatever lively rhetorical appearance we evoke. It has very little to do with the actual cultural diversity of the world.

The campus aviary, of course, exists mostly in the minds of the bureaucrats who attempt to organize it. Their idyllic vision appears in thousands of college brochures and web pages. Here is a specimen of the common house sparrow version from California State University, San Bernardino:

> CSUSB will be a university community where all individuals are secure to explore and develop their cultural and diverse identities. All persons will be provided opportunity and encouragement to explore and discover the richness of the tapestry of human experience. The university community is united in the condemnation of acts of hatred & intolerance.

With a little patience, however, one can spot the rare species, the arctic terns or whooping cranes of campus *diversity*. Here, for example, is a remarkable statement from the University of Michigan's 1995 "Preamble" to *Understanding the Difference That Diversity Makes: Assessing Diversity and Tolerance Initiatives on College and University Campuses*, in which the splendor of *diversity* scholarship is recognized:

> In the same period in which the student body has changed so dramatically, so too has the scholarship upon which knowledge is constructed. With the new scholarship on formerly understudied groups, an intellectual resurgence comparable to the Renaissance has taken place, invigorating academic disciplines, disrupting former ways of understanding things, and challenging

higher education to rethink what it teaches, the way it teaches, and why it teaches what it does.

In addition to issues of access, retention, and climate, there has been an increasing recognition by colleges and universities that if they are to educate students to assume leadership in an increasingly diverse society and the internationalized context in which we function, the educational process, the campus community, and the curriculum must reflect that mission. Education that does not engage these issues, may become increasingly irrelevant to the current and future world which we inhabit. Thus, providing students with knowledge about diversity has been incorporated into the vast majority of college and university mission statements within the past two decades.

While some college administrators may see in *diversity* "an intellectual resurgence comparable to the Renaissance," the aviary has a less certain appeal to students. A great many students buy into the vision promoted by their schools and colleges, but complain that the promised idyll never quite materializes.

For example, Deborah Burke, an anthropologist and "Diversity Web Site Coordinator" at Oregon State University, conducted interviews with students about their views of *diversity* for OSU's "2002 Pride Celebration. From Silence to Celebration: It's a Rainbow World After All." On the whole, the students she spoke to were enthusiastic about the concept of *diversity* but somewhat disappointed by the practice.

John Sykes, a gay student, showed he had learned the key lessons:

> I have always thought of diversity in the terms of what you learn in biology class; it is the wide representation of different kinds of things or people. What I have learned now, and I've taken a lot of DPD (Difference, Power, and Discrimination) (I am in two right now), is that it is not just tolerating people with differences, it is embracing them and supporting them. It is one thing being tolerated and that is totally not the same thing as being embraced and celebrated.

And Mr. Sykes appreciated what Oregon State University had to offer. When Ms. Burke asked him to describe his "ideal regarding a community," he replied:

> I would say OSU is pretty close as far as, like there is the OSU community and ... student involvement, and the cultural center

community. In the student government we do affirmative action. We actively recruit LGBTs and it just feels like my issues matter. I am a part of the community. They will be talking, "Well we have to go to this thing for this USSA (United States Student Association)." They have quotas to go to their legislative conference; they go and lobby their congressman.... So many delegates need to be women to send there, and one of them needs to be an LGTB. You know like proportionate to the size of the university, so I am like, "Wow!" You know it feels like I matter, like again I am being embraced.

He loves the quotas, but even OSU falls short of perfection. As Sykes notes, his university still has fraternities and the real diversiphiles exist a little outside the mainstream:

> Greeks are not diverse and they are white, upper-class, and they have a lot of clout in this university, so it is just kind of the smaller underground community that you have to get in to really know about, and I like it a lot.
> I feel like they [the Greek fraternity members] are the bosses even though they comprise a minority of like 12 to 20% of the campus.... They can force people to do stuff and then they have money because they are upper-class. They have clout because the predominant leadership in this community is the white male, so it is like they don't even have to work. I think they need to recognize their privilege for one thing and try to give it up a little.

While John Sykes, like, objects to the alleged privileges of the fraternity members, other diversiphilic students at Oregon State and elsewhere unreel a long list of complaints about *diversity*'s deeds falling short of *diversity*'s promises. Angel Wilson at Oklahoma State University, for example, writes:

> It's not uncommon for me to go an entire day without seeing someone who looks like me. It also is not unusual for me to be the only Black person in a class. This really bothered me my freshman year. How could a university be so far behind in terms of diversity?

Wilson also complains about the pressures of being a minority student in a diversity-minded social system: "I hate to admit it, but any one that happens to be a minority is viewed under a microscope, especially on our campus." But she acknowledges that she enjoys the attention too, though she "resents the fact" that she often has to explain that she speaks for herself and not all "the other men and women of my race."

Ms. Wilson's classmate Sarah Gonzales offers an account that points to the idyll of *diversity* breaking down in a different way. She loves Oklahoma State's approach to *diversity* seemingly because it helps her retreat into an ethnic sanctuary:

> Being a Latina, I was used to my family always being around for everything and this time I was on my own.... From the moment I stepped onto the patio and heard the speaker preaching about Latino pride, I was hooked. The members instantly became my brothers and sisters. For me it was a great relief to learn the similarities between us....
>
> From there on the Hispanic Student Association and other diverse organizations were a major part of my life. I eventually became President of H.S.A. and recruited others in the same way I had been found, getting out and talking to people. Letting Latinos know that there is a family that exists on this college campus.

The statements by Mr. Sykes, Ms. Wilson and Ms. Gonzales are part of a growing genre of *diversity* testimonials. Some colleges, such as Michigan State University, run annual "What diversity means to me" essay contests. Others, such as Oklahoma State University, solicit statements from likely prospects. Elsewhere, one can find student discussion groups with long sophomoric rants about the need for more black/brown/female/GLBT professors. The result is that we have an abundant public record of student endorsements for and gripes about *diversity*. And from what Sykes, Wilson, Gonzales and thousands of others say, it is clear that whatever else college *diversity* is, it is not the simple extension of the real world of social and cultural difference into the groves of academe. The LGBT quotas that please John Sykes, the microscopic attention that alternately pleases and displeases Angel Wilson, and the ethnic cocooning that pleases Sarah Gonzales have some counterparts elsewhere in our society, but they definitely don't reflect the real diversity of American life.

Concocted diversity imagines the world as divisible into neatly defined social groups, each with its own thriving cultural traditions. Once upon a time we anthropologists thought the world might actually be like that. Ruth Benedict's famous *Patterns of Culture* (1934) offers such a vision, and the notion of one tribe=one culture provided the basic rubric for ethnographies of sub-Saharan Africa until perhaps the 1960s. But the facts kept getting in the way. Everywhere we anthropologists looked, we found people on the move, changing languages, borrowing customs, merging traditions, intermarrying, creating hybrid cultures, reinventing themselves, acting as the custodian of ancient laws in the morning and participating in the global market that afternoon. In sub-Saharan Africa, for example, by the 1960s anthropologists began to relinquish the idea of the "tribe" in favor of more open forms of social organization. Books began appearing, such as *Strangers in African Societies* (1979) and *The African Frontier* (1987), that focused on social diversity and mobility, and anthropologists turned their attention to groups such as the Chamba in West Africa, who possess some kind of common ethnic identity but comprise communities that speak different languages and organize along different social principles.

And so far as anthropologists are concerned, we came to see culture as immensely important but also immensely mercurial and virtually impossible to pin down and label. Pinning down and labeling, however, are precisely what concocted cultural *diversity* requires. Perhaps because of this, when anthropologists lend support to the *diversity* movement—as many do—they frequently turn obscurantist by invoking the aid of postmodern irony or neo-Marxist dialectic. The categories of concocted *diversity* plainly do not make sense without such aid.

But if we stick to arguments that can be considered in the light of day, the distinction between the actual diversity of American life and a political ideal of arranging access to social goods in proportion to the size and strength of social groups—the distinction between *diversity I* and *diversity II*—can be both expanded and sharpened. We really experience two *kinds* of diversity: the kind that is an inextricable part of the world in which we live; and the kind that we create in artificial imitation of that world.

The diversity that is inextricably part of the world includes natural diversity (of the Aru Islands, for example), but it also includes much of human social and cultural diversity. In the world as we know it, people have always spoken different languages, held different and incompatible worldviews, conceived and practiced conflicting beliefs, pursued irreconcilable goals, and organized themselves into separate and often hostile groups. There is no reason, despite the fantasies of globalizers and the fears of antiglobalizers, to think that our species is on the verge of total homogenization and uniformity. The inextricable fact of social and cultural diversity is evident in the bellicosity between Pakistan and India and in the separatists of Quebec. With skill and luck, political leaders can negotiate across the lines of such divisions and occasionally they are worn away by conquest, intermarriage or oppression, but division itself cannot be eradicated. It is part of the human condition.

The temptation to build little imitation diversities, however, is not written into our fate. It is a political movement within American society (and some other Western nations) with a recent and particular history. The artificial imitations of human diversity have some precedents, such as the living tableaus of native peoples that were assembled for the 1893 World's Columbian Exposition in Chicago, and the "It's a Small World After All" pavilion at Disneyland. The League of Nations and the United Nations may provide models of a sort for artificial diversity too—not in the representation of nations per se, but in the elaborate formulae for cultural balancing. The fullest expression of artificial diversity, however, is the contemporary American college campus with its (sometimes illegal but real) admissions quotas, its multicultural affairs offices, its division of students into ethnic clubs, and its curriculum aimed at convincing students that these strange impositions are simultaneously justified as corrections of past wrongs and as preparation for living and working in American society.

The real diversity of the world is one of its crucial characteristics. We have a moral duty to understand the world as best we can, and that includes coming to terms with its real diversity. Sometimes that is a diversity that awes us with its Aru Island beauty; sometimes it is a diversity that appalls us with its Rwanda-like cruelty; and often it is a diversity that baffles us with its Marquesan-like strangeness. Natural diversity is not, in and of itself, good or bad. It simply *is,* and our goal as men and women seeking to become educated is to comprehend it in its full complexity.

But artificial diversity merits no such respect. It is, at best, a morally neutral pedagogical contrivance. But it is sometimes much worse: a set of social arrangements that are unjust and that thwart our higher aspirations.

Real diversity has its own perils, as those missionaries who could not cope with Polynesian strangeness found out. But real diversity can produce misfortunes in more mundane ways as well.

In September 1999, the $125 million Mars Climate Orbiter plunged into the Martian atmosphere and burned up. It turned out that one team of people writing its navigational software used metric units and another used English units, and no one had noticed the difference. The diversity of metric and English scales is part of the real diversity of the world, produced by diverse social systems evolving over thousands of years; and failure to agree clearly to rely on one convention of measurement led to catastrophe. The diversity of conventions in the world probably will not send us, like the Mars Climate Orbiter, hurtling to oblivion, but it does frustrate conversations, delay projects, and even end friendships.

The greater danger we face, however, comes from artificial diversity—from its false assurances and from what it robs us of. Diversity that is achieved by racial, ethnic or any other quotas in college admissions; diversity that consists of syllabi in which books have been included or excluded because of the race, nationality, gender or gender preference of the authors; diversity that takes the form of hiring or not hiring faculty members because of the social category they are alleged to inhabit; diversity that prompts one to praise or blame in the spirit of demonstrating his openness to other cultures—these are, every one of them, pernicious forms of diversity.

Thinking Outside the Cave

The false assurances of artificial diversity are the shadows on the wall in our version of Plato's allegorical cave: images that we mistake for substance. In Plato's allegory, those who watch the shadows believe they are the only reality and strongly resist looking outside the cave.

Artificial diversity has just that kind of grip on American campuses—and not *just* on campuses. To be in favor of this kind of diversity is to lay claim to a kind of righteousness tinged with modesty. It connotes a willingness to accommodate others who are not like one's self. To favor diversity is thought to place one on the side of kindness, generosity and openness to the world. And to be against it is evidence of small-mindedness.

But these are mere illusions. The real small-mindedness is to think that the Aru Islands can be fitted inside a greenhouse on Pittsburgh's Northside, or that it is generous to lower college admissions standards for people because of their race. To admit students in this fashion is to tell them that the college—and perhaps society at large—does not believe they could succeed on their own abilities. It plants the idea that "equality" itself is an artificial social arrangement imposed by the actions of others, and it negates the idea of equality as the underlying and inherent condition of all humanity. To induct people into college even partly because of race is to hand down a life sentence of corrosive self-doubt, based on the suspicion that one couldn't have succeeded on merit alone. And those who serve this sentence also come under intense psychological pressure to perpetuate the arrangement, so that others might "benefit" from the same "breaks."

These last two points, of course, are hotly disputed. The black newspaper columnist Clarence Page, for example, writes:

> So, of all the arguments I have heard various people make against affirmative action, I find the least persuasive to be the charge that it makes its recipients feel bad. . . . Most white males have not felt particularly bad about the special preferences they have received because of their race and gender for thousands of years. Why should we? Believe me, compared to the alternative, preferential treatment feels better.

But Page mistakes the criticism. He is very likely right that most of the beneficiaries of racial preferences in college admissions (or the newsroom jobs and presidential appointments he refers to) do not "feel bad" about receiving an unearned benefit. Far from it. But at a deeper level, the human mind distrusts—perhaps it even abhors— the violation of human reciprocity that comes from taking what's not rightfully ours. Even criminals who live by depriving others of their possessions typically develop rationalizations for why they deserve what they steal and why their victims deserve to be robbed.

The beneficiaries of affirmative action likewise are forced by the logic of their situation to seize explanations that somehow they deserve their good fortune. Page's comments illustrate the rationalization at work: the hallucination of "white males" benefiting from "race" preferences for "thousands of years," and the glib assertion that *the* alternative to affirmative action is racial (and gender) discrimination. This sort of grasping at nonexistent straws is one illustration of the psychological legacy of affirmative action. It shows that "corrosive self-doubt" fully at work. In its small-mindedness, however, the *diversity* movement is unable to take in this sort of criticism.

Racial preferences in college admissions are but one component of concocted diversity in higher education, but they are surely the foundational idea of the whole movement. It is the racial preference component of diversity that most demands hypocrisy of faculty members, students and administrators. And in these respects, favoring artificial diversity is *not* righteous; it is arrogant and bigoted. It jeopardizes the integrity of everyone's education for the sake of maintaining a fleeting illusion of fairness.

Artificial diversity's illusion of fairness is really a flickering of several separate fires on the cave walls. One is the idea that educational access in the present can make up for denial of educational opportunity in the past. Clearly this is false at the level of individuals. My opportunity to go to college does nothing to repair my grandmother's lack of such opportunity. Making the present generation pay for the mistakes of past generations only makes sense if we assume a kind of "group right." If a group's rights were infringed in the past and the group still exists, it can be compensated.

But the logic of this position, once exposed, ought to make us wonder: Do we really want to configure ourselves into a society based on group rights? When we think through the implications of group rights, we see a long and frightening road out of democracy and individual freedom, and into tyranny and the straitjacket of stereotypes. We have a recent historical model for such a society: South Africa under apartheid. Or, if that enormity seems too distant to contemplate, we can consider India's attempts to abolish caste hierarchy while promoting group rights for low-caste and untouchable groups. And near at hand, we have the example of Canada wrestling with "Quebec's distinctiveness" (as it was called in the 1991 constitutional reform proposals) and the rights of its aboriginal peoples.

Group rights may not necessarily devolve into apartheid-style hierarchy, but they clearly have led to deeper divisions and fiercer resentments in the countries that have experimented with them. Once we allocate political rights by group identity, the assignment of group identity becomes the crucial determinant of everything else for the individual; the group gains a strong interest in ensuring the conformity of its members; the individual faces powerful pressure to conform; and the resentments only multiply.

Artificial diversity's illusion of fairness is also based on the spurious idea that group affiliation by birth is a reasonable stand-in for worldview or cultural outlook. What we really want, say some advocates of artificial diversity, is cultural and intellectual diversity, but that's hard to arrange. But, say these advocates, we get a good enough approximation by assuming that most African-Americans think like African-Americans, most Latinos think like Latinos, most gays think like gays, and so on.

One of the greatest moral gains of the Civil Rights Movement was the widespread recognition in American society that stereotyping is pernicious. The *diversity* movement, however, doubles back on that lesson. It offers a justification of sorts for reviving and maintaining racial stereotypes that should be recognized as morally repellent.

In a recent article in the *New Republic*, for example, Jeffrey Rosen extolled one of his African-American law students for articulating what Rosen thought was an appropriately African-American view of racial profiling. Having such authentic black views expressed in class, argued Rosen, is a good reason to maintain affirmative action in admissions. But Rosen does recognize that not all African-Americans think alike. He also wrote:

> One of the most committed conservative students in my recent constitutional law class was an African American woman who, like Clarence Thomas, bitterly resented the claim that African Americans think and vote alike. But her position, too, contributed to the diversity of the class.

Rosen's condescension to this student is crushing. Her earnest claim to individuality is flicked away as he assigns her to her proper role as a specimen of a rare subspecies, a black conservative. It is not that her views actually matter, but that she too contributes to "the diversity of the class."

The truth is that she and the other student both deserve to be treated as complex individuals whose lives reflect many influences.

To single out their race as *the* defining feature of their identities is simplistic—and mean.

Rosen is by no means exceptional in employing this form of supposedly benevolent racial stereotyping. Professor G. Pritchy Smith teaches in the College of Education and Human Services at the University of North Florida and is the co-author of *Common Sense about Uncommon Knowledge: The Knowledge Bases of Diversity.* At the November 2001 convention in Las Vegas of the National Association of Multicultural Education, Professor Smith made a presentation where, as reported by Robert Holland, he declared that "African-Americans learn holistically. They are not so concerned about specific little details. Most white kids have respect for validated knowledge. In other cultures, it has to feel like the truth." These sorts of glib generalizations now pass, under the banner of *diversity*, as sensitivity to cultural differences, rather than the soft bigotry they actually are.

One defender of racial *diversity* quotas attempts to head off this criticism in an interesting way. Jonathan R. Alger, writing in 1997 on "The Educational Value of Diversity," suggested:

> The range of similarities and differences within and among racial groups is precisely what gives diversity in higher education its educational value. For example, by seeing firsthand that all black or Hispanic students in their classes do not act or think alike, white students can overcome learned prejudices that may have arisen in part from a lack of direct exposure to individuals of other races.

Alger would be right about the wholesomeness of *diversity* if he were right about what actually happens in the classroom and elsewhere on campus. But he has the psychological dynamics of campus *diversity* entirely wrong. Recruited in the name of *diversity*, students quickly understand they have a part to play involving their ethnic identities (or other recognized classification). They find, as Angel Wilson at Oklahoma State University found, that they are expected to be "representative" of their group. They are invited, as Sarah Gonzales was invited to experience "Latino pride," to join ethnic sodalities. They are taught, as John Sykes was taught in his Difference, Power and Discrimination classes at Oregon State University, that group identity is to be "celebrated" and "embraced." And they encounter teachers like Professors Rosen and Pritchy who seem less intent on fostering individualistic thought among minority students than encouraging conformity to stereotypical expectations.

Minority students are particularly vulnerable to the lure of self-stereotyping that *diversity* dangles. Faced with tough academic challenges, some middle-class black and Hispanic students suddenly adopt the stance of the ethnic outsider who rejects academic standards, blames the system, and acts too tough to care. Such actions, rooted in insecurity, offer no valid educational path; but within the culture of *diversity*, few in higher education dare resist minority students' descent into the faux authenticity of street personae. *Diversity* legitimates such destructive play-acting as a valid form of seeking one's identity.

Grounded

In the wake of the 9-11 terrorist attacks, many Americans seemed to revert to the older language of tolerance and fairness toward others and put aside, at least temporarily, the newer language of deference and celebration. The switch merely shows that we still have the cultural resources to invoke different sets of cultural ideals depending on the national circumstances and mood. The Left grumbled, but most Americans cheered as the U.S. military pressed its campaign in Afghanistan in the fall and winter of 2001–2002. In the midst of this, the U.S. Postal Service issued a Ramadan stamp, the reception of which was an apt symbol of the shifting balance between old-style tolerance and new-style *diversity*. The stamp occasioned no outrage or protest, but it sold poorly.

It would be a mistake, however, to think that *diversity* is exclusively an ideological preoccupation of the American Left. It indeed has a strong base on the Left, but it also has appeal in many other precincts in American politics. President George W. Bush famously made his 2000 nominating convention into a display and celebration of ethnic diversity and followed up by appointing a conspicuously *diverse* cabinet. Within that cabinet, several individuals appear as strongly committed to the *diversity* ideology as anyone on the American Left.

In the wake of 9-11, for example, the U.S. secretary of transportation, Norman Mineta, issued orders that prevented security guards at airports from "profiling" for Middle Easterners. Instead, the nation's airports became snarled as the guards performed random searches of travelers who fit no known pattern of security threat.

Secretary Mineta is a Japanese-American who was interned in Wyoming with his family by the U.S. government during World War II. The episode is central to his life and he has made much of it since 9-11. In a newspaper interview in October 2001, Mineta commented:

> In 1942, 120,000 of us were rounded up and put in these camps simply because of our race. We were behind barbed wire, with military guard towers every 200 or 300 feet, spotlights and machine guns. Even as an 11-year-old kid, I looked up at those towers and thought, "If we're in here for our own protection, why are the machine guns pointed in at us—and not out?"

Determined not to treat others unjustly, Mineta proved susceptible to the argument that it would be *unfair* to focus the security efforts on people who, on the basis of apparent age, sex, cultural background and ethnicity, were most likely to be affiliated with terrorist groups. To Mineta, profiling people whose characteristics fit those of known terrorists would be a form of "discrimination." And he asserted that "Surrendering to actions of hate and discrimination makes us no different than the despicable terrorists who rained such hatred on our people."

Equating reasonable searches of individuals who fit a profile with "hate" and "discrimination" is pretty far from common sense, but it is entirely consonant with the ideals of *diversity*. Profiling violates *diversity*'s paradoxical injunction that social differences ought to be recognized only for such purposes as dispensing contracts, awards and government patronage, and for rooting out discrimination. Any other application is quickly—and often thoughtlessly—denounced as motivated by hatred, bias or other bad motives.

Autonomy

Artificial *diversity* presents itself as benign, but is far from it. We may *feel* that to be in favor of diversity is to be in favor of fairness, but if we stop to look at and think about the mechanisms by which artificial *diversity* is pursued, we should recognize that those feelings are a false guide. Artificial *diversity* is, essentially, dehumanizing. It turns us each into mere exponents of social groups; it denies us our individuality; and it makes us complicit in denying the full humanity of others.

Pursued as social policy, *diversity* is a form of systematic injustice and it makes us accomplices to injustice. To treat people as objects, as though they are the residuum of their race, class, gender and other such superficialities, and not individuals who define themselves through their ideas and creative acts—that is injustice. But it is not the only injustice that we have licensed as we have allowed artificial *diversity* to sweep through the university and through society.

Artificial *diversity*, for example, hollows out religion, turning communities of faith into centers of multiculturalism. The movement is pan-denominational and the current "monthly quote" on one of its websites, multicultural-church.com, captures the manner in which the essentially secular message of *diversity* is clipped on to religious rhetoric. General Superintendent Paul Cunningham at the 1994 Multicultural Ministries Quadrennial Conference at Nashville First Church of the Nazarene writes:

> I believe cultural diversity is providing us with one of the greatest opportunities the church has ever had, because we have the message that enables us to live together and enjoy each other at God's table. That is what our message does for us. You can't hate somebody and have holiness of heart and life. You can't be discriminating against somebody if you have holiness of heart and life. The two do not go together, you see. They just don't go together. That's why this message is a message that the world needs to hear.

Reverend Cunningham, in other words, derives the essential Christian message of universal fellowship not from Jesus or anything else in the New Testament, but from the much newer gospel of "cultural diversity." It is not a wise trade. Christian fellowship is grounded in the profound idea that we are equal in the eyes of God. In that light, cultural *diversity* makes no difference. To search for fellowship by means of cultural *diversity* is to puff with pride those differences that Christianity, in principle, sets out to abolish.

But it is not just religion, or education, or any limited number of institutions in which *diversity* has made its transforming mark. It has, rather, swept through the culture.

When Alfred Russel Wallace traveled through the Malay Archipelago, he found the diversity of species astounding. During one two-week period in Borneo, he discovered more than 320 new species of beetles—34 in one day. As he reflected on all this variety, Wallace had to abandon the Sunday-school theology that God created each species to serve some human need: "all living things," he wrote,

> were *not* made for man. Many of them have no relation to him. The cycle of their existence has gone on independently of his . . . and their happiness and enjoyments, their loves and hates, their struggles for existence, their vigorous life and early death, would seem to be immediately related to their own well-being and perpetuation alone, limited only by the equal well-being and perpetuation of the numberless other organisms with which each is more or less intimately connected.

What Wallace glimpsed in the natural world was its independence of being. And indeed, real diversity calls us to understand that others were not created for our convenience or edification.

We are creatures with an infinite capacity for self-consciousness and a desire to tinker with the world, but our aviaries are simply enchanting illusions. When it comes to the serious question of how to prepare ourselves for the real world, we should shun illusion no matter how enchanting and strive to take our places amidst the magnificent diversity of things real.

THREE

DIVERSITY BEFORE *DIVERSITY*

Facing the title page of many old books (and few new ones) is a full-page illustration, a frontispiece. It is an advertisement, though a little out of the way. To get to it, the reader has to go to the trouble of taking the book in hand, and because books naturally open in the middle, page back to the beginning. There, sometimes under a sheet of tissue, might be a work of gaudy artistry, a staid portrait of the author, or a steel-point etching of some dramatic scene with a cryptic caption, such as: "Daphne smiled mischievously as she gave Robert the walnut."

During the great era of frontispieces, before dust jackets and paperbacks began their full frontal beckoning to passersby, one especially rich tradition of frontispieces developed: the tableau of human diversity, or, as it is titled in volume two of Reverend J. G. Wood's *The Uncivilized Races or Natural History of Mankind* (1870), the "Allegorical Representation of the Races of Man."

The artist in this instance has drawn a droopy-eyed Caucasian missionary, enthroned amidst a crowd of natives. His right hand rests on a Bible while his left reaches out languidly over a pineapple and some nondescript tropical fruit. He seems to be watching a young man in a weed girdle who kneels before him, about to unravel a decorated roll of tapa or bark cloth. Judging from the tattoos on his thigh, he is a Polynesian, and the garlanded woman next to him who is gazing raptly at the missionary must be that personification of unfettered sexuality, the Polynesian woman.

Crowded around these three are fourteen other figures, including an Eastern Woodland Indian, a Mayan, a Plains warrior with a raised tomahawk, an Australian aborigine, an Abyssinian, two Chinese, a Hindu, a Pashtun, a Thai, a mounted Mongol warrior, and a couple of classic barbarians having at each other with spear and battleaxe. In the middle distance, two people sit at the base of some trees smoking and sewing, while offshore, two Inuit in kayaks attempt to harpoon a right whale.

Reverend Wood leaves the interpretation of this allegory up to us. But I get the point. The missionary represents the modern university, comfortably ensconced left of center. His own intellectual traditions are the closed book that serves him only as a casual prop, while he reaches out in an ambiguous gesture: welcoming all kinds of human difference to his august presence, but expecting something in return too.

What does he expect? The men in the picture are variously suspicious, disgusted or enraged, but the three women look on the missionary with definite interest. The allegory shows us that the university understands that commitment to diversity is sexy.

Goshoot

Alas, no. My interpretation, though highly plausible as an account of the attitudes of contemporary American college professors, probably does not suit a book published in 1870. Such a book could not have a playfully positive view of diversity because, as we all know, this was the era of humorless cultural imperialism. In his placid superiority, the missionary depicted in the frontispiece to Reverend Wood's work must represent the self-assured superiority of Western civilization and Christendom over the subjugated native peoples of the earth.

Let me at once concede the point. Nineteenth-century writers in the West generally did not feel a terrible weight of guilt about the missionaries sent to convert non-Christian peoples, merchants sent to stimulate a trade in Western goods, colonizers sent to promote new native industries, administrators sent to impose Western ideas of law and order, or gunboats sent to secure the territorial claims of Western governments.

Reverend John George Wood (1827–1889; no relation) was an English clergyman best known for his popular works on nature, such as

My Feathered Friends (1856) and *Man and Beast* (1874). I first noticed him, however, in a passage in Mark Twain's *Roughing It*, where Twain is racking his brain for a way to explain how low in the scale of humanity he considered the Goshoot Indians (i.e. Western Shoshones, Gosha-Utes, now usually spelled Gosiute) he encountered in Nevada:

> On the morning of the sixteenth day out from St. Joseph we arrived at the entrance of Rocky Canyon, two hundred and fifty miles from Salt Lake. It was along in this wild country somewhere, and far from any habitation of white men, except the stage stations, that we came across the wretchedest type of mankind I have ever seen, up to this writing. I refer to the Goshoot Indians. From what we could see and all we could learn, they are very considerably inferior to even the despised Digger Indians of California; inferior to all races of savages on our continent; inferior to even the Tierra del Fuegans; inferior to the Hottentots; and actually inferior in some respects to the Kytches of Africa. Indeed, I have been obliged to look the bulky volumes of Wood's *Uncivilized Races of Men* clear through in order to find a savage tribe degraded enough to take rank with the Goshoots.

Twain's conceit that the "savages" of the world could be arrayed on a single scale of wretchedness, with some "considerably inferior" to others, is a very stale joke today.

For one thing, Twain's sardonic invective about the Goshoots is almost indistinguishable from some of the serious scientific opinion of his time. Anthropologists and others still took it as a matter of course that the various tribes and nations of the world could be arranged on a single scale of progress, from the most primitive to the most advanced. Some of the great formative debates in anthropology were over the proper calibration of this scale. Which contemporary peoples most resembled the hypothetical state of "primitive man"? In what order and by what steps should man's advancement up the scale of civilization be measured? And who—the English? the French? Americans?—should represent the furthermost march of civilization?

Because I teach first-year graduate students in anthropology the history of their discipline, and because I believe that the best way to learn history is to read original sources, I have spent considerable time among the nineteenth-century social theorists who asked these questions. Within anthropology as it is taught and practiced today, the nineteenth-century debates over the social progress of mankind are treated as an embarrassment. They reveal how blind and ignorant the discipline was in its origins; how early anthropology was so closely allied in spirit with the subjugation of mankind to Western economic, political, religious and cultural interests. The founders of anthropology—figures such as the American lawyer Lewis Henry Morgan (1818–1881), the English Quaker turned Oxford anthropologist Edward Burnett Tylor (1832–1917), and the Scottish folklorist Sir James George Frazer (1854–1941)—are remembered, if at all, according to the contemporary consensus, for compiling giant works that are vitiated from the outset by false assumptions and specious methods.

Being of a contrary turn of mind, naturally I like to defend Morgan, Tylor, Frazer and the large contingent of ambitious but now forgotten scholars of which they were part. And my basic line of defense is that these scholars gave us our first genuinely complex and detailed account of human cultural diversity.

Sheaves

Nineteenth-century anthropology is most frequently dismissed today with the all-purpose curse, "Social evolutionists!" Sometimes this curse can be wrapped into a more specific insult, "unilinear social evolutionist," which distinguishes Morgan, Tylor and company from later thinkers who argued that societies *do* evolve, but along separate paths. The "social evolutionist" tag, however, is more a matter of contemporary mythology than an accurate historical assessment. For while nineteenth-century anthropologists struggled mightily with the idea of human *progress,* most found only limited use for the idea of *evolution.* Their central project was to make some kind of sense of the bewildering variety of human customs suddenly thrust into view by the West's excited commercial expansion into the rest of the world. "Progress" and to a lesser extent "evolution" provided rough ways to sort the data, but it is always the facts, the burgeoning richness of human invention and the strangeness of human experience, that animate these writers. A new world opens up before them. Their writing sparkles with the freshness of intellectual discovery. Others, they seem to say, have seen these things only with their eyes; but suddenly, we *understand.* Anthropology is thus born of the effort to comprehend human diversity with the full imagination and the mind.

The works of these early anthropologists stand in contrast to those of some more famous and influential thinkers, who were indeed focused on progress itself, not on its utility for organizing ethnography. Georg W. F. Hegel (1770–1831), Auguste Comte (1798–1857), who invented the word "sociology," and Herbert Spencer (1820–1903) offered elaborate accounts of the nature of progress, and Spencer explicitly yoked his version to a theory of social evolution. Karl Marx (1818–1883), borrowing liberally from Hegel, offered yet another account of the nature of social progress. But these thinkers, who remain—sometimes painfully—present in our intellectual world, have virtually nothing to teach us about actual human diversity. They simply mow the world down and leave it to be stacked in sheaves.

When Mark Twain insults the Goshoots, however, he does not call upon the ghost of Hegel or the specter of Marx. Nor does he turn to the erudite anthropology of Edward Tylor or the wildly ambitious researches of his fellow American Lewis Henry Morgan. Instead, Reverend J. G. Wood's *The Uncivilized Races* comes to hand.

Partly this is a matter of timing. *The Uncivilized Races* was published in 1870, two years before *Roughing It.* But Tylor's *Researches into the Early History of Mankind and the Development of Civilization* was first published in 1865 and had run through several printings, and Tylor's masterwork, *Primitive Culture,* was published in 1871. Lewis Henry Morgan's magnificent *Systems of Consanguinity and Affinity of the Human Family* was published by the Smithsonian Institution in 1870.

Tylor and Morgan, however, addressed themselves to the audience of scholars, scientists and that portion of the lay public in love with the great intellectual adventures of the age. Even if, by chance, Twain knew of their works, they would not have provided the kind of popular reference he needed to nail his joke on the Goshoots. *The Uncivilized Races,* on the other hand, had just the right air of Victorian stuffiness and familiarity. Probably every American household prosperous enough to have a library had something like Reverend Wood's profusely illustrated tomes.

The genre of the popular ethnographic compendium is now extinct. Perhaps the closest we come today is the *National Geographic* magazine, which was founded in 1888 and is thus a survivor of an earlier cultural era. But for more than a century, beginning in the 1830s, books that offered a tour of all mankind were highly popular.

Whoever Travels Among Them

Among the early examples of this genre was Charles A. Goodrich's *The Universal Traveller* (1838), which, though it lacks a frontispiece, has a considerable subtitle:

THE
UNIVERSAL TRAVELLER
DESIGNED TO INTRODUCE
READERS AT HOME
TO AN ACQUAINTANCE WITH THE
ARTS, CUSTOMS, AND MANNERS,
OF THE
PRINCIPAL MODERN NATIONS ON THE GLOBE
EMBRACING A VIEW OF THEIR
PERSONS—CHARACTER—EMPLOYMENTS—AMUSEMENTS—RELIGION—DRESS—
HABITATIONS—MODES OF WARFARE—FOOD—ARTS—AGRICULTURE—
MANUFACTURES—SUPERSTITIONS—GOVERNMENT—
LITERATURE, &C. &C.
DERIVED FROM THE RESEARCHES OF
RECENT TRAVELLERS
OF
ACKNOWLEDGED ENTERPRISE, INTELLIGENCE, AND FIDELITY;
AND EMBODYING
A GREAT AMOUNT OF ENTERTAINING AND INSTRUCTIVE INFORMATION

Americans today tend to pride themselves on the largeness of their outlook, and to assume that earlier generations were, by comparison, parochial. In this light, we might expect that, despite the huge compass of his title, Goodrich would spend most of his universal traveling going by coach from one European city to another, and perhaps sparing a glance here and there for the rest of the world. But this does not remotely describe what Goodrich actually did.

The book in fact comes very close to living up to the author's vaunting claims. Goodrich admits in the preface that he "has been obliged to omit notice altogether of a few countries, and to abridge

somewhat more than he would wish," but *The Universal Traveller* "visits" (usually by way of summary and extract from the reports of real travelers) an extraordinary range of peoples around the world. It begins with a survey of the United States, considering regional and ethnic differences, and then proceeds to "Indian Tribes, Canada, Esquimaux, Greenlanders, Iceland, Mexico, and the West Indies." Other sections offer country-by-country surveys of South America, Europe and Asia (including Java and New Zealand). In surveying Africa, Goodrich distinguishes the Barbary States, Nubia, Abyssinia, "Caffraria" (East Africa), Southern Africa, Central Africa and West Africa, and he presents specific accounts of various tribes, including "The Amaxor Tribe," "The Corannas," "The Fellatahs" and "Ashantee." Among the "few countries" that Goodrich omitted from *The Universal Traveller* were India, Australia and most of the Pacific Islands.

Some of what Goodrich has to say about the inhabitants of faraway places—and not so faraway places—would surely offend the sensibilities of Americans today. Speaking of the Welsh, he writes:

> The *women* of the *higher class* are generally well informed and possess great volubility of speech, with a considerable portion of satirical wit. The men, who pay much less attention to mental attainments, are great sportsmen, and hospitable but often addicted to excessive drinking; and so irritable, that trifling provocations have engendered quarrels that have not subsided through many generations. They are very litigious; and there are few countries in which lawyers are so numerous, or so much employed.

Today, we would most likely condemn this sort of description as a collection of stereotypes—and perhaps in doing so impoverish our chances of perceiving some genuine aspects of cultural patterning.

Goodrich rarely uses the word "diversity," but an exception occurs as he attempts to describe the Central African kingdom of Bornou:

> The population of Bornou, estimated by Major Denham at 5,000,000 souls, is composed of a great diversity of races and tribes; and no fewer than ten different dialects are spoken in the empire.

(Major Denham is one of those "recent travellers of acknowledged enterprise, intelligence, and fidelity" whose published accounts

Goodrich mined for his book.) He also quotes Denham disparaging the people of Bornou:

> The women are particularly cleanly, but not good looking; they have large mouths, very thick lips, and high foreheads. The manner of dressing their hair is also very unbecoming. It is brought over the top of the head in three thick rolls, joining in front in a point, and thickly plastered with indigo and beeswax. Behind the point, it is wiry, very finely platted, and turned up like a drake's tail.

He proceeds in this vein to describe in detail and criticize as "unbecoming" the "tattoos" (actually scarifications) of the inhabitants of Bornou.

Today, we prohibit our travel writers from expressing dislike of the persons or the adornments of the people they encounter, and many Americans shy from any frank expression of their aesthetic reactions to people who look different from themselves lest they be accused of racism. Clearly Goodrich suffers none of these inhibitions. He is, to the contrary, exuberantly interested in what people look like, and he expresses distaste and admiration in about equal measure. Of the East Africans he writes:

> Barrow pronounced the Caffres to be "the finest race of men he ever beheld." Ray, in his "Researches," speaks less highly of their personal appearance, but admits that there are "many remarkably fine and well made men among them." Many of them, this latter writer adds, are tall, robust, and very muscular: their habits of life induce a firmness of carriage, and an open, manly demeanor, which is altogether free from that apparent consciousness of fear and superstition which generally characterizes uncivilized nations.

Physical appearances in Goodrich's accounts usually shade into moral assessments. These too are so out of fashion today that the modern reader laughs or blushes at the naïve nineteenth-century writer in his gross assumption of cultural superiority.

Lest we laugh too hard, we should glance at Goodrich on the Hottentots ("or Quaigua, as they call themselves") in South Africa. Goodrich does not especially admire them, but his criticisms are tempered and he finds more to blame in their white neighbors:

> Indolence has been the bane of these people, while sensuality and filth, its usual concomitants, are evils that have been strengthened by the contempt and oppression of the Dutch settlers. They have not, indeed, the same inducement to labor as more civilized tribes.... Not withstanding this savage mode of living, the Hottentots are kind and affectionate towards each other; and ready to share their last morsel with their companions. They are harmless, honest, faithful; but extremely phlegmatic.... If accused of crimes, of which they know themselves guilty, they generally divulge the truth; and they rarely quarrel among themselves, or use provoking language. Though naturally of a quiet and timid disposition, they will run into the face of danger, if led on by their superiors; and they endure pain with great fortitude. Whoever travels among them, may be sure of finding food and lodging, such as they have to bestow; and though they will receive presents, they ask for nothing.

In Goodrich's account, the Hottentots come off considerably better than the Boers, but his assessment is no mere exercise in conjuring up generic "noble savages." The Hottentots are indolent, sensual, timid; Hottentot women are "the most ill-formed and ill-proportioned of the human race"; women and men alike resemble "a European in the last stages of jaundice"; they do not trouble themselves to find food but, when they get it, the Hottentots are "voracious." This is hardly an idealized portrait.

Goodrich is not much more than a workmanlike writer. His book has no claim on our attention as an example of stylistic brilliance or intellectual daring. And yet *The Universal Traveller* possesses an imaginative scope and openness to some of the possibilities of human diversity that is beyond our reach today.

Just Delineations

At the beginning of *The Universal Traveller,* Goodrich offers a few words of justification for his project. One of his appeals to the reader is the idea that his literary "mode of traveling" will "serve to enlarge and enrich the mind." This is, of course, just a variation on a very old idea of the benefits of travel, transferred to reading *about* travel. But Goodrich then takes a step further. He says that "nothing is better calculated" to produce this enlargement and enrichment of the mind "than just delineations of human nature—of human life, and manners, and character—of man in all the varieties of his condition, as an inhabitant of the earth."

Let us try for a just delineation of where Goodrich's book stands in the tradition of writing about other cultures. Behind stands a very old tradition. *The History* of Herodotus offers a fifth-century-B.C. traveler's view of the circum-Mediterranean world, with some excursions to points further north, east and south. We can still turn to Tacitus and read his stern accounts of the Britons and the Germans in the first century A.D. for instruction on how to see one's own society more clearly by reflecting on the customs of other peoples. Marco Polo (c. 1254–1324) left us with his strangely bare account of eighteen years in Kublai Khan's China, but in the centuries that followed, the number of travelers multiplied and the precision of their memories improved. When the English diplomat and spy Richard Hakluyt (c. 1551–1616) collected his anthology, *The Principal Navigations, Voyages, Traiffiques and Discoveries of the English Nation* (second edition, 1598–1600), it ran into three volumes and over 1.5 million words.

After Hakluyt's death, his manuscript collection was acquired by Reverend Samuel Purchas (PUR-kas), chaplain to the archbishop of Canterbury, who drew on it for successive editions of his own book, *Purchas His Pilgrimage; Or Relations of the world and the religions obserued in all ages and places discouered, from the creation vnto this present: Contayning a theologicall and geographicall historie of Asia, Africa, and America,* which in the fourth edition (1625) was an even longer— 4-million-word—account of world travels and discoveries. Jack Beeching, a modern editor of Hakluyt, credits Reverend Purchas with realizing the market opportunity in "stay-at-home" readers with a "taste for closet travel." *Purchas His Pilgrims* (as it is usually called) is pretty clearly an ancestor of Goodrich's *The Universal Traveller.*

Travel writing became a major literary genre in the seventeenth and eighteenth centuries. In the third edition of his essays (1625), Francis Bacon included a brief set of instructions ("Of Travaile") to would-be travelers. ("Travaile, in the younger Sort, is a Part of Education; In the Elder, a Part of Experience.") As the number of accounts of overland adventures and overseas voyages grew into the many thousands, the opportunities for imitation and satire occurred to some writers.

In *Robinson Crusoe* (1719) and *Captain Singleton* (1720), Daniel Defoe (c. 1659–1731) created wonderfully imaginary travel narratives. The lesser-known work, *Captain Singleton*, offers an invented trek across Africa. Defoe showed one way of exploiting the fictional possibilities of the genre; Jonathan Swift (1667–1745) showed another use of travel fantasy. In *Gulliver's Travels* (1726), Swift returned to Tacitus' technique of making the description of supposedly distant people a mirror for the follies of his own society.

Fiction and satire, however, did not slow the industry that Hakluyt and Purchas had inaugurated. Published accounts of travels and broader surveys of mankind remained one of the most popular forms of writing. *An Entertaining Account of All the Countries of the Known World Describing the Different Religions, Habits, Tempers, Customs, Traffick, and Manufactures of Their Inhabitants* by Georgius Candidius, Evert Ysbrant Ides and Sir Thomas Roe appeared in its fourth edition in 1752.

But this takes us perhaps far enough. By the time Goodrich attempted *The Universal Traveller,* the English-speaking world was full of accounts by ordinary travelers, artful liars, extraordinary fabulists, sentimental journeyers, castaway sailors, heroic explorers and many others. Goodrich also had predecessors in the attempt to synthesize the abundance of travelers' reports into one account, but I have not encountered any work prior to *The Universal Traveller* that aims directly at an American audience thirsty for its own comprehensive account of human diversity. Goodrich was on to something.

Diversity Diversifies

In the decades that followed Goodrich's 1838 volume, American interest in cultural diversity diversified. One strand led to intensive research. Henry Rowe Schoolcraft (1793–1864), for example, became a sort of Audubon of the American Indians. From 1822 to 1841, he was the U.S. government's agent to the Chippewa and Ottawa tribes in Michigan and Wisconsin. Schoolcraft's marriage in 1825 to Jane Johnston, who was half Chippewa, fired his interest in Native American life, and he began to collect and publish folktales. His first major anthology of these appeared as *Algic Researches* in 1839. Schoolcraft's magnum opus,

Information Respecting the History, Condition and Prospects of the Indian Tribes of the United States, was a six-volume extravaganza published between 1851 and 1857. Along the way, he co-founded the American Ethnological Society, influenced the first secretary of the Smithsonian Institution to make the study of Indians a priority, and inspired the young Lewis Henry Morgan to write the first great American ethnography, *League of the Ho-De'-No-Sau-Nee, Iroquois* (1851).

This path eventually led to the creation of the Bureau of American Ethnology (in 1879) and the founding in the United States of a formal discipline devoted, at least initially, to the study of native peoples. But Schoolcraft's influences also led in other directions. Henry Longfellow's *The Song of Hiawatha* (1855) arose, as Longfellow said, from his reading of Schoolcraft's *Algic Researches* (Vol. I, p. 154) and his *Information Respecting ... the Indian Tribes* (Part III, p. 314). Longfellow adds:

> Into this old tradition I have woven other curious Indian legends, drawn chiefly from the various and valuable writings of Mr. Schoolcraft, to whom the literary world is greatly indebted for his indefatigable zeal in rescuing from oblivion so much of the legendary lore of the Indians.

Thus Longfellow's *Haiwatha* stands indebted to Schoolcraft much as T. S. Eliot's *The Waste Land* stands indebted to Frazer's *The Golden Bough.* But it is also important to know that when Longfellow was writing:

> By the shore of Gitche Gumee,
> By the shining Big-Sea-Water,
> At the doorway of his wigwam,
> In the pleasant summer morning,
> Haiwatha stood and waited.

he was also consciously modeling his folkloric epic on the Finnish folk epic, the *Kalevala.* Diversity thus entered American artistic conceptions early on and with considerable imaginative force.

Another expression of that force was the art of George Catlin (1796–1872), who spent eight years (1832–1839) among the Plains Indians, painting their portraits, sketching their ceremonies and creating an irreplaceable visual record of their cultures. Catlin published reproductions of his paintings in *Letters and Notes on the Manners, Customs, and Conditions of North American Indians* (1844), and *O-Kee-Pa: A Religious Ceremony and Other Customs of the Mandan* (1867). He was an artist more of remarkable opportunities than of remarkable talent, but his books are full of shrewd and careful observation of his subjects.

American interest in the diversity of mankind had still other strands. Some writers set out treatises on race, which, as compendia of all sorts of observations about humanity, do not differ much in character from *The Universal Traveller*. Charles Pickering (1805–1878) in *The Races of Man and Their Geographical Distribution* (1850), for example, offers comments on the Hottentots that partly buttress and partly contradict Goodrich's:

> I have found many points of interest in the Hottentot character, as portrayed by travelers, who universally bear testimony to the faithfulness, efficiency, and courage of their guides in trying situations, amid the dangers of this difficult and desolate country.... [R]eadily adopting the habits of civilization, these people have ever proved active and useful assistants to the colonist.... [They] deserved a better return than unequal legislation.

"Universally bear testimony"? Well, not quite. Efficiency and the qualities of being "active and useful" are not what Goodrich emphasized, but the two authors agree on faithfulness and share a dim view of how the Boers treated the Hottentots. Pickering's account is supplemented with a finely executed and sensitive portrait of a Hottentot boy.

Pickering himself was a physician and naturalist assigned to the United States Exploring Expedition (1838–1842), and his book originated as part of its official report. The U.S. Exploring Expedition, under the command of Lieutenant Wilkes, toured coastal South America, much of the Pacific and the coast of Antarctica, and touched at Australia. Though poorly organized and badly managed, the expedition produced an abundance of scientific results but, like Pickering himself, it has fallen into obscurity. Pickering originally had been appointed as the expedition's naturalist, but the American Philosophical Society, citing Pickering's nearsightedness, insisted that the expedition needed a sharpshooter in the role, and Pickering found himself sharing his naturalist duties with a heavily armed taxidermist named Titian Ramsay Peale. In his recent book on the Wilkes Expedition, Barry Alan Joyce suggests that Pickering's turn to the study of native

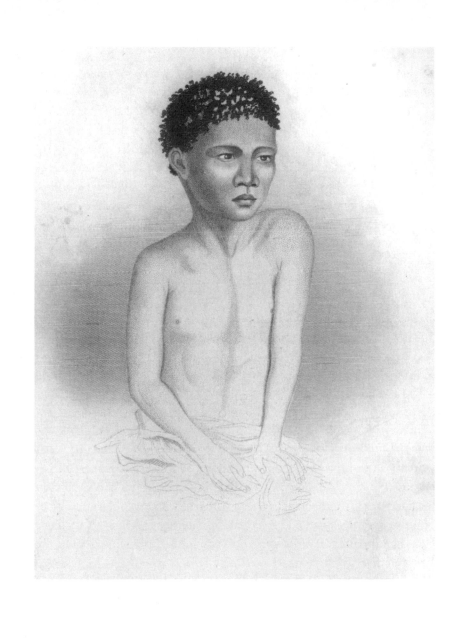

peoples during the voyage may have begun as a way to avoid the taxidermist. Diversity has many points of departure.

In more direct lineage from *The Universal Traveller* are works such as Reverend J. L. Blake's *The World As Exhibited in the Manners, Customs, and Characteristics of All Nations* (1853), which improves on Goodrich by including better illustrations and by venturing to spots that Goodrich missed, such as the Pelew Islands and the New Hebrides. Reverend Blake perhaps has taken advantage of the vastly increased familiarity with the Pacific that Americans had acquired through the China trade and the whaling industry in the years since 1838.

The impulse to write a relatively short but nonetheless all-embracing overview of cultural diversity was gradually compromised in the direction of more and more detail. What Goodrich and Blake aspired to do in one small volume took Reverend Wood, in 1870, two large volumes. By the end of the nineteenth century, we begin to encounter overgrown forests such as John Clark Ridpath's *History of the World; Being an Account of the Ethnic Origin, Primitive Estate, Early Migrations, Social Conditions and Present Promise of the Principal Families of Men; Together with a Preliminary Inquiry on the Time, Place and Manner of the Beginning Comprising the Evolution of Mankind and the Story of all Races; Complete in Four Volumes* (1894). Nor did the bloat stop at Ridpath's four volumes. Soon, multivolume series appeared, such as *Peeps at Many Lands*. By the 1920s, publishers had perfected the geographic extravaganza in series such as Charles F. Horne's seven-volume *The World and Its People or A Comprehensive Tour of All Lands* (1924) and Holland Thompson's thirty-volume *Lands and Peoples: The World in Color* (1929–1932).

Such works clearly no longer aspire to be readable syntheses, but they do retain at least some of the spirit of *The Universal Traveller:* they answer a genuine curiosity about what the world away from home looks like, and they sustain Goodrich's idea that learning about the diversity of mankind enlarges and enriches the mind.

Dust Is Not Dirt

That spirit is even more evident in another strand of the American fascination with cultural diversity before we called it that: children's books and schoolbooks were filled with the topic too. Geography was an important part of the American school curriculum from early on, and Americans felt a need for their own geography textbooks. By midcentury there were several, including Roswell C. Smith's *Smith's Geography: Geography on the Productive System for Schools, Academies, and Families* (1854). But Americans also continued to feed their children's fascination for the exotic with more lurid foreign books, such as James Greenwood's *Savage Habits and Customs* (1865), which was published as part of the English Beeton's Boy's Own Library series. Greenwood's book is full of terrific stuff that children today would never be allowed to read. In an account of an assembly among the "Ojibeways," Greenwood relates:

> One of the fellows, with one eye painted white, the other coal black, was not ashamed to tell loudly, and with a beaming face, how he once fell upon a poor solitary Sioux girl and scalped her. He gave us the minutest details of the atrocity, and yet at the end of the harangue, he was applauded, or at least behowled, like the other orators.

A safer excursion, however, could be found in Jane Andrews' *Seven Little Sisters, Who Live on the Round Ball That Floats in the Air* (1861). The seven little sisters from remote climates and continents (including Agoonack, the Esquimau Sister; Gemila, the Child of the Desert; Pen-se, who lives on a Chinese junk; and Manenko, whose father hunts for game on the plains of East Africa) are equally sweet and endearing, despite cultural differences.

But the Goodrich urge to capture an image of the whole world in its bustling variety is alive in children's books too. One such is Milton Hadley's *Little Men and Women; Or Boys and Girls of Many Lands, Containing Full Descriptions of the Children and Youth of France, Norway, Italy, Sicily, India, Africa, Arabia, China, Egypt, Mexico, Canada, Kaffir Tribes, Hawaii, Cuba, Greenland and Other Countries; Little Folks of All Countries with Captivating Accounts of the Manners, Dress, Amusements, Social Customs, Education, Employments, Etc. Etc. Including Charming Stories of the Little Indian Boys and Girls in Our Western States and Territories, Etc.* (1903). Hadley delights in correcting misimpressions:

> It is often said that Egyptian children are dirty. They are almost never dirty. The children of the masses, and frequently the

> children of the middle classes, are often dusty in the extreme, because they live in and move about in a land of extreme dust. But dust and dirt are two very different things. Dust is not necessarily dirt. Sandy dust, such as Egypt's dust, is most clean matter.

And he sometimes presents appalling caricatures:

> The Algerian blacks are ugly, thick of lip, coarse of skin, flat and lumpy of nose, hopeless of brow, and impudent of chin.
>
> But yet they escape entire hideousness. They have three great beauties: lovely, loving, pleading eyes; splendid white teeth; and faces that, though muddy of skin and thick and blurred of feature, beam with real kindness and inexhaustible good nature. The Negro children have, in addition to these, the beauty of youth.

Perhaps aimed at a slightly younger age, Grace Duffie Boyan and Ike Morgan's *Kids of Many Colors* (1901) offers an illustrated collection of verses that depict children among the Pygmies, Laplanders, Hawaiians, Gypsies, Cubans and many others. Boyan and Morgan explain:

> All our little boys and girls wonder how 't would be
> If they lived in other lands, across some distant sea;
> And over there, in ev'ry land, the children say: "O dear!
> How do children look and play around the world from here?"

And they conclude:

> The kids of many colors, hair straight and kinked and curled,
> Are just the little people that make the little world.

Boyan and Morgan do not exhibit the kind of deference to other cultures that is standard in today's children's books, but they are clearly universal in spirit. Their theme stands in contrast, for example, to Robert Louis Stevenson's "Foreign Children," which begins:

> Little Indian, Sioux or Crow,
> Little frosty Eskimo,
> Little Turk or Japanee,
> Oh! Don't you wish that you were me?

Stevenson pokes gentle fun in the poem at the English boy who assumes he is the envy of mankind, but the subject occurs far more readily to the Scots-English writer than to Americans, who, as exemplified by Boyan and Morgan, assume the world is filled with curiosity, not envy.

The tradition of teaching children unabashedly about cultural variety lived on at least into the 1930s with the "Uncle Ben" series, in which Uncle Ben takes young readers in a succession of short pamphlets to central Africa, Polynesia, India and many other destinations. Beyond the 1930s, however, it becomes increasingly difficult to find evidence of the American capacity to register cultural diversity in a direct way. The spirit of confident curiosity seems to wither. We grow more "sensitive" to the people in these no longer quite so faraway places, more reluctant to generalize about their cultures, and strongly averse to responding openly to their physical appearance.

How Pocahontas Lost Her Groove

The story of how Americans reckoned with human diversity would be incomplete without at least some mention of its erotic dimension. Part of our interest in diversity is the sexual attraction people often feel toward others who are dramatically unlike themselves. Cultural difference, in the right circumstances, turns people on. When Americans in the nineteenth century thought about diversity, they were, at least part of the time, also thinking about sex. That is probably the deeper meaning of all those passages in *The Universal Traveller,* Pickering's *The Races of Man,* and similar books in which the author marvels at the physical ugliness or beauty of women and men among some faraway people.

The theme was not always hidden. Melville's raptures over the beautiful (and, he implies, willing) Marquesan girl, Fayaway, helped to make *Typee* a bestseller. And Americans today are slowly coming to admit that their countrymen always experienced sexual attraction across the color line. The story of Pocahontas (c. 1595–1617) wrapping her arms around the head of Captain John Smith to save him from being clubbed to death by Powhattan's warriors no doubt spoke more clearly to earlier generations, but we can still sense the cross-cultural frisson.

Americans of both sexes have long fantasized and sometimes acted across such cultural boundaries. In some cases, no doubt, the boundary was merely irrelevant to an attraction between two individuals, but very often such attractions were fraught with pent-up feelings about hierarchy and subordination. That theme has been explored by some of our best writers, such as William Faulkner in *Light in August*. But as Americans today, priding ourselves on our frankness, come to admit that earlier generations of our countrymen frequently mated across racial and cultural boundaries, we are in some danger of turning this complex fact into another myth: that the attraction was really just about domination and that it is to be understood primarily in terms of powerful but hypocritical white men exploiting vulnerable black, Indian and other nonwhite women. We think of World War II GIs coming home with Japanese war brides and older American bachelors advertising in Korean publications for mail-order brides. One stereotype depicts insecure white men who, in an era of emancipated white women, seek submissive "Oriental" women that they think they can dominate.

The story we tell ourselves today that epitomizes our view of this situation is Thomas Jefferson's supposed liaison with his mulatto slave Sally Hemmings. In the absence of a documentary record, advocates of this view have turned to DNA comparison of Hemmings' descendents and acknowledged members of the Jefferson family. But genetic details may never provide conclusive evidence that Jefferson (as opposed to another member of his family) fathered some of Hemmings' children. Even the uncertainty, however, fuels the depiction of Jefferson as carelessly gratifying himself, so unconcerned for Sally or his children by her that he abandoned them to historical oblivion. The same faint facts, however, could mean many different things. If Jefferson was the father of some of Hemmings' children, could their relationship have been based on mutual love rather than exploitation? The question is, in our current way of thinking, off the table, even though Jefferson did, after all, direct that Hemmings' children be emancipated after his death.

The story of Pocahontas and Captain John Smith is charged with the erotic idea that a European male, reduced to a position of powerlessness and imminent death, might still excite the interest of a woman from an uncivilized tribe. Pocahontas *chooses* Smith. The historical Pocahontas did, in fact, save him, although she ended up marrying a different Englishman. The story of Sally Hemmings and Thomas

Jefferson, by contrast, is charged with the entirely different erotic idea of the European-American male as immensely powerful over his subordinates and acting as he wishes. Sally Hemmings' feelings, let alone her capacity to act on her own volition, are unknown and irrelevant. Hemmings is Jefferson's victim.

The two stories together tell us much about the differences between the old and new concepts of diversity. The old one indulges the idea that the erotic attractions between individuals of different races and cultures are mutual. In the case of Jefferson, the new idea of diversity emphasizes that sexual exploitation was just another facet of slavery, colonialism and imperialism.

The old idea of diversity evoked a world in which much of the erotic potential lay in its mystery. Americans were attuned to the reality that their own sexual customs, rules and expectations were not shared by other peoples. Some reacted to this with Victorian disgust and reforming zeal, but many others were lured to the differences. The new idea of diversity attempts to nullify the mysteriousness of the world. Americans do not now expect to encounter people less inhibited than themselves, although we retain a few strands of the older view.

The 1998 movie *How Stella Got Her Groove Back*, for example, offers a fable of a forty-year-old African-American woman who is successful as a stockbroker, but unfulfilled. Stella is erotically recharged by a vacation to Jamaica during which she has an affair with Winston, a twenty-year-old Jamaican man. The movie was based on a novel by Terry McMillan that reflects her own experience.

Stella is one of numerous reminders that the cultural recognition of the erotic potential of diversity hasn't completely disappeared, but in other ways, the movie clearly belongs to our epoch of diversity, not the older tradition. Despite the playfulness with stereotypes, *How Stella Got Her Groove Back* can't quite escape framing the cross-cultural affair between Stella and Winston as another instance of the rich and powerful American taking advantage of the younger, poorer, vulnerable native.

As in so many other ways, the older idea of diversity seems truer to human experience and richer in texture than our current one. I do not, however, mean to neglect its seamier side. The attraction to people who are different from oneself and the familiar world of one's own culture turned, for some Americans, toward a form of smuttiness. In the 1890s, a French army physician, who wrote under the name Jacobus X, began publishing a kind of amateur sexual ethnography, with works such as *L'Amour aux Colonies: Singularities, Physiologiques et Passionnelles* (1893) and *Lois Génitales: Etude des Phenomenes Presidant aux Fonctions de L'Amour Normal et de la Procreation Humaine* (1906). Some of his work was quickly translated into English and republished in the United States, in the guise of scholarship.

The first of these, a translation of *L'Amour aux Colonies,* was *Untrodden Fields of Anthropology: Observations on the Esoteric Manners and Customs of Semi-Civilized Peoples; Being a Record of Thirty Years Experience in Asia, Africa, America and Oceania; By a French Army-Surgeon,* which was published circa 1898 by the enterprising Charles Carrington, under the imprimatur of the fictional "American Anthropological Society." Dr. Jacobus X (sometimes identified as Jacobus Sutor) thus began a long career as America's favorite ethnopornographer. Well into the 1930s, the "Falstaff Press" continued to issue "privately printed" works attributed to Dr. X, sometimes accompanied by grainy photographs of topless native women.

Dr. X's reports contain little if anything that would shock contemporary Americans. Their interest lies, rather, in the appetite they catered to: the breathless excitement in thinking about the sexual lives of people in some distant place, whose experience of the world is different from one's own. That thought is presumably what lies behind some of the other cultural detritus of the era, such as the five anonymous volumes of carefully captioned ethnographic photographs that appeared in 1935, *The Secret Museum of Mankind.* I hesitate to ascribe an erotic motive to *The Secret Museum,* which is filled with myriad posed formal photographs of men and women in ethnic costume, or engaged in such activities as playing musical instruments, practicing archery or paddling canoes. But the title suggests a purpose, and there are perhaps enough bare breasts and undraped limbs to hint what that purpose was. Some of the captions too are lubricious. One photograph shows an ornately bespangled Berber girl in northern Algeria gazing at the camera, her arm raised as if to shield her from the sun, and is captioned:

A DANGEROUS BEAUTY IN SULLEN MOOD

> She has stood, until weary of attracting attention, by a wall in
> Biskra, this geisha of the Sahara, with her hard-won dowry of
> gold and silver adorning her person. She can sing Arab love-
> songs, play flute, hautboy, and zither, and dance more seduc-
> tively than girls of any other tribe. Her skill in making cigarettes
> and coffee is famous, and all her charms and accomplishments
> are for hire.

The Secret Museum of Mankind is, oddly, back in print, perhaps as an
object of curiosity. The world turns and turns, and what was once a
means to gape at other peoples becomes itself an object of gaping. It
is, so far as I know, the only book among the multitude of works that
constitute the written testament of America's older fascination with
diversity that has been resurrected for a contemporary audience.

Judging Cultural Difference

The new diversity may be, as we tend to think it is, an ethical advance,
but it is worth taking note of what this possible advance has cost us.
In a crucial sense, we have banished our ability to engage freely and
creatively with cultural diversity. We live instead with a myth that all
diversity is good, and that to respond appropriately to cultural difference we must shut off that portion of our brain that automatically
assesses. If diversity really does enlarge and enrich us, surely it is
because diversity puts strenuous demands on our judgment. When
we encounter real diversity, we need to make intellectual, moral and
aesthetic sense of it, and the further it lies from our previous experience, the more our intellectual, moral and aesthetic judgment will be
challenged.

But in the current epoch of all-diversity-is-good-diversity, we are
faced with a new prime directive: do not judge. The new spirit of diversity finds its ethical mandate in a form of supposed open-mindedness
that is inimical to the impulse to judge other cultures. According to
this view, to judge is to be ethnocentric and to be unworried about
being ethnocentric is to license bigotry.

This criticism is overdrawn and unwarranted. It is overdrawn in
that making judgments about other cultures is *not* evidence of a closed
and ethnocentric mind. Some *forms* of judging may indeed fall into

that deserved condemnation, but the act of judging cultural differences need not be a sterile exercise in applying fixed categories. We learn by judging and by correcting our judgments when they prove faulty. The Hottentots may be by nature indolent or energetic, faithful or treacherous. We don't know until we attempt to frame the generalization and assess how well it comports with the facts. A generalization that we stick to despite the facts is an unwarranted stereotype, and there is always the risk that we will make our generalizations come true by acting as if they already are.

But is this the risk that is evident in Goodrich's or Pickering's accounts of the Hottentots? Both seem, on the contrary, to find that the gravest defect in Hottentot life is their unfair and unfortunate subjection to the Boer settlers. The generalizations that Goodrich and Pickering offer do not blind them to the effects of social inequality. To the contrary, those generalizations seem to bring social inequality into focus by helping us to see that, whatever the faults of their moral character, the privations suffered by the Hottentots are unjustifiable.

In any case, the contemporary attempt to proscribe judging is doomed to failure, for we will judge anyway, even if we feel ashamed of it or blocked from expressing our judgments. Judging cultural difference is simply how humans naturally encounter the world. We should aim not to forestall judging but to make it explicit and therefore within easy reach of further consideration and correction.

Then and Now

Our nineteenth- and early-twentieth-century predecessors made quick and sometimes harsh generalizations about other peoples. Present-day disdain for those sorts of judgments and for the people who made them, however, is foolish. Our quick-to-judge cultural ancestors almost always saw deeper into cultural diversity than we do. Our understanding of diversity, uprooted from genuine human reactions and sterilized, is comparatively shallow. We no longer have access to the unalloyed feelings of amazement, repugnance, pity and horror that some cultural differences might indeed warrant. We no longer allow our senses to take in the uncanny, the horribly ugly, or the provocative in the appearance of foreign bodies or their strange dress. The more cautious and limited reactions we allow ourselves may reward us with a sense of achieved virtue, but they also wall us off from reality.

What Americans Mean by "Culture"

Many contemporary Americans, ignorant of the actual past, credit themselves with a level of sensitivity to cultural differences that eluded our supposedly unreflective predecessors. It is a sad delusion. The truth is our predecessors have left us an amazingly rich record of their curiosity about and reflection on cultural differences. Perhaps we ignore this record because those earlier generations used other words, the term "cultural difference" being of fairly recent vintage.

"Culture" in the broad sense of a collective whole comprising a distinct view of the world, intellectual dispositions, traditions, and habits of mind and manner is a specialized use of an older word essentially invented in English around 1900 by the German-born anthropologist Franz Boas (1858–1942). For decades it was a technical term (in this peculiar sense) found only in anthropology journals and monographs, but Boas' numerous students included some of the most skilled academic propagandists of the twentieth century. Some of these students, such as Alfred Kroeber (1876–1960) and Robert Lowie (1883–1957), are no longer well-known names, though they were famous and influential at one time. Others, especially Margaret Mead (1901–1978) and Ruth Benedict (1887–1948), remain prominent. It is probably to Mead and Benedict above all others that we owe the vast popularization of the anthropological idea of "culture."

The word "culture" as it is popularly used, however, creates a problem. It is a magnifying glass of a word, one that makes mountains out of molehills and prevents us from seeing the real mountains because our attention is fixed at the level of feldspar crystals and mica flakes. We use "culture" for almost any and every difference between two people, two institutions, two places. Yankees fans and Red Sox fans have two "cultures." The difference between Fox News and CNN is a matter of "culture." Harvard and MIT are near neighbors, but they are "culturally different."

To say that a difference is a *cultural* difference may be to imply that one does not have to judge the merits of the case. *Cultural* differences call for toleration of both sides because, after all, how can we decide between two whole ways of life? But there is another, almost opposite, way to use the word, which, instead of putting the speaker above the fray, inserts him aggressively into the middle of it. For example, Elizabeth Hays, writing for the *Daily News* (New York), reported on a Gerritsen Beach boat owner who, at a public hearing on some proposed regulations, declared:

> "It's my culture to be able to waterski. It's my culture to be able to fish," he continued. "And that's what I'm going to do until I die," he concluded, as the standing-room only crowd erupted into cheers and applause.

Calling something "my culture" or "our culture" can work as a "Keep Off" sign, but it obviously works better for some social groups than for others. The command "Respect my culture!" is better suited to the groups that define themselves partly or mostly through a history of victimization than to groups that are heirs to cultural privilege. The Gerritsen Beach motorboat aficionado is attempting to qualify for beleaguered-group status on the basis of social class. It is a longer shot for him than, say, for a Native American who speaks of "my culture," but the motorboater still has a better chance to play this angle than, say, the Boston Symphony Orchestra.

Americans fluidly switch back and forth between the two meanings, the aggressive "It's my culture" and the relativist "It's their culture." The seeming contradiction is bridged by the idea that pride in one's own culture is the foundation of tolerance toward other cultures. In a recent letter to the editor of the *Atlanta Constitution,* for example, a woman named Neers Mehta Miller explained:

> I am of Indian Hindu descent (born and raised in the United States) and have been happily married for the last five-and-a-half years to a Caucasian (Methodist). I want to be able to impart my culture and heritage to our children one day and want to raise them to be accepting of the different types of people, faiths and traditions in our world.

Mrs. Miller's hopes for her children are laudable and eminently achievable, at least as long as she is content with passing on to her children a "culture and heritage" that are suitably modified for American taste.

In fact, that doesn't look like it will be a problem, since the view she expresses in her letter is itself thoroughly American and not, in any obvious sense, informed by a Hindu worldview.

The Diversity Paradox

Thus when contemporary Americans speak of "cultural difference," they are usually pumping up their own specific heritage, exaggerating slight differences of temperament and attitude that separate rival sports teams or colleges, or simply acting like know-it-alls. They are not thinking about "culture" in the sense Boas intended or about any of the academic battles that anthropologists subsequently fought over the right manner to construe the differences between the traditional ways of Fiji Islanders and Samoans, or Goshoot Indians and Hopi Indians, or any of these people and the heirs of Western civilization living in Massachusetts. *Those* kinds of cultural differences require a very different frame of reference, and are only very vaguely swept into the category of "cultural diversity."

In fact, the more we dwell on the idea of "cultural diversity" as an aspect of American society, the less attention we seem to pay to the real and substantial cultural diversity of the rest of the world. This loss goes beyond the trivialization of a word. Nineteenth-century writers were able to convey rich impressions of the variety of mankind without using the *words* "culture" or "diversity" at all in their current meanings. We don't need the word or the concept "culture" to achieve a rich understanding of human diversity. It is a possible aid, but it is also—and it has become—a possible obstacle. The real loss, however, is not in our vocabulary but in our experience, in the attenuation of our ability to respond as fully and richly to human differences as did people like Goodrich, Wood—and Twain.

Ambush

Twain's politically incorrect assault on the character of the Goshoots has not passed unnoticed. The anthropologist Warren L. D'Azevedo writes that "It stands as probably the most malicious characterization of a conquered people in the history of White contact with native Americans." D'Azevedo associates Twain's screed with the attitudes that rationalized "the domination of White intruders over a people who already had been brought to a state of degradation by decades of aggressive contact." And to show the lingering effects of Twain's spite, he cites a writer from the 1940s who declared that the passage is "a classic every Nevadan loves. He reads it more often than he does the Bible."

Mark Twain's attack on the Goshoots does not end where we left it, with the invocation of Reverend Wood's *Uncivilized Races of Men*. Appalled by the degraded state of these Indians, Twain says that he had to consult Wood's "bulky volumes" to find another "savage tribe" of equal debasement. He continues:

> I find but one people fairly open to that shameful verdict. It is the Bosjesmans (bushmen) of South Africa. Such of the Goshoots as we saw, along the road and hanging about the stations, were small, lean, "scrawny" creatures; in complexion a dull black like the ordinary American Negro; their faces and hands bearing dirt which they had been hoarding and accumulating for months, years, and even generations, according to the age of the proprietor; a silent, sneaking, treacherous looking race; taking note of everything, covertly, like all the other "Noble Red Men" that we (do not) read about, and betraying no sign in their countenances; indolent, everlastingly patient and tireless, like all other Indians; prideless beggars—for if the beggar instinct were left out of an Indian he would not "go," any more than a clock without a pendulum; hungry, always hungry, and yet never refusing anything that a hog would eat, though often eating what a hog would decline; hunters, but having no higher ambition than to kill and eat jackass rabbits, crickets and grasshoppers, and embezzle carrion from the buzzards and cayotes; savages who, when asked if they have the common Indian belief in a Great Spirit show a something which almost amounts to emotion, thinking whiskey is referred to; a thin, scattering race of almost naked black children, these Goshoots are, who produce nothing at all, have no villages, and no gatherings together into strictly defined tribal communities—a people whose only shelter is a rag cast on a bush to keep off a portion of the snow, and yet who inhabit one of the most rocky, wintry, repulsive wastes that our country or any other can exhibit.

> The Bushman and our Goshoots are manifestly descended from the self-same gorilla, or kangaroo, or Norway rat, whichever animal-Adam the Darwinians trace them to.
>
> One would as soon expect the rabbits to fight as the Goshoots, and yet they used to live off the offal and refuse of the stations a few months and then come some dark night when no mischief was expected, and burn down the buildings and kill the men from ambush as they rushed out.

Twain's caricature of the Goshoots is indeed awful. Is it forgivable?

Mark Twain was a man of powerful prejudices and strange *idées fixes.* He talked himself into believing that Shakespeare could not have written Shakespeare's works; late in life, he talked himself out of finding any redeeming good in human nature. We cannot turn to Twain expecting to find someone immune to stereotypes and biases. His writing is full of them—except that, against all odds, he so often turns out better than himself. The same man who mocked the starving and dispossessed Goshoots gave us the prejudice-annihilating *Adventures of Huckleberry Finn,* in which the real hero, Jim, is an escaped slave.

Twain's invective against the Goshoots is also, at a certain level, at war with itself. He attacks their character unrelentingly, but (inadvertently?) conveys a picture of suffering and extremity. I suppose today we are less apt to be shocked that hunters and gatherers in the Great Basin would include crickets, grasshoppers and carrion in their diets, but if we look past Twain the polemist, we see Twain the newspaper reporter attending to the plain details. Who is it that offers alcoholic spirits to the Goshoots in the name of religion? Are patience, tirelessness and humility so clearly evidence of a degraded state?

Twain has twisted every factual observation into a clause in his indictment of the Goshoots, but the case is so absurdly overstated that we may well be prompted to consider the alternatives.

In this sense, Twain captures both what is admirable and what is forlorn about the American experience of diversity before the advent of *diversity.* On one hand, he possessed the quickness of imagination to recognize the profound debasement of the Goshoots, and the boldness of expression to convey that recognition so well that it is remembered to this day. On the other hand, by venting such extreme distaste in so humorous a manner, Twain gave encouragement to many who saw in his words license to sneer at the unfortunate Indians.

Sneering at the dispossessed is one of the emotional roots of racism, and it is clear that the open-mindedness toward human diversity that was characteristic of much nineteenth-century American thought had racism as its evil twin. Looking back today and assessing the American past by means of our brittle new creed of *diversity*, we tend to see mostly the racism, seldom the open-mindedness.

Diversity After *Diversity*

Paging through Reverend J. G. Wood's *The Uncivilized Races* and other volumes mentioned in this chapter, I am repeatedly struck by their assurance that a popular readership would be interested in such things as the domestic lives of Aborigines or Tongan dress. Today, such topics are the province of specialists and the substance of scholarly monographs. But for a time—more than a century—interest in cultural diversity was so strong among Americans that publishers could roll out volume after volume of *The Universal Traveller* and its progeny, and expect good sales.

Today we chatter endlessly about cultural diversity; we admire and extol cultural differences; and we admire our own admiration of those differences as evidence of our ethical enlightenment and aesthetic sophistication. But we are, at least by comparison with our cultural forebears, vastly ignorant of what we are talking about. Once upon a time, Americans encountered the world's diversity with awe, anger, prejudice, disgust, erotic excitement, pity, delight—and curiosity. Then we recast ourselves as champions of tolerant diversity, became fearful of inconvenient facts, and lost interest.

FOUR

THE LANGUAGE OF DIVERSITY

Words possess a bit of magic. They are seldom merely arbitrary globs of sound. Rather, many words—especially important words—in addition to their plain meanings have associations that deepen and color their psychological significance. Americans could as easily call the mixing of people from different ethnic backgrounds, different genders, different religions and different sexual orientations something other than *diversity*. The word *heterogeneity*, for example, means virtually the same thing. But it is highly unlikely that ordinary Americans would ever warm to an appeal for "more heterogeneity" in schools or in the workplace. This is not merely a matter of our suspicion of polysyllabic constructions descended from the Greek. English provides several other simple words that designate diversity.

Party, for example, used to mean "diverse," a sense that survives in the expression "parti-colored." The adjective *party* often referred to color (c. 1440: "Party clothe, or clothe made of dyuers colowrys."), but sometimes meant "internally divided" (c. 1420: "Fortune, the goddesse, with her party face.") and sometimes designated internal contradiction (1717: "It was, as I hear, a party per pale sermon, viz. both for the whiggs and for the tories."). But contemporary usage has passed this possibility by. When we say that some university is a "party school," we do not mean that it has an ethnically diverse enrollment.

English provides a host of simple words that *can* convey the essential idea of diversity: a *mix*, a *stir*, a *mingling*, a *medley*, to name a few. We also have metaphoric candidates: a *marl* is a rich soil made of diverse parts; an *olio* is a dish made of diverse ingredients or any heterogeneous mixture (1847, Disraeli: "An olio of all ages and all countries."). And we have other fancy words, like *heterogeneity*, that convey similar points: *allotropic* (of an element that exists in two or more molecular forms), *multifarious, variegated.*

Why, out of all these and many more possibilities, do we choose to speak of our social differences as *diversity?* I suspect some would answer that the word *diversity* sounds more positive than most of the alternatives. That answer has some merit, but why does *diversity* sound good to us? In fact, over its long history in English, the word *diversity* has often had bad connotations, and when not meant pejoratively, it usually fell short of approbation.

In one of its earliest recorded uses, Chaucer, in "The Man of Law's Tale" (c. 1386), referred to the irreconcilable conflict between two laws: "Ther was swich diuersitie Bitwene hir bothe lawes." ("There was such diversity between the laws [of two countries].") Caxton in 1481 identified *diversities* with political factions ("many dyuersetees, & facions not lyke"), and two years later employed the word in one of its old meanings as something contrary to goodness and justice: "This quene ... made unto the peple grete dyuersytees." (The Queen stirred up conflict in the kingdom by inciting factions.) That negative idea of *diversity*, borrowed from French, seems to show up most frequently in political discourse. In 1513, for example, Henry Bradshaw wrote, "In all his realme was no dyuersyte, Malyce was subdued."

But diversity also had a range of more neutral applications. The *Oxford English Dictionary* offers examples of "diversity" in other fields, including grammar:

> 1530. Jehan Palsgrave. "Dyversite of gendre is expressed onely in pronownes of the thirde persone."

and botany:

> 1665. John Rea. *Flora, seu de florum cultura, or a complete florilege.* vii. 42. "The White lily affordeth three diversities, two besides the common kind."

And Sir Thomas Browne in *Religio Medici* (1643) offers a paradoxical meditation on the infinite variety of human faces, in which "diversity" is part of God's plan, even while it separates the human from the divine:

> Nor doth the similitude of creatures disparage the variety of nature, nor any way confound the works of God. For even in things alike there is diversity, and those that do seem to accord do manifestly disagree. And thus is man like God; for in the same things that we resemble him, we are utterly different from him.

None of these, however, would seem to infuse the word with the positive feeling that Americans now find in it. So how did diversity achieve its healthy glow? When did it cease to mean unwelcome conflict and conditions rife with malice? Or escape from pallid neutrality?

Part of the answer is the Romantic movement in the arts, which found much to admire in the diversity of nature. When Nathaniel Hawthorne sat down by some trees in Sleepy Hollow at ten in the morning, July 27, 1844, notebook in hand, he noted not only the exact time and place but also the "beautiful diversity of green" all around him. Hawthorne was hardly alone in harboring such feelings, but I suspect the real source of our higher estimation of diversity lies elsewhere: the publication in 1859 of Charles Darwin's *The Origin of Species by Means of Natural Selection*.

This may surprise some who think kindly of social diversity and not so kindly of the harsh principles of Darwinian evolution, but the connection is strong. Darwin put biological diversity at the center of his theory, and in so doing gave diversity a wholly new positive connotation. He argued that nature's capacity to produce new species arose directly from natural variation within species, and he saw this diversity as crucial to each species' ability to adapt and survive. Darwin speaks much more frequently of "variation" than he does of "diversity," but when he does employ the word "diversity," its positive associations are unmistakable. In his chapter "Struggle for Existence" he writes:

> When we look at the plants and bushes clothing an entangled bank, we are tempted to attribute their proportional numbers and kinds to what we call chance. But how false a view is this! Every one has heard that when an American forest is cut down, a very different vegetation springs up; but it has been observed that the trees now growing on the ancient Indian mounds, in the Southern United States, display the same *beautiful diversity* and proportion of kinds as in the surrounding virgin forests. [emphasis added]

Darwin, noting that animal breeders can, over time, turn barely appreciable differences into divergent breeds, continues:

> But how, it may be asked, can any analogous principle apply in nature? I believe it can and does apply most efficiently, from the simple circumstance that the more diversified the descendants from any one species become in structure, constitution, and habits, by so much will they be better enabled to seize on many and widely diversified places in the polity of nature, and so be enabled to increase in numbers.

Darwin's argument elevated diversity (or "variation") within a species from incidental fact to crucial determinant of a species' biological success.

This was a radical break with scientific tradition. At least since Aristotle, Western scientific inquiry had focused on the *essential* qualities of species. If one wanted to know what a wombat was, one attempted to find the attributes necessary and sufficient to *define* the species of wombat. Darwin's revolutionary idea was to pay close attention to the data that such *essentializing* definitions threw away: the incidental variation among wombats that did *not* determine whether an animal was a wombat rather than, say, a walrus. For Darwin, natural variation among the existing members of a species—their *diversity*—was both the foundation for species' survival in an ever-changing world, and the root of new species. In the chapter "Variation Under Nature" he notes that "a well-marked variety may be justly called an incipient species."

Darwin's revaluation of intraspecies diversity slowly worked its way into mainstream thought accompanied by a second idea: the incredible variety of species, especially in the tropical regions of the world. Darwin's contemporary Alfred Russel Wallace was perhaps the more evocative writer on this topic. Wallace was the itinerant bug collector and all-round amateur naturalist whose independent discovery in 1858 of the idea of the origin of species through natural selection finally roused Charles Darwin to announce the theory that *he* had been deliberating for twenty years. Together with Darwin, Wallace prompted the nineteenth-century revolution in biology which stands, largely unacknowledged, behind our culture's current elevation of *diversity* into a high social principle.

From what we know today, it is clear that biological diversity is very different from cultural diversity. But what is clear today has not always been clear. For at least a century before Darwin published *The Origin of Species* and for half a century after, the dominant theory linking human biological diversity and cultural diversity was the theory of race. Racialist theories are attempts to account for human diversity as though that diversity were *primarily* a matter of distinct biological varieties.

Darwin himself, and Wallace too for that matter, were not especially concerned with racialist theories. Even so, neither drew firm lines between his observations of plants and animals and his observations of humans. At the very beginning of his career as the naturalist on the HMS *Beagle,* Darwin was a sharp-eyed observer of the natives of Tierra del Fuego and Tahiti. And Wallace freely mixed his accounts of his searches for exotic insects and birds with his accounts of native peoples.

We are, for better and for worse, the inheritors of this tradition. Through Darwin and his many successors, we have learned to see natural diversity as a tremendously positive aspect of our world. When contemporary Americans talk about diversity, of course, very few of us are thinking about Darwin or Wallace; but we are thinking *by means of* their ideas about who and what we are. If we see ourselves as having some responsibility to respect diversity, it is because we have learned from them and their scientific successors that diversity is a deeply creative principle in nature.

The bit of magic in the word *diversity* is this association with a powerful scientific idea. Diversity in nature turns out to be crucial to the health of individuals, the well-being and adaptability of species, and the course of evolutionary change. The contemporary appropriation of the word "diversity" refers to matters logically and substantively quite different from what the old biologists had in mind, but even so, it borrows some of their heft and prestige.

But it also puts racialist thinking at the unacknowledged center of the *diversity* doctrine. Diversiphiles twist and squirm around this fact, always attempting to redefine race as a *cultural* concept, but never quite willing to relinquish the sense that races are a flesh-and-blood reality. Diversiphiles, of course, emphasize many other social *diversities* in addition to race. Language, nationality, gender, religion, disability and gender preference are bundled into contemporary notions of *diversity* as well. Yet race remains *diversity par excellence,* and diversiphiles frequently claim that the other *diversities* they hope to turn into sources of social privilege are "just like race"—i.e., like race, they are stigmatized categories that disadvantage those who are forced to occupy them and are perpetuated one generation to the next.

This is an odd situation, in that diversiphiles seem to be running away from and at the same time running toward race, and it is odder still in that the idea of race itself has long since been abandoned by serious science. Race, however, has had a stubborn afterlife in American culture. Many Americans still unknowingly employ the vocabulary of discredited nineteenth-century racial theories. (What, after all, is a "Caucasian"?) And the biologically nonsensical premises of racialism repeatedly find their way into our sober considerations of public policy. We continue, for example, to create legislative districts based on race; we award government contracts based on the supposed racial identity of the owners of businesses; and we tolerate different default rates on student loans depending on the racial classification of the college.

Race and *diversity* thus make an interesting pair. The repulsion between them is real. Race insists on the importance of biology; diversity insists on the importance of culture. The word *race* appears in contemporary English fraught with misgivings; *diversity* exudes confident generosity. *Race* lumbers under the double burden of mournful history and dubious science; *diversity* skips cheerfully ahead. The idea that racial *diversity* is only one of several socially valuable *diversities* implicitly demotes race from its position as the primary division in American life. And the rhetoric of *diversity* is better adapted to "celebrating difference" than to grasping racial hierarchy, inequality and stigma. The positive connotations of the word *diversity* are at war with the negative connotations of the word *race.*

And yet the attraction between *race* and *diversity* is real too. When Americans began in the 1970s to praise *diversity* and to seek policies to increase *diversity,* they were originally thinking about race, and even today, when people speak of *diversity,* they tend to think first of racial issues. Race remains the focal meaning of *diversity,* but this is best seen by examining actual usage.

How the Word *Diversity* Is Actually Used

Although the ideology of diversity was born in the discussion of differences between blacks and whites, it quickly subsumed other differences, such as ethnicity, sex (gender) and region. And it has continued to expand so that, depending on context, when Americans speak of diversity they may be referring not only to differences between whites and "people of color," but also to religious differences, sexual preferences, physical or mental handicaps, or still other social differentiations.

This scatter of meanings does have an approximate consistency within the ideology of *diversity.* All of the differences that are sometimes wrapped into *diversity* are asserted to be the subject of society's intolerance and invidious treatment. So to be in favor of *diversity* is to take a stand in opposition to what one supposes are forces of intolerance, usually conceived as a hierarchy of privilege that historically favored and still favors heterosexual, nonhandicapped, white males. Still, the word as used by diversiphiles doesn't always mean the same thing.

Most Americans probably don't notice this multiplicity of meanings. We are so used to switching from one meaning to another that it comes automatically. But let's turn off the automatic pilot for a moment and examine the variety. *Diversity* seems to have four main meanings, having to do with categorization, representation, ideology and what might be called social scientific bumbling. Let's take these, and their subvarieties, one by one.

I. CATEGORIZATION: The word *diversity* is sometimes shorthand for "human social or cultural diversity."
This usage has three main variations:
   A. As a euphemism for one or more unnamed categories of people. The speaker wishes to denote the real or desired presence of individuals belonging to certain recognized categories in American society without naming the categories. He might say, "Our company needs more diversity." Depending on context, *diversity* in this sentence might mean, *Our company needs more:*
      A1. African-Americans
      A2. African-Americans, Latinos and Native Americans

A3. African-Americans, Latinos, Native Americans and
   Asians

A4. All of the above plus women

A5. All of the above plus gays and lesbians

A6. All of the above plus disabled people

Note that the list is hierarchical. "Diversity" can refer just to African-Americans without further specification, but it cannot normally refer just to women, gays and lesbians, or disabled people without an additional modifier, e.g. "Our company needs more gender diversity."

These usages are extremely common. For example, a newspaper story calling for more minority-group athletes to participate in Winter Olympic sports ran under the headline:

> All-American Ideals; Olympics: Call for More Diversity on U.S.
> Winter Teams Comes from Athletes Who Have Overcome Odds
> (*Baltimore Sun*, February 24, 2002, p. 2F.)

The text that follows indicates that "diversity" in this instance stands for "athletes of color," which in turn includes African-American bobsledder Vonetta Flowers, Cuban-American speed skater Jennifer Rodriguez, and Asian-American figure skater Michelle Kwan. A nearly perfect A3, missing only a Native American—unless Derek Parra, the Mexican-American speed skater, is to be classified Native American as well as Latino.

A news story about minority actors pressuring television networks to give them more roles refers to a coalition of ethnic interest groups that came to the actors' aid:

> The coalition has given low marks to the networks' diversity attempts.
> (Greg Braxton and Dana Calvo, "Everyone into the Talent Pool,"
> *Los Angeles Times*, March 17, 2002, part 6, p. 6.)

Outside its original context this sentence is indecipherable, but in the middle of the article it is perfectly clear. The "coalition" is composed of the NAACP, the National Latino Media Council, American Indians in Film and Television, and the Asian Pacific Media Coalition. Hence "diversity" in the quoted sentence is again an A3.

B. As a shorthand way to refer to *cultural* diversity in general. The speaker wishes to denote the variety of customs and beliefs that are characteristic of humanity without acknowledging any specific custom, belief or culture.

For example, after 150 current and former employees of AT&T accused the company in November 2001 of "sexual harassment, racial discrimination and bias against the disabled," AT&T "spokeswoman" Cindy Neale said,

> AT&T has a very strong, long-standing commitment to diversity in the workplace, and in fact, it's our company policy that we treat all individuals with dignity and respect.
> (Carrie Mason-Draffen, "AT&T Bias Charge," *Newsday*, November 30, 2001, p. A7.)

Ms. Neale is constructively vague. We have no idea what AT&T is really committed to. (Does the company's commitment to "diversity in the workplace" include hiring lazy people? Alcoholics? The litigious? Proven incompetents?) But we are invited to assume a meaning in keeping with the contemporary usage. Miss Neale means something to the effect that "AT&T doesn't discriminate against people on the basis of sex, race or handicap."

The word "diversity" can be especially tricky when it is used in this vague and encompassing fashion (B), and it might therefore be helpful to distinguish a few subtypes:

B1. *Diversity as what's left over after specifying all the groups that have come to mind.*

For example, Elizabeth Bennett, a psychology professor at Washington and Jefferson College, told a reporter that campus offices of multicultural affairs

> are shifting to include not only blacks but also Latinos, gays, lesbians, international students, the disabled and the whole range of diversity existing within American culture.
> ("Defining Diversity: Success Is Hard to Gauge Because the Meaning of Multiculturalism Has Changed," *Pittsburgh Post-Gazette*, December 23, 2001, p. W3.)

Of course, Professor Bennett doesn't literally mean the *whole* range of diversity in American culture. The Office of Multicultural Affairs at Washington and Jefferson probably isn't catering to campus conservatives, heterosexual white males or people who enjoy smoking. The "whole range of diversity" means something like "and any other victim groups I forgot to mention."

B2. *"Cultural diversity" can also be used as a compressed statement for the broader banality that the world is a big place, full of human variety.*

For example, Katie Johnson Hoffman, student at Cheektowwaga Central High School near Buffalo, told the organizers of the school's multicultural awareness day:

> How wonderful for a school district to welcome the world and truly promote cultural diversity.
> ("Day Promotes Multicultural Awareness," *Buffalo News*, February 6, 2002, p. C3.)

Katie's school district, however, only staged some performances by Native American, African-American, Irish and Polish dancers, and held forty "workshops." It seems unlikely that any of these uplifting events actually increased the amount of cultural diversity in the world at large, or even in Buffalo. What Katie meant by saying the school promoted "cultural diversity" was something to the effect that "the school encouraged us students to form positive emotional associations with the general idea that the world is full of different cultures, all of them pretty nice and deserving our respect."

II. REPRESENTATION: The word *diversity* sometimes refers not to actual human variety but to *representations* of such variety. This usage of "diversity" builds on all of the previous ones by seizing the principle of categorization. But in this instance, instead of a category of people, "diversity" refers to images of people.

For example, a newspaper story about video games began:

> Violence in video games is commonplace, even games developed for the youngest players, while racial and gender diversity is barely existent, a children's research group said Monday.
> (Michelle Healy, "Video Game Verdict: Violent, Not Diverse," *USA Today*, December 11, 2001, p. 9D.)

From the text we learn that only 16 percent of the video game "human" heroes are women, that there are "no Latina characters," and that "African-American and Latino men were typically athletes."

This use of "diversity" to mean something like "depictions of social categories" leads to some very peculiar formulations in which the speaker or writer seems to lose touch with the difference between real people and mere representations of people. It is common in academic writing.

III. IDEOLOGY: The word *diversity* sometimes refers to a set of beliefs.

This is a frequently encountered use of the word "diversity" that would have baffled any speaker of English before 1978, the year of the Supreme Court's *Bakke* decision. In this usage, "diversity" does not refer to real people or even representations of people, but to a set of beliefs.

Usually, the writer who employs "diversity" in this sense assumes the reader's familiarity with multiculturalism. For example:

> Diversity, political correctness, opportunism, mandated recognition of other cultures—all combine further to promote tolerance —or the illusion of tolerance—for once barely tolerated immigrant groups.
> (Wendy Law-Yone, "Persian Delights," *Washington Post*, December 19, 1999, p. X14.)

> This is the diversity president speaking, a man who sees nearly every issue—at home and aboard—through the prism of multiculturalism.
> (Francine Kiefer, "Why 'Togetherness' Is a Cornerstone for Clinton," *Christian Science Monitor*, May 20, 1999, p. 1.)

> Defenders of amending school curricula to include diversity requirements do not want to take away from the proud heritage of America; they want to add to that heritage by including the contributions of all Americans.
> (Susan D. Moeller, "Multiculturalism: An Effort to Let Every Voice Be Heard," *Seattle Times*, November 12, 1991, p. A13.)

> In Oak Park, a suburb with a history of attention to diversity and the rights of all, gay and lesbian activists say it is their turn now.
> ("Metro Briefings," *Chicago Sun-Times*, August 17, 1992, p. 4.)

Occasionally, however, "diversity" in this broad sense crops up in a different ideological context. For example, in February 2002, Jean Popp, the president of the city council of Canonsburg, Pennsylvania, proposed a council resolution supporting an amendment to the U.S. Constitution to allow prayer and other religious expression on public property:

> Popp's resolution states, "... our country was founded on the precepts of freedom, liberty, diversity, and the right of people to acknowledge God according to the dictates of conscience."
> ("News Briefs," *Pittsburgh Post-Gazette*, February 17, 2002, p. W9.)

Ms. Popp appears to think that whatever works for the multicultural Left might work just as well for the Religious Right.

But in its most familiar form, the *diversity* ideology asserts that American society is a hierarchy in which whites oppress other groups, and that individuals participate in the perpetuation of this hierarchy by harboring hurtful stereotypes about the members of the oppressed groups. The word "diversity" in this context refers to the set of beliefs that liberates the individual from his attachment to these stereotypes by allowing him to see the worthiness of the oppressed groups.

Thus we frequently hear of "diversity training." For example, in the wake of the September 11 terrorist attack, police officers of Temple Terrace near Tampa learned some special skills. A news report relates:

> During diversity training last week, police officers discussed how to approach veiled women and how to persuade Muslims to report crimes.
> (Babita Persaud, "In Pursuit of Knowledge," *St. Petersburg Times*, October 6, 2001, p. 1B.)

After a classmate hit Atlanta high school student Keishuna Young with his car in what police said was a "racially-motivated attack," Keishuna and her mother:

> said the incident served as a wake-up call for the need for additional racial diversity training in schools.
> (Andrea Jones, "Attack Victim, Mom Push Diversity Training," *Atlanta Constitution*, November 5, 2001, p. 1JJ.)

And American Express settled a sex discrimination suit by agreeing to pay out $31 million and also:

> to name a diversity officer and start mandatory diversity training for financial advisors, a company spokeswoman said.
> ("American Express to Pay $31 Million in Suit," *Los Angeles Times*, February 22, 2002, part 3, p. 2.)

The police discussions in Temple Terrace, the school program that Keishuna Young calls for, and the regimen that lies ahead for AMEX employees are focused on changing people's attitudes. To be "trained" in "diversity" in this sense is to become convinced of the rightness of a particular worldview, which will lead one to recognize and overcome religious, racial and gender biases. *Diversity* training is therefore one kind of "sensitivity training."

The ideology of "diversity," however, is mercurial, and the listener or reader has to pay close attention to exactly what social categories are being elevated by the training that comes along with it. Dotti Berry is a lesbian in Lexington, Kentucky, who runs a diversity training business called EmpoweringDiversity.com. Her brand of *diversity* aims at "affirming gay people as being among God's children."

And "diversity training" is sometimes just a metaphor for life experience leading to cultural broadmindedness. In a newspaper article, a musician known as "DJ Logic" describes how, growing up in the Bronx in the 1980s, he encountered hip-hop, alternative rock and jazz. The reporter comments:

> It all started with his mom buying him a pair of turntables for Christmas 1985. The diversity training, he got on the streets.
> (Scott Mervis, "Logical Leap," *Pittsburgh Post-Gazette*, November 9, 2001, p. 24.)

IV. SOCIAL SCIENTIFIC BUMBLING: The word *diversity* sometimes refers to some more or less indecipherable formulation of a diversiphile savant.

The diversity movement has intellectual roots in the social sciences, and it might be said that social science contributed the word *diversity* to popular thought about social order. Some social scientists, however, seem intent on wresting the word back. To this end, they propose formal definitions that attempt to eliminate the word's many ambiguities. For example, writing about Department of Defense "work-groups," two psychologists observe:

> Originally, the word [diversity] served as a way to communicate information on the variation of race, sex, religion, and national origin (RSRNO) characteristics among workers within an organization. As researchers explored the deeper meanings of the term, it became clear that diversity might refer to qualities associated with or attributed to RSRNO characteristics. The "valuing diversity" movement led to further implicit (unstated) refinements of the term and possibly greater confusion as to its definition.
> (Robert M. McIntyre and Judith L. Johnson, "Personality and Leadership in Diverse DoD Workgroups and Teams," 2001.)

Greater confusion than RSRNO? What could these psychologists be thinking? They go on to quote another worker in the social scientific vineyards, K. L. Larkey, who offers this clarifying view:

> For purposes of understanding current theory, diversity is defined as (a) differences in worldviews or subjective culture, resulting in potential behaviors that may have moral differences among cultural groups ... and (b) differences in identity among group members in relation to other groups.

The phrase "resulting in potential behaviors" deserves its own little warm corner in language hell. But never mind; there is worse to come.

A professor of management and decision sciences takes his bearing from some other colleagues:

> Milliken and Martins (1996) suggested a typology of diversity dimensions: "observable" and "less observable." Observable attributes of diversity include such characteristics as race, ethnic background, age, or gender. Less observable attributes include such attributes as education, technical abilities, functional background, tenure in the system, social economic background, and personality characteristics or values.
> (Gary L. Whaley, "Three Levels of Diversity: An Examination of the Complex Relationship between Diversity, Group Cohesiveness, Sexual Harassment, Group Performance, and Time," 2001.)

Enough, enough, enough.

The social scientific debauch of "diversity" is clearly worse than all the ambiguities of popular usage put together. I will take my chances attempting to figure out from context what the reporters at the *Buffalo News* and the *St. Petersburg Times* have to say, and I would advise the reader to slam shut any book that attempts to transform the word "diversity" into a meaning akin to the definitions cited above.

Diversity Metaphors

A friend of mine, Sam, who was a child survivor of one of the Nazi death camps, sometimes brings me interesting books and other objects he has scavenged from the Wellesley town dump. He is a quiet, meditative man who has a keen eye for details. Sam is a biologist, a professor before he retired, and we share an interest in odd words such as "formication," which refers to the feeling that bugs are crawling over your skin. He also taught me how to recognize the distinctive gait of someone with advanced syphilis (which, among other things, destroys nerves in the feet), and he once gave me a copy of a collection of sermons by Father Charles Coughlin, which he found perfectly preserved in the dump. Father Coughlin was the Michigan priest whose national radio broadcasts in the 1930s veered from endorsement of Roosevelt's New Deal to anti-Semitic diatribes.

I have not seen Sam at work in the town dump, but I imagine him taking pleasure in the unexpected juxtapositions—the dented shovel beside the unbroken egg—that come to light. I expect he finds some solace in saving what can be saved.

Sam's pastime came to mind as I was considering the metaphoric side of *diversity*, which luxuriates in images of disparate things combined into harmonious wholes. *Diversity* is said to be, among other things, a rainbow, a quilt, a rich stew, a box of crayons, a Noah's ark. The town dump, in this regard, has a certain overlooked potential.

Diversiphiles turn to metaphor not just to popularize their ideas but to cover over a contradiction that would be hard to hide in plain speech: the contradiction between the diversiphiles' insistence that the differences among cultural traditions are vast and irreconcilable, and their simultaneous assertion that diversity is a path to overcoming division and achieving national (or pan-national) unity.

The favored metaphors of rainbows, quilts, stews, crayons and arks are easily visualized images of many-ness in unity, but they fail in one key way: All of them smuggle in the underlying commonality that the doctrine of *diversity* usually attacks. The parts of the rainbow are all spectra of visible light; the quilt is stitched from swatches of fabric; the stew comprises edible foodstuffs; the crayons are part of a palate of colors; and the ark has on board the fauna that will inhabit the postdiluvian earth. What's missing is the radical separateness of each of the parts: the color that does not *want* to be part of the rainbow, the fabric that dangles outside the quilt. Those diversiphiles who respond to Martin Luther King's image of the "single garment of destiny" by bringing up "loose threads" are, in their way, closer to the metaphoric mark.

To get all the way to a satisfactory image of *diversity*, we would have to construct some metaphor in which each component possesses its own autonomy and insists on its own importance, and the whole would be overseen by a power who simultaneously credits and ignores each part's claim to precedence. The town dump seems to me to be the ideal form of a conglomerate unity where completely unrelated things of disparate origin end up side by side, kept in their place by the apotheosis of the modern multicultural teacher, the guy who drives the bulldozer.

As Sam has taught me, the town dump is full both of aesthetic wonders and useful stuff. The moralist can find worthy lessons there, and the materialist a bit of plunder. It is, however, a place that speaks constantly of the past, and is more melancholy than any graveyard. The dump is where the unmemorial odds and ends of our lives end up. Dumps tell our history, but not in the way that we would like to remember it.

I must admit that the town dump will probably not catch on as the metaphor of choice among diversidacts in the schools. They would resist the metaphoric implication, even as they embrace the hard reality that *diversity* is a way of situating children amidst the debris of broken dreams and spent lives.

Diversidacts and diversiphiles of all sorts prefer a more upbeat imagery of unity. When the Advisory Board of President Clinton's Initiative on Race issued its final report in September 1998, it was characteristically titled *One America in the Twenty-first Century: Forging a New Future.* The title is meant seriously. Although the Initiative on Race had often served only to elevate and accentuate racial and ethnic differences, Chairman John Hope Franklin and his colleagues saw nothing odd in proclaiming their work as a step toward "One America."

Appendix H of *One America in the Twenty-first Century* lists hundreds of organizations across the nation that the Advisory Board of the Initiative on Race considered as offering "promising practices." The annotated list amounts to a kind of encyclopedia of multiculturalism's institutional presence as of 1998, and *diversity* metaphors abound.

Voices United in Miami, Florida, "empowers young people to cultivate solutions to community problems and to promote intercultural appreciation and understanding"; *We're All on the Same Team Cultural Diversity Education Program* in Phoenix, Arizona, promotes "the value of cultural diversity and [creates] opportunities for positive exchange among diverse groups of people"; *Interfaith Bridge Builders Coalition* in Utica, New York, "celebrates and upholds the cultural and ethnic diversity in the community and promotes racial reconciliation"; *Mosaic Harmony*, a choir in Washington, D.C., "believes that the rich and inspiring tones of gospel music can bridge racial and ethnic barriers" and brings "a message of unity and diversity to the community." And the *Color Me Human Program* in Hixson, Tennessee, "encourages organizations to use the Color Me Human logo and products as a symbol that the organization is supportive of diversity issues." The list is rich with *common destinies, common grounds* and other commonalities, and offers numerous kinds of *together*ness, *one*ness and *unity*—all in the name of helping us celebrate difference.

To secure its place on the national agenda, *diversity* relies to an extraordinary degree on images and metaphors. But We're-All-on-the-Same-Team/Bridge Builders/Mosaic Harmony/Color-Me-Human *diversity; diversity* with its rainbows, patchwork quilts, rich gumbos and Noah's arks; the *diversity* of *One America in the Twenty-first Century*—all these diversities are, in the end, species of illusion. They pump life and energy into the assertion of the radical separateness of all the parts, and then childishly prate about the unity that is sure to follow.

FIVE

BAKKE AND BEYOND

The idea of *diversity* as a legitimate goal for those who shape the future of our society sprang into existence on June 28, 1978, when Justice Lewis Powell of the United States Supreme Court issued his opinion in *Regents of the University of California v. Bakke.* In the decades since, the idea of diversity that Powell articulated in the *Bakke* decision has been cited by both plaintiffs and defendants in thousands of cases involving racial set-asides, differential admissions standards and other forms of discrimination. And courts at almost every level of the American judicial system have issued opinions derived from *Bakke* in which "diversity" is accepted as a worthy consideration in weighing conflicting social goods.

Despite its historical importance and its fame, the *Bakke* decision is murky. The case involved Allan Bakke, who had been denied admission to the University of California, Davis, School of Medicine, despite his having substantially better credentials than those of some other applicants who were accepted. The school acknowledged that Bakke had been passed over in favor of less-qualified minority candidates, but claimed that it had the right to do so as part of its affirmative action ("Special Admissions") program. Bakke prevailed with the California Supreme Court, but the Regents of the University of California then appealed to the U.S. Supreme Court. The broader public interpretation of the case was that it provided a test of the theory of "reverse discrimination"—the idea that laws prohibiting discrimination against blacks and other minorities must also prohibit discrimination against whites.

The Supreme Court ultimately found in favor of Bakke and stated that he was entitled to an order of admission to the UC Davis Medical School. The vote, however, was narrow (5 to 4) and the written opinion resembles a crazy quilt. There were six separate opinions among the nine justices, stitched together by coalitions on a few narrow points.

In the history of the U.S. Supreme Court, only a few other cases have produced so fractured a result. The six separate opinions show a Court that didn't know what to think. Four of the justices—Stevens, Burger, Stewart and Rehnquist—would have left the matter to the State of California, a decision that might have led other state supreme courts to deliver similar opinions and thus quickly sweep away all such state-sponsored affirmative action admissions programs. Four of the justices—Brennan, White, Marshall and Blackmun—were, to the contrary, eager to find in favor of the University of California and thus uphold the use of race in admissions to college and graduate programs.

With the 4–4 split, the deciding vote was Powell's, and Justice Powell, it is said, relished the role. Between the oral arguments in the case on October 12, 1977, and the announcement of the decision on June 28, 1978, he danced in the middle, refusing to associate himself clearly with either Chief Justice Burger's view (that the University of California special admissions policy was in "plain conflict" with Title VI of the Civil Rights Act of 1964, and that Bakke's victory should therefore be upheld on statutory grounds), or Justice Brennan's view (that the UC program should be upheld on constitutional grounds, citing the Fourteenth Amendment). Powell agreed that the Fourteenth Amendment should be invoked and that it *did*, in principle, permit affirmative action, but he viewed the UC program as a flawed and excessive application of the principle. Powell held out for the standard of "strict scrutiny" in affirmative action admissions—which meant that a strong burden of proof would fall on the proponents of such programs to prove they are justified and necessary.

In the end, instead of joining either side, Powell composed his own wildly eccentric opinion. In it, he cited some tough-sounding principles that favored the elimination of invidious racial distinctions:

> "Distinctions between citizens solely because of their ancestry are by their very nature odious to a free people whose institutions

are founded upon the doctrine of equality." *Hirabayashi,* 320 U.S. at 100. *University of California v. Bakke,* 348 U.S. at 290–91 (1978).

Indeed, it is not unlikely that among the framers were many who would have applauded a reading of the Equal Protection Clause that states a principle of universal application and is responsive to the racial, ethnic, and cultural diversity of the Nation. *Bakke,* 348 U.S. at 293.

It is far too late to argue that the guarantee of equal protection to *all* persons permits the recognition of special wards entitled to a degree of protection greater than that accorded others. *Bakke,* 348 U.S. at 295.

But no sooner had Powell zigged in the direction of a colorblind interpretation of the Fourteenth Amendment, than he zagged in the direction of spectrographic sensitivity:

As I am in agreement with the view that race may be taken into account as a factor in an admissions program, I agree with my Brothers BRENNAN, WHITE, MARSHALL, and BLACKMUN that the portion of the judgment that would proscribe all consideration of race must be reversed. *Bakke,* 348 U.S. at 297.

Powell's decision frustrated Brennan, White, Marshall and Blackmun in several ways. They had hoped to overrule the California Supreme Court and reinstate the UC Davis Medical School's affirmative action program. But Powell joined the other four justices in upholding the part of the California Supreme Court's decision that ended that program. The Brennan quartet was also eager to have the *Bakke* case decided on constitutional rather than statutory grounds. Powell agreed, but added his insistence on the "strict scrutiny" standard, which three of the four (White excluded) bitterly rejected. Brennan, White, Marshall and Blackmun thus ended up with only two of their points backed by a five-member majority: the shunting aside of Title VI so that the case could be framed as a constitutional decision, and the agreement that under *some* unspecified condition a state-sponsored racial classification could be constitutional.

The five-member majority held together on this point, but just barely. The Brennan quartet was angry with Powell. Marshall in particular found him unbearable, and Brennan recorded in his diary that

Marshall viewed Powell's opinion about the need for strict scrutiny as "racist."

Given the 4–4 deadlock on the Court, presumably neither side dared to mention that Powell had served up an incoherent and self-contradictory mess. The best that Brennan, White, Marshall and Blackmun could do was to agree with it selectively and then add further clarifications. So it is that we end up with the concurring votes on two sections: the summary and the brief section in which Powell declared that race classification is sometimes acceptable. White also joined Powell in insisting on the need to subject racial classifications to "strict scrutiny." The Brennan wing of the Court thereby ignored four-fifths of Powell's opinion, and the important section they did endorse was merely a two-sentence paragraph:

> In enjoining petitioner from ever considering the race of any applicant, however, the courts below failed to recognize that the State has a substantial interest that legitimately may be served by a properly devised admissions program involving the competitive consideration of race and ethnic origin. For this reason, so much of the California court's judgment as enjoins petitioner from any consideration of the race of any applicant must be reversed. *Bakke*, 348 U.S. at 320.

This vague endorsement of the idea that admissions programs may consider race is therefore the only real majority opinion to come from the *Bakke* case.

That, in turn, leaves Powell's other arguments stranded in the limbo of Supreme Court dicta. His declarations about *diversity* are left high and dry on the beach. His claim that the goal of attaining "a diverse student body" is "constitutionally permissible" was met with the cold silence of his fellow justices, as was his now-famous "plus factor" argument in the section in which he imagined:

> The file of a particular black applicant may be examined for his potential contribution to diversity without the factor of race being decisive when compared, for example, with that of an applicant identified as Italian-American if the latter is thought to exhibit qualities more likely to promote beneficial educational pluralism.

Powell's worry that the UC Davis Medical School had been, in effect, scanting the Asian and Chicano applicants' "potential for contribution to educational diversity" moved not a single fellow justice to utter a peep of concurrence. *None* of the other eight justices endorsed any of these points. Yet they were to become the single most important part of the *Bakke* case and the foundation for all subsequent diversity litigation.

Afterthoughts

The *Bakke* decision is a watershed at least as much for cultural as for legal reasons. It invigorated both sides of the national debate over how best to promote equal rights for all Americans. On one side, those who doubted the justice and fairness of affirmative action took heart that Allan Bakke had won. The principle that racial quotas in college admissions are simply wrong had been, at least in some sense, vindicated. Indeed, part of the *Bakke* legacy is the enduring stigmatization of "quotas" and the consequent need for diversiphiles to deny strenuously that they are installing them in our institutions, even as they do exactly that.

On the other side, those who believed that racial inequities lie so deep in American society that only systematic race-minded remedies can correct them took heart that Justice Burger and his colleagues had *lost*. Affirmative action would live to fight another day, and in the meantime, Justice Powell had breathed life into a tentative new rationalization for affirmative action, the *diversity* defense.

But the prominence that Powell's opinion thrust upon the concept of *diversity* was disconcerting. The idea of defending racial quotas by citing the advantages of *diversity* had indeed been kicking around for several years, but it was just one of several hypothetical sales pitches for countering the increasingly sharp attacks on the unfairness of affirmative action. To get the measure of how far out of orbit Powell's decision really was, it is useful to look back at the body of the case, including the California Supreme Court's decision and the various pleadings that Powell and his fellow justices considered.

The California Supreme Court's opinion in the earlier stage of the *Bakke* case makes clear that the *diversity* argument had already come up, but that it played no great role. It is mentioned four times in passing in the majority's decision—three times in paraphrase of the University of California's arguments and once in reference to the single dissent in the case, by Judge J. Tobriner. This dissent mentions the word four times as well, but neither the majority opinion nor the dissent engages in any actual assessment of the merit of the argument. The majority brushed it aside as irrelevant; Judge Tobriner accepted it at face value.

Diversity next appears as a minor theme in the University of California's petition to the Supreme Court to review the California Supreme Court decision. The petition frames the university's racial preferences as primarily an effort to realize "the goal of educational opportunity unimpaired by the effects of racial discrimination" that was the center of *Brown v. The Board of Education* in 1954.

One problem, however, was that the UC Davis Medical School did *not* have a history of racial discrimination against minorities. It had opened only in 1968. Its initial class of fifty students had only three minority students (all "Asians") and the school's faculty immediately formed a "Task Force" to develop a program "to compensate for the effects of societal discrimination on disadvantaged applicants of racial or ethnic minority group status."

The University of California's petition summarizes the result of the Task Force program:

> In 1970, the first year of operation of the program, eight minority students were specially admitted (five Blacks and three Chicanos) and, out of a total entering class of 50 students, there were 12 minority students. In 1971, the total class was increased to 100, the level at which it has remained. In 1971, 15 minority students entered through special admissions (four Blacks, nine Chicanos and two Asians) and there were a total of 24 minority students in the class. In 1972, there were 27 minority admittees, 16 of whom came through special admissions (five Blacks, six Chicanos and five Asians). The entering group of 1973 contained 31 minority students, 16 selected under the special admissions program (six Blacks, eight Chicanos and two Asians). Finally, in 1974 twenty-five minority students accepted offers of admission, nine through regular admissions and 16 through the special program (six Blacks, seven Chicanos and three Asians).

Almost no Blacks entered Davis through regular admissions from 1970 to 1974. The numbers for each year were: 1970 (0); 1971 (1); 1972 (0); 1973 (0); 1974 (0).

Allan Bakke had applied for admission in 1973 and again in 1974, and both times was rated by the school as "qualified" for admission. In 1973, the school, using a 500-point scale for evaluating applicants, rated Bakke a 468; in 1974, using a 600-point scale, it rated him a 549. In the brief that Bakke filed in opposition to the University of California petition, he included a chart showing how his credentials stacked up against both the regular admittees and the special admittees in those two years:

Class Entering in Fall 1973						
	SGPA	OGPA	Verb.	Quan.	Sci.	Gen. Info.
Allan Bakke	3.45	3.51	96	94	97	72
Average of Regular Admittees	3.51	3.49	81	76	83	69
Average of Special Admittees	2.62	2.88	46	24	35	33

SGPA: undergraduate grade point average in science courses
OGPA: overall undergraduate grade point average
Verb./Quan./Sci./Gen. Info.: scores on the Verbal, Quantitative, Science and General Information sections of the Medical College Admissions Test

Class Entering in Fall 1974						
	SGPA	OGPA	Verb.	Quan.	Sci.	Gen. Info.
Allan Bakke	3.45	3.51	96	94	97	72
Average of Regular Admittees	3.36	3.29	69	67	82	72
Average of Special Admittees	2.42	2.62	34	30	37	18

If we put together both parts—the University of California's petition and Bakke's response—the case that the Supreme Court agreed to hear in 1977 looks far more like a dispute over numbers than a debate about *diversity*. UC wanted larger numbers of minority students in its School of Medicine; Allan Bakke wanted to be judged for admission on the numbers that showed he was measurably better qualified than the "special admittees." The *diversity* argument does not appear in the section of the UC petition giving reasons why the Supreme Court should hear the case.

But the idea of *diversity* was definitely present in the petition, in one key sentence in which the University of California explained that:

> previously used admissions standards failed to make adequate provision for the educational advantages of a racially and culturally diverse student body, the societal need for adequate professional services in underserved minority communities, and the educational and career opportunities of minority students.

Each of these subsidiary arguments—(1) diversity has educational advantages, (2) minority communities need more doctors, and (3) minority students need more opportunities—reappeared in the University of California's October 1977 brief in the case.

They remained, however, in the position of props for the main argument, the defense of the "special admissions" policy at UC Davis Medical School as a step intended "to counteract effects of generations or pervasive discrimination" against minorities (p. 2). *Diversity* comes into this larger picture several times by way of short comments, but in view of the historical importance those comments gained from Powell's opinion, it is useful to see them together. Sometimes the UC brief alludes to the *diversity* rationale without using the word:

> Today, only a race-conscious plan for minority admissions will permit qualified applicants from disadvantaged minorities to attend medical schools, law schools and other institutions of higher learning in sufficient numbers *to enhance the quality of education for all students;* to broaden the professions and increase their services to the entire community; to destroy pernicious stereotypes; and to demonstrate to the young that educational opportunities and rewarding careers are truly open regardless of ethnic origin. [p. 13; emphasis added]

Sometimes the word "diversity" appears without any connection to the rationale:

> Formal barriers against minority participation in medical schools did not fall till very recently and, by itself, the elimination of those restraints did not produce racial diversity. [p. 26]

But here and there, the UC brief glances toward the *diversity* rationale per se:

> The first step away from the doctor-as-scientist model was aimed at producing a more diverse student body and profession. But this step did not, by itself, lead to racial diversity in the medical schools, nor a substantial number of minority physicians. [p. 31]

> The ends [of the UC Davis Special Admissions program] include ... obtaining the educational and societal benefits that flow from racial and ethnic diversity in a medical school student body. [p. 32]

> The goals also include increasing the skills of non-minority medical school students and physicians. As a result of the integrated education made possible by the Davis program, white students will develop an enhanced awareness of the medical concerns of minorities and of the difficulties of effective delivery of health care services in minority communities. They will also stand a better chance of developing a rapport with their future minority patients, no matter where they encounter such patients. [p. 33]

At one point, the brief attacks:

> the assumption, or the set of assumptions, that the best medical education necessarily occurs in the company of other students selected solely on the basis of formal credentials and without encountering significant diversity, in other students. [p. 51]

And the word "diversity" crops up several times in contexts of school desegregation. For example:

> Numerous state and lower federal courts have upheld the utilization of racial criteria to increase racial diversity in schools and to counter the effects of discrimination, despite the absence of *de jure* discrimination.

With incidental exceptions, these are the only statements in the University of California's eighty-seven-page brief that deal in any substantive manner with *diversity*. The topic is notably absent from the brief's "Conclusion."

In oral arguments, former U.S. solicitor general Archibald Cox, arguing on behalf of the University of California, used the word "diversity" once during his forty-four-minute presentation, and that in answer to a question from one of the justices. Cox said:

> Certainly the objective of improving education through great diversity is perhaps even more important in an undergraduate school than it is in a professional school, but I wouldn't minimize its importance in a professional school and I would emphasize it is important when it comes to membership in the professions so that the professions will be aware of all the segments of society.

His comment clearly does *not* advance the argument from the brief that diversity is educationally enriching for all involved.

Diversity, in sum, was a small, intellectually unelaborated part of the University of California's case before the Supreme Court. The arguments that UC put first were that it needed to make up its past deficit of black students; that it needed to serve the larger cause of societal equity toward blacks; and that it needed to assist in supplying more physicians to black neighborhoods. *Diversity* was present more in the form of a rhetorical gesture than a serious argument—and almost like an afterthought.

Intimations of Things to Come

The strangeness of Powell's invocation of the diversity rationale for affirmative action cannot be fully gauged without seeing just how rare this idea was in American life before Powell put it on the table.

Before the *Bakke* decision, when people spoke of "diversity" in education, they almost always meant the variety of colleges and universities in America. Lacking a single national system of higher education, like France and many other countries, the United States had developed a vibrant mixture of public and private, sectarian and secular, large and small, technical and liberal arts colleges and universities. Occasionally someone would note a financial threat to one category of college or someone would float a proposal to centralize a state university; then some college president would reply to the effect, "We must do all we can to preserve the diversity of higher education."

Search through the newspapers of the 1970s before *Bakke,* and that is what you find, except here and there the faintest whisper of a new idea. The earliest such whisper I can find is an article in the *New York Times*, October 10, 1973, describing the final report of the $6 million multiyear study by the Carnegie Commission on Higher Education, chaired by former University of California president Clark Kerr. The *Times* summarized the report, in part, by saying the commission was calling on colleges and universities to enhance their "diversity." The idea seems vaguely associated with admitting different kinds of students. (The report itself is written mostly in the pre-*diversity* language of "equal opportunity.")

Here and there an article appeared speaking of the need to diversify the faculty. In March 1975, the *New York Times* reported on efforts by New York University and the City University of New York to find faculty members with more diverse backgrounds. The story says that some faculty members criticized the initiative as latently anti-Semitic. But the reporter quotes a college report that captures the *diversity* rationale, except that it speaks of faculty members rather than of students:

> Diversity in the backgrounds of City University faculty is described by the report as a way of encouraging "new perspectives and outlooks, different teaching approaches, greater variety of academic opinion, and a richer heritage."

The first unambiguous mention in the news of the idea that "diversity" among *students* is educationally worthwhile, however, does not appear until November 23, 1977—seven months before the *Bakke* decision. The *Washington Post* took notice of a screed by sociologist Edward A. Wynne, who argued that the isolation of living in the suburbs stunted children's emotional growth:

> This leads, he says, to antisocial and self-destructive conduct, including high suicide rates, drug use, delinquency and introverted behavior. Sociologist Wynne lays the blame on many things that have made suburban living attractive to two generations of Americans: big lawns, shopping centers, safe streets and large, modern schools.

Professor Wynne, judged from the distance of a quarter-century, looks a bit quaint in his pronouncements:

Children who grow up in suburbs, he adds, "are uniquely isolated from diversity," outside stimulations and most real-life
situations, making it hard for them to adjust to later life.

What evidence he had that suburban kids find it difficult to get along
in life is to be found, I suppose, in his book *Growing Up Suburban* (1977),
but it might be worth adding that Professor Wynne's fondness for
diversity came from a particular moment in his life, when "he gave
up his career in government and went back to school at the University of California at Berkeley in 1968, the height of the student protest
movement." He recalls, "I was 36 and the place looked pretty darn
good to me."

So is the intellectual origin of the diversity movement really a
middle-aged sociologist grousing that the suburbs aren't as stimulating as Berkeley, circa 1968?

No, not exactly. I recall heated debates at Haverford College when
I was an undergraduate there in the early 1970s and students fretted
with heartsick sincerity that the college lacked *diversity*. They were
decrying the relatively low numbers of blacks and Hispanics, not the
absence of women at the single-sex school.

And in the summer of 1976, I worked for a few weeks in the library
of a little start-up center at Rutgers University in New Brunswick,
where the goal seemed to be to popularize the idea that the *experience*
of ethnic diversity is a fundamental part of a good education.

Professor Wynne's promotion of the idea that *diversity* is a positive condition for education was in the cultural air, as was his distaste
for the suburbs, which had already been a countercultural standard
for twenty years, stretching back to the Beat Generation. But the sociological antithesis *good diversity / bad suburbs* deserves to be noted on
the eve of Allan Bakke's troubles.

The scarcity in the newspapers of the 1970s of the idea that *diversity* is, in and of itself, educationally worthwhile does not mean that
the idea was not being bruited in other contexts. What about the law?
Wouldn't it make sense that, before the Bakke case, lawyers and the
courts had, at least tentatively, begun to explore this terrain? After all,
this was the era of forced desegregation in the nation's schools and
court-ordered bussing. It would be surprising if the courts had not, at
some point, hit on the diversity-is-educationally-worthwhile argument.

Indeed, there are instances in the legal record in which the idea is mentioned, but they are very few, and very brief. There is not a single law review article pre-*Bakke* that focuses on diversity in this sense, or, so far as I can tell, even mentions the idea. The only pre-*Bakke* case involving a claim of reverse discrimination in college admissions was *DeFunis v. Odegaard* (1973). Marco DeFunis was a Sephardic Jew from Washington State who sued the University of Washington School of Law for denying him admission because of its illegally discriminatory affirmative action policy. A state trial judge, however, had issued an injunction that allowed Mr. DeFunis to attend the school, and by the time the Supreme Court was ready to issue its decision, DeFunis was set to graduate. A five-member majority of the Court decided that the case was therefore moot and it resulted in no opinion. In any event, the diversity-is-educationally-worthwhile argument was not part of the University of Washington's pleadings, and the term "diversity" does not appear at all in the record of the case.

Presumably, Powell himself would have cited any major decision or case that buttressed his view of *diversity*, and his silence on that score is evidence of a kind that no such case existed. But Powell and his clerks did not have the computerized legal databases we have today and it is possible he overlooked something. Did he? As far as I can tell, no. The pre-*Bakke* record on the idea that diversity is educationally worthwhile seems to be limited to scant mentions in a handful of district court episodes in long-running school desegregation cases.*

Just three weeks before the *Bakke* decision, the district court in eastern New York issued an opinion in *Lora et al. v. Board of Education of the City of New York,* 456 F. Supp. 1211 (1978) that adds an interesting sidelight on the intellectual milieu of *Bakke*. This was a class action suit brought on behalf of a group of emotionally disturbed black and Hispanic children, claiming that the New York "Special Day Schools" to which they had been assigned because of "severe acting-out and aggression in school" were "intentionally segregated dumping grounds

---

Swann v. Charlotte-Mecklenburg Board of Education (1971) in North Carolina; *Bradley v. The School Board of the City of Richmond* (1972) in Virginia; and *Bradley v. Milliken,* 345 F. Supp. 914 (1972) all include decisions in which the concept of diversity is mentioned but not elaborated into a diversity-is-educationally-worthwhile doctrine.

for minorities." In reaching his opinion—essentially, that the situation had already been resolved—the judge observed:

> Generally shared by thoughtful proponents of this approach [of keeping mildly handicapped students in mainstream classes] is a commitment to encouraging acceptance of diversity. Average children are considered to benefit as much from having the handicapped in their classrooms as are exceptional pupils.

The judge also quotes W. C. Rhodes, an expert on "mainstreaming" the handicapped, to the effect that special educators have a duty to change "the educational structures and processes to embrace diversity and pluralism."

The *Lora* decision gives a peculiar flavor to the idea of *diversity*'s educational merits, as it segues from the desegregationist idea of mixing people in the classroom who are racially or culturally *different* to the idea of mixing in people who are distinctly less *capable.*

Taking the popular press and the world of legal decisions and commentary together, however, it seems safe to say that *diversity* was a fairly marginal idea at the time that the *Bakke* case made its way to the Supreme Court. But *Bakke* was about to change that. The *Washington Post*'s November 1977 notice of Professor Wynne's book decrying the lack of diversity in the suburbs was preceded by an October 1977 column by *New York Times* writer Russell Baker, who took a swipe at Allan Bakke for being so sore at not getting into medical school. Baker said that policies aimed at promoting racial diversity are sensible, and that Allan Bakke wouldn't have had a case at all had the admissions office chosen "16 academically inferior football players." Baker's analogy also deserves a special memorial, in that it seems to be the first time that someone seriously offered the argument that skin color is a specialized skill akin to excelling at sports.

From that point on, there is a dribble of articles that connect ethnic diversity with educational goals. The *Washington Post* (March 1978) editorializes against a legislative proposal to increase diversity among schools because "The greater the diversity among schools, the less diversity each child will see in the classroom where it counts." The day after the *Bakke* decision was announced, the *New York Times* (June 29, 1978) pats Harvard on the back for winning Justice Powell's praise as a place that considers "diversity" without sacrificing academic merit; a Silver Springs, Maryland, primary school (September 1978) discovers that racial integration can improve the classroom ("Finding Advantages in Diversity"); a dean at the University of Pennsylvania School of Law (December 1978) declares that she will continue to seek diversity in the student body. And Carter administration Treasury official Donald Lubick and his wife, Susan, who put their children in Washington, D.C., public schools, explain (1979): "We were looking for a school that was both intellectually stimulating and urban, in terms of racial and economic diversity." Clearly, by the time the Lubicks speak, the diversity idea—that diversity in and of itself is educationally worthwhile—has crystallized for people of left-leaning cultural outlook.

Within a few years, the rivulet of articles grows to a gushing stream, and by the late 1990s a full flood. At this point, the *diversity* rationale is so widespread in the culture that it is second nature to high school students, who turn out college admissions essays by the yard on how diversity has enhanced their education.

Did all this come from Justice Powell's fishing for some way to split the difference on a divided Court?

Yes and no. Yes, Powell's decision unquestionably transformed what had been a minor legal argument into an idea that people had to take seriously. Without *Bakke*, the *diversity* argument—the conceit that ethnic and racial diversity are *educationally* constructive—might have languished along with the labor theory of value and a thousand other bits of leftist rhetoric that never caught on. Powell's *Bakke* opinion, however, lifted *diversity* out of obscurity and gave it the respectability of seeming law. Millions of people, in fact, probably assumed—and still do—that it *was* law. The happenstance that none of his Supreme Court colleagues joined Powell in extolling *diversity* tends to be overlooked, and those who are now committed to promoting the idea are perhaps reluctant to remember that the widely cited legal foundation for pursuing diversity in schools and colleges rests on one man's unsupported opinion.

But no, Powell cannot be credited with having invented the idea. Diversity as a cultural principle—including the idea that ethnically and racially mixed classrooms are educationally stimulating—had been floating around in leftist American intellectual culture for about a decade. The immediate reaction to Powell's opinion suggests that leftist

intellectuals were taken by surprise that such an incidental concern—
that racially mixed classrooms might benefit white folks too—should
have played a significant role in rescuing affirmative action from the conservative justices. It took a little while for the Left to realize that it had
been handed a potentially powerful new weapon in the culture wars.

But for *diversity* to succeed in the culture and not just the courts,
the idea would have to be elaborated. As it turned out, the important
connections were to link the pursuit of ethnic and racial quotas in
classrooms with notions of cultural relativity and with the conception of education as a quest for personal identity. These conceits were
already well established on campus since the 1960s, but they had not
coalesced into a single dogma. Powell, in effect, lit the match in the
fireworks factory.

Today, when the single word *diversity* has become a synecdoche
for the whole skein of arguments and assumptions that went into the
original position, as well as for an ideology that has moved far beyond
simply justifying affirmative action, it is difficult to recover just how
narrow and peculiar Powell's opinion really was. Having rejected both
of the coherent principled stands available to him—Brennan's robust
call for getting out of the way of affirmative action and Burger's robust
call for colorblind legal rights—Powell was left with no obvious way
forward. In opposition to the Brennan faction, he was determined to
say that affirmative action could be used only under very strict and
limiting conditions, and he found that the UC version of affirmative
action failed to meet these conditions. The University of California
simply reserved sixteen places in the class of one hundred for "minority group" applicants, and judged applicants assigned to this pool by
a completely separate—and much lower—set of standards. That left
Powell in need of identifying some situation in which a university
had a constitutionally legitimate *interest* in classifying people by race,
and in which the university could *act* on that classification without
violating other constitutional rights. His answer was the university's
interest in pursuing racial diversity in the classroom by means of a
system in which race was not the sole determinant of admission but
only, as he put it, "a plus factor."

Powell seemed untroubled and even unaware that he had attributed moment and solemnity to a featherweight idea. If race could be
"a plus factor," in the case of any individual student, it would be the

determining factor. By his reckoning, principles of human equality for which the nation had fought a revolution and a civil war, and principles of fairness for which the nation had struggled for more than one hundred years after the Confederacy surrendered, could both be trumped by a university's interest in attaining "a heterogeneous student body." His colleagues sat by in—one hopes stunned—silence.

Before *Bakke*

Affirmative action is usually reckoned to have come into existence thirteen years before the *Bakke* decision. President Johnson, giving a commencement address, "To Fulfill These Rights," at Howard University on June 4, 1965, had presented the essential idea. American Negroes, he said, had gained their basic freedoms through such measures as the Voting Rights Act, but, added Johnson, "Freedom is not enough."

> You do not wipe away the scars of centuries by saying: Now you are free to go where you want, and do as you desire, and choose the leaders you please.
>
> You do not take a person who, for years, has been hobbled by chains and liberate him, bring him up to the starting line of a race and then say, "you are free to compete with all the others," and still justly believe that you have been completely fair.
>
> Thus it is not enough just to open the gates of opportunity. All our citizens must have the ability to walk through those gates.
>
> This is the next and the more profound stage of the battle for civil rights. We seek not just freedom but opportunity. We seek not just legal equity but human ability, not just equality as a right and a theory but equality as a fact and equality as a result.

President Johnson's view that "equal opportunity is essential, but not enough" eventually found legal form in Executive Order 11246, which required federal contractors to "take affirmative action to ensure that applicants are employed, and that employees are treated during employment, without regard to their race, creed, color, or national origin."

Executive Order 11246 crops up in every history of affirmative action as a momentous event, but it appeared at the time to be little more than bureaucratic housekeeping. We owe the journalist Nicholas Lemann a debt for having sifted through the dust of this period to capture a glimpse of the origins of ideas and expressions in which we are still enmeshed. According to Lemann, the phrase "affirmative action," in the sense of race-conscious hiring to increase the number of black employees, had been around since 1961 when Hobart Taylor Jr. (a young black lawyer from Detroit who was asked by Vice President Johnson to lend a hand) added it to a draft of what would become President Kennedy's Executive Order 10925. That order, says Lemann, "merged two obscure Eisenhower Administration committees that were supposed to prevent discriminatory hiring." Johnson's more famous EO 11246 sounds, at first, very similar. It abolished two White House committees, one of them headed by Hubert Humphrey, and transferred "affirmative action" enforcement to the Labor Department.

Lemann, appropriately, calls Executive Order 11246 an "invisible milestone." The transfer of power meant nothing much to the press or the public at the time, but as Lemann points out, it took affirmative action out of the hands of busy White House staff and gave it to "more permanent staff" devoted to the task. I think the point could be sharpened. The White House itself is not the place to grow a national bureaucracy. It is the right place to enunciate principles and shape the contours of a new program, but if a president is finished persuading and still determined to impose a program, he turns it over to the agencies. People who are in no sense ennobled by the original conception are best at devising ways to grind the country into submission.

Once in the hands of the Labor Department (to which EO 11246 gave the primary power to enforce) and other federal agencies, affirmative action proceeded by the usual course, attracting some true believers and, especially in higher education, winning a large following of cynical opportunists who could parade their betrayal of academic standards as a new kind of idealism. But unlike many government initiatives handed off to the federal agencies, affirmative action proved lastingly unpopular.

Just as large numbers of Americans had risen to the challenge of setting aside racial differences and seeing each other as equals, affirmative action required them to do an about-face and swallow the idea that an individual's race *should* count more than his ability in getting a job or a promotion, or gaining admission to a college. And just as the legal barriers of Jim Crow were torn down across the South and individuals had immensely better opportunities to compete on the basis of their hard work, their ambition and their talents, the nation was asked in the name of affirmative action to accept new racial barriers that trumped hard work, ambition and talent. Racism had not disappeared from American life, but it had lost its respectability and most of its cultural force.

Some people of good will could persuade themselves that these exceptions to the rule of legal and moral equality could and should be endured because affirmative action would be a temporary step, as President Johnson had declared, to bring people "up to the starting line." But others were doubtful that equality could be achieved by inequality and were troubled by the open-ended nature of the program. When would we be ready to say that the beneficiaries of affirmative action had reached the starting line?

Still more corrosive was the tendency of affirmative action's supporters to impute racism to its opponents. No doubt some were indeed racists, but the great majority were innocent of this charge. They were well-meaning people disturbed by the ethical raggedness of affirmative action and unwilling to swallow a doctrine of collective guilt. But the supporters of affirmative action, concentrated in education, the press and government, were relentless in denying that the policy's critics had any reasonable points.

The critics, however, kept growing stronger. They challenged the petty indignities of affirmative action publicly and sometimes legally. Powell observed that the Supreme Court "has not sustained a racial classification since the wartime cases" involving Japanese-Americans, and he cited a long list of cases that accepted affirmative action in hiring *only* in connection with evidence of previous discrimination.

By the mid-1970s, many of affirmative action's supporters could see plainly that they were losing the battle for broad public consent. *They* were committed to a system of "racial justice" based on set-asides and quotas, but the popular will was turning against them. What was needed was a way to make "racial justice"—actually, systematic *injustice*—palatable to the country at large.

Enter *diversity*.

Powell's View of Diversity

Powell's remarks about diversity in his *Bakke* decision deserve a closer look. There are two key sections. The first argues that universities have a legitimate *educational* interest in pursuing racial diversity; the second repudiates the University of California's "Special Admissions" program as an acceptable means to attain that legitimate end. In addition to these two sections, Powell has an appendix to his opinion in which he extols Harvard College's approach to achieving diversity.*

Powell's *diversity* argument begins with the flat assertion that the goal of attaining "a diverse student body" is "constitutionally permissible." Powell grounds this in "academic freedom," which he holds is implied in the First Amendment, and says, "The freedom of a university to make its own judgments as to education includes the selec-

---

*Harvard University's statements about its pursuit of *diversity* among the undergraduate students it admits have played a disproportionately large role in the *diversity* debate. One of the key documents is a four-page appendix to the Brief of *Amici Curiae* filed in support of the University of California in the *Bakke* case by Columbia University, Harvard University, Stanford University and the University of Pennsylvania. It has an appendix, titled "Harvard College Admissions Program," which Powell cited and relied on heavily in his *Bakke* opinion. It describes Harvard's policy for "the past 30 years" of not making "scholarly excellence ... the sole or even predominant criterion" for offering an applicant admission.

Were it to do so, the document explains, "Harvard College would lose a great deal of its vitality and intellectual excellence" and "the quality of the educational experience offered to all students would suffer." To avoid these calamities, Harvard selects "those students whose intellectual potential will seem extraordinary to the faculty— perhaps 150 or so of an entering class of over 1,100," and then turns to other criteria. These other criteria include "interests, backgrounds and career goals."

Writing in 1977, the unnamed author of the statement interprets this concern for breadth as a commitment to "diversity" and as "an essential ingredient to the educational process." He allows, however, that diversity hasn't always meant the same thing. "Fifteen or twenty years ago ... diversity meant students from California, New York and Massachusetts; city dwellers and farm boys; violinists, painters and football players; biologists, historians and classicists; potential stockbrokers, academics and politicians." But times have changed and Harvard "now recruits" others, including "blacks, Chicanos and other minority students." This means that, yes, "race has been a factor in some admissions decisions." This is, in principle, no different from preferring a "farm boy from Idaho" to a Bostonian. "Similarly, a black student can usually bring something a white person cannot offer."

The author vigorously denies that Harvard uses "target-quotas for the number of blacks." The approach is more diffuse. "It means only that in choosing among thousands of applicants who are not only 'admissible' academically but have other strong qualities, the Committee, with a number of criteria in mind, pays some attention to distribution among many types and categories of students." The statement ends with

Bakke *and Beyond* 119

tion of its student body." He cites various cases in which the Court expressed its respect for academic freedom, and then (partially quoting from another opinion) suggests that "'the nation's future depends upon leaders trained through wide exposure' to the ideas and mores of students as diverse as this Nation of many peoples."

By this Powell reaches the idea that the "robust exchange of ideas" makes the goal of racial diversity "of paramount importance in the fulfillment of [the university's] mission." Let's pause here, because Powell's step is a very big one. It requires us to assume that the diversity of ideas and their "robust exchange" is promoted by stocking the classroom with people who are *racially* diverse. Does racial diversity really equal intellectual diversity? In later legal writing, this assumption is often called the "racial proxy" argument, i.e. racial diversity is a proxy for intellectual diversity.

---

a paragraph on some "further refinements" that "illustrate the kind of significance attached to race." Given a choice between "the child of a successful black physician ... with promise of superior academic performance" and a "black who grew up in an inner-city ghetto of semi-literate parents whose academic achievement was lower but who had demonstrated energy and leadership," the committee "might prefer" to admit the latter, but either could be edged out by "a white student with extraordinary artistic talent."

Justice Powell was deeply impressed by this document and cited it repeatedly in his opinion.

It is perhaps worth adding that African-Americans did not have to wait for the 1970s revision of Harvard's diversity policy to gain admission to Harvard. In 1865, Harvard Medical School admitted an African-American named Edwin J. C. T. Howard and the undergraduate college admitted an African-American named Richard T. Greener. The number of African-Americans who were admitted was small but far from negligible. Perhaps the most famous was W. E. B. Du Bois, who graduated in 1890 with a degree in philosophy *cum laude.*

In recent years, Harvard has busily re-remembered its past commitment to *diversity* in some creative ways. Former president Neil Rudenstine, for example, published an essay titled "Student Diversity and Higher Learning," arguing that "Contrary to popular belief, the deliberate, conscious effort to achieve greater student diversity on our campuses was not born in the 1960s. In fact, it reaches back to the mid-nineteenth century." He credits pre–Civil War Harvard president Cornelius C. Felton with pursuing geographic diversity and makes Charles W. Eliot, the educational reformer who served as president of Harvard 1869–1909, an apostle of *diversity.*

Why is Rudenstein, like other Harvard diversiphiles, so intent on giving *diversity* this imaginary older pedigree? The point is to smooth over the introduction of racial quotas to college admissions by rhetorically assimilating them to a more wholesome tradition of seeking out students with many different talents and backgrounds. Being of a certain race, however, is not a talent and not clearly a background either, as it indicates nothing definite about a person's character or experience. The Harvard approach to *diversity* is to employ racial classifications and pretend they are something else.

Many of us find the racial proxy argument very unconvincing on its face—and racist. Knowing what color someone's skin is tells us nothing certain about what the person thinks. One might depend on stereotypes to venture a guess, and some of these guesses might be highly probable. (For example, the odds are strong that an African-American who voted in the 2000 presidential election voted for Al Gore.) But do we really want to justify preferential college admissions by relying on racial stereotypes? That seems the unavoidable destination of Powell's logic.

But stay a moment longer. Are we really sure that we know what *racial* diversity is? Clearly, to admit students by race implies that we know what race is and can recognize racial differences with sufficient accuracy to make these judgments. Powell and his Supreme Court colleagues merely assumed that this kind of classification was feasible. In doing so, they elevated American folk belief over established scientific evidence that, even in 1978, left no real room for the validity of the kinds of racial classifications that Powell had in mind. It is important to note that, right from the start of its *legal* career, "diversity" has been entangled with dubious conceptions of race.

Back to *Bakke*. Powell next argues that although medical school is primarily focused on "professional competency" rather than trading opinions, "the contribution of diversity is substantial." He cites a case about legal education in which the Court held that it was useful for law students not to be isolated "from the individuals and institutions with which the law interacts." Likewise, "Physicians serve a heterogeneous population." And to that end, doctors in training benefit from meeting other doctors who have different "experiences, outlooks and ideas."

This is another statement of the race-as-proxy-for-diversity-of-the-mind conceit, and it is also a false inference. Powell has no evidence nor even a mildly plausible argument that physicians are better able to serve a "heterogeneous population" by studying in a medical school cohort designed to match that population's demographic profile. In fact, a great many successful physicians in the United States are immigrants from nations such as India in which the demographic profile of the medical schools they attended bears virtually no relation to the demographic profile of their American patients.

Powell concludes this part of his opinion with a reservation: "Ethnic diversity, however, is only one element in a range of factors a university properly may consider in attaining the goal of a heterogeneous student body." He is willing to have race considered as one factor among many, but not as one factor of two. The University of California at Davis's "dual admissions program is a racial classification that impermissibly infringes [Bakke's] rights under the 14th Amendment."

At this point, Powell has inflated "a heterogeneous student body" out of proportion to its actual importance in education; insinuated that "race" and "ethnicity" can reasonably be considered as components of that diversity; and recklessly assumed that "race" is a valid proxy for intellectual outlook. In the following section of his opinion, Powell explains in more detail how the University of California's approach, which involved reserving sixteen places out of a hundred for "minority group" applicants, failed to meet his standard for constitutionality.

As Powell puts it, the "state interest" in allowing the university to take account of "race or ethnic background" is "not an interest in simple ethnic diversity, in which a specified percentage of the student body is in effect guaranteed to be members of selected ethnic groups." The state instead is interested in "a far broader array of qualifications and characteristics of which racial or ethnic origin is but a single though important element." To explain how this obfuscation of an underlying quota can be accomplished, Powell cites (at length) how Harvard does it and concludes:

> In such an admission program, race or ethnic background may be deemed a "plus" in a particular applicant's file, yet it does not insulate the individual from comparison with all other candidates for the available seats.

This approach supposedly makes the losers feel better:

> The applicant who loses out on the last available seat to another candidate receiving a "plus" on the basis of ethnic background will not have been foreclosed from all consideration for that set simply because he was not the right color or had the wrong surname.

The guarantee to all applicants would be that their "qualifications would have been weighed fairly and competitively," and they would have no grounds "to complain of unequal treatment under the 14th Amendment."

Of course, as the years went on and some white students who had highly competitive applications were turned down in favor of less-qualified minority applicants, quite a few individuals *did* find grounds for complaining that they had received "unequal treatment." Here and there, a law review article appeared; conservative commentators began giving voice to those who found themselves on the losing side of racial preferences; and the matter eventually produced a cluster of *Bakke*-style reverse discrimination lawsuits.

The most important of these, so far, is *Hopwood v. Texas.* In 1996 and 2000, the U.S. Court of Appeals for the Fifth Circuit ruled in this case that *diversity* was not the kind of compelling interest that could justify racial preferences in college admissions. The initial *Hopwood* ruling stunned the diversiphiles, who had assumed that Powell's race-as-proxy-for-outlook doctrine was settled law. Gary Orfield, professor of education and social policy at Harvard and one of the nation's leading defenders of the diversity doctrine, described the event as "The Hopwood Shock"—

> Academic leaders ... were stunned by the 1996 Texas decision prohibiting affirmative action and the California state referendum that made it clear that no consensus existed on the benefits of diversity, and by the fact that the academic world, whose leaders were overwhelmingly committed to maintaining diverse campuses, had not done its homework. The research had not been done to prove the academic benefits and the necessity of affirmative action policies.

But in May 2002, the Sixth U.S. Circuit Court in *Grutter v. Bollinger* took a position opposite to that of the Fifth Circuit in *Hopwood*. It found full justification in a *diversity* rationale for racial preferences in admissions to the University of Michigan Law School. We clearly stand in need of a clarifying ruling from the Supreme Court, and can reasonably expect to get it when the *Grutter* case and its pending companion, *Gratz et al. v. Bollinger,* are accepted for review. For contrary to Powell's vapid assertion that under his scheme, no one would have cause "to complain of unequal treatment under the 14th Amendment," his *Bakke* legacy has been one of bitter grievance.

His race-as-proxy-for-outlook fallacy vitiates Powell's whole approach, but the slipshod logic of Powellian *diversity* never really got in the way of the colleges and universities. They simply nodded to the *Bakke* decision by disguising their old racial quotas as "plus factor" systems and got on with the business of discriminating. It seems odd that Powell, who was proud of his pragmatism, did not foresee that his "plus factor" approach would be an open invitation to such abuse. Perhaps he truly believed that colleges and universities would consider the "plus factor" of race just one of many lively attributes students might have, like ability to the play the oboe, success on the high school swim team, or a record of achievement at 4-H Club fairs. But race is not and never could be a qualification in the sense of denoting ability or merit, and the higher education establishment took the new rule for what it was: superficial and practically unenforceable. The new priority on "plus factor" diversity instead of blatant set-asides meant mainly that college and university admissions offices now had to hide racial preferences behind walls of nondisclosure, in confusing thickets of statistical irrelevancies, and underneath effusive language about inclusiveness.

Powell's Sources

Powell's confidence in the idea that racial diversity would serve higher education as a valid proxy for intellectual diversity has puzzled many people over the years and embarrassed some diversity advocates who understood how thin the ice was on which Powell skated. In 1998, William Bowen and Derek Bok, former presidents of Princeton and Harvard, published a book (*The Shape of the River: Long-Term Consequences of Considering Race in College and University Admissions*) that was intended to provide some empirical support for the claims that affirmative action in college admissions has accomplished what its proponents promised. At one point, Bowen and Bok take up the challenge of justifying the claims of diversity, saying that "such an accounting is overdue." They glance back to *Bakke* (misstating the year, 1978):

> A sense of the educational value of diversity led Justice Powell in
> the Bakke case to affirm the continued use of race in admissions
> decisions. Writing in 1976, he was willing to rely on the state-
> ments of university officials. Valuable as such declarations are, the
> time has come, after twenty years, to test them against the views
> and impressions of those who have actually experienced racial
> diversity first-hand.

They are too modest. Who are those "university officials" who
made the valuable declarations upon which Justice Powell relies? As
it happened, Powell's praise of Harvard's admissions policies was
based on the "friend of the court" (*amicus curiae*) brief in support of
the University of California that was jointly filed by Columbia University, Harvard University, Stanford University and the University
of Pennsylvania. Derek Bok, of course, was Harvard's president
(1971–1990) at the time. Bowen's influence on Powell was even more
direct. The *only* evidence that Powell cites in favor of the idea that
diversity benefits students is a long excerpt from the *Princeton Alumni
Weekly* (September 26, 1977) in which then-President Bowen asserted
that a "great deal of learning occurs informally" on campus. Bowen
couldn't quite say where it happened or how, but he was sure that
"learning through diversity" was real, and that instances of it "can be
subtle yet powerful sources of improved understanding and personal
growth." Subtle and powerful, *diversity* works its ineffable way into
the broader education of the student.

So taken is he with the evidentiary weight of President Bowen's
alumni magazine remarks on "Admissions and the Relevance of Race"
that Powell returns to them in the next section of his opinion and
quotes another paragraph to show that Princeton, like Harvard, understood how to use race as a "plus factor." Bowen had assured his alumni
that "race is not in and of itself a consideration in determining basic
qualifications" for getting into Princeton, but "in conjunction with"
other factors "race can be helpful information."

Is there some sheepishness in Bowen and Bok's later acknowledgement of Powell's willingness "to rely on the statements of university officials" in drafting his *Bakke* opinion? Probably not. For more
than twenty years, as far as I can tell, they kept their silence as most
of the nation's 3,800-plus colleges and universities tried to twist their
admissions policies into conformity with Justice Powell's opinion about

the educational importance of diversity. All that time, Bowen and Bok knew that the policy was based on nothing more than a public relations statement (the four-page "Harvard College Admissions Program" Appendix to the *amicus* brief) intended to gloss over Harvard's dabbling in identity politics and an ad hoc justification to alumni of Princeton's race-based admissions practices.

And when, in *The Shape of the River,* Bowen and Bok get their chance to show that racial and ethnic diversity are *educationally* valuable, their case turns out to be amazingly thin, despite all the years they had after Powell's decision to make it convincing. They have statistics to show that black students who graduate from top-drawer colleges and universities on average benefit, intellectually and materially, from the experience. (Who would expect otherwise?) And they have statistics to show that most students say they like and believe in the value of *diversity.* (Data that tell us nothing about whether diversity is educationally constructive, or how to weigh the trade-offs when the pursuit of diversity displaces other goods, such as fairness and academic standards.)

Bowen and Bok's soggy apology for diversity in *The Shape of the River* has unleashed a new rush to find *some* kind of evidence that *diversity* works as advertised. Faced with continuing lawsuits that challenge the *diversity* rationale, universities have sought experts to bolster the idea. When a group of students filed suit against the University of Michigan claiming that its affirmative action admissions program unlawfully discriminated against them on the basis of race (*Gratz et al. v. Bollinger,* and a separate case filed by students against the University of Michigan School of Law, *Grutter v. Bollinger*), the university asked Patricia Gurin, a professor of psychology and women's studies, to prove that a "racially and ethnically diverse student body has ... benefits for all students, non-minorities and minorities alike." The Gurin report is everything that Powell might have dreamed. In fact, it is little more than that.

In the years following *Bakke,* the Supreme Court narrowed the conditions under which affirmative action programs could be considered constitutional. In *Wygant v. Board of Education,* 476 U.S. 267 (1986), a five-member Court majority (Burger, Powell, White, Rehnquist and O'Connor) voted down a Michigan school board's layoff plan that favored minorities over white teachers who had more seniority. The plan failed the "strict scrutiny" test of the Fourteenth Amendment that Powell enunciated in *Bakke*—the test that racial classifications have to serve a legitimate state interest and be necessary to meet that interest.

In *Richmond, Virginia v. J. A. Croson Co.*, 488 U.S. 469 (1989), a six-member Court majority struck down a city ordinance that set aside 30 percent of municipal contracts to minority businesses. Writing for the majority, Justice O'Connor concluded that the City of Richmond had trespassed on Congress's power to decide how to enforce the Fourteenth Amendment, and that the city had also failed to show the need for "remedial action." And in 1995, in *Adarand Constructors v. Pena*, 4515 U.S. 200, a five-member Court majority overturned a U.S. Department of Transportation minority set-aside program as—once again—failing to pass the "strict scrutiny" standard.

Wygant, Croson and *Adarand* were not about "diversity," but they each strengthened the principle that affirmative action programs could be squared with the Fourteenth Amendment only if they passed the "strict scrutiny" test. Powell had stood alone on that point in his *Bakke* opinion. But if Powell's view of the need for strict scrutiny of affirmative action had gathered a durable majority on the Court, what about his other stand-alone idea, diversity? On this the Court has remained essentially silent. Between 1978 and 2002, the Court cited *Bakke* in forty-six other cases, but it never affirmed the overriding importance of "diversity" or judged whether affirmative action admissions programs designed to enhance "diversity" could pass "strict scrutiny."

That silence, however, is not the whole story. When President Reagan nominated Robert Bork in 1987 to replace Powell on the Supreme Court, Bork was known for, among other things, his sharp criticism of the *Bakke* decision and affirmative action in general. Reagan had already replaced two Supreme Court justices (Stewart and Burger), but they had been part of the four-member *Bakke* dissent, and their replacements (O'Connor, 1981, and Scalia, 1986) were uncontroversial. Replacing Powell, however, threatened the pro–affirmative action majority on the Court. The campaign to vilify Bork, which drew much of its energy from this issue, led to his 58–42 defeat in the Senate and the creation of a new verb, to *bork*—to attempt to scuttle a candidate's nomination through a combination of exaggerated scrutiny, innuendo and whipping up opposition among interest groups.

In the years since, numerous other presidential nominees for positions requiring Senate confirmation have been borked, and the mere threat of a borking has derailed some nominations before they were made. That this loss of comity owes something to the *Bakke* decision must have been especially painful to Powell in his final years. The Virginia gentleman, who prided himself on moderation, thought he had found in *diversity* a calming middle way to deal with a politically divisive issue. Instead, he had patented the litmus test by which conservatives and liberals would henceforth judge—and bork—each other's candidates.

After Bork's nomination was voted down (and another candidate, Douglas Ginsburg, withdrew), Reagan successfully appointed Anthony Kennedy to the Court, and Kennedy proceeded to become the fifth anti–affirmative action vote. The *Bakke* opinion, however, has one other connection to the current Supreme Court. In 1993, President Clinton successfully nominated Ruth Bader Ginsburg to the Court. As it happens, she had been one of three American Civil Liberties Union lawyers who wrote the ACLU's *amicus* brief supporting the University of California in the *Bakke* case. In that instance, she had argued that Allan Bakke deserved no relief because UC's decision not to admit him hadn't caused him any "stigmatic injury."

Thus the *Bakke* decision is more than just an important legal document; it is woven into the lives and careers of all the Supreme Court justices. The silence of the Court on the *diversity* theme in Powell's opinion grows louder every year.

Circuit Court Diversity

While the Supreme Court has been waiting for exactly the right case with which to reconsider *diversity*, lower courts have been more adventuresome. By coincidence, in December 2000 three separate courts issued important decisions about Powell's *diversity* doctrine; eight months later, yet another lower court weighed in.

On December 4, 2000, the Ninth Circuit Court (California, Oregon, Washington, Montana, Idaho, Nevada, Arizona, Alaska and Hawaii) ruled in *Smith v. University of Washington* that Powell's comments on diversity have the status of "binding Supreme Court precedent." On December 13, 2000, U.S. district judge Patrick Duggan in Michigan (in the Sixth Circuit—Michigan, Ohio, Kentucky and Tennessee) ruled in *Gratz v. Bollinger* that nothing the Supreme Court has said so far prohibits lower courts from treating *diversity* as a "compelling state interest" if there is "sufficient evidence regarding the educational benefits that flow from a diverse student body." On December 21, 2000, the Fifth Circuit (Texas, Louisiana and Mississippi) issued its third (and final) opinion in *Hopwood v. Texas*, declaring that the pursuit of diversity as a justification for affirmative action in admissions is unconstitutional. On August 27, 2001, a three-judge panel of the Eleventh Circuit (Georgia, Alabama and Florida) ruled unanimously in *Johnson v. The University of Georgia* to overturn the University of Georgia's *diversity*-based admissions policy. The Eleventh Circuit declined to overrule Powell's Bakke decision but dryly noted that "a majority of the Supreme Court has never agreed that student-body diversity is, or may be, a compelling interest sufficient to justify a university's consideration of race."*

This diversity of opinions among the federal circuits about the constitutional merits of *diversity* will have to be ironed out by the Supreme Court at some point, but until then we are left with a basic conflict. The University of Michigan case is interesting because it features Professor Gurin's social-psychological attempt to prove that *diversity* is educationally worthwhile. I'll come back to that in a moment. But first some more on *Hopwood*, the case that so shocked Professor Orfield at Harvard and many other diversiphiles.

The case began in 1992 when Cheryl Hopwood and several other individuals sued the University of Texas, saying that they had been denied admission to the UT Law School because of its preferred admissions of black and Mexican-American students. In March 1996, the Fifth Circuit Court of Appeals ruled that any consideration of race in college admissions is unconstitutional. The U.S. Supreme Court declined to review this decision. In March 1998, U.S. district judge Sam Sparks ruled that neither Hopwood nor any of the other students would have gotten into the School of Law even if it had not had an affirmative action program. Ms. Hopwood and the other plaintiffs

---

*Johnson v. The University of Georgia, 263 F. 3d at 1245 (11th Cir. 2001).

appealed again to the Fifth Circuit Court of Appeals, which issued its decision on December 21, 2000. The court upheld Judge Sparks on the likelihood that Hopwood and the others wouldn't have been admitted anyway, but it also took the occasion to affirm its 1996 ruling that the pursuit of *diversity* offers no acceptable grounds for preferential admissions. In June 2001, the U.S. Supreme Court again declined to review the *Hopwood* decision.

The effect of *Hopwood* on how the University of Texas Law School admits students has been substantial. Professor Olin Guy Wellborn, who oversaw admissions to the school in 1992, admitted that of the 96 offers of admission to "resident minority applicants" that year, only 18 would have been admitted "under a race-blind system." The other 78 were admitted in place of better-qualified candidates.

The court's 1996 ruling covered other points besides *diversity*. It cleared away arguments that the School of Law could use race in deciding admissions "to combat the perceived effects of a hostile environment at the law school," to alleviate the school's "poor reputation in the minority community," and to eliminate "present effects of past discrimination" by parties other than the school itself. But chiefly, the court focused on the *diversity* rationale, since that was the University of Texas's main defense of its program. In its December 2000 opinion, the court offered its strongest explanation of its position. For the first time, a court took explicit notice that when Powell invoked the ideal of *diversity*, he spoke for himself, not for the majority:

> The diversity rationale was first advanced by Justice Powell in his swing opinion in Bakke, in which he wrote only for himself. Although four Justices joined Justice Powell in holding that "the State has a substantial interest that legitimately may be served by a properly devised admissions program involving the competitive consideration of race and ethnic origin," the same four disagreed with him as to the rationale that is necessary to justify constitutionally the government's use of racial preferences. Justice Brennan wrote separately on behalf of the four concurring Justices to express the view that the Constitution permits the government to use racial preferences only "to remedy disadvantages cast on minorities by past racial prejudice." None of the four other Justices would go the extra step proposed by Justice Powell and approve student body diversity as a justification for a race-based admission criterion. *Hopwood v. Texas*, 236 F. 3d at 274–75 (5th Cir. 2000).

The Fifth Circuit Court defended its position against the Ninth Circuit's decision in *Smith v. University of Washington* a few weeks earlier, in which that court had ruled that the right approach in light of the fragmented nature of the *Bakke* opinion would be to embrace the rule that the Supreme Court majority "would have embraced if need be." That is a roundabout way of saying that Brennan, White, Marshall and Blackmun would have gotten on board with Powell's *diversity* doctrine if they had known what was coming. To this, the Fifth Circuit offers the judicial equivalent of "Ha!"

> With respect, however, we do not read Marks [the opinion cited by the Ninth Circuit to justify its claim] as an invitation from the Supreme Court to read its fragmented opinions like tea leaves, attempting to divine what the Justices "would have" held. Rather, in the absence of subsequent Supreme Court precedent squarely and unequivocally holding that diversity can never be a compelling state interest, we read Bakke as not foreclosing (but certainly not requiring) the acceptance by lower courts of diversity as a compelling state interest. *Hopwood*, 236 F. 3d at 275.

The Fifth Circuit then reiterated its most important point, that "the Constitution does permit the government to use racial preferences for the purpose of remedying the present effects of past discrimination, but that the government cannot constitutionally use racial preferences for the purpose of fostering student body diversity."

By this standard, it does not matter whether *diversity* actually works as Powell believed it would and Bok and Bowen claim it has. Even if *diversity* were proven to be a splendid way to enhance education and entirely reliable when achieved through quotas, set-asides or admissions preferences, it would still be unconstitutional. The Fifth Circuit concluded simply that the alleged benefits of *diversity* do not outweigh the constitutional right to equal protection under the law.

Bunker Hill

As I write, the latest entry in the Circuit Court Diversity competition is an opinion in the University of Michigan Law School case, *Grutter v. Bollinger*, 288 F.3d 732 (6th Cir. 2002). On May 14, 2002, the United States Court of Appeals for the Sixth Circuit, in a 5–4 decision, upheld the *Bakke*-based claims of the Law School that its racial preferences are a justified pursuit of *diversity* for legitimate educational goals. The case also produced a very notable dissent by Judge Danny J. Boggs, who demolished the majority opinion, rejected Powell's *diversity* doctrine, and added a "Procedural Appendix" exposing the unethical and possibly illegal maneuvers by Chief Judge Boyce C. Martin to ensure a majority on the court for his view of the case.

When the British finally captured Bunker Hill from the American rebels on June 17, 1775, the long expanse of meadow down to the Mystic and Charles Rivers was strewn with fallen British soldiers. The American forces took some heavy casualties too, but most made a clean getaway, and an American general, Nathanael Greene, remarked, "I wish we could sell them another hill at the same price."

Grutter v. Bollinger may be the *diversity* movement's equivalent of the British victory at Bunker Hill. Noted legal journalist Stuart Taylor, writing in the *National Journal* a week after the decision, captured the sense among *diversity* skeptics:

> A prediction: The Supreme Court will almost certainly reverse the 6th Circuit decision, *Grutter v. Bollinger*—which conflicts squarely with a 1996 decision by the 5th Circuit called *Hopwood v. State of Texas*—and will strike down the blatant preferences used by the law school.

Those preferences are nothing subtle. As Judge Boggs noted in his dissent:

> The figures indicate that race is worth over one full grade point of college average or at least an 11-point and 20-point percentile boost on the LSAT. In effect, the Law School admits students by giving very substantial additional weight to virtually every candidate designated as an "under-represented minority" or, equivalently, by substantially discounting the credentials earned by every student who happens to fall outside the Law School's minority designation.
>
> More shocking is the comparison of the chances of admission for applicants with the same academic credentials (at least numerically). Taking a middle-range applicant with an LSAT score 164–66 and GPA of 3.25–3.49, the chances of admission for a white or Asian applicant are around 22 percent. For an under-represented minority applicant, the chances of admission (100%)

would be better called a guarantee of admission. *Grutter v. Bollinger,* 288 F. 3d 732 at 796–97 (6th Cir. 2002).

Judge Boggs' dissent is a remarkable document that might indeed foretell what the U.S. Supreme Court has to say about *Grutter v. Bollinger,* but the majority opinion he dissented from is also quite interesting. Writing for the majority, Chief Judge Boyce Martin unleashes a pack of new diversity rationales, or rather reformulations of the discredited old ones. "Quotas," for example, are in bad odor, so the University of Michigan offered a new euphemism. For *diversity* to work, it said, the school must attain a "critical mass" of minority students. Chief Judge Martin quotes the Law School's current director of admissions, Erica Munzel: "According to Director Munzel, 'critical mass' is a number sufficient to enable under-represented minority students to contribute to classroom dialogue without feeling isolated" (288 F. 3d 732 at 737).

But perhaps Martin's most audacious move is his attempt to transform Powell's views about *diversity* in the *Bakke* case—which, as we have seen, were his views alone, unsupported by any of the other justices—into a "majority" opinion with full force of law. Martin attempts this bit of magic by invoking an older Supreme Court opinion in a pornography case, *Marks v. United States,* 430 U.S. 188 (1977), in which the Court decided that under certain circumstances, it could deduce a majority view from previous opinions even if, in fact, there had not been an actual majority. Martin takes it upon himself to decide that, unbeknownst to the Supreme Court in 1978 and overlooked for the intervening twenty-four years, the *Bakke* decision did amount to a majority endorsement of Powell's *diversity* doctrine.

Chief Judge Martin's opinion airily bypasses the Supreme Court's requirement that racial classifications pass the "strict scrutiny" test of being "narrowly tailored." The Martin majority was persuaded by Director Munzel and other Law School officials that other approaches to recruiting minority students would fail "to enroll a 'critical mass' of underrepresented minority students."

Martin's decision also absorbs another important modification in the diversity rationale. Powell's idea was that *diversity* was a legitimate educational goal because race could serve as a proxy for *ideas,* and his *Bakke* opinion makes much of the need for universities to serve as places for the "robust exchange of ideas." But the stereotype of people of the same supposed "race" having therefore the same ideas has worn thin, and diversiphiles in the intervening years have quietly shifted ground. They now tend to say comparatively little about the supposed *diversity* of ideas encoded in racial categories and much more about the supposed diversity of *experience* encoded in racial categories. Thus, as Martin's opinion notes, the University of Michigan Law School's official admissions policy:

> provides that the Law School "seeks a mix of students with varying backgrounds and experiences who will respect and learn from each other." (288 F. 3d 732 at 736)

And:

> its admissions policy describes "a commitment to racial and ethnic diversity with special reference to the inclusion of students from groups which have been historically discriminated against, like African-Americans, Hispanics and Native Americans, who without this commitment might not be represented in our student body in meaningful numbers." Students from such racial and ethnic groups "are particularly likely to have experiences and perspectives of special importance to our mission." (288 F. 3d 732 at 737)

The shift from racial and ethnic diversity for the sake of diverse *ideas* to racial and ethnic diversity for the sake of diverse *experiences* is shrewd, in a way, for it introduces a tautology. What is the "experience" of being an African American, Hispanic or Native American other than the mere fact of fitting oneself to the categorizations "African-American," "Hispanic" or "Native American"?

The translation of diversity from the realm of proxy-for-ideas to proxy-for-experience still rests, at bottom, on group stereotypes. There is no "black experience" as such, nor a Hispanic experience as such, and so on. To justify college admissions preferences in these terms is to indulge in a racial essentialism that, were it made explicit, would be quickly recognized for the racism it really is.

If our experiences as members of racial groups were such good stand-ins for our ideas and opinions, we could cancel all future elections and just rely on the census. Most of us realize that our life experience has *some* bearing on our ideas, but to turn that vague approximation into an excuse for racial discrimination is educational malfeasance. And in the case of the University of Michigan, not just a tiny whiff of malfeasance, but an Ann Arbor sized Camembert of malfeasance.

Chief Judge Martin has inadvertently buoyed the spirits of those of us who would like to see Powell's *diversity* doctrine retired. *Grutter v. Bollinger* is as ripe for reversal as a case can get. Even if the U.S. Supreme Court uses it to knock down the legal *diversity* doctrine, the *diversity movement* won't simply disappear. But getting rid of Powell's *Bakke* opinion would be a lot like the American success in 1776 in driving the British out of Boston: a key victory at the start of a long war. Those of us who are doubtful about the *diversity* doctrine were certainly defeated in the Sixth Circuit. But I wish we could sell them another hill at the same price.

Logging Diversity

In the 1970s, before Justice Powell turned the idea into a legal pillar supporting affirmative action, *diversity* had a quiet life. The idea and sometimes the word itself came up in conversations about the advantages of racial integration, and it played a role as well in speculation on other topics, some of which I will pursue elsewhere in this book. But *diversity* as a vague term of approbation for mingling with people of heterogeneous backgrounds was neither controversial nor especially exciting. Most people enjoy some variety in life and common sense accords with the notion that college is a good place to expand one's horizons, in part by meeting new and different people. Likewise, there is not much controversial in the idea that meeting people of other ethnic backgrounds often contributes to those widening horizons.

The problem with Powell's formulation is not that it strains credulity to find educational merit in racial and ethnic diversity, but that Powell wanted to take this weedy sprout as the basis for a logging industry. It is one thing to recognize that the mixing of people from various backgrounds encourages a broader view of one's country and the world; it is quite another to make view-broadening a justification for selectively lowering admissions standards to favor some ethnic groups and disfavor others. It is one thing to observe that the informal side of campus life encourages people to form friendships across social boundaries; it is quite another to set aside equality and fairness in order to foster such contacts. And it is one thing to achieve insights into the common human nature that underlies our numerous diversities; it is quite another to impose an artificial *diversity* based on privileges and exclusions.

Critics of the *diversity* that stemmed from Powell's opinion have often been attentive to what makes the idea appealing in the first place. I don't know of anyone who argues that social "uniformity" or ethnic "homogeneity" make for a better education or a more just society. The opposite of Powell's version of "plus factor" pursuit of ethnic diversity in college admissions is not a "minus factor" or resegregation, but a robust university that welcomes everyone on the same bases of ability and deep and serious commitment to the academic, ethical and intellectual goals of higher education.

Diversity became a major theme in the legal and cultural sides of American life through the *Bakke* decision, which was, first of all, concerned with college admissions; and it is through legal battles over college admissions that the concept continues to receive the most explicit critical attention.

Among the critics of *diversity* who recognize what is appealing in the idea is Professor Eugene Volokh at UCLA School of Law. Professor Volokh notes, "Diversity is appealing because of what it is not." We can speak of diversity, he says, without calling up theories of racial responsibility, group rights, compensation for past wrongs, or agreement about how much people in our society still suffer from discrimination. People *do*, of course, invoke all these grievances, but *diversity* offers a language for promoting racial togetherness that, on its face, is grievance-free. As Professor Volokh puts it, "Diversity is appealing because it's forward-looking."

Volokh offers what I take to be one of the most important critiques of diversity, for he connects its central strength—its call for "evaluating the whole person, including the regrettably but undeniably important factor of race"—with its central weakness: that it validates and reinforces the dehumanizing habit of judging people by stereotypes. *Diversity* advocates never tire of telling us that stereotyping is wrong, but the *diversity programs* they defend are rooted in the idea of race-as-proxy-for-opinion, and therefore are themselves covertly imbued with stereotyping. Indeed, in many of these programs the stereotyping is not covert at all. Black students, for example, are routinely called on to present "black" points of view and are criticized if their views do not fit what their teachers consider appropriate to the students' "social position." Woe to the black student who supports the views of Clarence Thomas or Ward Connerly and thereby commits the unpardonable sin of "race treason," which carries with it a loss of racial authenticity.

Volokh's analysis suggests, I think correctly, that while diversity plain and simple may be educationally worthwhile, *diversity* as a program may have been philosophically corrupt from its inception. Justice Powell's idea of rescuing the giant enterprise of affirmative action by appealing to the virtues of diversity was thus misconceived. Diversity does indeed have virtues, but their pursuit is not the central task of higher education. Moreover, by elevating diversity to a position of importance disproportionate to its actual role in education, the Powell doctrine compromises what was good about diversity in the first place.

The central task of higher education is, of course, a matter of important and no doubt interminable dispute. We do not have one good answer that satisfies all, but several answers that contend: higher education centers on the pursuit of truth; it centers on the cultivation of good character; it centers on no single thing but is where many fields each strive for their own form of excellence; its task is the transmission to the next generation of the legacy of knowledge and the high aspirations of the generations that have gone before; or its task is to prepare a generation to make the world anew.

I am partial to the idea that higher education is, above all else, the pursuit of truth and that this concept encompasses the others. But no matter which premise one starts with, it is a struggle to turn the pursuit of ethnic and racial *diversity* into much more than useless ornament: the intellectual equivalent of the filigree on the diploma. *Diversity* as we have come to know it is seldom a friend of the pursuit of truth. The double standards in admissions tempt colleges and universities into public deception; unwanted disclosures prompt censorship; and campus discussions chill into polite avoidance of some hard and potentially embarrassing topics. While encounters with *real* diversity unveil some important truths, the *diversity* regime is one of settled falsehood.

Is *diversity* better suited to the pursuit of good character? Not if good character means putting aside stereotypes and treating individuals as individuals. Does *diversity* assist in the pragmatist's project of promoting many different kinds of excellence? It seems more closely associated with lower admissions standards, grade inflation, undemanding undergraduate majors, and a falling off in what we expect high schools to teach college-bound students. Does *diversity* play its part in passing on a valuable legacy to a new generation? Only if one considers the perpetuation of racialist categories a legacy worth having. Does *diversity* help the young on their way to making the world anew? It seems rather to insist that the future will be patterned on the divisions of the past—or on new divisions adopted in reaction to the old.

It is easy to recognize in ordinary and uncontrived diversity some educational merits, but they are accent marks, not full words. As valuable as it is to get to know people of many different backgrounds, doing so is ultimately of less importance than such things as learning how to write well, how to speak and read a foreign language, and how to use calculus. But not everyone agrees. For instance, there is Professor Gurin.

Complex Thinking in Michigan

The "Expert Report of Patricia Gurin," submitted by the University of Michigan to U.S. district judge Patrick Duggan in *Gratz v. Bollinger*, is a fascinating attempt to put the ideological claims of diversity on some kind of scientific footing. I suspect Gurin's report is more likely to be cited than read by the legions of *diversity* apologists in the press and in the universities who have lived on the short rations of sheer assertion since *Bakke*. Gurin's report, however, deserves close attention because it is one of very few attempts of its kind.

In completing the task she was assigned by the university, Gurin offers a double thesis: students "learn better in a diverse educational environment"; and that environment better prepares them "to become active participants in our pluralistic, democratic society." The "learns better" idea is built up from a series of postulates borrowed from Erik Erikson, Jean Piaget and some other psychological theorists. Essentially, Gurin accepts a strong distinction between the mental activity of simply plodding along in one's accustomed path and the "complex thinking" that occurs when one is confronted with new and unexpected situations. *Diversity,* according to Gurin, encourages the active and complex kind of thinking because it puts students in exactly those sorts of situations.

It never seems to occur to Professor Gurin that for most students, *diversity* is among the most scripted and routine parts of their education. Students are never slow to comprehend the social codes of peer groups or the numbingly simplistic expectations of *diversity* trainers. The canned *diversity* on college campuses is, all in all, a pretty unlikely context to stimulate "complex thinking" after the first week of freshman year. In any case, the distinction between the automatic-pilot and the dynamically involved forms of learning is misleading. We learn a great deal during our ordinary attentive and even half-attentive states, and the notion that students are better served when they are brought to an excited pitch of "critical thinking" is delusory.

But it is not hard to see what Professor Gurin is driving at. The rhetoric of "critical thinking" is a familiar part of contemporary campus life. "Critical thinking" sounds like a worthy effort to uncover buried assumptions and biases in plausible but misleading arguments and to check the logic and examine the evidence behind theoretical claims. But the term has been taken over by the ideologues for whom it denotes training students to reduce any and every argument to a set of race-class-gender and sexual preference coordinates. Gurin associates herself precisely with this approach as she summarizes the work of a "higher education researcher" named Patricia King:

> King further argues that social diversity—having multiple voices in the classroom—and the multicultural teaching strategy of presenting multiple perspectives from the points of view of race, class, and gender foster fully reflective thinking.

Gurin is enamored with the idea that *diversity* promotes escape from a stultifying worldview. Her report is rich in synonyms for her basic equations of "segregated backgrounds" with passive and immature thinking, and *diversity* with "growth in intellectual engagement and motivation." She cautions against "replicating the home community's social life" on campus, because it "impedes the personal struggle and consciousness of thought" that social psychologist Erik Erikson says late adolescents need to endure. *Diversity,* by contrast, offers the right kinds of "discontinuity and discrepancy" or "incongruity or dissonance." Short of this, we are likely to fall back into "mindlessness." Being plunged into diversity's "heterogeneity of group members" promotes critical thinking because it eliminates "group think" by which "members mindlessly conform."

So here we have a document attacking group-think and mindless conformity in support of the notion that people's opinions naturally reflect their membership in an ethnic or racial group. It is worth reading the Gurin report for this alone.

Gurin's other thesis, that diversity prepares students "to become active participants in our pluralistic, democratic society," is fairly obvious. The students who have learned to become "critical thinkers" are now positioned to live "racially and ethnically integrated lives." Gurin quotes the Association of American Colleges and Universities to the effect that this is a good idea, and notes that "corporate leaders" also extol the idea of colleges preparing students to have "empathy with other workers' perspectives." Later she acknowledges that *diversity* prepares students less for life in America as it has been, than for life as it may become. In our political tradition, Gurin says, "democracy and citizenship are believed to require social homogeneity, simplicity, and an overarching common identity, rather than social diversity, complexity, and multiple identities." But times are changing, and maybe with a more "heterogeneous population in the United States," *diversity* training will be more important:

> Our students, as leaders of the future, need to learn how to accept diversity, negotiate conflicts, and form coalitions with individuals and groups if they are to become prepared to be leaders in an increasingly heterogeneous and complex society.

This recipe for future leadership is a masterpiece of doublespeak. No one would disagree that leaders must "accept diversity" in the sense of the real variety of the nation, but Gurin's phrasing implies that those leaders must also accept *diversity* in the sense of racial and ethnic preferences. Clearly a leader must "negotiate conflicts" in the ordinary sense of this phrase, but the *diversity* cognoscenti will recognize a second meaning to the effect of "validating the unfounded but deeply felt views of oppressed groups." Forming coalitions is what pragmatic political leaders always have done. Gurin's double meaning is that our future leaders must buy into the multicultural Left's vision of society as a patchwork of ethnic interest groups.

Read at the level of its plain meaning, Gurin's account of the situation facing future leaders is utterly banal and provides no justification at all for imposing a *diversity* regimen on students. But read at the level of its double meanings, her account points only to her own political commitments.

That, it seems to me, is the theoretical scope of Gurin's argument. It has only one other dimension worth mentioning: her claim that these points can be demonstrated with regression analysis on various statistical surveys. Here, I must draw the curtain. Read the numbers if you must. Plough through the Cooperative Institutional Research Program (CIRP) data, the Michigan Student Survey, and the classroom data from Michigan's Intergroup Relations, Conflict and Community Program. And pay careful attention to the actual data used to define the variables. Gurin, for example, discovers "classroom diversity" in the CIRP study by counting "students' enrollment in ethnic studies courses." And see if you, like Judge Duggan, are convinced that here at least we have proof that *diversity* is indeed the educational bolus that Justice Powell imagined.

Or, if you prefer, tackle Thomas Wood and Malcolm Sherman's *Race and Higher Education: Why Justice Powell's Diversity Rationale for Racial Preferences in Higher Education Must Be Rejected* (2001), published by the National Association of Scholars (NAS). This organization entered the *Bollinger* case in opposition to the University of Michigan, as "a friend" to the students who were suing. Wood and Sherman (who is a professor of mathematics and statistics) review Gurin's report and give Judge Duggan a drubbing too, for his gullibility.

Complex Thinking in Cambridge

Diversity eventually sloshed over the sides of its affirmative action bucket. As an ideology, it entered into popular ways of thinking about lots of other subjects that had nothing to do with rectifying racial disparities. But at its start, on June 28, 1978, *diversity* was a legalistic gambit intended to protect the principle of race-based admissions preferences from the plain meaning of the Equal Protection Clause.

Many Americans—then and now—did not believe affirmative action deserved to be protected, and would have preferred a *Bakke* decision that ended racial preferences. But since President Johnson initiated it in Executive Order 11246, affirmative action has always had loyal supporters and, after *Bakke,* many of these supporters made the shift from a rhetorical emphasis on overcoming the lingering effects of slavery and Jim Crow to the softer appeals of diversity.

Supporters of racial preferences in admissions know that they face a dubious American public. Since the mid-1970s, opinion polls have consistently shown that large majorities of Americans oppose affirmative action. A July 2001 national survey by the *Washington Post,* the Henry J. Kaiser Family Foundation and Harvard University, for example, reported that 86 percent of blacks, 94 percent of whites, 88 percent of Hispanics and 84 percent of Asians said that hiring and college admissions "should be based strictly on merit and qualifications other than race or ethnicity." In November 1996, California voters by a 54 percent majority passed Proposition 209, which, in principle, abolished affirmative action programs in employment, education and public contracting. In November 1998, voters in Washington State did the same.

Confronted with the deep unpopularity of affirmative action, its academic supporters have turned more and more to the soothing rationale of diversity to accomplish affirmative action by other means. Bowen-and-Bok and Gurin are outstanding examples of this special pleading, but they have company. On May 17, 2001, for example, the "Harvard University Civil Rights Project," codirected by education professor Gary Orfield, issued a report called *Diversity Challenged,* which aimed to show "the educational value of diversity is sufficiently compelling to justify consideration of race in deciding whom to admit to colleges and universities." The gist of the report was that school districts in Louisville, Kentucky, and students at Harvard Law School had benefited from exposure to "different views" and cultures. How so? Diversity "affected the complexity of their thought and even deeply affected their future life plans." Along with the report, the Civil Rights Project issued poll results purporting to show that 64 percent of Americans support affirmative action and 25 percent oppose it. This is pretty lightweight stuff anchored to pretty implausible numbers.

One other such attempt to justify affirmative-action-*cum*-diversity bears an interesting institutional pedigree, for it deals with the medical school at the center of the *Bakke* case. In 1997, two faculty members at the UC Davis Medical School, R. C. Davidson and E. L. Lewis, published a widely noted article in the *Journal of the American Medical Association* offering what they said was evidence from student records and opinion surveys that showed that ethnic preferences in the school's admissions policies yielded "powerful effects on the diversity of the student population," but showed "no evidence of diluting the quality of the graduates."

The doctors examined all students admitted through affirmative action between 1968 and 1987 and reviewed their "academic progress, national board examination scores, graduation, residency evaluations, and practice characteristics." For the twenty years covered by the study, the school admitted 20 percent of its students under "special consideration." About half (53.5 percent) of these were minority students, but "When only underrepresented minority groups are analyzed, 42.7% of special consideration admissions and 4.0% of regular admissions were minorities."

Drs. Davidson and Lewis collected three kinds of data: first, the sorts of information collected by admissions offices from applicants, including undergraduate grade point averages (GPA), Medical College Admission Test (MCAT) scores, and age, sex and ethnicity; second, the sorts of data that indicate degree of success within medical school, including graduation, scores of the medical students on Parts I and II of the National Board of Medical Examiners' (NBME) Examination, school honors and invitations to join the Medical Honors Society; and third, the answers of graduates to a questionnaire intended to illuminate their subsequent careers. The results:

	Study Population	Control Population
Mean GPA	3.06	3.50
Mean MCAT (before 1982)	544	613
Mean MCAT (after 1981)	9.0	11.0
Med. School Grad. Rate	94%	98%
NBME Exam, Part I	444	580
NBME Exam, Part II	437	527
% Invited to Join Med. Honors Society	5%	14%

These data show that on average, students admitted under "special consideration" (the "Study Population") did less well in medical school than those admitted without such consideration (the "Control Population"). If the difference in graduation rates seems relatively slight, it should be weighed in the context of typical medical school policy: once a student is admitted, most medical schools work extremely hard to get the student all the way through the program. Once admitted, any student is highly unlikely not to finish medical school. Thus the discrepancy between a 98 percent graduation rate for the control group and a 94 percent rate for the "specially admitted" is significant.

The third leg of the study, however, shows something entirely different. Only 73 percent of the study group returned the questionnaire; 79 percent of the control did so. But those who did respond from the two groups gave very similar answers: 82 percent of both said they completed their residencies. Other answers:

	Study Population	Control Population
Special Honors (Best Resident/ Chief Resident)	16%	21%
Family Practice Residency	25%	24%
Primary Care Residency	74%	76%
Board Certification	80%	85%
Failed Board Certification	2	0
Percent of Patients who are white	55%	59%
Percent of Patients who do not speak English	17%	13%

On this basis, Drs. Davidson and Lewis reach their conclusion that UC Davis Medical School had succeeded in promoting diversity without "diluting the quality of the graduates." Of course, what it really shows is that, on average, the less-accomplished graduates of UC Davis Medical School have careers that look much like the other graduates. Let's bear this in mind a moment.

Legacy

Justice Powell, who retired from the Supreme Court in June 1987, died on August 25, 1998. He had written other notable decisions, but *Bakke* was his chief legacy. And *diversity,* by the mere accident of Powell's adopting it in the unusually divided circumstance that confronted the Court in that case, won its chance to become both a legal concept and a broader cultural ideal.

Allan Bakke completed his medical training at UC Davis and went on to become a successful anesthesiologist at the Mayo Clinic in Minnesota. Perhaps he is represented somewhere in the "control population" of Davidson and Lewis's 1997 study. The less-qualified minority student that UC Davis originally admitted instead of Bakke was Patrick Chavis. He is presumably represented in Davidson and Lewis's "study population."

For a time, Dr. Chavis's career was celebrated. Senator Edward Kennedy spoke of him in a statement to the Senate Labor and Human Resources Committee on April 30, 1996: "Today, Dr. Chavis is a successful ob-gyn in central Los Angeles, serving a disadvantaged community and making a difference in the lives of scores of poor families." He was also extolled in the pages of the *Nation* by Tom Hayden and by Connie Rice of the NAACP's Legal Defense Fund. "Bakke's scores were higher," said Rice, "but who made the most of his medical school education?" And he is the heroic figure with whom Nicholas Lemann led his important article defending affirmative action in the *New York Times Magazine* in 1995. (In the "down-at-the-heels," mostly black and Hispanic neighborhood of Compton, there's "a fancy new house with a BMW parked in its bricked front courtyard." It belongs to Dr. Chavis, who has "an enormous practice comprising entirely poor people on Medicaid.")

But in June 1997, the Medical Board of California suspended Patrick Chavis's license to practice, citing his "inability to perform some of the most basic duties required of a physician." He was found guilty of "gross negligence" in treating three patients.

Chavis's success in Compton was based not just on his ob-gyn practice, but also on his liposuction business ("New Attitude Body Sculpting"). One of his patients lost 70 percent of her blood. Another suffered a severe infection, but survived. A third was less fortunate. Dr. Chavis had performed liposuction on her at his New Attitude office and then rushed away to deal with another patient who had checked out of a hospital emergency room and been taken to Chavis's private house. Meanwhile, the liposuction patient was left back in his office, where her condition deteriorated. She went into cardiac arrest from loss of blood and died as her husband rushed her to a hospital emergency room.*

I do not want to make too much of this sad story, but it is important that we not forget the difference between high-flown rhetoric extolling social diversity and the practical reality that academic admissions standards exist for good reason. The best qualified are the best qualified, regardless of race, and society ends up paying a very large price when it scants that reality. The "deep thinking" that diversity may excite is no substitute for the actual knowledge that a surgeon needs to carry out his tasks without jeopardizing the welfare or the lives of his patients.

In the end, Justice Powell's *Bakke* decision was a case of wish fulfillment: a search for a painless way to accelerate racial and ethnic integration in higher education by detouring around academic standards. But "race" is *not* a "plus factor" in performing surgery, practicing law, or any other form of advanced study; it is an irrelevancy. And the kind of *diversity* achieved by racially preferential admissions is not educationally invigorating; it is intellectually threadbare and ethically contemptible.

Far from being a painless solution to the nation's racial divisions, Powell's exaggeration of the importance of *diversity* only deepened our racial problems, and affirmative action remains an unsettled and vexing issue. But as large and important as it is, that debate is not the central legacy of *Bakke,* or the primary subject of this book. The *Bakke* decision's even larger legacy was to give scope, legitimacy and force to a new way of thinking about social diversity, which would prove to have cultural applications far beyond college admissions and even race.

---

*Patrick Chavis, age fifty, died July 23, 2002, from a gunshot wound. Los Angeles police believe he was the victim of an attempted carjacking. His death initially received scant notice from the mainstream press, but on August 15 the *New York Times* belatedly printed an obituary that acknowledged Dr. Chavis's short-lived celebrity as an affirmative action success story and his subsequent disgrace.

SIX

DIVERSE GODS

I began my academic career in the 1970s as an anthropologist studying American religion. Between 1977 and 1981, I made a series of trips to the central Wisconsin village of Necedah (Ne-SEE-da) to learn about the nearby community of followers of Mary Ann Van Hoof, who had been having visions of the Virgin Mary and other "celestials" since 1949. On the site of her former farm where all of the early visions occurred, her followers had erected an elaborate complex of stone grottos, constituting "The Queen of the Holy Rosary, Mediatrix of Peace Shrine." People from around the country (though mostly from the upper Midwest) had moved to this remote rural village to be near Mary Ann and the Shrine. They were known locally and somewhat pejoratively as Shriners, but usually referred to themselves as Shrine People. (The movement also has a legally organized identity as "For My God and My Country, Incorporated.") I estimated that the Shrine People numbered about five hundred during the period of my research, but the Shrine also had a more diffuse national following that was manifest in the large number of "pilgrims" who arrived on the "Anniversary Days" commemorating the nine original apparitions of the Virgin Mary in 1949 and 1950. I estimated that perhaps twenty thousand followers made a pilgrimage to the Shrine at least once a year.

Mary Ann and the Shrine People provided an overabundance of things for an anthropologist to think about. The movement combined bits and pieces of dozens of separate folk traditions, including spiritualism, in an ostensibly traditionalist Roman Catholic framework, and married the whole to a homegrown apocalyptic vision. The Shrine itself was a fantastic mélange of evocations from European shrines, such as Lourdes and Fatima, with images of Washington and Lincoln, and representations of Mary Ann herself. And all this overlay a dark conspiratorial view of world history. Mary Ann's "messages and revelations" expressed a gnawing fear of communism. Senator Joe McCarthy, whose hometown is not far from Necedah, appeared in person in some of Mary Ann's visions. But her vision of the "One World Conspiracy" showed that communism was only one tentacle of a larger conspiracy that also included capitalism and Judaism.

Sorting through all of this was difficult, and every time I thought I had figured out the movement's real character, I fell into more complications. Necedah, it turned out, was home not just to one unconventional religious movement, but also to an abundance of shadow movements. Would-be rival prophets had attracted small followings of their own; individuals who were outwardly Shrine People had privately defected, some back to the Roman Catholic Church, others onward into even more esoteric groups; and former members of the movement lingered around Necedah to preach warnings to the passing pilgrims.

My original reason for undertaking an anthropological study of the community that had gathered around Mrs. Van Hoof was to explore how religion can become a way of escaping from and rethinking the dominant social order. America, of course, traces part of its genealogy as a nation to such an escape. The Pilgrims and the Puritans were recusants who saw a temporary settlement in New England—their "errand in the Wilderness"—as a way of creating a new, more godly, and better society. The dream of radical social reform to be attained, first of all, by drastic retreat from the prevailing order may be the original American Dream. The Shrine People were living out a very old tradition—although they didn't see it that way.

I indeed found a small community of religious believers who had chosen to step out of the mainstream of American society. But like a lot of other anthropologists who have gone to the field expecting one thing and finding another, I was disconcerted. I wanted to find the Shrine People reflecting on the larger social order they had (partially) abandoned, but that turned out not to be actively on their minds. Shrine People generally were much more absorbed with the topic of their personal histories and how these intertwined with the Shrine community. And I wanted to find Shrine People vigorously imagining and (partially) creating the new world vividly conjured up in Mary Ann's prophecies and in the sometimes lurid displays on the Shrine grounds. But it was as if the Shrine, in its own exuberance, had left the Shrine People with little more to imagine. The Shrine People turned out not to be the tribe of social critics and utopians I had postulated.

But they did teach me a lot about the self-invention of American religion.

Circulation

Perhaps the most important thing I learned in Necedah was that American religious seekers often make a career of it. Only a handful of Shrine People had been active in the movement for more than ten years. The typical pattern of involvement was a long period of flirtation as a pilgrim, in which the individual maintained ordinary membership in a Roman Catholic parish in the suburbs of some Midwestern city in Ohio or Illinois. At a crucial juncture, the individual would experience a "miracle" while visiting the Shrine. The most common such miracle was the discovery that an ordinary rosary chain had been transformed into gold. The individual—most often a married woman—would then move with her family to Necedah and commence a period of strenuous involvement in Shrine affairs. Within a few years, some members of the family would become deeply alienated from the Shrine, and the entire family would then leave.

I found very few second-generation Shrine People. But I also found that the movement seemed to replenish itself year after year. Even after a particularly disastrous decision by Mary Ann that caused a major wave of defections, the movement rebounded. (On May 28, 1979, she brought in her own "Catholic" clergy—"the American National Catholic Church, Roman Catholic Ultrajectine"—and thereby abandoned the pretense that the Roman Catholic Church itself would reverse its condemnation of the movement.) I couldn't say with precision whether the number of adherents was in a steady state, but the movement was clearly not in peril of extinction after thirty years of heterodoxy.

What I learned from my fieldwork I subsequently found confirmed by large-scale sociological studies. Americans are indeed a churchgoing people, but a sizable percentage of us go from one church to another. The saints circulate—or the sinners shop around.

The Church of Diversity

The *diversity* movement is playing a conspicuous part in contemporary American religion. Seminaries—which are currently among the weakest intellectual links in higher education—are avid perpetrators of hiring by race, ethnicity, gender and sexual orientation. Some of the loopier forms of sentimental multiculturalism are promulgated in pulpits and Sunday schools across the land, and thus the celebration of human difference frequently triumphs in the very places formally dedicated to the idea of universal values and truths. In ordinary life, we meet with an unprecedented fluidity of disparate traditions, in which ecumenical efforts give way to freelance borrowing across formerly insurmountable barriers of ritual and creed. Intermarriage among Catholics, Protestants and Jews is at a historic high. Moreover, millions of individuals whose ancestors were exclusively Protestant, Catholic or Jewish for hundreds of years convert with minimal social friction to Buddhism, Hinduism, Islam, Bahai or other sects, some unknown in the West a generation ago. Brand new religions and we'll-make-it-up-as-we-go-along forms of Neo-Paganism now draw substantial followings. At the level of theological reflection, *diversity* is manifest both in a new emphasis on the plurality of being and in wildly implausible attempts to synthesize traditions that have almost nothing in common. (Boston University theologian Robert Neville, for example, has launched a synthesis of Methodism with Confucianism.)

The *diversity* movement has thus entered deep into the bloodstream of American religion. Its symptoms are many, but they are easily recognized as stemming from a single idea. *Diversity* in religion is a nullification of the claims of every particular religion to having *exclusive* access to some divine or ultimate truth. *Diversity* preaches that each religion (probably) has a piece of the truth; or in any event, its followers are striving up the same mountain as everyone else, even if they pursue the ascent by a different path.

Diversity enunciates what looks like a new and highly relativist kind of religious tolerance. It issues in an ethical injunction to treat those who profess a different faith than one's own with deep respect, and it impels a modesty about one's own faith, which becomes, after all, only one of many equally valid possibilities and possesses no privilege from the mere happenstance that one professes it to be "true." *Diversity* thus leans very far in the direction of nonjudgmentalism. One ought not, according to Diversified Religion, make negative judgments about the worthiness of other people's religious beliefs or practices. To do so is to engage in one or both of the key ethical failings recognized by *diversity:* allowing oneself to be swayed by prejudice, or perceiving other people through stereotypes.

The ethic of nonjudgmentalism promoted by *diversity* demands more than just keeping one's invidious judgments to oneself; it is a profound inner commandment that one not make such judgments in the first place; and it is further a commandment that if one discovers oneself making such judgments, one should seek to overcome them and, ideally, atone for having made them.

In this sense, the religion of *diversity,* though immensely tolerant of religious difference, still preserves an emotionally powerful sense of sin and guilt. It is sinful to judge, but we are all prone to this sin and therefore in need of some kind of forgiveness, grace or redemption. The precise vocabulary for this constellation of ideas about recognizing and correcting our errors against Toleration varies among denominations of the Church of Diversity, but it is found in all of them. (In the event that there actually is a "Church of Diversity," my apologies. The expression is intended to cover the vast number of nominally different congregations—Christian, Jewish, Buddhist and so on—for which the ethic of nonjudgmentalism overrides traditional, more exclusive religious claims.)

Nonjudgmentalism thus has an internal limit: it does not apply to one's own transgressions against toleration. It also has an external limit: it does not apply to (most) forms of fundamentalism. Fundamentalists, at least seen from the perspective of *diversity,* do not play the game. They continue to make exclusive claims to religious truth; they eschew the ideal of tolerating difference; and they are openly judgmental toward nonbelievers. The Church of Diversity judges Christian fundamentalists worst of all, perhaps because the heresy, as they see it, is close to home for adherents to the large number of Christian churches that have embraced *diversity* as a cardinal principle. The fundamentalisms found in non-Christian faiths have the same exclusive approach to religious truth, disdain for tolerance, and uninhibited readiness to judge as do Christian fundamentalists, but are remitted a little of their collective sin by reason of their *cultural* difference and situation in the Third World.

On this point, *diversity* feels an inner conflict. Islamic fundamentalists deserve to be included within the charmed circle of *diversity* because they are "different." But they deserve to be outside the circle of *diversity* because so many of them refuse to accept the relativistic account of religion that is the sine qua non of enlightened believers. *Diversity* stands in need of Muslims who are conservative enough to be characterized as "fundamentalist," but open-minded enough to see Islam as just one of many valid paths to salvation. There are not enough of them.

In fact, Islam poses some deep conceptual challenges to *diversity*. It is a world religion that has not developed much of a relativistic bent. Its traditions of tolerance toward nonbelievers are thin, while its spirit of aggrandizement and aggressive *in*tolerance toward those of other faiths is robust. President Bush speaks of a distinction between a "good Islam" that respects the rights of people of other faiths, and a "bad Islam" which is a perversion of this otherwise fine religion. But it is not a distinction that is easy to maintain historically or theologically. Islam indeed has quietist sects such as the Sufis, and Islam in America has some moderate intellectual spokesmen such as UCLA law professor Khaled Abou El Fadi, but taken as a whole, Islam comprises a complex of religious, political and philosophical traditions that are irreconcilable with the principles of *diversity*.

And in crucial ways, our imprisonment within the conceptual world of *diversity* hinders our ability to comprehend the challenge to American civilization posed by Islamic radicals and their millions of sympathizers in the Muslim world. *Diversity* makes us think that, deep down, all religions say the same thing. But all religions *don't* say the same thing, and Islam especially dissents from the idea that its Truth is merely a local variant of the generic truth available in other flavors at other stores. To the extent that it blinds us to the kind of intellectual inquiry we need to understand these matters, *diversity* is not just folly; it is dangerous folly.

Religious toleration is, of course, nothing new, and if we are to understand the religion of *diversity*, we have to distinguish between

several kinds of toleration. One form, which might be called Jeffersonian tolerance, regards all religions as more or less the same sort of
mistake, and therefore equally due condescension. Tolerance of this
nature may be based on deism, agnosticism, atheism or mere indifference. It proceeds by a principle of prudence, to the effect that, as
people believe many and conflicting things, the common good is best
served by not making an issue out of anyone's faith.

The other old form of religious toleration is that which is grounded
in the faiths themselves. Many, if not most, faiths have at least one
strand of tradition that demands of their adherents generosity toward
those who profess different faiths. The grounds of this generosity vary
considerably. Some view nonbelievers as souls potentially to be won
over; others cast nonbelievers as protected by some ancestral privilege; still others urge the underlying identity of the gods, regardless
of the faith. Herodotus, writing in the fifth century B.C., said that "All
men know equally of the Gods," and held it to be sheer lunacy to disrespect someone else's religion. By Herodotus' account, the Egyptians
believe the gods drove the Persian King Cambyses mad because he
committed sacrilege against their god Apis. But Herodotus disagreed,
and said Cambyses "could not have been in true possession of his
wits before."

Millennia of religious conflict attest that Herodotus' tolerant conviction has often failed to stay the hand of the religious oppressor.
And more modern intrafaith traditions of toleration have only occasionally prevailed over sanguinary impulses. But within every major
faith represented in contemporary America, some ideals of religious
toleration were strongly present before the *diversity* movement began
to take hold in the 1970s. Somehow, without giving an inch of their
own claims to the possession of exclusive truth, many faiths found
their own ways to promote tolerance.

The Credulous Community

In my assessment, the *diversity* movement's most profound effect on
American religion lies in the manner in which we conceive of religion
itself. Instead of a world of contending faiths, each attempting to establish the validity of its own claims to ultimate truth, *diversity* evokes a

world in which all faiths are automatically credited with more or less the same degree of validity. Instead of a society where faiths are typically rooted in a durable, multigenerational community and conversion to a new faith is exceptional, *diversity* promotes a society in which faith communities consist of temporary constellations of adherents and faith-switching is ordinary and expected. Under the creed of *diversity*, attention shifts away from the absolute value of the sect's teachings and focuses instead on the relative value of those teachings to the individual who is in search of a good expression of his spiritual longings.

But in casting *diversity* as something that primarily has changed the meaning of religion in America, I don't want to overlook entirely the race-class-gender gerrymandering, multicultural mythologizing and other insults to spiritual intelligence that *diversity* has authorized in churches and seminaries. The energy and imagination that the churches once directed to religion is, in many churches, now directed to these familiar leftist ideologies of social reform. A few examples may suffice.

In March 2000, one of my Boston University colleagues, walking through the School of Theology, noticed a flyer taped near an elevator: a picture of the earth from outer space, with the title "Crafting the Critical Community" arranged in an arc. And then the text:

EXPLORING THE UNDERSTANDING OF CULTURE, RACE AND IDENTITY IN THE SEMINARY CONTEXT
You are invited to an open discussion about the development of
Multicultural Education Programs
at Boston University School of Theology
led by
Joan Schoenhals and Cooper Thompson
Project Consultants of VISIONS, Inc.

And below this was a curious schedule:

Tuesday, March 21, 2000

International Students with April Willingham	12:00–1:30	Hartman Room (B-23)
Korean Students with Cooper Thompson & Dr. Park	12:00–1:30	Room 325
Students of Color with Renae Gray	12:00–1:30	Dean's Office (Room 110)

Wednesday, March 22, 2000		
White Women Students with Joan Schoenhals	12:00–1:30	Room 325
White Male Students with Cooper Thompson	12:00–1:30	Hartman Room (B-23)
White Male Faculty with Cooper Thompson & John Capitman	1:30–3:00	Hartman Room (B-23)
White Women Faculty with Joan Schoenhals	1:30–3:00	Room 325
Faculty/Staff of Color with April Willingham & Cooper Thompson	3:00–4:30	Hartman Room (B-23)

I reproduce this in its specificity because it provides such a pure example of the mindless categorization of people that the multiculturalist branch of *diversity* ideology imposes. One might think that a seminary dedicated to teaching students the pursuit of transcendent truths would be the last place to segregate international students, Korean students, "students of color," white women students, white male students and such, but that would be to miss the incredible dumbing-down of seminary education during the *diversity* era.

The consultants on this particular project, Visions Inc., as I discovered when I looked them up, operate out of Arlington, Massachusetts, and have been in business since 1984. According to its mission statement, Visions Inc.

> was founded and remains committed to the belief that a multicultural environment can be created by understanding and eliminating racism, sexism, ageism, classism, heterosexism, anti-semitism, adultism, ableism, violence and other forms of oppression and internalized oppression.

Clearly, in some important way, the secular utopian vision exemplified by Visions Inc. has displaced the visions of brotherhood and salvation that the churches once thought themselves qualified to offer. Far from "Crafting the Critical Community," this seminary, like a great many others, seems intent on absorbing uncritically the tiny-steps-for-baby-feet Marxism, racialism and radical feminism that are abroad in today's academy.

And lest it seem that I am slighting my own university in citing this example, I will add that former BU president Jon Westling, on learning about it, inquired and then directed that the contract with Visions Inc. be terminated.

So much for the seminary version of race-class-gender gerrymandering. As to the multicultural mythologizing of the churches themselves, it is, I imagine, familiar to any reader who sets foot in an American church, but to anchor our thoughts on the matter, let's consider the Community-Building Campaign at St. Mark's Church in the Dorchester neighborhood of Boston. A recent newspaper article captures the scene of some fifty people, "Irish, African, Haitian, and Vietnamese," who "sit in a semicircle of metal folding chairs." Reverend Dan Finn explains:

> Each person commits to meeting two other people during the week to talk about who they are, where they came from, and what they care about.... Relationship building is critical. Unless we do this, we don't have the capacity to take action on issues of community concern.

The St. Mark's Church Community-Building Campaign probably does some good, and I cite it not as an example of *diversity* creating divisiveness. But it is indeed an example of *diversity* diverting religion into furthering an essentially secularist vision. Reverend Finn observes: "Historically, religion hasn't always worked this way, but at its best, that's what it's about—building bridges and crossing boundaries.... We're trying to grow the community from the inside out."

The good will of Reverend Finn and the participants in the Community-Building Campaign is heartening and helps to explain why *diversity* is such an appealing idea to so many Americans. We might pause just a little, however, on the thought that religion "at its best" is about "building bridges and crossing boundaries." The ideal of *diversity* can fuel the *social* mission of the churches, but its connection to any of the other legitimate missions of the churches is tenuous.

Neo-Pagan *Diversity*

Diversity ideals have become part of almost every American religion, but in one case, *diversity* has achieved an almost complete fusion with a form of religious expression. Neo-Paganism (a term that I will use to include witchcraft, or Wicca, as its practitioners prefer to call it) is essentially a mystified version of *diversity* itself conjoined to a vague form of nature worship. Neo-Paganism is a movement mainly of rebellion. It defines itself against Western civilization and its religious traditions, which it attacks as intolerant and oppressive. Neo-Paganism, by contrast, sees itself as profoundly tolerant, benign, open-minded, nonexclusivist and liberating, not to speak of being profoundly originalist.

Neo-Paganism's account of itself, however, is a mixture of half-truths and falsehoods. The movement is indeed tolerant in the sense that it proliferates new Neo-Pagan ideas and practices without end, and Neo-Pagans have no concern about reducing the ever-growing abundance of different views to an orthodoxy. The movement is intolerant, however, in its underlying disdain for what Neo-Pagans usually see as the stultifying creedal religions, with their "arbitrary rules about moral issues," as one Neo-Pagan writer puts it.

Neo-Paganism is above all a religion of the Self, in which the individual practitioner is offered an imaginary omnipotence and exemption from other people's judgments. The nonjudgmentalism that characterizes the Church of Diversity becomes radicalized in Neo-Paganism. In many ways, it is the perfect consumer "religion." It beckons to those who are dissatisfied with the demands of their faith to turn away and invent a new faith tailored exactly to their spiritual wishes. Neo-Paganism is thus a free market religiosity for a free market society, and one in which the Self is sovereign over secular and sacred alike. "I have many personal reasons why the modern mainstream religions have failed for me," writes one Neo-Pagan, "and why I choose to go back to my pre-Christian roots to seek my answers. It has not been the easy road either, but it certainly works for me."

This phrase *works for me* appears frequently in Neo-Pagan writing. "I only know that worshipping the Goddess as well as God," says another communicant, "works for me." The phrase gives voice to the self-help movement aspect of Neo-Paganism, but seems a little anemic before the majesty of the cosmos. (Job to Yahweh: "This isn't work-ing for me.")

The primary ethical rule cited by Wiccans, the Wiccan Rede, is "An it harm none, do as thou wilt." Wiccans also frequently cite the Threefold Law: "Whatsoever you do returns to you threefold." The antique diction in both cases is an affectation. Wicca for the most part traces its ancestry to the mid-twentieth century and the pronounce-ments of Gerald Gardner (1884–1964). Gardner was a British citizen who had managed tea and rubber plantations in Ceylon, Borneo and Malaya, and later served as a customs inspector in the colonial Malay civil service. During his years abroad he developed a lively interest in folklore and the occult. When he retired from his government job in 1936, he returned to England and got involved in the occult. In 1939 he was initiated into a coven of witches, and from that point on he considered himself a witch.

Gardner's importance to modern Neo-Paganism arose from his skill as a publicist. In 1949 he published a novel, *High Magic's Aid*, which included descriptions of contemporary English witchcraft, and followed it up with *Witchcraft Today* (1954), in which, as the historian Ronald Hutton noted, Gardner "posed as a disinterested anthropol-ogist who had been lucky enough to discover [witchcraft's] survival as a secret and initiatory system of pagan religion."

Few knowledgeable people believed the accuracy of Gardner's descriptions or accepted his claims about the antiquity of the cult, but he nonetheless established the Wiccan version of modern Neo-Paganism and gave it its primary texts. Many Neo-Pagans character-ize Gardner's formulation, "An it harm none, do as thou wilt," as an *elite* ethical stance. M. Rose Bohusch, vice president of the Kent Neo-Pagan Coalition, for example, wrote to me saying that the Wiccan Rede is "the highest end of ethical statements" because it embodies "the concept of Radical Responsibility." Cecylyna Dewr, writing on behalf of the Pagan Pride Project, explains:

> Pagan ethics allow personal freedom with a framework of per-sonal responsibility. The primary basis for Pagan ethics is the understanding that everything is interconnected, that nothing exists without affecting others, and that every action has a conse-quence. There is no concept of forgiveness for sin in the Pagan ethical system; the consequences of one's actions must be faced

and reparations made as necessary against anyone whom you have harmed. There are no arbitrary rules about moral issues; instead, every action must be weighed against the awareness of what harm it could cause.

And a Boston University Neo-Pagan student group, Nemeton, adds, "Having knowledge of this universal law of return, we assume sole personal responsibility for our behavior and actions. Therefore, we neither support nor condone any activities which may cause harm to others, whether magickal or mundane."

These assurances, however, are pretty thin. The Neo-Pagans I have met and corresponded with often flatter themselves as having what Ms. Bohusch called "a highly developed sense of reflection and radical responsibility." But their self-assurance is not matched by much actual knowledge of history, a concern for logical consistency among their beliefs, or a focus on the connection between ethical instruction and responsible conduct in a democratic society.

Although I believe Neo-Pagans should be perfectly free to believe as they wish, my willingness to state my doubts about the movement have sometimes resulted in Neo-Pagans accusing me of intolerance. The real issue is that in the Church of Diversity, it is not enough to tolerate religious differences; the differences must be extolled, the beliefs granted lavish statements of respect, and doubts and reservations not uttered at all, lest they give offense.

Despite the widespread sense among Neo-Pagans that they are the most open-minded of all believers, Neo-Pagans do not much care for discussion of the actual history of the cults they would like to revive. Indeed, historical amnesia appears to be a rather prominent characteristic of Neo-Pagan thought. Neo-Pagans are generally surprised, for example, to learn that the nature and folk-spirit worship of the Nazis is very similar to today's Neo-Paganism. A few recognize the parallel and attempt to banish it. In "Dispelling the Nazi Curse on Germanic Paganism," for example, John C. Mayer declares, "I am a Germanic Wiccan. That does not mean that I am a fascist or a racist." Mayer is right, but he ignores the great Neo-Pagan Loophole. Because Neo-Pagans vociferously proclaim their unwillingness to judge or exclude other Neo-Pagans and because, after all, "An it harm none, do as thou wilt" puts the responsibility of deciding what is or isn't harmful entirely on the individual practitioner, Neo-Paganism has no principled basis for keeping the Nazis out.

The historical amnesia of Neo-Paganism issues in moral flaccidity in other ways too. It is a movement that seeks to resurrect many ancient religions, which it extols as being closer to nature than Christianity and Judaism. But Neo-Pagans tend to have little to say about the torture and human sacrifice that were frequently at the center of the very cults they hope to revive. Neo-Pagan silence on that heritage, however, is not quite total. For example, one of the people moved to write to me after I published my article about Neo-Paganism at Boston University wanted to set me straight about human sacrifice. She wrote, "In most cases, the people sacrificed were prisoners of war, and it was a way to keep from having to feed and house them for the next umpteen years, while they potentially caused more trouble."

Now that's reassuring.

The Center That Didn't Hold

Neo-Paganism is a *diversity* ideology that has intellectually run amuck, but it is virtually exempt from criticism in the mainline churches. Neo-Pagans often find fault with Christianity, saying that it is narrow-minded, repressive and intolerant. But the mainline Christian churches, in their zeal to prove their own commitment to *diversity,* typically go out of their way to show respect for Neo-Paganism.

The triumph of *diversity* in the mainline churches leaves them practically defenseless against their adversaries, both in the antinomian pagan Left and in the fundamentalist Right. The fundamentalist—or more broadly, the conservative—churches do not hesitate to denounce Neo-Paganism as conducive to immorality, evil and insult to God, and are often blunt as well in finding the mainline churches to be spiritually weak and hopelessly compromised by their accommodations to secular society. The mainline churches usually ignore these breaches of *diversity* etiquette, but they do have in waiting the reply that we noted before: Christian fundamentalism, they say, is *intolerant.* The fundamentalists and other conservative churches shrug this off. Of course they are intolerant; virtue does not reside in tolerating error.

These contretemps are worth mentioning because they connect
the rise of *diversity* to the larger story of the decline of the liberal
churches and the rise of their evangelical rivals. This historical trend
has proceeded uninterrupted since the 1960s and has been widely
noted. Compare the growth in adherents of four "conservative"
churches to three mainline churches for the period 1952 to 1990:

Church	Adherents 1952	Adherents 1990	Percent Change 1952–1990
Assemblies of God	459,256	2,139,826	353.0
Church of Jesus Christ of Latter-Day Saints (Mormons)	845,689	3,540,820	318.6
Seventh Day Adventists	252,917	903,062	257.1
Southern Baptist Convention	8,122,346	18,891,633	133.2
Episcopal	2,555,063	2,427,350	−4.3
United Methodist	9,509,418	11,077,728	16.6
Presbyterian	3,415,837	3,553,335	4

The newest figures from the National Council of Churches show
that the Mormons, for the first time, number among the five churches
with the largest number of adherents, while the Methodists continue
to fade:

Denomination	Membership as of 2002
Roman Catholic Church	63,683,030
Southern Baptist Convention	15,960,308
United Methodist Church	8,340,954
Church of God in Christ	5,499,875
Church of Jesus Christ of Latter-Day Saints	5,208,827

Catholic membership continues to grow, but only because of an influx
of immigrants who are already Catholic.

The most compelling explanation of this vast change in the landscape of American organized religion, I think, is that which was put

forward some years ago by Dean M. Kelley in *Why Conservative Churches Are Growing* (1972). Kelley argues that the patterns of growth and decline cannot be tied to any specific doctrinal differences, but line up perfectly with the degree to which the churches demand strict discipline and obedience. The demanding churches continue to grow, while the come-as-you-are-and-remain-that-way churches stagnate or decline. Mildness does not attract large numbers of new members to organized religion in America. Severity does.

To the detriment of the churches that have most embraced it, *diversity* is inevitably a doctrine of religious mildness. It has no theological point beyond tolerance; no stirring ideal beyond Visions Inc.'s attempts to eliminate "internalized oppression" by having separate encounter groups for Asians, People of Color and Whites; and no heroic commitment beyond Reverend Finn's innocuous Community-Building Campaign.

I take this as a serious loss for American culture. The mainline churches were once a gyroscope for our society. They insisted on the importance of distinct traditions and impeded social change just enough to ensure that people had time to think it through and adjust. They blended tolerance and skepticism, accepting the right of others to exist without abandoning their own right to doubt the wisdom of other points of view. They were sufficiently starched to hold a crease, but sufficiently flexible to kneel.

That vision is now lost—not only discarded, but derided by all sides. The mainline churches themselves are embarrassed by their former gentility, and the antinomian Left and evangelical Right mock it. How did this happen? Much of it was the result of a surfeit of open-mindedness among church leaders in the 1960s. The Presbyterian minister who was chaplain at Yale from 1958 to 1975, Reverend William Sloane Coffin Jr., stands out among his generation. At first a supporter of the Civil Rights movement and a Freedom Rider in 1961, Reverend Coffin went on to become an activist in the movement against the war in Vietnam. He traveled to Hanoi in 1972, while the war was still being prosecuted. On his return he grew more and more interested in the "human potential" movement.

In 1973, on sabbatical from Yale, as he tells in his autobiography, Reverend Coffin spent "considerable time" with human potential "gurus" around San Francisco. He was "particularly drawn" to Michael

Murphy, who had "studied and meditated in an Indian ashram absorbing in particular the wisdom of the remarkable mystic, Sri Aurobindo." Murphy was one of the founders of Esalen, the famous center of the human potential movement at Big Sur. Reverend Coffin, a national figure for his antiwar exploits, found this to be heady company: "The only thing that put me off," he said, "was the tendency of some movement members to bounce from guru to guru, as if the discovery of significant truth didn't require a person to stop at some point and start digging for himself." Thus Coffin glanced at and then put aside the reality that religious searchers go on searching and do not become regular Presbyterian congregants.

The human potential movement in turn led Reverend Coffin to an ever-broadening taste for religious exotica. "The people I most liked," he confessed, "were the Zen Buddhists." And, "one group in the human potential movement whose philosophy and methods I was unable to swallow was est (Erhard Seminars Training)," because Werner Erhard "never talks of the downtrodden" and was not critical of "the structures and values of American society."

At this point, although the word "diversity" has not yet appeared to crystallize this cluster of ideas, the concept is fully present. All religions, in Coffin's view, are really *one,* and the celebration of defanged differences takes on an air of portentous importance:

> Clearly the survival unit in our time was no longer an individual nation or an individual anything; it was the entire human race, plus its environment.
>
> To recognize this formula as the sole formula for survival was, I realized, to affirm the validity of the ancient religious belief that we all belong to one another, every one on this planet. That is the way God made us. From a Christian point of view, Christ died to keep us that way so that, quite simply, our sin is that we are constantly trying to put asunder what God has joined together. Human unity is not even something we are called on to create, only something we are called on to recognize.... We should have the courage to live in accordance with our conviction that territorial discrimination is just as evil as racial discrimination.

This is a long way from Presbyterianism, but not nearly the end of Reverend Coffin's spiritual journey.

In time, he would become a full-fledged advocate of *diversity*. In an essay published in 1999, for example, he commences:

> Let me start with a few words about diversity. Clearly, God is more comfortable with diversity than we are. After all, She made it! We, on the other hand, tend to fear our differences more than we celebrate them.

This is *diversity* distilled to its ideological essence. What happened to the mainline churches in America? Read Reverend Coffin.

The Hooper Principle

The Shrine People in central Wisconsin and the Neo-Pagan movement across the country are but a tiny part of the variety—the actual diversity—of American religion. And they differ enormously. The Shrine People inhabit a tight-knit residential community and profess a traditionalist version of Christianity; Neo-Pagans participate in an amorphous and scattered movement in which one of the few constants is a rejection of Christianity. The Shrine People emphasize the prophet Mary Ann's one-of-a-kind and exclusive access to divine powers; Neo-Pagans emphasize that all comers have access to the divine. The Shrine community is organized on the basis of hierarchical authority; Neo-Paganism abhors hierarchy and recognizes authority only in narrow contexts and attenuated forms.

But while I could multiply such differences, it would paint a false picture. For, at a key level, the movements aren't that different. An individual participant in either one could, quite plausibly, migrate to the other over the course of a few years, or over a lifetime of religious questing. The Shrine emphatically asserts its Catholic identity, but in crucial respects, it is a folk religion that incorporates pagan elements. The "sacred spot" beneath the "sacred ash trees" on which the Virgin Mary normally appeared to Mary Ann Van Hoof connects to very old folk traditions in rural Europe. Mary Ann's trance-induced visions and channeling of celestial voices drew from her childhood experience with her mother, who was a practicing spiritualist. The incorporation into Shrine mythology of UFOs, magic pyramids and sinister secret agents who prowled the Necedah night owe nothing to main-stream Christianity.

The Shrine appealed to American Catholics who had somehow become unmoored from their church and were searching for a more fully convincing account of the world. They seldom realized that, once adrift, they would probably remain adrift the rest of their lives, moving from one island of faith to another and never wholly coming to rest.

The deeper commonalities that link the Shrine and Neo-Paganism are evidence, at least to an anthropologist, that the great variety—again, the actual diversity—of American religion is much less than the natives think it is. The differences among religions are conspicuous and often emotionally emphasized but, below the fractured surface of competing theologies and disparate gods, American culture provides a fairly calm uniformity of fundamental assumptions. The most important of these is the idea enunciated in the First Amendment that religion is *really* a form of personal expression. The recognition of an unlimited right to pursue one's own religious expression puts virtually every religion on the table as a potential option.

Until very recently, few Americans carried this assumption through to its logical limits. Historically, the vision of religion as what-ever-I-choose-today has been strongly limited by the claims of family, community and faith itself. Religion in the sense of an enduring moral community held its own against the idea of unlimited wandering in search of the best fit. Most people stayed within their parents' tradition, their ethnic group's tradition, and the traditions that held sway in their geographical region.

Family and community remain powerful predictors of an individual's likely religious affiliation, but they are considerably less powerful than they once were. Some observers treat this as a generational event. Wade Clark Roof, chairman of the Religious Studies Department at the University of California, Santa Barbara, for example, sees the weakening of family as a factor in religious affiliation as a result of the cultural circumstances in which Baby Boomers grew up:

> The postwar generation grew up with pluralism of all forms—cultural, religious, lifestyle. Its members were not exposed, except possibly as young children, to the religious culture that the preceding generations of Americans had known as constituting the

core of American experience.... Hence, as adults, the new generation has not known a strong religious center in American life.
Religion was whatever one *chose* as one's own.... For them, the
American practice of speaking of religion as a "preference"
assumed a taken-for-granted quality. What else could it be but a
personal choice?

Roof's account may be overgeneralized, but he captures a key aspect
of contemporary American religion: the transformation of *all* religious
expression into the language of "preference."

One day at the Episcopal Church in which I grew up, a new family appeared a few pews in front of ours. After the service my mother
greeted the newcomers—the Hooper family—and came away
shocked. They had informed her that they were new in town and were
just "church shopping." Each Sunday they were going to a different
church in a different denomination to find the one they liked best. Mr.
Hooper, as I recall, was a professional labor mediator. Presumably, he
wanted to see all the evidence before making a decision.

The Hooper approach to religious affiliation was a perfectly
rational procedure from the perspective of religion as a personal choice,
but a strange and unsettling behavior from the perspective of religion
as a moral community or the perspective of religion as a set of claims
about ultimate truth.

Tolerance and Discord

America has been religiously diverse since the beginning of English
colonization and the tensions between the Puritans of Massachusetts
Bay Colony and the earlier Pilgrims at Plymouth. Through the decades
and centuries we further diversified and, more importantly, discovered practical ways to accommodate religious differences. The path
was not always smooth—Catholics and Jews especially faced a long
era of discrimination—but freedom of religious expression and social
tolerance prevailed legally and, at length, in the broader culture.

But this history of religious diversity in America is one story, and
the rise of the contemporary *diversity* movement in religion is another.
The imposition of the new ideal of *diversity* onto the old practical reality of diversity often involves a drastic reinterpretation of history,

which plays down centuries of relative religious amity and amplifies every note of discord. *Diversity* insists that the American past was mainly a matter of powerful Protestant churches crushing dissenters, burning witches, hanging Quakers, exiling Antinomians, forcing conversions on the Indians, persecuting Catholics, and worse. The story continues to the near present when, finally, enlightened people of all faiths discover *diversity* and begin the hard work of turning back the deep-rooted biases that have caused untold pain and have so often belied the First Amendment.

Those who espouse this view see contemporary America as still rife with religious and other prejudices. For example, E. Allen Richardson, who is a professor of religious studies at Cedar Crest College in Allentown, Pennsylvania, writes:

> In the majority of communities across the United States, there are few ways that a member of a religioethnic minority can experience the major institutions of mainstream life without extraordinary difficulty. Contacts with a welfare office, a courtroom, a hospital, or a mainstream religious institution are all potentially traumatic experiences.

This emphasis on *diversity* has transformed the whole field of historical study of American religion, too. In the preface to a recent collection of scholarly essays, *Religious Diversity and American Religious History,* the editors, Walter H. Consur Jr. and Sumner B. Twiss, distinguish between the current fashion and the "consensus historians" of American religion who, in the period after World War II, emphasized "the unity of American religious life" and "the shared national faith." But since the 1970s, according to Consur and Twiss, a new era has dawned, "one that has discarded the image of the melting pot for that of the salad bowl." The new focus on religious pluralism, "that rambunctious and dynamic spiritual variety," attempts to draw our attention away from commonalities and toward differences, including "groups often considered peripheral, if not morally aberrant, by an earlier period."

Some of this new work strikes me as very constructive, in that it traces the steps by which religious leaders, once zealous in defending the exclusive claims and political privileges of their own denominations, gradually came to embrace a more pluralistic view. Matthew

Backes, a historian at Columbia University, for example, has written about the Connecticut Congregationalist minister Lyman Beecher (1775–1863), who between 1815 and 1818 argued vehemently against "an alliance of Jeffersonians, Episcopalians, and dissenters known as the Toleration Party" who threatened Congregationalist supremacy in the state. Beecher lost this battle, and Connecticut disestablished the Congregationalist Church in 1818. But in defeat, Reverend Beecher had a sudden change of heart. Backes quotes Beecher proclaiming in an 1819 sermon:

> [W]ith trumpet-tongue, the providence of God is calling upon Christians of every denomination, to cease from their limited views, and selfish ends, and to unite in the conflict which is to achieve the subjugation of the world to Christ.

Beecher's new, more expansive view was still far from an embrace of tolerance of all religions, but it was a large step in the direction of a system of beliefs that could accommodate doctrinal differences. He had found a way to argue that Christians should "delight in the virtues of other sects," and even to embrace doctrinal controversy as the best way to reach the truth. His transformation, however, went only so far. In the 1840s, Beecher was one of the leaders in the anti-Catholic nativist movement.

Reverend Beecher's discovery of theological grounds for tolerating some opposing religious views illustrates the young nation's sometimes-difficult ascent toward broader toleration. Moving from a mere plurality of religious opinions, most with strong regional roots, to a culture in which religious variety was generally reckoned a strength took many decades. The startling thing about it is not that it was slow and at times uncertain, but that it happened at all. The profusion of sects in America, most of them promoting exclusive claims to religious truth, had no significant historical precedent. Thus the effort of many contemporary historians of religion to play down the hard-won American consensus over religious toleration in favor of tensions, conflict, discord, and "groups often considered peripheral, if not morally aberrant, by an earlier period" seems a bit perverse.

Why have the historians of American religion swung in line with this approach? There seems to be no answer other than their susceptibility to the leftist ideology of *diversity*, an ideology that automatically prefers a historical account emphasizing social division, mistreatment of minorities and the less powerful, and the failure of noble ideals over an account of real cultural achievement.

Peripheral Lessons

This is not to say that we cannot learn something important from studying "groups often considered peripheral, if not morally aberrant." The Shrine People and the Neo-Pagans, for example, have much to teach us about religion in America—only what they teach us is *not* what the pro-*diversity* historians of religion expect. The externally imposed tribulations that these peripheral movements have suffered are almost entirely trivial. Though they are often eager to portray themselves as victims of prejudice, the reality is that they are cocooned by American tolerance and must work hard to rouse any reaction from others beyond bored indifference. Some of the more flamboyant antics of marginal religious groups seem aimed precisely at shaking the complacency of an external world that is more inclined to shrug than to find fault.

If one wishes to believe that the Virgin Mary appeared on Mrs. Van Hoof's potato farm, or if one wishes to wear a pentangle and bay at the moon, most Americans will say, in effect, "Do whatever you like." Conflict might arise, however, if one pushes for institutional recognition among those who hold different commitments. Mary Ann Van Hoof and her followers precipitated one crisis after another in seeking recognition from the Roman Catholic Church. Neo-Pagans generally have found little resistance on campuses, but they did at Boston University when the student group Nemeton sought formal recognition as a campus *religious* group. Live and let live is one thing; demanding social approbation is another.

This is perhaps one of the areas in which the *diversity* movement in American religion illuminates the larger *diversity* movement. For the *diversity* movement over all pushes hard on the claim that tolerance is not enough and that what is wanted is a kind of affirmation of group identity. The diversiphiles hope to replace America's live-and-let-live pluralism with an edgier respect-my-group-or-else pluralism. And the kind of respect that is demanded is exemplified by the Church of Diversity: I must show that I regard your group as, in every respect, the full moral equivalent of my own. Anything less would imply that I secretly harbor the judgment that your group is not good enough—and that way, say the diversiphiles, lies oppression.

What the Shrine People and the Neo-Pagans really teach us is that the peripheral American religious groups are not radically disjoined from the broader American religious experience, but are part of that experience. The Shrine People and the Neo-Pagans simply rearrange and exaggerate some of the familiar elements of mainstream religions. In so doing, they may lose sight of important principles of balance and moderation, and they may transgress ethical boundaries. The Shrine community and Neo-Paganism generally do not win my endorsement as intelligent and morally impressive forms of religious expression. But their conceptual ordinariness is unmistakable once one gets beyond the surface glitter of divine apparitions in one case or the mumbo-jumbo of Celtic deities and ancient spells in the other.

The deep secret of the form of religious *diversity* found among "groups often considered peripheral, if not morally aberrant" is that it is mostly a story of religious banality. The underlying ordinariness of these movements, however, is key to understanding the fluidity of participation in them. The reason that people can and do move in and out of them so easily is that the jumps from one set of beliefs to another—the conceptual discontinuities—are much smaller than are generally supposed. Those small differences, however, can have profound spiritual and moral consequences.

As I gauge it, the differences among American religions are small though important; but construed through the lens of *diversity*, the inverse image appears: the differences are huge yet somehow inconsequential.

Although the pursuit of *diversity* is illuminated in some ways by considering the out-of-the-way cases such as the Shrine People and the Neo-Pagans, *diversity* must also be understood on the vaster scale of American denominationalism. In my view, the most revealing part of the picture is the evidence of how fluid religious affiliation has become in American life.

One indication of this fluidity is the median age of members of various denominations. The older the median age is, the weaker the ability of the denomination to hold on to the children and grandchildren of members. The 1990 *National Survey of Religious Identification* provides a wealth of statistical information on this and other interesting matters. That study found the oldest median age among Presbyterians (48.3 years), with the Methodists (48 years), Episcopalians (45.7 years) and Lutherans (45.4 years) not far behind. The youngest median ages of members were found among Pentecostals (39.9 years), Catholics (40.1 years) and Mormons (41.6 years). The study also offered some refinements: "Female Methodists are 14% of the oldest cohort [over age 75] but only 6% of the youngest [under age 25], indicating significant intergenerational losses."

Of course, loss of affiliation with one denomination doesn't necessarily mean that another denomination gains. Perhaps the most relevant statistic would be a measure of how likely Americans are to *change* a denominational affiliation, and Barry Kosmin and Seymour Lachman, who summarized the 1990 *National Survey of Religious Identification* in their book *One Nation Under God*, offer us this:

> Various polls suggest that somewhere in the range of 25% to 30% of the American public switch denominations in their lifetime. Some acquire the habit and go on to become "multiple switchers." Of course those who change religion tend to be people who take religion seriously, since change is an active experience. The largest reasons for religious change, in descending order of importance, are marriage with someone of a different religious background, shift in religious stance or belief, and migration to a new geographical community.

So a quarter or more of church-affiliated Americans change their denominations over the course of their lives. In practical terms, this is a lot of fluidity. The National Council of Churches counts over 152 million Americans as affiliated with the 66 largest denominations. If is true that 25 to 30 percent have changed or will change their affiliations, we must imagine 38 to 45.6 million religious seekers likely to change their minds.

It is no doubt important to register this as a mass phenomenon, but it is helpful too, I think, to see it on a more intimate scale. Statistical surveys of religious groups are fairly abundant, but let's consider one small case. The Mennonites, generally considered a conservative faith, as of 1990 had 1,242 churches in the United States and a total membership of 154,259, according to the *Atlas of American Religion*. In

1989, J. Howard Kauffman and Leland Harder pursued a survey of 3,083 Mennonites in the United States and Canada. Of these, 30.7 percent said they had belonged to a different denomination before joining the Mennonite Church, and many had come from affiliations that would seem to have little in common with the Mennonite heritage: 8 had been Episcopalians, 52 Lutherans, 41 Presbyterians, 142 Methodists, 155 Baptists and 34 Catholics. And marriage clearly did have something to do with this pattern: 1,069 of the survey's married respondents of this question—41.6 percent—said they did not belong to the same church as their spouses at the time of their wedding.

It seems to me that whether we look at the population of the United States at large or zoom in on particular groups, the basic story is the same. Even among old established denominations, and even in small conservative sects, a large portion of the membership consists of people who have spent a part of their lives committed to some other faith. This is not the situation that has prevailed over most of Western history, or world history for that matter. Such fluidity is partly the outcome of America's pluralistic religious tradition, partly the outcome of the *diversity* movement's further leveling of sectarian differences, and partly also a *cause* of *diversity*'s accelerating appeal.

Converting to Thin Air

When someone quits the religion he was raised in and converts to another, what generally is the relation between his new faith and his former one? Does the childhood faith remain a kind of standard against which the new faith is measured? Or is the convert drawn so completely into the new faith that he sees it only in its own exclusive terms? Do the two faiths subtly blend together?

No doubt the answers to these questions depend on the individual. It would not be too difficult to find instances of each of these ratios of old to new faith among converts. Still, I think the evidence is mounting that we have entered an era of conversion, one in which religious affiliation means far less than ever before. *Diversity* has altered the equation in two ways: it has homogenized the churches, so that it is far more difficult to find a distinct theological flavor in any particular church; and it has flattened the religious sensibility of individuals, so that they experience religion more like consumers and less like pilgrims thirsting for salvation.

The deep religion of America seems at this juncture to be a kind of pragmatic pluralism. That idea is implicit in the First Amendment and has been crafted as doctrine for over a century by American philosophers and theologians. But with the elevation of *diversity* to an overriding principle of American life, the familiar paradox once again emerges: the more we extol *diversity*, the less of it we really have. The principle of *diversity* is a leveler of real differences.

Religious toleration has deep roots in America, roots that stretch back to Roger Williams' founding of Rhode Island and William Penn's founding of Pennsylvania. Williams and Penn promoted toleration essentially on the basis of freedom of conscience: that people should be free from external coercion so that they might respond without impediment to the voice of divinity that is found in all men. Williams wrote of his colony as "a shelter for persons distressed for conscience," and Penn's book, *The Great Case of Liberty of Conscience Once More Debated and Defended* (1670), remains one of the great arguments for religious freedom.

Thomas Jefferson's 1777 *Bill for Establishing Religious Freedom* in Virginia begins with an echo of this older tradition:

> Well aware that the opinions and beliefs of men depend not on their own will, but follow involuntarily the evidence proposed to their minds; that Almighty God hath created the mind free, and manifested his supreme will that free it shall remain by making it altogether insusceptible of restraint ...

But Jefferson quickly moved on to the "impious presumption of legislators and rulers" who attempt to set up "their own opinions and modes of thinking as the only true and infallible."

Jefferson inveighed against the abuse of liberty in making men pay alms for pastors not of their choosing, and the violation of "natural right" that comes from requiring an individual to profess a religious opinion as a condition of office. And he found particular danger in the "civil magistrate" who intrudes "his powers into the field of opinion." Jefferson then identified religious freedom as the essential condition for overcoming false ideas:

> [T]ruth is great and will prevail if left to herself; that she is the
> proper and sufficient antagonist to error, and has nothing to fear
> from the conflict unless by human interposition disarmed of her
> natural weapons, free argument and debate; errors ceasing to be
> dangerous when it is permitted freely to contradict them.

The end of this great argument was the specification that "all men shall be free to profess, and by argument to maintain, their opinions in matters of religion, and that the same shall in no wise diminish, enlarge, or affect their civil capacities."

While Williams and Penn founded an ideal of tolerance on the capacity of men to discover the light of truth *within* themselves, Jefferson seemed to justify religious tolerance as a condition for truth to prevail in some broader debate in the society at large. Jeffersonian man seems better equipped to uncover error than to intuit truth, and the *Bill for Establishing Religious Freedom* aims above all at keeping religious opinion disentangled from lawmaking, where it could give its mistakes the added edge of civil power.

It is Jefferson's vision of toleration based on distrust, not Williams' or Penn's visions of toleration based on trust, that became the stronger voice in our culture. Jefferson's view, which assimilates religion to the broader category of personal expression, was embodied in the First Amendment and remained a powerful tool in the early republic for winning the debates against the established churches in the other states. Reverend Lyman Beecher's defeat by the Toleration Party was but one episode in that larger trend.

The last two centuries of American history cannot plausibly be read as a retreat from this legacy. Legislation, judicial decisions, and above all the broader American culture have steadily advanced the claims of religious toleration. And along with increasing toleration, we have experienced a continuing proliferation and diversification of sects. Against this background we might well wonder: What purchase has the *diversity* movement found on the American religious conscience? Where are the abuses to be rooted out?

The *diversity* movement has nothing particularly to say about *religious* differences in the United States; it treats them simply as matters of personal taste and expression, and is roused to the task of defending freedom of expression only on those occasions when someone on the Religious Right, such as Pat Robertson or Jerry Falwell, makes a pejorative comment on some other faith, such as Islam. The more day-to-day, active focus of the *diversity* movement in American religion is not religious difference but social categories, and *diversity*-minded clergy and congregants spend their time, like college administrators and business executives, plying the calculus of race, class and gender—and ethnic group, immigrant status, sexual orientation, et cetera.

But at this point, we pass beyond the distinctive issues that make *diversity* in religion worth thinking about and find ourselves back in the dreary world of treating people not as individuals who have souls, but as social coordinates who have skin color, sexual preference and so on.

Whither tolerance? Religious tolerance is cheap and easy when religious differences are trivialized. But as the *diversity* principle leads us ever further away from recognizing real religious difference, we may well be losing hard-won and deeper traditions of toleration—and religious traditions worth tolerating.

SEVEN

DIVERSITY AFFLICTS THE ARTS

Among the actors honored in the 2002 Academy Awards were Halle Berry, the first black woman to win Best Actress, and Denzel Washington, the second black man to win Best Actor. The first black actor to win an Oscar, Sidney Poitier, received a lifetime achievement award at the ceremony. The telecast host for the event was Whoopi Goldberg, who in her opening monologue wryly observed that "So much mud has been thrown this year, all the nominees look black." (She was referring to the rumor that the movie *A Beautiful Mind*, based on the life of the Princeton mathematician John Nash, had suppressed his homosexuality and anti-Semitism.) Joe Williams, film critic for the *St. Louis Post-Dispatch*, summed up the ceremony using a familiar word: "After an Oscar build-up with more subplots than a Robert Altman movie, the big story turned out to be diversity."

Diversity ex Nihilo

The success of African-Americans in movies and popular entertainment, however, is only a small part of the story of *diversity* in the arts. The larger story is like an Icelandic saga, stretching over many generations and involving obscure feuds that even the combatants have lost track of by the time the elders gather at the *Althing* (the parliament) to straighten out the mess. Or, to take a popular art closer to home, the story of *diversity* is like one of those nine-hundred-page grocery-store novels tracing the fortunes of a family from its fabled patriarch and matriarch to their lightweight but history-conscious descendants today.

By the 1970s, when the *diversity* movement first stirred in the United States as one of the ways in which affirmative action might transform American society, the arts were well primed with their own forms of identity-consciousness. Americans readily assumed that art expressed the struggle, the vision, the trial of the artist. Alternative conceptions, such as the artist as a faithful adherent to tradition or the artist as one who strives to approximate a timeless ideal of beauty, had no significant presence in American culture.

An art world preoccupied with the idea of creative self-expression and a public conditioned to see the arts in terms of the personal identities of the artists had no natural resistance to the *diversity* ideology. When it emerged in the late 1970s as a new way of thinking about race, ethnicity and gender, *diversity* almost instantly became an established standard. Henceforth, it would be mandatory to consider the manner in which an actor's race contributed to his performance, what bearing a musician's ethnicity had on her interpretation, and in what manner the combination of race and gender contributed to a writer's new novel. A subtle affirmative action arose affecting which writers got published and who received awards. In the jargon of the times, the "social location" of the artist was to be seen as crucial, and social location—always and everywhere—meant primarily race, class, gender.

Individuals Without Individuality

In some artistic traditions, the identity of the artist has been of little concern to the people who enjoy or make use of the art. The traditional Eskimo stone carver, the Trobriand canoe prow expert, or the Tongan tapa cloth maker might be known for exceptional skill, but their works were valued exclusively as a stone carving, a canoe prow, or a decorated bark cloth, not as an exemplar of a particular artist's vision.

Not so for us. We are, at least since the rise of Romanticism, obsessed with the personal vision of the artist. Even eccentric movements like William Morris's attempts to restore impersonal medieval craftsmanship got quickly recast as matters of personal inspiration.

I repeat this point to underscore the deep irony of *diversity*'s triumph in the arts. Its way paved by a culture that eagerly cast the artist as one who possesses a uniquely individual vision, *diversity* turned the artist into a mere spokesman for his race, her gender, our race-class-gender. The *diversity* artist was allowed to keep a morsel of individual identity, but only to the extent that one person's experience of prejudice or oppression is always a tiny bit different from the next person's. The business of the *diversity* artist is to grind out endless permutations of one and only one theme: "Oppression of People Like Me."

Having only one theme, of course, does not necessarily mean that the works are uniform in artistic quality. Medieval religious art essentially has only one theme—glorifying God—but over the centuries, artists made it a large theme, and medieval art has moments of transcendent beauty as well as dull lifelessness. Likewise, some *diversity* art is imaginative, some pedestrian, some just stupidly propagandistic.

Diversity on the whole has been a deadening influence on the arts not because the theme is entirely antithetical to artistic achievement, but because it boxes the artist into such a narrow role. The *diversity* artist accepts the duty to illustrate the travail of the social group to which he or she belongs. But I use the word "group" loosely, since part of the *diversity* artist's task in some cases is to convince the audience that the social coordinates on display (e.g. lesbian Hispanics from the upper Midwest) mean something more than static on the identity politics dial.

Diversity artists are often painfully aware of the spiritually corrupt bargain they have struck. In reward for casting themselves as the artistic spokesmen for their victim groups, they receive recognition and a niche in the market. But they accept this reward at the price of giving up—perhaps permanently—any hope of transcending the race/gender/omni-victim niche. Holland Cotter, in a perceptive article in the *New York Times*, observed:

> Race and class are a problem, though, for minority artists. And multiculturalism ended up being as much a hindrance as a help. It made ethno-racial identity a source for gaining cultural power, but it also turned into a trap.

Cotter argued that the trap is "particularly frustrating to artists born in the '60s and '70s" who are "as interested in the unfolding span of art history as in the immediacies of agitprop." But it is *diversity* agit-prop, of course, that gets the reviews and opens the doors to galleries.

God Is Pleased

Diversity in the arts has several dimensions. The celebration of African-American performers exemplified by the 2002 Academy Awards ceremony belongs to one dimension: a focus on the group affiliations of individual artists. But *diversity* in the arts also means juxtaposing or merging disparate cultural traditions; insisting on quotas in hiring and staging; harnessing art to the didactic goals of *diversity*; and promoting the political agendas of the various interest groups that gather under the rubric of *diversity*.

These are familiar parts of the current cultural landscape and can be illustrated with a handful of news reports from any given week. For instance, the *Columbus Dispatch,* on March 1, 2002, announces under the headline "Diversity Fosters Beauty, Gospel Singers Learn" an upcoming charity concert at the Ohio Theatre, in which "the mostly white Columbus Symphony Orchestra" will perform with the "racially mixed gospel choir from New Salem Missionary Baptist Church." According to the newspaper account, this juxtaposing of separate cultural traditions is extolled by various Columbians in the familiar language of *diversity*. Adam Troy, a member of the board of Action for Children, the charity that sponsored the concert, is quoted: "I think the vision has been to hold the event up as Columbus's premier diversity event." Terry Finneran, a bass singer in the gospel choir, added, "Diversity strengthened all of central Ohio." And Patricia Winbush, who also sings in the choir, observed, "I feel that God gave us music to reach people where they are, but it's all God's music: bluegrass, classical, gospel, hip-hop. As long as God is pleased, it's cool with me." The term "diversity event" seems apt, and these combinations of disparate artistic traditions that also offer opportunities to mix performers from different backgrounds are very common.

Music, however, appears to be the medium in which *diversity*-by-juxtaposition is most frequent, and gospel music seems an especially strong magnet for those who are drawn to this expression. Reporting on the 2001 Christmas concert of the Oakland Interfaith Gospel Choir, for example, the *San Francisco Chronicle* described the sixty-two-voice ensemble as encompassing "more than just three religions":

> Since its founding in 1986, its members have included Buddhists, agnostics, and a psychic minister. For many choir and audience members, this diversity is especially meaningful at the end of a year marked by violent cultural conflicts and religious extremism.

Thus *diversity*-by-juxtaposition lends itself to the agenda of the Church of Diversity (see the previous chapter) as well as to racial and ethnic versions of *diversity*.

A less cheerful dimension of *diversity* in the arts is the insistence on quotas in hiring and staging. I referred in passing in Chapter Four (p. 89) to the recent alliance of the NAACP, the National Latino Media Council, American Indians in Film and Television, and the Asian Pacific Media Coalition in an effort to press television networks to give minority actors more roles. Their pressure tactic has many precedents. In 1990, a controversy broke out over the casting of the Welsh actor Jonathan Pryce in a lead role as a Eurasian pimp in the Broadway production of *Miss Saigon*. Actors' Equity opposed Pryce on the grounds that he was not Asian, but eventually backed down when the show's producers threatened to cancel the production. In December 1991, when Pryce left the show, he was replaced by a Filipino-Chinese actor, Francis Ruivivar. The union also objected to the casting of a Filipino actress, Lea Salonga, in the title role, saying that the part should have been reserved for an Asian-American actress.

The *Miss Saigon* controversy began in the summer of 1990 when an Asian-American playwright, David Henry Hwang, and an Asian-American actor, B. D. Wong, filed a complaint with the Asian division of the "Ethnic Minorities Committee" of Actors' Equity. In one of his letters to the president of Actors' Equity, Mr. Wong wrote:

> There is no doubt in my mind of the irreparable damage to my rights as an actor that would be wrought if (at the threshold of the 21st century) Asian actors are kept from bringing their unique dignity to the specifically Asian roles in "Miss Saigon," and therefore to all racially specific roles in every future production which will look to the precedent "Miss Saigon" is about to set as a concrete model.

"Unique dignity?" In another letter to the chairman of the Actors' Equity committee for racial equality, Mr. Wong wrote:

> We may never be able to do the real work we dream to do if a Caucasian actor with taped eyelids hops on the Concorde.... Chances to nail the big guys like this don't come often. Let's do it.

The union debated the issue and in August 1990 decided to deny Mr. Pryce the opportunity to act the role in New York that he had performed in the London production of the play. Actors' Equity executive secretary Alan Eisenberg read a statement at a news conference, declaring that "The casting of a Caucasian actor made up to appear Asian is an affront to the Asian community." Mr. Eisenberg characterized the action as "a moral decision."

But it was too much even for the left-leaning American press. The *Washington Post* editorialized that the Actors' Equity position had rightly prompted a "flood of ridicule," and added that the decision "demonstrated the silliness of taking an initially well-intentioned sentiment to absurd and legalistic extremes." The "solution," said the *Post,* was more "nontraditional casting," in which the race of the actor was ignored in favor of "talent at creating illusion."

But the chairman of Actors' Equity's Commission on Racial Equality, Chuck Patterson, held the union's line, telling the *New York Times:* "This is a moral issue, to correct decades of injustice to actors of color." And the union's call for racial casting found other supporters. Asian-American actor Ernest Harada was quoted by the *Los Angeles Times:*

> "There is no way we can stop 'yellowface' in the lead roles unless we take a stand," says Harada, president of the Assn. of Asian Pacific American Artists, "and this is the one the union finally agreed with us on."

Mr. Harada's union was also prepared with statistics showing the "underrepresentation" of minorities in American entertainment:

> Although the non-white ethnic groups in the 1989 census estimates made up 22.5% of the American population, the Screen Actors Guild says that only 15%-16% of film and television jobs went to minority actors, slightly up from 14.3% in 1987.

Other actors and playwrights rushed in with ill-considered declarations. Actors Robin Bartlett, Victor Garber and Ellen Parker joined playwrights Craig Lucas, Terrence McNally and Larry Kramer in a letter to the *New York Times* declaring that the *Miss Saigon* issue wasn't about "free speech" but about "civil rights," and saying they would "like to believe" that "no American producer would think to cast a white actor in any Asian part at this time."

In the end, however, the union backed down and Mr. Pryce reprised his role for an American audience. Those who had complained so vociferously nonetheless probably achieved their main objective. The producers of plays and the makers of movies now realized that, while it would be safe to cast minority actors in "nontraditional" roles, casting nonminority actors as minorities would be to court all kinds of trouble.

The era of *diversity* in casting—the era of not-quite-quotas but where's-our-share?—begins with the *Miss Saigon* controversy, but it continues to roll on. Not wishing to risk a *Miss Saigon* sort of fiasco occurring again, most producers have quietly conformed to the rule of casting only minority actors in minority parts. Moreover, the theatre is fuller than ever before with parts intended to be played by minority actors. The dynamics of the theatrical world, of course, always mean that there is a much greater supply of aspiring actors than of good parts, and people in the profession always complain. But it does seem that the *Miss Saigon* style complaints have trailed off, simply because folks like David Henry Hwang and B. D. Wong eventually got their way. It will be a very long time before an actor like Mr. Pryce is again the beneficiary of "nontraditional casting."

It is less clear to me that the *diversity*-inspired ban on whites playing Asian roles will preclude Asians and African-Americans playing traditionally white roles. Robert Brustein, the long-serving (but now retired) artistic director of the American Repertory Theatre in Cambridge, Massachusetts, for example, was one of many directors who have supported "colorblind casting" in the sense of casting African-Americans across the color line. The matter, however, is not exactly settled. In June 1996, the playwright August Wilson (author of *Ma Rainey's Black Bottom; Fences; Two Trains Running; The Piano Lesson,* etc.) gave a speech at the Theatre Communications Group in which, as *Newsweek* reported it, he "scolded black performers for taking white roles in so-called colorblind casting." It was quite a scolding and included words for white directors—Brustein seemed to be among the intended targets—whom Wilson called "cultural imperialists."

Brustein quickly replied in the pages of the *New Republic,* where he serves as drama critic, to what he called Wilson's "rambling jeremiad." He excoriated Wilson's promotion of "separatism" and "divisiveness," lamented his black nationalist vitriol, and wondered:

> Is a man [Wilson] who has garnered such extraordinary media attention—not to mention every conceivable playwriting fellowship—really in a position to say that blacks are being excluded from the American theater or that these institutions only "preserve, promote, and perpetuate white culture?"

Brustein concluded by calling Wilson's speech "melancholy testimony to the rabid identity politics and poisonous racial consciousness that have been infecting our country in recent years."

The bitter disagreement between the two men got a public airing on January 27, 1997, when they debated at New York's Town Hall, and Brustein offered one more round in another essay in the *New Republic,* in which he stood pat on his own approach to *diversity:* "My writing and my actions are clear testimony to my support for the richness of multiculturalism—as long as it is not a pretext for promoting race hatred or generating separatism." He took care, however, to point out Wilson's longstanding commitment to a different vision of the role of *diversity* in art:

> [Wilson] recently denied ever saying he would not work with a white director, and so I must remind him of his article in the *New York Times* in 1990 called "I Want a Black Director," where he refused to allow *Fences* to be filmed by a white director. "Let's make a rule," he wrote. "Blacks don't direct Italian films. Italians don't direct Jewish films. Jews don't direct black American films."

Wilson, so far as I can tell, has suffered no injury to his career for his espousal of racial exclusiveness and his outright contempt for efforts to integrate theatre. The newspapers generally reported on his altercation with Brustein as a stimulating give and take. (The *Boston Globe,* for example, editorialized after the debate, "Bravo! August Wilson and Robert Brustein!")

Wilson, I think, is not to be understood as a diversiphile at all. He is the son of a white father and black mother, who defines himself as "culturally" African-American. ("The cultural environment of my life is black and always has been.") His embrace of racial identity may owe a great deal to the *diversity* movement, which opened up the possibility of making a successful career in the arts out of the posturings of identity politics. His two Pulitzer Prizes speak of the success. But Wilson is better classified as a diversiphage than a diversiphile: one who lives off of *diversity* rather than one who loves it. Taken at his own word, he is a black nationalist; but the more complicated truth is that he plays to an audience of diversiphiles for whom the black nationalist rhetoric serves as a proof of authenticity.

Miss Saigon was clearly the most visible of *diversity*-inspired fights over racial casting, but the Wilson/Brustein affair suggests that the underlying controversy continues. Social identity is now set firmly in the minds of those in the theatre world as a central problem, and it has expanded from actors to virtually all the other personnel. Recently the New York State Council on the Arts, for example, issued a report lamenting the "underrepresentation" of women among playwrights, producers and directors.

Big Bird

Still another dimension of *diversity* in the arts is the attempt to harness art to the didactic goals of the movement. *Diversity,* after all, takes much of its energy from its moralistic claims. In addition to making society a fairer place for groups that have suffered (or are continuing to suffer) oppression, *diversity* is supposed to free people from their reliance on stereotypes and inspire us all to be more tolerant. The arts have avidly taken up this program of moral reform.

In January 2002, the *Los Angeles Times* previewed the coming season of *Sesame Street* and noted: "Other shows this season focus on diversity and tolerance (Big Bird's visiting pen pal is aghast to find that his buddy is friendly with species other than birds)." Other bird watchers are tuned in to this sort of thing. Children Now, a San Francisco based children's advocacy group, watches to see what *diversity* lessons are proffered by television for the very young. The *St. Petersburg Times* reports that Katie Heintz-Knowles, a Children Now consultant, was concerned about "a lot of shows where race is ignored." Katie lamented: "I don't think color blindness is a good thing. . . . We're looking for acknowledgement of some sort of difference, when you can tell people are aware of and respectful of the difference."

The pedagogical applications of *diversity* in the arts are also a prominent part of many school programs. The *Rocky Mountain News* reported on the "Nonviolence Project" sponsored by the "diversity club" at Littleton High School in Colorado in spring 2002 and directed by art teacher Mary Rosenberg. She prompted her students to paint their ideas, and the students talked "about the importance of solving problems without anger or violence." Three girls painted white swans in a "garden of harmony" with blue teardrops "representing hate, anger, pain, and violence" excluded from the garden. *Diversity*, evidently, is something like Eden—and Ms. Rosenberg's students had not yet encountered real swans, which often attempt to solve problems with cygnine displays of anger and violence.

Education these days slides easily into political advocacy, but it is still worth distinguishing between the two. Big Bird is part of a play intended to teach children about the folly of narrow-mindedly seeking one's friends only among others of one's own group. If this were the only instruction that *diversity* in the arts had to offer, we might well conclude that it is a wholesome if rather bland form of moral suasion. But *diversity* in the arts actually spends a much greater proportion of its effort tendentiously promoting the grievances of the usual (and some unusual) victim groups.

Anne Marie Welsh, theatre critic for the *San Diego Union-Tribune*, begins a preview of the coming season of a local theatre: "With its performance standards raised and it diversity flags flying, Diversionary Theatre has announced a 2002–03 season." The executive director of the theatre, Chuck Zito, explained that the plays would focus on "immigration, Hispanic gay men, [and] the fate of a lesbian who is not closeted 'enough' for her employers." The season includes a play titled *Deporting the Divas*, which Mr. Zito described as exploring "the borders not only between the United States and Mexico, but between Chicano and Anglo, gay and straight."

The Diversionary Theatre may have an excellent season of drama in the works, but even if not, the season is chock-full of political advocacy. What the Diversionary Theatre is doing, of course, so are dozens or perhaps hundreds of other local theatres. "Theatre Offensive" in Boston announced its May 2002 offering:

> *Hamartia Blues.* Letta Neely, The Boston Phoenix's "Best Local Author 2001," blows the whistle on life in the American gridlock. JaySan [f.] is building a life with her lover Neferdia [f.], but her jailed brother's desperate calls are a constant reminder of the dire choices both siblings face. Will the secret that binds them destroy the whole family or help to confront the cycle of violence, poverty and racism?

Diversity provides such an all-round artistic justification for pushing the demimonde into the mainstream that other denizens of the twilight are catching on. In Buffalo, Mr. James E. Hellerer, manager of Rick's Tally Ho, recently proposed adding a club with topless dancers across from a local Hyatt Regency. According to the *Buffalo News*, Mr. Hellerer argued that his "classy elaborate place" would "offer diversity in the city's entertainment district." Mr. Hellerer, attuned to his times, wrote to the city council explaining that "diversity is good."

Discontents

Mr. Hellerer's dictum suggests a robust confidence in the idea of *diversity* in the arts, but other friends of *diversity* have had second thoughts from time to time. Back in 1990, when the American art community was still vexed with the question of *Miss Saigon*, Richard Bernstein worried:

> The independence of the artist can be compromised by the requirement of sensitivity to social goals. The quest for diversity can turn into its opposite, a conformity that masquerades as diversity, or just plain mediocrity. And given the sanctimonious current atmosphere that surrounds the issue of race and minorities, it seems possible that nobody will point the mediocrity out.

Bernstein concluded, somewhat darkly, "The last thing needed is a cultural consensus, even a consensus dressed in the mantle of diversity."
    Eleven years later, Holland Cotter voices some similar reservations. No simple opponent of *diversity* in the arts, Cotter says:

"Multiculturalism, more than an attitude, but less than a theory, was a propelling force behind American art of the last two decades. It will define the 1990's in the history books." Mr. Cotter has still more praise for the movement that "changed the art world's demographics and expanded its frame of reference beyond Western horizons." Multiculturalism also "reversed old patterns of exclusion" and brought new "voices into the mainstream."

Yet for all this, as we noted above, Mr. Cotter harbors the view that multiculturalism is a "trap" that frustrates artists who would like to be more than ethnic baggage handlers. Hence he was intrigued by a show in the Studio Museum in Harlem titled "Freestyle," which featured works by African-American artists who were trying something other than the standard *diversity* themes. The show's curator, Thelma Golden, suggested that the works exemplified what she called "post-black art." Cotter mentions a similar term, "postethnicity," proposed by the historian David A. Hollinger. Both words point, in Cotter's view, to the attempt of artists to break out of the *diversity* box.

That box, he says, is constructed out of several panels. First, those who fit a demographic description such as "African American, Latino, Indian, or any blend of these" are forced by American society to reflect a lot on issues of ethnicity, so the subject naturally comes up in their art. Second, in a "severely depressed art market in the late 1970's and again in the late 1980's," the ethnic card provided an opening: "In came street-based graffiti, self-taught and so-called outsider art, identity-oriented work of all types, as well as art from non-Western cultures." Third, "a generation of teachers, writers, historians and museum personnel educated in the 60's and 70's" achieved positions of prominence that allowed them to act on their "clear perspective on the effects of racism."

Cotter is right on all three points, although he has phrased them with excessive delicacy. The third point is an especially precious way of saying that the ruthless reign of Political Correctness has begun. *Diversity* in the arts got some of its lift from ideologues committed to the simplistic thesis that Western society is essentially an exploitative economic system founded on the oppression of women and people of color. When it came to the arts, those who held this view were interested in seeing emphatic agreement with their mono-thesis and nothing else.

As to African-American artists thinking a lot about African-American experiences, and likewise with members of other stigmatized groups—of course; but Cotter offers a one-sided statement of a complex situation, since many artists addressed themselves to themes that were not group-specific or conspicuously "ethnic." As to seizing market opportunities and then finding it difficult to break out, it is just the weary way of the world. Live by the graffiti-sprayed mural, die by the graffiti-sprayed mural. The next generation always has to come up with a new angle.

Plural Pronoun, Singular Object

Bernstein and Cotter stand out for offering highly articulate doubts about the *diversity* movement in the arts. They are sympathetic to the movement, but have come to see its limitations. But Bernstein, writing in 1990, had no discernible effect on the trend; and I would be surprised to find Cotter's 2001 article turning out to have any greater intellectual grip. Here and there, a critic expresses some frustration.

James Auer, writing in 1991 in the *Milwaukee Journal Sentinel*, gripes about the aesthetic emptiness of art shows based on group identification:

> I'm always a little suspicious of shows whose only common bond is the race, ethnicity or gender of the exhibitors. Somehow, in our multicultural age, there should be room for diversity in the arts, rather than a supportive clannishness.

Perhaps Mr. Auer is having his little jest. Just what does he think "diversity in the arts" is if not "supportive clannishness"? But he quickly shows he understands the game: "... an all-female, all-Asian or all-Islamic juried show is no less discriminatory than, say, an all-white-male-Methodist imagefest." Mr. Auer piquantly adds that the artists who frequently show up in these segregated shows are *not* seeking such venues because they "couldn't otherwise find opportunities to exhibit." He mentions for example, a Milwaukee show limited to African-American artists that included works by Kara Walker, who regularly exhibits in a gallery, has works in major museums, and was "featured" in 2000 "on the cover of *The New York Times Magazine*."

Other critics express a milder chaffing at the *diversity* collar. Glenn McNatt, writing in 2002 for the *Baltimore Sun*, observes: "Despite the tendency to lump all African-American art into a tradition of protest and racial pride, black artists have explored a surprisingly broad range of styles, materials and methods to express their experience."

Whose tendency is it to lump all African-American art this way? And why and to whom is it surprising that the stereotype doesn't fit? Glenn McNatt seems to see the world through eyes that never before encountered African-American art outside the mode of self-conscious *diversity;* eyes that, even as he discovers the possibility of something else, remain focused on that narrow field of vision, group consciousness. Note that whatever else African-American arts are, they are arts that "express *their* experience." Plural pronoun, singular object.

I don't want to be too hard on Mr. McNatt. He is groping his way out of the cave: "... while there is no homogeneous style of black art, black artists can draw on a rich visual legacy that reflects the great diversity among African-Americans themselves and the various ways they have experienced and responded to their situation." But the road back from *diversity*-think is hard.

McNatt might, however, take some inspiration from Ellen Pfeifer, who writes for the *Boston Herald,* and who, reviewing a Boston Pops concert in 1999, reached the end of her tether for *diversity* clichés:

> I have a dream ... a dream for the millennium.
> A dream that all composers and librettists of cantatas, oratorios and operas would seek other themes and texts than those enshrined in the P.C. pantheon. I have a dream that such creative teams would voluntarily place a moratorium on the writings of Walt Whitman, Sojourner Truth, Martin Luther King, Jr., John Fitzgerald Kennedy, Maya Angelou, and Malcolm X, among others. I have a dream that the subjects of liberation, diversity, and empowerment would be considered exhausted, spent, depleted and that poets would cast their nets for fresh material.

Dream on, Ms. Pfeifer, dream on.

Final Dress Rehearsal

For every crack that appears in the Great Wall of Diversity in the arts, there are squads of *diversity* workers with caulking guns, masons with quick-drying cement, and morale officers to keep up their fighting spirit.

To catch this process, scroll back to the beginning of the 1990s when *diversity* ideology began to take the form of organized pressure groups. In 1991, for example, Peggy Cooper Cafritz, chairman of the Cultural Education Committee of the Smithsonian and cofounder of the Duke Ellington School of the Arts, published a substantial article in the *Washington Post* decrying the limited space devoted to African-American artists in the capitol's museums. Perhaps the oddest part of her complaint was the view that not only does "cultural exclusion" continue today, but "in some ways it is getting worse." Getting worse? In the age of *diversity?*

Ms. Cooper Cafritz notes that, as of 1991, the National Gallery of Art "does not have a single black on its curatorial staff" and has never had "an exhibit by an African American artist." She wonders, "How can a gallery proclaim itself as national in scope (while receiving considerable public funding) and ignore the cultures of Asian, African, Indian and Latino-Americans? African, Latino- and Asian Americans pay taxes too." She goes on to mention that the Phillips Gallery, the Washington Opera and the Washington Ballet have had "no sustained interest" in developing "culturally diverse programs." And that the National Symphony "has never played a regular-season program of black composers," though it was about to.

This is art nakedly held to the standard of ethnic appeasement. If there are painters who happen to be African-American who deserve a place in the National Gallery, very few Americans would wish to exclude them. But the National Gallery does not exhibit a large collection, and one has to wonder which deserving works have been neglected? The Washington Opera and the Washington Ballet presumably have faced even greater challenges in accommodating a demand for greater "cultural diversity," as they specialize in art forms rooted in particular traditions in which African-Americans have played relatively little part. To be sure, opera and ballet can train new performers who are specifically selected because they are African-American, and commission new works by composers and choreographers likewise selected on the basis of race as well as talent, but why? Why not simply eliminate any barriers and let those who seek out these rarified arts compete for them?

There are a hundred familiar answers to that question, all of which suppose that subtle and not so subtle barriers would prevent African-Americans in particular or *diversity* in general from succeeding in these venues without organized pressure on the opera, ballet, symphony or museum. And this critique may be, to some extent, valid. Barriers do exist, although the arts are hardly bastions of ethnic prejudice. The real issue is finding a proportion between the scale of the problem and the scale of the solution. Peggy Cooper Cafritz, writing in 1991, sounded an ominous note. Her article may have been the final dress rehearsal for the screed that arts organizations have to get their *diversity* numbers right.

That position is now in long-running performance. Arts organizations know what can happen. Back in 1989, according to the *Los Angeles Times,* the California Arts Council "slashed its grant to Costa Mesa's South Coast Repertory by 23% from 1988—despite top praise for artistic and management strength—in part because of weak "ethnic diversity" on the theatre's board and staff." The California Arts Council took its cue from a National Endowment for the Arts report on "cultural diversity" faulting arts organizations for not recruiting enough "minorities on the staff."

Diversity enforcement today is much further along. In 1999 and 2000, for example, the Lila Wallace–Reader's Digest Fund's LEAP initiative—Leadership and Excellence in Arts Participation—handed out over $25 million to arts organizations "to encourage broader and more diverse audiences in the arts." The Seattle Art Museum received a $1.2 million "diversity grant," which the *Seattle Times* said would "be used to increase the racial and socioeconomic diversity of the museum staff, its board and its programming the next four years."

This is just ordinary stuff in American arts management today, barely worth a passing thought, but it reflects decisions deliberated not so many years earlier. In 1993, the American Symphony Orchestra League issued a report that, as the *New York Times* summarized it, "urged orchestras to redecorate their halls, introduce more popular music, enforce racial diversity onstage and reach out to new audiences by changing focus and mission." In general, the boards of American arts organizations are keenly aware that some of their funding may depend on vigorous commitment to *diversity,* both where the public can see it and behind the scenes where the government agencies and foundations can still count it.

For some arts, it remains an intractable problem. The jobs don't pay well and the sorts of people who normally gravitate to them are those with a strong interest in "high culture." While this includes people of every ethnic background, it doesn't necessarily produce the same proportions of ethnically identified staff members and performers as are found in the general population.

Portraits of Diversity

Art, of course, is everywhere, and there is no logical place where *diversity's* attempt to transform art in its own image is likely to stop. In May 2001, the *Washington Post* managed to describe the hanging of the portraits of two senators, Margaret Chase Smith of Maine and Blanche Kelso Bruce of Mississippi, under the headline "Senate Takes Step Toward Artistic Diversity." The idea proved infectious. In December, Charles Barron, a newly elected councilman in Brooklyn, said his first step would be to sponsor a resolution "to allow portraits of black and Latino historical figures" to be added to City Hall. He thought Malcolm X and Ella Barker would be good pictures to add.

Diversity portraiture, however, can provoke strong feelings. In January 2002, the New York City Fire Department proposed to turn a photograph of three white firemen who were raising a flag on the wreckage of the World Trade Center into a nineteen-foot representation of a trio of white, black and Hispanic firefighters to memorialize the 343 firefighters who were killed on 9-11. But white firefighters—and many other people—bitterly complained about the falsification of the photographic image, and eventually the memorial was scrapped.

Masks

Diversity often casts the artist as though he or she were the exemplar of a group and thereby in an especially advantageous position to interpret the group's collective experience both to the group itself and to the outside world. The artist is thus anointed to a position both as the voice of an otherwise inarticulate body and as a mediator between social worlds.

A moment's reflection ought to be enough to make one wonder whether this anointment is warranted. It requires, first of all, that we conceive ethnic groups as actually having the sort of collective "experience" that the artist-as-spokesman could draw on. But many of the so-called groups assembled under the rubric of *diversity* are more sociological artifact than a people of unified historical experience and consistent outlook. Diversity within the group is at least as great as diversity between the group and its imagined alters. *Diversity* deals with this, if at all, as a deep mystery. Over and over we hear of artists revealing that "Well, actually, my art speaks to the *diversity* of experience among my people."

Even if the artist happens to speak directly to the real collective experience of a real group, he rarely possesses more than ordinary insight into that common experience. A good artist is hard at work cultivating his own imagination and talent; a rare and extraordinary artist will capture something of broader significance. The ordinary artist hardly carries an entitlement to serve as Profound Interpreter of the Collective Mind.

Of course, we inherit some of the assumption that the artist is the voice of the collective unconscious from the Romantic tradition lying behind the *diversity* movement, but that doesn't give the supposition any better warrant. For the most part, the assumption serves as a doormat for people with unconvincing ideas about their interpretive credentials.

Consider Willis "Bing" Davis, "painter, sculptor, photographer, and ceramist," according to the *Columbus Dispatch.* The newspaper's art critic, Jacqueline Hall, observes that "The dominant factor in his existence is his African heritage, reflected in every aspect of his art." Davis works in many media, but Hall takes particular note of his color photograph series, "Urban Masks," in which "He captures close-up views of a city's least-photogenic aspects—a manhole cover, a cracked concrete wall, a dried-up wooden palisade...." These may or may not be wonderful photographs, but it is crucial to hear what Mr. Davis says about them: "'I see things in a very Africa-like manner, like masks.' ...'I'm mentally reconnecting with my past.'" Perhaps, but it is not *his* past in the usual sense. Although Davis has "made numerous pilgrimages to Africa," he was born in South Carolina, grew up in Dayton, graduated from DePauw University in Indiana in 1959, attended the Dayton Art Institute, and received a master's degree in education from Miami University.

I don't know "Bing" Davis's work at all, but sight unseen, I would be far more likely to take his photographs of manhole covers and cracked walls seriously if he offered them as interpretations of Dayton or Columbus rather than as insights into the immemorial past and the distant continent he has visited.

Parades

Prince George's County, Maryland, is the "wealthiest black majority county in the United States." On April 23, 1996, it held a celebration to commemorate its 300th anniversary. The *Washington Post* tagged it a "Happy Diversity Party."

Many of the day's events catered to "the county's emerging black majority, tens of thousands of affluent and educated African Americans." The twenty "high school military units" composed mostly of African-Americans that marched in parade in Prince George's County that day were part of a community with no recent history of exclusionary practices to atone for and little reason to meditate on cultural grievances. The affluent county of 750,000, of whom 55 percent were African-American, might not seem the setting where *diversity* ideology would need to be strongly asserted.

Our public discourse is often so dominated by the conceits of *diversity*, however, that we turn to them even when they seem beside the point. Wayne K. Curry, the county executive, spoke that day of "the marvelous achievement of our diversity," and extolled the people who "all share a dream and reverence for freedom, for fairness." Freedom and fairness, yes, but "diversity"?

Diversity might be understood in this context as a broader historical claim. Even though African-Americans form a prosperous and politically dominant community in Prince George's County *today*, they were not always so, and the day's events were, from beginning to end, reminders of the past that had been overcome: "The day began at a plantation manor, evoking images of the county's slave past." And it ended with a gala dinner where guests were "greeted by county residents dressed in colonial-era garb." Mr. Curry spoke of the county's "checkered past" and said the day was a time to "celebrate all the sacrifices made by our ancestors."

An event like this points toward the likelihood that the theme of *diversity* will endure at least in the public side of the arts. Individual artists may conclude it is too constricting an ideology, but politicians like Wayne Curry correctly recognize *diversity* as a rhetorical resource for asserting, displaying and enacting rituals of group identity. The level of aesthetic ambition in public ceremonials of this sort may be low, but pageants and parades are undeniably a form of public art, and one that is readily adapted to the bromides of *diversity*.

Consider Westchester County, New York, which is also a very prosperous place, but not a very black one. Since 1991, Westchester County has hosted an annual "Music America" benefit concert to assist nonprofit human service organizations "devoted to Dr. King's goals of nonviolence and racial harmony." The *New York Times,* reporting on the December 2001 concert ("A Music Tradition That Plays On in the Key of D, for Diversity"), said the program draws a mixed audience and quoted Winston A. Ross, executive director of the Westchester Community Opportunity Program, as saying that the concert "symbolizes the diversity of Westchester coming together in a community event." Sylvia Bloom, director of communications for the Center for Preventive Psychiatry in White Plains, echoed the sentiment: "This event represents diversity at its best."

I don't know that Mr. Curry in Prince George's County would necessarily agree with Ms. Bloom in Westchester County, but no matter. The real point here is that while *diversity* in the arts may wear the grim face of reproach in the context of forcing open more job opportunities in arts organizations, while it may wear the scornful face of anger in the context of telling its stories of group victimization, while it may wear the calm mask of authority when asserting the privileged perspective of group identity, *diversity* in the context of public life is an altogether cheerful fellow, full of harmony, tolerance and good will.

This cheerfulness rings false to some critics, who complain that it is so untruthful to the real experience of life in American society as to be damaging. Paul Farhi, a staff writer for the *Washington Post,* for example, groused in February 2000 against the NAACP's campaign to get more blacks on network television:

> T.V.'s biggest racial problem isn't that it excludes or demeans blacks. It's the other way around. Television programming is already far more integrated—and provides far more uplifting

black role models—than almost any other institution in American life. Indeed, T.V.'s real problem is that it can't shake its own hopeful lies: that America is an integrated, largely harmonious, race-blind society.

Diversity has no easy answer to complaints like this, since it encompasses conflicting demands for realistic portrayal of American society and idealization of component groups. *Diversity* in the arts aims simultaneously at abolishing and projecting group stereotypes. This is *diversity's* own destructive version of "damned if you do, damned if you don't."

Aesthetic Objections?

I've woven most of this chapter out of stories ripped from the back pages and art sections of newspapers, rather than from academic treatises, art magazines, concert programs or gallery guides. The advantage of the newspaper stories is that they give the unvarnished cultural history, without obscurantist jargon and impenetrable theory. I have also moved, without distinction, between the worlds of high and low culture. That distinction is one that I continue to uphold as valid, but it has only slight bearing on *diversity* in the arts. Broadly speaking, low culture, such as parades, network television and popular music, can absorb *diversity* more easily. Since the standards are low to begin with, little in the way of artistic integrity or imaginative freedom is compromised by the insistence that groups be catered to in casting, behind-the-scenes appointments, programming decisions and the like. It might well be important to oppose *diversity* on other grounds—for example, as a violation of legal rights or the principles of freedom and equality—but these are not *aesthetic* objections.

   Diversity poses a more difficult challenge to high culture, such as serious poetry, Western art music, studio painting, opera and ballet. At first, *diversity* may seem simply irreconcilable with the deeper aesthetic purposes of these traditions. After all, art that aspires to the summit of human excellence cannot pause to check whether it squares with parochial group preferences. But the story is really more complicated.

The high art traditions were often already badly damaged in various ways before the *diversity* assault was mounted. The elevation of the inward-seeking artist had sealed off huge territories of aesthetic experience known to earlier centuries; secularization had silenced key themes in the arts for many performers and a large portion of the audience; and we had already lost much of the common vocabulary in the high arts and imposed on audiences an impossible demand to approach each artist's works on whatever novel terms he demanded.

These developments left serious high art in a strange and weak position when the *diversity* movement first appeared—a position exemplified by the makeup of the audience, which was (and is) large, but fractious. Connoisseurs mingle with enthusiasts; self-improvers accompany ingenuous lookers-on; the educated, half-educated and uneducated join in democratic exuberance. The high arts in America could do a lot worse than be swept up in the free-for-all of American taste, but at the same time, it would be very hard to make the case that it is an art world ruled by actual aesthetic standards shared by any sizable portion of the public. It is, rather, (in another sense of the term) a diverse art world, in which real standards, mere fashion and utter superficiality go to the theatre, museum or concert hall together.

Diversity has indeed furthered some of the meretricious trends. When radical chic politics overcame good sense in the 1960s and the *culturati* began to speak of museums and galleries as "contested sites" in a war between the old elite and the oppressed, the stage was set for a flood of ugly, uninteresting art. The anti-aesthetic created by this movement is that art must be "challenging"; and the art world developed a knack for convincing itself that an offense against good taste, traditional morality, conventional religious piety or patriotism, or any other kind of decorum was a blow struck for human liberation. The art world's elite could be relied on to praise as worthwhile anything that seemed likely to irritate ordinary people, and by the 1980s and '90s it was praising Robert Mapplethorpe's bullwhip in a rectum and Andres Serrano's crucifix in a jar of urine.

Diversity gained ground in the high arts as a complement to the school of offense-for-the-sake-of-offending. Museum directors who wished to be seen as *au courant* could vary the routine between shows aimed to shock and more positive exhibits that showcased self-styled ethnic artists. Either way, their "contested space" was being put to use to aid the oppressed. Thus *diversity* and offensiveness worked together in a good cop/bad cop routine.

The peak moments—the solar eclipses—for what might be called the diversiphile-Mapplethorpe alliance have been those occasions when an exhibit hits both registers at once: *diversity* and offensiveness. That's what the Brooklyn Museum achieved, for example, in "Sensation," its 1999 show that featured Chris Ofili's painting comprising an image of the Virgin Mary with elephant dung on one of her breasts, surrounded by pornographic photographs. Mr. Ofili, who was born in Britain, says he uses elephant dung in his art as a tribute to his African roots. He has thus perfected a synthesis of *diversity*-mongering and Mapplethorpery. In any case, the "Sensation" exhibit raised the ire of New York mayor Rudolph Guliani, who unsuccessfully sought to shut it down, and the disdain of Dennis Heiner, a seventy-three-year-old retired teacher and unhappy Catholic layman, who in December 1999 successfully squirted white paint on Ofili's painting.

Diversity and the high art establishment do not, however, always see eye to eye. For insance, in spring 2002, Thelma Golden, curator of the Studio Museum in Harlem, mounted a show titled "Black Romantic," which featured realistic figurative paintings by thirty African-American artists such as James Hoston and Shamek Weddle. Because the artists were defiantly realist in an age that views realism as aesthetically retrograde, the art establishment gave the show a chilly reception; but because the artists were not only African-American but also self-consciously producing "black art," the art critics were in a bind.

Vanessa Jones, a reporter for the *Boston Globe,* wrote that "Flustered art critics offered backhanded compliments as they reviewed saccharine images of winged lovers and haloed black men created without the irony that often marks contemporary work." The exquisite balance of condescension and forbearance is evident, for example, in the comment of Natalie Hopkinson, a writer for the *Washington Post,* who warned that "it would be wrong to dismiss the genre as chocolate-covered kitsch." The opportunity to deploy the great art world cliché—the idea of the gallery as a "contested" space—surely couldn't be far from the lips of some critic. Ah, here it is. Michael Kimmelman, reviewing the show in the *New York Times,* wrote:

> Ms. Golden in her catalog describes this division of taste as hav-
> ing parallels in the rift between fans of Toni Morrison and Terry
> McMillan, or between Wynton Marsalis and hip-hop. It's the
> high-low battleground, where her show, groundbreaking for the
> Studio Museum, now begs to be contested.

Thelma Golden's catalog received quite a bit of attention in the
reviews. Vanessa Jones, in the *Boston Globe*, quoted Golden explaining
that black art

> combines the social and political pulse of the Black community
> into an artistic reflection.... [It] seeks to step beyond the white
> western framework of American art which has enclosed and
> smothered any previous expression of Blackness.

And some of the artists seemed to agree. Mr. Hoston, for example,
explained that his goal was to "document the black middle class." He
aimed "to do paintings that show that we do exist, OK, 'cause there's
just not enough of that around." His painting "Hot Day In" depicts a
young woman seated in the dappled sunlight of a plant-filled room,
gazing out of an open window. It is a fine and memorable painting,
but if it documents the black middle class, it does so only in the sense
that it is quiet and unperturbed by any suggestion of social pathology.

Diversity and the contemporary art establishment usually get
along swimmingly, but the "Black Romantic" exhibit points to a hidden tension. As Mr. Kimmelman opined, "To snicker at the exhibition
would be patronizing. To brush it off as a hoot would be worse." But,
of course, he did both.

Against this background, I am not at all certain that the infliction
of *diversity* on high art is so great a catastrophe. *Diversity*, in any of
the forms I've discussed, has little prospect of enriching serious art;
but neither will it impoverish the arts any further than they already
have been. The real artists, I suppose—the individuals of surpassing
imagination and genuine creativity and essential indifference to the
trivialities of group identity—will find their way despite all the obsta-
cles, including *diversity*.

So, while the arts are not improved by *diversity*, they can probably bear it. I am less sanguine, however, about the effect of *diversity*
on the aesthetic sensibilities of artists and ordinary people. *Diversity*

diverts us into seeing ourselves not as autonomous individuals who bring what light we can to our lives, but primarily as members of groups. The artist who absorbs this lesson with any degree of enthusiasm has, in a key respect, resigned his commission as an artist and abandoned his muse. He has become a servant of an ideology and given up the harder task of seeing the world as both ancient and new. The ordinary person who sees art through the lens of *diversity* probably doesn't see art at all, and thereby impoverishes his life. But the ordinary person is also, by rights, an autonomous individual who is charged, as are we all, with comprehending himself as a moral agent and free-willed actor in the world. Self-expression is a crucial dimension of that autonomy and ought not to be lightly thrown away by adopting a simplistic answer to the question "Who am I?" All of us are, in part, shaped by the social groups in which we voluntarily or involuntarily participate. Yet we must come to terms with those realities without clinging to the spurious answer that group identity is our only identity.

Diversity in its most compelling sense is *within* us. The arts are important, not least for their capacity to illuminate those inner diversities in ourselves and in others. *Diversity* in the sense of the movement that insists on the preeminence of group identity, however, trivializes art, and to that extent, it is an affliction that truly does diminish us.

Exemptions

Diversity afflicts most of the arts in America, but not all. We don't seem to look for *diversity* in the art of engraving burial markers, although the recently introduced techniques of implanting porcelainized photographs and etching elaborate designs by laser may change that. Grave art may be one of the next frontiers of *diversity*. We expect aesthetically-pleasing bouquets from our florists, but this is a trade seemingly untouched by *diversity*. And what about gardening?

Not far from my office at Boston University is a city park that has been partly turned over to residents to plant gardens. What began as World War II Victory Gardens has expanded over the years and become a lush maze of horticultural delights. Exotic hibiscus blossoms twine with old New England favorites, like hydrangeas; here someone is husbanding a tomato crop, while a few feet away, buddleia bushes attract a profusion of butterflies. Some gardeners have excavated stone grottos in their assigned plots; others have planted dwarf apple trees. The Fenway Gardens, teeming with birds, comprise more than five hundred individual plots awarded by lottery and cultivated inch by inch. Amid this sheer abundance, the illusion of escape from the city is complete. One looks up in genuine surprise to see the Prudential skyscraper a quarter-mile away. I take the Fenway Gardens as a fair image of gardening *diversity*.

Perhaps a hundred yards beyond the Fenway Gardens on the banks of the aptly named Muddy River, one comes to the next modern link in Frederick Law Olmsted's Emerald Necklace encircling the neck of Boston. This link is a high hedge ringing the James P. Kelleher Rose Garden. At the right time of day, one can enter and stroll around a tidy path between carefully tended rose bushes, each with a black and white placard announcing the variety: Early Morn, Break o' Day, Elegance. At intervals one comes to shaded benches that invite quiet contemplation of these austerities. At the end of one avenue is a statue titled *Disconsula,* showing a woman in the extremity of grief. It is a gift from the city of Barcelona, devastated in the Spanish Civil War.

The abundance and vivacity of the Fenway Gardens seems to me infinitely preferable to poor *Disconsula* among her hybrid roses. Perhaps she is mindful that her time has passed.

EIGHT

IDENTITY BUSINESS

In the opening of Hermann Melville's enigmatic novel *The Confidence-Man, His Masquerade* (1857), a stranger steps on board the steamboat *Fidèle* as it prepares for a trip from St. Louis to New Orleans. He comes to a placard near the captain's office "offering a reward for the capture of a mysterious imposter, supposed to have recently arrived from the East," and near the crowd that has gathered to read the reward poster he chalks a message onto a small slate: "Charity thinketh no evil." An apparent deaf-mute, he is pummeled and pushed aside for his efforts, and soon is seen no more, perhaps having disembarked at one of the many landings along the way.

Or perhaps not. For as Melville's novel proceeds, a succession of characters in different dress, in a variety of dialects and of different races trick the passengers of the *Fidèle* into offers of cash or trust. The title of the book suggests that the tricksters are all one and the same "mysterious imposter," but Melville does not spoil his masquerade with an easy answer.

Today, the art of manipulating identity has been taken to a vastly more sophisticated level in the business world by *diversity* officers, trainers and consultants. Unlike Melville's confidence man, however, *diversity* generally operates within the bounds of the law. Indeed, it is wrapped in all the sanctimony that the commercial world can muster. Companies boast of their commitment to *diversity* as though it were self-evidently a virtue.

But the ethical basis of the *diversity* business hasn't really advanced beyond the voyage of the ironically named *Fidèle*. It still depends on people not recognizing the real past and on the improvising of new identities calculated to gain people's sympathies. *Diversity* practitioners ask us to see a person not in terms of his real life, but as an embodiment of the history of an oppressed group. If we fall for this, it is partly because it is an audacious simplification of our national life. Rather than face the sheer and sometimes bewildering variety of people in their real diversity, we accede to the script in which an accent, a skin shade or a surname is automatically taken as evidence that an individual suffered prejudice, was denied educational opportunities, and has overcome the odds.

Diversity practitioners likewise depend on telling stories that they figure will deflect scrutiny from their actual ends. The master narrative of *diversity* is that it is a way to overcome a legacy of unfairness and discrimination by giving us a workplace that "looks like America." The story is meant to sound so wholesome that to question it would be to demonstrate a poverty of fellow feeling. But the story bears scant relation to the facts. *Diversity* as it is practiced in hiring and on the job does not eliminate but rather imposes unfairness and discrimination; and the "looks like America" image works only if one imagines America as composed of a rigid grid of ethnicities.

The Empty Quarter

The introduction and institutionalization of *diversity* ideology in American commerce has been superbly chronicled by the sociologist Frederick R. Lynch in *The Diversity Machine* (1997). Lynch sportingly attended workshops where he played *BaFa, Diversophy, Name Five* and other games run by dour *diversity* consultants. He interviewed dozens of *diversity* trainers such as Lewis Griggs, a Nixon White House aid turned New Age *diversity* guru; R. Roosevelt Thomas Jr., a former Harvard Business School professor and founder of the American Institute for Managing Diversity at Morehouse College; and Lillian Roybal Rose, rooter-out of internalized "negative societal stereotypes" ("The best workshops have been where white males burst out crying.").

Lynch attended not just one but three of Lewis Griggs' annual National Diversity Conferences (1991, 1992, 1993); observed *diversity* training firsthand at the Los Angeles Sheriff's Department in 1991 and

1992; and sat in on debates about *diversity* at four annual conventions (including "Unity through Diversity" in 1990 and "Beyond Parity to Managing Diversity" in 1991) of the California Community College system. Lynch devoted particular attention to faculty and student views on *diversity* at his alma mater, the University of Michigan, which, as we have seen, has become a key battleground in the legal dispute over the *diversity* justification for ethnic and racial preferences. And Lynch perused *diversity* manifestos, ploughed through the *diversity* journal articles, and soldiered across the Death Valleys and Gobi Deserts of how-to *diversity* books.

Later travelers through these bleak and arid regions must consult Lynch's *The Diversity Machine* in gratitude—and wonder at the wisdom of proceeding further. Ahead lie trackless expanses barren of any real thought, alternately scorched with accusations and chilled with conformity. Here and there one spies a cairn, a little pile of stones set up by the intrepid Lynch to mark the grave of a missed opportunity (Why didn't the Reagan White House kill affirmative action when it had the chance?) or to mark an invisible fracture (When exactly did affirmative action transmute into proportional representation of victim groups?). But otherwise, this is the Empty Quarter.

It is empty of real thought because the American business community has decided, in effect, passively to absorb the ideology of *diversity* without thinking through its ethical, social or even business implications. Lynch completed his seven-year study of the movement in 1997, and left little doubt that what he called "the diversity machine" was on a destructive course:

> Both the ends and the means of this policy movement pose a substantial threat to the values of the generic liberalism enshrined in American law and culture; free speech, individualism; nondiscrimination on the basis of ethnicity, gender, or religion; equality of opportunity; equal treatment under universalistic laws, standards, and procedures; democratic process; and, above all, a sense of national unity and cohesion embodied in the spirit of *E Pluribus Unum*.

Unheeded warnings, of course, have an honored place in the history of human folly, from Laocoön's attempt to warn his fellow Trojans not to drag that wooden horse inside the city gates, to actor James Woods telling the flight attendant on a Boston to Los Angeles trip a month before 9-11 that the four Middle Eastern men sharing the seats in first class were acting suspiciously.

Lynch's warnings—carefully framed, balanced, precise, grounded in close observation, and sympathetic to the issues that business executives face—have been, as far as I can tell, ignored. But he sent me an e-mail last year, which suggested that, unlike Laocoön, he has not been strangled by a sea serpent, and he continues to hope, having recently brought out a new edition of *The Diversity Machine*.

By the Numbers

In 1994, journalist Andrew Ferguson estimated that there were about five thousand "diversity trainers" in the United States. He traced their origins to a 1987 report titled *Workforce 2000*, written by Arnold Packer and William Johnston for the Hudson Institute. Lynch too credits the *Workforce 2000* warnings of "rapid demographic change" with creating a sense of "crisis, urgency, and purpose" for the *diversity* movement. Why the urgency? The report contained a breathtaking projection of demographic change. As the *New York Times* reported in January 1988:

> The study estimates that 25 million entrants to the labor force will be needed by the year 2000. Most of these will be nonwhite, female or immigrant workers. Native white males, who now constitute 47 percent of the labor force, will account for only 15 percent of the entrants to the labor force by the year 2000.

From 47 percent total to a 15 percent replacement rate is an astounding drop for little over a decade. What did the Hudson Institute think was going to happen? Lynch refers to the number as a "misprint." I asked Professor Packer, who explained:

> It was not a misprint but the writing should have been clearer. The 15% refers to the NET increase in the workforce where "net" refers to the total increase minus the withdrawals (retirees, deaths). We should have had a sentence explaining this appear at a few times in the book.

In other words, the 15 percent referred to the sliver of the workforce composed of white males over and above those who replaced the number of white males already in the workforce.

Professor Packer and his colleague pointed to a real phenomenon, but they phrased their observation in a manner that invited serious misunderstanding of its scale. By their calculations, the percentage of white males in the workforce could be expected to fall by year 2000 to about 45 percent of the total workforce. But what journalists and many others *thought* they said was that by year 2000 only 15 percent of the workforce would consist of white males. Some slightly more sophisticated readers realized that this interpretation made no sense, but then fell into a second trap: they assumed that Packer and Johnston meant that of the total pool of new recruits in year 2000, only 15 percent would be white males. But no, that is not what they meant either. Packer and Johnston's "15 percent" is just the percentage of white males within that small subset of the workforce that represents net new jobs added between 1988 and 2000.

American society, viewed from a certain angle, is a sea of statistics. What does it matter that one number was misunderstood for a while? In this case, it mattered because that number was cited in print hundreds of times—and perhaps tens of thousands of times in conversation—to justify a huge shift in the management strategies of U.S. corporations, to mandate changes in business school curricula, and to sway public opinion. Arguably hundreds of millions of dollars, perhaps billions, were spent in pursuit of the agenda for which the "15 percent" claim was the primary argument.

It is also striking that American business and the press looked on this imaginary demographic change mostly with approbation. White males had become so disdained a category that their supposed demise was worth hardly a shrug.

A combination of factors visible in the mid-1980s indeed meant that an interesting shift was afoot in the demographic profile of American workers. Low birthrates among non-Hispanic whites, higher birthrates among Hispanics and blacks, high immigration rates of nonwhites, and above all the huge increase in the percentage of women in the workforce meant that "white males" would constitute a somewhat smaller portion of the whole. But virtually nobody in the press or in the business community understood the claim to be this limited.

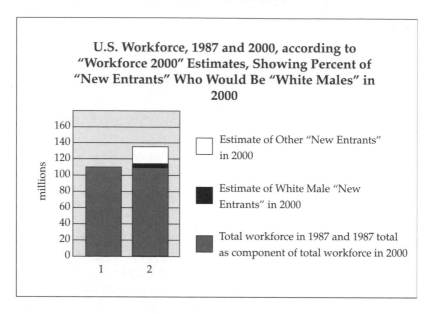

The actual percentage of "white male workers" in the labor force has minimal importance and should be a matter for robust indifference. But that is not how either *diversity* advocates or the business community at large received the news that so few new workers in the decade ahead would be white males. Instead, the figure was used to declare a labor emergency. Corporate America, it was argued, was shaped around the outlook and cultural assumptions of white males and thus wholly unready to recruit and manage a workforce in which white males would dwindle to a mere 15 percent. Bludgeoned with this supposed fact, many companies conceded that they needed the help of the new experts who offered to teach them the ways of *diversity*.

The will to believe in the number was strong, and somehow what should have been obvious—that the number was way off—didn't strike people who wrote and spoke about such things. Perhaps it was just too good an idea to give up. In April 1988, the *New York Times* repeated its erroneous interpretation of the number:

> White males will account for only about 15 percent of the
> entrants to the nation's work force by the end of the century,
> according to Work Force 2000, a study by the Hudson Institute.

And the faux statistic was well launched. The *Times* cited it only once again—August 14, 1988—but by then it had been taken up by the *Washington Post*, in a slightly different form:

> Yet between now and the year 2000, about 80 percent of new workers will be women and minorities.

Then it moved north. The *Boston Globe*, December 27, 1988, quoted the president of New England Telephone declaring:

> Look at the demographics for the 1990s: 15 percent of new people in the work force will be white males.

And then west. The *St. Louis Post-Dispatch* cited it on May 14, 1989:

> Among the young people starting out to work in the next decade, only 15 percent will be white males, the historic core of the work force.

The bogus number took more than a year to get to St. Louis, but once there, it found a lasting welcome. The *Post-Dispatch* mentioned it again on November 20, 1989, in a story on Caterpillar Inc.'s efforts to attract female and minority-race workers, and again on January 22, 1990, as it reported on a speech by John E. Jacob, president of the National Urban League. And yet again on July 30, 1990, in an editorial, "Fairness, Not Quotas," by Clarence Page.

Meanwhile, the *Toronto Star* had acquired the virus, which first appeared in an August 28, 1989, business page article about changes in the U.S. workforce, gestated for a year and then reemerged on August 7, 1990, in a revised version of Clarence Page's editorial. From there the phony stat found its way into a December 28, 1990, article about job discrimination in Ontario, attributed now to Trevor Wilson, the president of "North America's leading head-hunting firm devoted solely to finding candidates who fill employment equity targets."

The number finally came to lodge in the *Seattle Times* on March 20, 1991:

> Only 15 percent of the new entrants into the labor force over the next 10 years will be native-born white males, compared with 47 percent today.

It lingered there a while, making its last continental appearance, so far as I can tell, in the *Seattle Times,* September 19, 1993, in an article on Seattle City Light's commitment to *diversity:*

> Census figures predict that only 15 percent of new workers will be white males in the year 2000.

By now, I suppose, the Hudson Institute's typo is being reported as news somewhere still farther west, perhaps in Guam.

The *diversity* movement in the business world boomed into existence partly on the basis of this misreported and endlessly repeated number. Those who cared for a more sensible-sounding figure could have turned after April 1990 to a U.S. Bureau of Labor Statistics report estimating that 32 percent of the workforce would consist of white males by year 2000, and that minorities and immigrants would hold 26 percent of all jobs.

How did the workforce really turn out in year 2000? It should perhaps not be too much of a surprise that by the mid-1990s, *diversity* advocates and their friends in the press simply lost interest in the subject. Lynch notes that R. Roosevelt Thomas caught and corrected the error in 1991, but by then the movement had other sources of momentum. There are no articles in the *New York Times,* the *Washington Post,* the *Boston Globe,* the *St. Louis Post-Dispatch,* the *Toronto Star,* the *Seattle Times* or any other major newspaper that follow up on the actual composition of the national workforce during this period, and the 2000 Census came and went without a murmur on the topic.

I have, however, looked at the U.S. Bureau of Labor Statistics reports. BLS says that the total of employed persons age sixteen and older in the United States in year 2000 was 135,208,000, of whom 61,696,000 were white males, which means that 45.6 percent of the employed workforce was composed of white males.

Clearly one can approach this data in other ways. Perhaps the "workforce" should include the unemployed. And it would be helpful to have the exact statistics for the *new* entrants to the labor force in 2000. The clues do suggest that white males are indeed declining as a percentage of the whole, but not by the radical jump imagined earlier by *diversity* advocates. Of the 2,756,000 individuals who graduated from high school in year 2000, the number classified as "white" is 2,219,000. The ratio of women to men within that 83 percent white majority is roughly 55:45. So a fair estimate of the number of white male high school graduates in 2000 would be about 998,550, or 36 percent of all high school graduates that year.

Of course, high school dropouts also enter the workforce, as do immigrants who never attended American high schools. And male and female high school graduates enter the workforce at different rates and different times. So the 36 percent estimate is merely a rough approximation of the rate at which white males were entering the workforce. I suspect, however, that it is considerably closer to the mark than the Hudson Institute's muff.

Calculus

A misleading statistic does not by itself prompt a movement as widespread and powerful as the *diversity* management movement, any more than a loose pebble automatically causes an avalanche. A pebble may, however, precipitate an avalanche if the conditions are right.

Workforce 2000 arrived at the right moment. The affirmative action rationale for racial, ethnic and gender preferences in hiring and promotion had become increasingly untenable due to the resistance of workers—usually white male workers—who refused to buy its premises. Some filed lawsuits, but many more offered passive resistance by continuing, whenever they could, to hire and promote on the basis of merit rather than racial quota. Left to their own, most major companies might have abandoned affirmative action as a policy that led to demoralization and poor hiring decisions, but of course corporate America didn't have this option. Companies that did business with the government—a category that includes virtually all major companies*—were still under the federal government's edict to continue with affirmative action. Thus by the mid-1980s, American business was trapped between legal compulsion to hire and promote on the

---

*Daniel Seligman, writing in 1991, observed: "The federal contract compliance program requires that all federal contractors, a category covering almost every Fortune 500 company and 250,000 other institutions, maintain goals and timetables for hiring more women and minority-group members." Daniel Seligman, "Buying Quotas," *Fortune*, 15 July 1991, p. 126.

basis of race, ethnicity and gender, and the antipathy of many employees, including managers, toward such preferences.

The solution: keep affirmative action but recast it as something new ("diversity"). The Hudson Institute's report came along just in time to give the business community what it needed, namely an empirical basis for shifting from the backward-looking, we're-making-up-for-past-injustices affirmative action rationale, to the forward-looking, we're-preparing-for-the-demographic-realities-of-tomorrow rationale. The new approach also handily offered a way to turn indoctrination into "technical training." The shift took a few years to accomplish. In March 1989, *Fortune* magazine reported that it had surveyed corporate CEOs and found that 68 percent of them agreed that the effect of affirmative action programs was "good, very good, or outstanding." And 42 percent of the CEOs said they "remained committed to affirmative action."

The 26-point discrepancy between those numbers seems to represent a cohort of CEOs who had thought affirmative action was good but were no longer committed to it. Perhaps these were the vanguard who had begun the switch from the "old" affirmative action rationale for quotas (good in its time) to the "new" *diversity* rationale (the wave of the future).

Full of Love

The moment when "diversity" became a key idea in American business was about a decade after Justice Powell's June 1978 opinion in the *Bakke* case. Powell's *diversity* rationale for racial and ethnic preferences in college admissions was taken up pretty quickly by college presidents and admissions officers, but the decision had no direct bearing on the business world. Moreover, three other Supreme Court decisions seemed to substantiate the older affirmative action rationales for discriminatory preferences in the workplace. In March 1971, the Supreme Court decided 8–0 in *Griggs v. Duke Power Company* that employers could not test applicants for jobs or promotions in a manner that restricted the opportunities for blacks. The case was brought by thirteen black workers at the power company who had been required to pass a high school equivalency examination to qualify for promotions. But to pass constitutional muster, the Court said, an employment test had to be a realistic measure of actual job qualifications. In the wake of *Griggs*, many companies abandoned general aptitude tests, but some switched to a form of testing in which the test-taker's score was compared only with the scores of others of the same race. In 1980, the federal government began applying this so-called "race norming" to the test scores of applicants for federal jobs. The practice went largely unnoticed for about a decade, but a public outcry led to a provision in the 1991 Civil Rights Act that outlawed race norming.

In June 1979, the Supreme Court ruled 5–2 in *Weber v. Kaiser Aluminum* that the company was permitted to use racial quotas in hiring in order to overcome imbalances in its workforce, even if the firm didn't have a history of racial discrimination. Brian Francis Weber was a white worker at a Louisiana factory who sued Kaiser Aluminum, claiming that he had been passed over for promotion because of his race under the company's affirmative action plan.

In July 1980, in *Fullilove v. Klutznick,* the Supreme Court ruled 6–3 that Congress had acted legally in 1977 in setting aside for minority-owned businesses 10 percent of government contracts in a $4 billion public works program. In May 1983, the Court backed out of a case it had previously agreed to consider in which white policemen and firemen challenged the constitutionality of a 1981 lower court order favoring blacks and Hispanics in the event of layoffs. The suit had been seen by the Reagan administration as a possible avenue for a ruling against affirmative action.

The high court's pro–affirmative action majority did not waver until June 1984, when it ruled 6–3 in *Firefighters Local Union No. 1784 v. Stotts* that a lower court had exceeded its powers when, in Justice White's words, it required "white employees to be laid off, when the otherwise applicable seniority system would have called for the layoff of black employees with less seniority." Carl Stotts was a black firefighter in Memphis who had filed a class action suit against the city in the 1970s, alleging that the fire department had discriminated against blacks in hiring and promotion. The case was temporarily resolved in 1980 with a consent decree involving immediate promotions for some black firefighters and various hiring and promotion goals. But in May 1981, Memphis announced layoffs that would proceed by a rule of last-hired-first-fired, which would have meant 15 out of 18 newly hired black firefighters would have lost their jobs. Stotts went to court again, seeking an injunction against layoffs of any black firefighters. The federal district court and the Sixth Circuit Court of Appeals ruled that the Memphis seniority system would indeed have to be scrapped. The U.S. Supreme Court overturned that decision, citing Title VII of the Civil Rights Act of 1964 to the effect that job seniority rules are protected unless they "intentionally discriminate."

The business world clearly recognized that the Reagan Justice Department was not friendly toward affirmative action, but in four years of office, President Reagan had only the small victory in *Firefighters v. Stotts*. The headline in the September 1984 issue of the American Bankers Association's trade magazine, *ABA Banking Journal*, drew the lesson that must have impressed many business leaders: "Supreme Court Didn't Kill Affirmative Action."

And while the Supreme Court was buttressing affirmative action against legal assaults, the other branches of government were busy building new on-ramps, adding better signs and increasing the speed limit. In June 1983, the *New York Times* reported that the Labor Department had compiled a huge study of 77,000 factories and more than twenty million employees between 1974 and 1980, showing that affirmative action "has been highly effective in promoting the employment of blacks, women and Hispanic people." The report was never officially released, but the story fed a constantly growing stream of advocacy in the press in favor of affirmative action—i.e., *plain old* "affirmative action," with nary a whisper of *diversity*.

That is not to say that the word "diversity" was unfamiliar among business leaders of this period. It appears with some frequency in the business press and management journals of the time, but only very rarely does it refer to *diversity* in the sense of the positive value of assembling people from disparate racial and ethnic backgrounds or incorporating women into formerly male workplaces. Rather, the business press is full of articles about managing conglomerates composed of diverse business enterprises:

> "Diversification Strategies and Organizational Policies of Large Diversified Firms" (1976);

offering a diverse line of products:

"John Hancock: Competing through Diversity" (1985);

and developing more diverse skills:

"Diversity Helps Risk Managers Move Up" (1983).

I have looked at abstracts of over five hundred business articles published from 1983 to 1985 with "diversity" somewhere in the text, without finding any in which "diversity" shows up in the sense of workforce *diversity* as a business goal.

A few articles seem to edge toward that meaning, but on closer look they edge away. Dillard B. Tinsley and Jose Angel Rodriguez, for example, contributed an article on "Mexican American Employees— Stereotypes or Individuals?" to the winter 1981 issue of *Business and Society*. The abstract says that "Business should treat Mexican Americans with special concern." This is promising, but what of *diversity*?

> Mexican Americans are a heterogeneous people. Recognition of their diversity and insight into common stereotypes are required for effective interactions with Mexican American business employees.

Alas, no. This is just a note about diversity *among* Mexican-Americans, and an old-fashioned appeal *not* to stereotype. We will have to wait a few years to reach the higher wisdom that *diversity* requires us to see the essential sameness of all Hispanics and that stereotyping, done with good will and cultural sensitivity, is correct.

In the fall of 1988, a seminal article by Regis McKenna, "Marketing in an Age of Diversity," appeared in the *Harvard Business Review*. McKenna offered a compelling account of how American business was transforming itself by pursuing niche markets. He observed, for example, that "today 75% of all machined parts are produced in batches of 50 or fewer," and he cited the proliferation of supermarket brands, "from 13,000 in 1981 to 21,000 in 1987." But what is perhaps most interesting about McKenna's article is that he spoke of this great differentiation of markets without even mentioning racial and ethnic *diversity*. The most prominent business article of the 1980s on diversity had nothing to say about *diversity*.

Diversity Arrives

The transformation in the American business world from a focus on rationalizing racial and ethnic (and sometimes other) preferences through the rhetoric of affirmative action, to justifying those preferences through the rhetoric of *diversity* probably began around 1987. The Hudson Institute's *Workforce 2000* could not have set off its avalanche late that year without there having been some psychological preparation. Yet it would take several more years before the *diversity* movement—or the *machine,* as Lynch calls it—was so well established that the business world was sure of the word's new meaning. As late as 1990, the titles of articles indicate the need to specify *which* diversity:

> "Managing Diversity (Minorities in the Workforce)" (*Across the Board,* March 1990)

> "Managing Diversity: Companies Must Be Prepared for a 'Rainbow' of Cultures in the Work Force" (*Business Journal,* April 1990)

But the ambiguity was soon gone. In the 1990s, *diversity* became far and away the dominant ideology in corporate personnel and human resource offices across the country, and it was an ideology loudly echoed in the executive suites.

Lynch's *Diversity Machine* ought to have clarified some basic points for the executives and boards of directors of American corporations, but by the time his book appeared, *diversity* had become a settled program. It offered a combination of appeals to American business that I think are best understood as mutually reinforcing. First, the *diversity* ideology no doubt gained some business converts—people who came to believe that *diversity*'s radical reordering of American society was a worthy end in its own right.

Whether muddled or coldly clear, some of America's corporate leaders support the *diversity* program as a way to transform American culture. Others, however, support it for more mundane reasons. A corporate *diversity* program might be accepted as part of the settlement of a discrimination suit, or adopted to forestall such a suit or limit its damages. The imposition of preemptive *diversity* to head off lawsuits or boycotts seems very common, but it is difficult to quantify. A company that pursues a preemptive *diversity* strategy is not, of course, likely to say so. Still, a great many *diversity* managers owe their positions to their CEOs' fears that employees might file complaints with the federal and state agencies or pursue lawsuits. A vigorous corporate *diversity* program might also be a form of insurance against the costly depredations of Jesse Jackson and Al Sharpton, should one of these gentlemen take an interest in the company's record of hiring or promoting minorities.

Still other corporate leaders have been convinced by Dr. Thomas and his epigones that *diversity* is just good business: that it will help their companies gain an edge in global and domestic markets, assist them in recruiting skilled workers, or spur creative work in business units.

Lynch reduces this tangle of motives to two, as he distinguishes between the "civil rights moralists" and the "image conscious pragmatists." He leans to the view that, over time, it is the pragmatists exemplified by Dr. Thomas's advocacy for "diversity management" who are really prevailing in corporate America. This may be so, but it is important to notice that the ideological side of the movement is still very much alive.

On the cover of the February 2002 issue of the magazine *U.S. Black Engineer and Information Technology* is the question "Will Diversity Survive the Downturn?" That downturn will be a fading memory in a few years, but if the people who speak for American business are right, *diversity* is here to stay. It will not only survive the downturn, it will come to be seen as an essential aspect of profitable enterprise.

The article in *U.S. Black Engineer and Information Technology* consists of a series of short statements from several dozen big companies and a few other employers in answer to the magazine's questioning them "about their continuing commitment to diversity during the economic downturn." They all gave essentially the same answer.

Abbott Laboratories: "The company's leadership team continues to promote new diversity efforts.... Abbott's continual ranking on Fortune's 50 Best Companies for Asians, Blacks, and Hispanics is one example of the company's ongoing commitment to inclusion and diversity."

Advanced Fibre Communications: "AFC prefers to maintain long-term relationships with its suppliers, including diversity suppliers." What is a "diversity supplier"? The folks at Advanced Fibre assume we already know—which is just one of many indications that we are eavesdropping on a long-running conversation.

The Aerospace Corporation declares that it "has five affinity groups that represent the diverse cultures, ethnicities, and lifestyles of our talented people." AT&T says, "We have ongoing, steadfast commitment to diversity." BellSouth Corporation adds: "We have increased our focus on internal affinity or networking groups by developing a Latino and Gay and Lesbian group in addition to our African American and Women's networking groups." Boeing also "remains focused on its commitment to established diversity objectives." Cisco Systems finds, "Diversity of our work force is a key link to our competitive advantage." And Coca-Cola says, in high third-person, "The Coca-Cola Company understands the value of diversity and has made it a top priority and business imperative." In fact, all fifty-four employers in *U.S. Black Engineer* magazine's survey say almost the same thing, from the consulting firm Booz-Allen & Hamilton, to Miller Brewing Company, which declares: "Full speed ahead. Diversity remains a business imperative."

The strong impression one gets from this litany of loyalty oaths is that American business speaks with one voice about *diversity*. Few if any other topics produce such uniformity of opinion. And that, I think, provides strong reason to doubt that the pragmatic version of *diversity* is really in the driver's seat. If the commitment to *diversity* in the business world were really driven by rational calculation of corporate interests, we would see the usual pattern of companies staking out distinct and sometimes opposed positions. Instead, we see the ritualistic repetition of a credo.

American business seems to see *diversity* as an unalloyed good. A testimonial to this consensus appeared in January 2002, when the Business–Higher Education Forum issued a report titled *Investing in People,* which concluded that "the challenge of our increasing diversity will shape both our national life and America's role in the global economy for decades to come." The Business–Higher Education Forum was composed of CEOs of pro-*diversity* businesses and *diversity*-committed college presidents. Their report is a solemn reiteration of many of the conventional pieties of modern multiculturalism brought forward in defense of maintaining and expanding the *diversity* regime in American education. I do not mean to suggest that it is a document of first-tier importance. It was timed, I think, as an effort to sway the courts in the pending decisions in two *diversity* lawsuits involving the University of Michigan, and it will quickly fade into the sea of *diversity* propaganda. It is, however, an especially succinct restatement of the *diversity* premises seen through the eyes of a large panel of corporate CEOs.

Investing in People received a lot of publicity, not all of it good. A review by one critic began: "The year is young, but it is not too soon to declare an early frontrunner in the increasingly crowded field of Stupid Pseudo-Scientific Reports in Desperate Defense of Racial and Ethnic Preferences."

Because it is aimed at showing how the business rationale for *diversity* dovetails with its educational rationale, *Investing in People* offers up a fuller version of the doctrine referred to in terser form by the companies quoted in the *U.S. Black Engineer* article. The full-blown rationale goes something like this: (1) American society is growing more ethnically diverse; (2) to fill the many jobs that our economy will create, we will have to recruit more heavily among minority groups; (3) those groups are typically not well served by our current educational system, and we must take steps to increase the educational preparation of members of minority groups to meet the coming demand for expert labor; (4) "inclusiveness" and "tolerance" have "helped build the foundation" for our "dynamic economy"; (5) diversity in school prepares individuals for "full participation in a diverse, democratic society"; (6) diversity on campus makes individuals into "better critical thinkers"; (7) diversity on campus produces workers who "collaborate harmoniously with co-workers" and enhances "innovation and problem-solving skills"; (8) a more diverse workforce would earn—and spend—more.

By these steps, the Business–Higher Education Forum reaches a series of eleven recommendations intended to shore up institutional and government support for "diversity." The first five are: strengthening "outreach programs"; providing resources to prepare teachers to work with "racially and ethnically diverse students"; and then the three major points, each in slightly coded language:

> **Review current strategies and policies designed to foster diversity** and ensure that they are meeting their goals, and publicize

the results of these reviews in the higher education and business communities.

Advocate that colleges and universities take the whole person into account when making admissions decisions; that is, consider all relevant qualities—not just grades and test scores—in assessing each applicant.

As part of the business employee recruitment process, emphasize to campuses the importance of being able to recruit personnel from a diverse student body.

In other words, meet the minority quotas and boast about the results; use racial and ethnic preferences in college admissions; and expect corporate recruiters to favor campuses that toe the *diversity* line and exercise racial and ethnic preferences in hiring too.

Old Favorites

The eight-step argument is a litany of familiar misrepresentations that updates the long-discredited 1987 Hudson Institute *Workforce 2000* warnings, compares growth *rates* without mentioning the relative magnitude of the original quantities, and leans on other statistical tricks. But points 3 and 4 deserve separate consideration. Points 5 and 6, and to some extent 7—that campus *diversity* creates better democratic citizens, more critical thinkers and more cooperative workmates—we met before in Professor Patricia Gurin's expert testimony on behalf of the University of Michigan in *Gratz et al. v. Bollinger. Investing in People* cites Gurin's and half a dozen other polemical assertions on the democratic and pedagogical benefits of force-fed *diversity*. The argument doesn't improve on second acquaintance. The successful imposition of undemocratic means does little to teach respect for real democratic values, and when "critical thinking" turns out to be a euphemism for learning to recite the mantra "Race-Class-Gender" in *diversity* classes, we ought to realize that *diversity* isn't really giving us a generation of students adept at extracting themselves from Plato's cave.

On the matter of whether *diversity* instills a spirit of cooperation that carries over to the workplace, I am also skeptical. *Diversity* on most campuses takes the form of a fairly high degree of racial and national self-segregation, and undercurrents of resentment aimed at those who have unearned privileges and self-doubt among recipients of such privileges. The carryover to the workplace is partly evident in reverse discrimination lawsuits and in the simmering resentments of people on the short end of *diversity*'s petty injustices.

Do Americans know how to put their differences aside and work together? For the most part, the answer is definitely yes. Does *diversity* augment this aspect of our national character? No, we manage it *despite* the imposition of *diversity*, which is often pulling in the opposite direction.

Diversity-Speak

That brings us to points 3 and 4. Point 3 asserts that many members of minority groups are often not well served by our current educational system—which is entirely true, although it might be added that many members of the "majority" are also ill served by that system. Point 4 is the idea that "inclusiveness" and "tolerance" have helped build the "dynamic economy" that has fueled globalization. This is a partial truth that needs to be weighed carefully. The exact wording in *Investing in People* is as follows:

> Inclusiveness and tolerance are in keeping with America's values of fairness and justice, and have helped to build the foundation for the most dynamic economy and society on earth. Forum members believe that the more we do to make schools, universities, and workplaces diverse, inclusive, and welcoming, the more our society benefits.

At one level this is unexceptionable, but a great deal depends on which of several possible meanings we attribute to particular words. The art of *diversity*-speak is to sound to the outsider blandly consonant with traditional values, while signaling to the insider one's espousal of the radical new doctrine. These sentences achieve just that.

Inclusiveness means something like "all are welcome" to the outsider; it means "special accommodations for ethnic preferences" in *diversity*-speak. *Tolerance* means to the outsider something like "I won't hassle you"; in *diversity*-speak it means "You will demonstrate to me your genuine respect for what I consider important." Inclusiveness and tolerance in the outsider senses are indeed "in keeping with" the values of fairness and justice as Americans have traditionally understood these values. But to square the *diversity*-speak versions of inclusiveness and tolerance with our sense of what is fair and just is a more doubtful undertaking. The word "fairness" can be teased into supporting an idea that some people deserve more than others, but we are naturally skeptical, and we want an explanation. *Diversity*-speak slides over the need to convince people that the best way to be "fair" is to be unfair.

Likewise with justice. The adroit dialectician can manage the idea that "justice" involves unearned privileges based on the principle that one's ancestors were disprivileged, but once the idea is stated openly, ordinary people are inclined to doubt it. The advantage of *diversity*-speak is that it sneaks the idea past the commonsense guards that protect us from intellectual flimflam. And is demanding "respect" for eccentric views really what we owe other people by way of tolerance? What we owe—most of the time—is noninterference. Respect should not be issued automatically on the premise that all cultural differences deserve it. Some do, some don't. Respect should be reserved for those ideas and cultural attainments in which we discover real worthiness.

Thus the first of the two sentences in *Investing in People* on the theme of *diversity*'s fundamental consistency with American values—"Inclusiveness and tolerance are in keeping with America's values of fairness and justice, and have helped build the foundation for the most dynamic economy and society on earth"—has two levels of meaning, one for the ordinary reader, another for the *diversity* insider.

What of the second sentence—"Forum members believe that the more we do to make schools, universities, and workplaces diverse, inclusive, and welcoming, the more our society benefits"? Here the double-hinged words are the triplet, "diverse, inclusive, and welcoming," and possibly also "society benefits." *Diverse,* as we have repeatedly seen, has the plain meaning of "made up of unlike parts," but also the ideological meaning, "composed of people from victim groups in the same proportions as occur in the general population." *Inclusive* we have just discussed in its secondary meaning as a warrant for special accommodations. And *welcoming* again rings the bell of unconditional "respect." Of course, we want schools, colleges and workplaces to be diverse, inclusive and welcoming, but we want them to be diverse, inclusive and welcoming in the plain English meaning of these words, not in the strained ideological senses of *diversity*-speak.

As to whether "society benefits" from the realization of these ideals, it all depends on which ideals we have in mind. To the extent that *diversity*-speak provides a cover for old-fashioned pre-*Bakke* affirmative action quotas, the answer is no. Those arrangements are fundamentally harmful to the society. To the extent that *diversity*-speak provides a cover for a program of radical cultural change in the direction of authorizing a structure of permanent ethnic and victim-group preferences, the answer is still no. We have little to gain by transforming American society into an ethnic caste system based on the purity of one's victimhood. But to the extent that the words "diverse, inclusive and welcoming" retain their dictionary definitions, yes, society *usually* benefits.

The last plank of the argument for *diversity* in *Investing in People* (point 8) is that a more diverse workforce would earn more and spend more. At bottom, I take this as a pitch to the nation that we should use every shortcut possible to speed African-Americans and Hispanics into the middle class. Implied here is the idea that academic standards shouldn't be allowed to stand in the way of hastening African-American and Hispanic students through college. Elsewhere in the report, this idea is explicit; recall, "Advocate that colleges and universities take the whole person into account when making admissions decisions; that is, consider all relevant qualities—not just grades and test scores—in assessing each applicant."

The argument appeals to a kind of base expediency. It is anti-intellectual in the sense that it views higher education as a mere credentialing service that can and should push real standards aside when they interfere with desired social outcomes. And it is shortsighted in its assumption that churning large numbers of unqualified students of any social background through college will really build prosperity. More likely it will simply erode both the intellectual and the market value of the college degree.

Banding

What exactly do *diversity* consultants do? How does the Vice President for Corporate Diversity spend his day? Where in the daily routine does the human resource professional pause and say, "Now I will carry out my *diversity* tasks"?

I come to the end of this chapter prepared to leave a little mystery. I have read Frederick Lynch's lucid account of the lives and works of *diversity* consultants and supplemented it by perusing the works of other writers who conjure up images of the diversiphiles at work in newsrooms, hospitals and schools. The story they tell is of people devoted to earnest make-work. *Diversity* advocates create the problems that *diversity* consultants are then hired to ameliorate. *Diversity* amelioration causes more problems, for which *diversity* experts propose the answer: more *diversity.*

Diversity in the workplace is supposed to make the company more agile, better equipped to reach out to new markets, and more creative in solving problems because, compared to the old, undiverse company, it has access to more styles of thinking. The diverse company is the company that has escaped from the rut of taken-for-granted ways. It is poised for creativity.

So goes *diversity* management theory. But there is a little rub. Not everyone is "comfortable" with *diversity.* A certain portion of the workforce is stuck in the old ways, and instead of being transformed into powerful new engines of creative ideas by *diversity,* they are vexed by the double standards in hiring and promotion and the implicit gag rules that the system requires. Enter the *diversity* trainers. Their job is to get the malcontents into line. Their techniques are, appropriately I suppose, diverse. Some try rational persuasion. ("Look at the demographics. Your company needs these workers. Bend a little. Performance will be better once workers really respect each other's differences.") Some organize role-playing games aimed at sensitizing workers to cultural difference. ("You are *alpha* people; you love peacefulness, generosity and simplicity. You others are the *beta* people, in love with hierarchy.") Some incite racial confrontations, on the grounds that only "honest" airing of the prejudices that the trainers know are deeply ingrained in their trainees will ever lead them past their psychological impasses.

Each of these approaches is doomed because, in the end, even people who say they want *diversity* want fairness too. Inevitably the attempt to run a company on the basis of group preferences collides with good business practice, which depends on the recognition of talent and the reward of actual performance. *Diversity*-speak obfuscates talent and performance by proposing that they cannot be judged by a single, consistent set of standards, but only by a different-strokes-for-different-folks approach.

The obfuscation took the practical form of "race norming" during the 1980s, but when race norming was outlawed by the 1991 Civil Rights Act, *diversity*-besotted companies turned to another dodge called "banding." The idea of banding is that everybody who scores within a certain range on a test—say, between the 70th and the 80th percentile—is assigned to a single band. For purposes of hiring or promotion, the actual scores are then ignored and the criteria shift to racial or ethnic identity, sex of the applicant, or whatever social identity desideratum the organization wants to promote. This technique minimizes the chances of identity preferences producing flagrant examples of abuse in which top-notch performers are passed over in favor of gross incompetents, but it leaves plenty of room for day-in, day-out petty injustices.

And when "banding" is eventually driven from the marketplace as a subterfuge that violates the Equal Protection Clause of the Fourteenth Amendment, *diversity* will adduce still more tricks. The model to keep in mind is state university systems faced with court decisions or popular referenda overturning affirmative action in admissions. Many have responded with ruses, such as admitting the "top 10 percent" of all high school graduates and assaults on standardized testing, rather than to strive honestly to obey the law.

"Top 10 percent" is just a handy way of identifying this particular ruse. The percent varies from plan to plan. The Texas legislature passed a top 10 percent rule in 1997 after the 1996 *Hopwood* decision; in 1999, Governor Jeb Bush successfully proposed a top 20 percent rule in Florida to go into effect in 2001; the University of California in 1999 adopted a top 4 percent rule for the class admitted in September 2001. Admitting the top 10 percent of every high school's graduating class may sound superficially like a fair way to distribute access to public universities, since it seems to offer the same chances to all students regardless of their home town or school district. But, as with other tricks intended to bypass the hard work of looking at the qualifications of individuals, the fairness is just an illusion. "Top 10 percent" approaches, in fact, end up denying opportunities to better-qualified students and rewarding incompetent high schools. They also diminish the educational opportunities of minority students who attend integrated schools: think of the African-American student who ranks just below the top 10 percent in a highly competitive integrated school district and loses out in college admissions to an African-American in the top 10 percent of an all-black, not very competitive school district.

Such programs exist solely to bump up minority student college enrollments without running afoul of the law, by circumventing the process of looking at the students' actual quality of preparation. The approach ends up admitting into college students who lack essential educational prerequisites; and the high schools that fail to teach worthy curricula are relieved of parental pressure, since the best students at these schools will be admitted to college no matter how poorly they are taught.

The ruse is not subtle. Its supporters often speak frankly of how such rules serve to advance the cause of *diversity.* The president of the University of Texas at Austin, Larry Faulkner, for example, wrote an op-ed article in the *Houston Chronicle* in October 2000, declaring:

> Meanwhile, the Top 10 Percent Law has enabled us to diversify enrollment at UT with talented students who succeed. Our 1999 enrollments levels for African American and Hispanic freshmen have returned to those of 1996, the year before the Hopwood decision prohibited the consideration of race in admission policies. And minority students earned higher grade point averages last year than in 1996 and have higher retention rates.

The higher GPAs and higher retention rates are good news, but are also backhanded evidence of what was wrong with the previous system of racial preferences, which the *Hopwood* decision outlawed.

President Faulkner happened to be writing this defensive op-ed article because the University of Texas flagship campus was coming under increasing criticism in 2000. Its enrollment had ballooned to more than fifty thousand students, even as the quality of students declined and many better-qualified students were rejected. According to the

Houston Chronicle, "Often the rejected students are whites who attended high-achieving schools in which it is more difficult to be ranked in the top 10 percent." But Faulkner disagreed with the idea that the 10 Percent Law was the culprit, blaming instead an inexplicable 46 percent increase in applications over the three previous years. The newspaper, however, found other university officials who "acknowledged that the 10 percent law has helped fuel the rise in applications."

So, from "race norming," to "banding," to "top 10 percent," the little game of subterfuges proceeds. *Diversity* in the minds of *diversity* consultants, diversicrats and diversiphiles is so worthy a goal that it warrants the endless search for loopholes, a relaxed attitude toward the truth, and some indifference toward the victims of every identity group.

Whether American business leaders will find a use for something like the top 10 percent rule, however, I wouldn't venture to say.

For the Ages?

Generally, in discussing *diversity* in American culture it seems sensible to refer to it as a *movement,* since its proponents are still engaged in the tasks of attempting to persuade, to impose, and to institutionalize their views. When it comes to American business, the word "movement" seems less apt, since the basic doctrines of *diversity* have already been institutionalized and no longer face serious opposition. *Diversity* has simply won the day in American business.

We do not know, however, how deep and how durable this triumph really is. American business has been conquered before—by Taylorism, by efficiency experts, by one-minute managers, and most recently by "total quality management." Some of the revolutions have a lasting legacy. We benefit (most of the time) from uniform accounting standards; and no one expects that American business will abandon networked computing or the search for more global markets. But I am skeptical that "diversity" has this staying power. The business inefficiency of maintaining a regime of ethnic and racial preferences will, I suspect, one day grow wearisome and, if the law allows, it will be quietly phased out in favor of sounder management principles.

NINE

DIVERSITY ON CAMPUS

An osage orange is about the size of a softball, with a beady texture and enough modest slopes and indentations to suggest that it isn't trying for the perfection of a sphere. It has just the right heft to be picked up and bounced in the palm of one's hand before going home to sit on a windowsill for a while, as a quizzical green trophy.

Osage orange trees don't grow around Boston, or Pittsburgh either. I encountered one for the first time when I was sixteen and spending the summer studying chemistry on the campus of DePauw University in Greencastle, Indiana. The tree inspired in me some of the same glow of wonder that I felt toward other examples of nature's prodigal strangeness: from dinosaur bones to giant shelf fungi. Osage oranges, so far as I know, serve no practical use. They are just large, inedible green fruit that fall on the shady lawns of Midwestern colleges, to be collected in due course by the groundskeepers and hauled off for compost.

I was therefore delighted when I recently read in *The Ghosts of Evolution,* by the science writer Connie Barlow, that the osage orange, *Maclura pomifera,* is a genuine oddity. Moreover, Ms. Barlow had seemingly borrowed my thoughts and relived my experience. She reports attending a conference at a college in Indiana at which one of the participants took her aside at lunch and:

> led me to a magnificent old tree. Strange fruit—about the size, weight, and firmness of a softball and the color of a glow-green tennis ball—decorated the ground beneath the tree and out to about as far as one would roll. We collected several, returned to

226

the conference hall, and placed one on the altar next to a photo of Earth from outer space and a bundle of ceremonial sage.

Barlow continues with other encounters with the tree and its fruit, "the fruit so strange its makes collectors of us all." But unlike most of us, she has an explanation.

The osage orange, she explains, is a fruit that evolved in a different environment from where it lives today. It is designed to attract and be eaten by the huge megafauna—the mammoths and other giant creatures that roamed North America before they died or were killed off by the ancestors of American Indians around eleven thousand years ago. The osage orange adapted to be tough enough to withstand the depredations of little animals, so that the big ones would carry its seeds away and propagate the tree far and wide over the plains.

It turns out that *Maclura pomifera* isn't the only tree to cater to the tastes of extinct megafauna. The giant pods of honey locusts, avocados, pawpaws and many other less-familiar species have similar evolutionary histories. They are all, as Barlow puts it, the ghosts of evolution. They are revenants who haunt the modern world waiting for their symbiotic animal partners to return and taste once again their delights.

Barlow gives due credit for this idea to the tropical ecologist Dan Janzen, who first proposed it after studying native fruit trees in Costa Rica in the 1970s, and to Paul Martin, a Pleistocene ecologist who coined the term "ghosts of evolution." The concept goes back to early notions of some animals and plants being "living fossils." The ginkgo tree and the wonderful coelacanth, a fish found in the Indian Ocean near South Africa in 1938 and later near the Comoros Islands, are the usual examples. But the Janzen hypothesis gives a new twist: species that embody in their current form evidence of a missing evolutionary partner.

The "ghost of evolution" concept also brings to mind a term suggested by a nineteenth-century anthropologist, Edward Tylor, for human customs that have endured beyond the circumstances from which they originally arose. Tylor called such customs "survivals," and thought they might provide a way to read back through time in the absence of historical records. He mentioned, for example, the "keeping up in stone architecture of designs belonging to wooden buildings," and the use of wooden tallies for tax receipts in England long after the introduction of paper and pen.

Tylor suggested that *survivals* of obsolete customs are especially likely to be found in "solemn ceremonies and other matters under the control of priests and officials, who are commonly averse to change." Attend a college commencement and observe the caps and gowns and ceremonial hoods, and you will know what Tylor meant. But in the age of *diversity*, perhaps the quaintest survival is the idea of liberal education itself. We continue to speak of it as both an ideal and an educational reality long after the conditions in which it thrived have disappeared.

The osage orange evolved in a world of club-tailed glyptodonts, shovel-tusked gomphotheres and imposing giant ground sloths who consumed it with gusto and propagated its seeds. The university evolved in relation to other extinct fauna: the high school graduate who was at ease in Latin and knew some Greek as well; the college freshman whose essays were a little stilted and perhaps too closely modeled on Joseph Addison, but for whom the preterit verb in the past subjunctive clause and the periodic sentence posed no mystery; the aspiring science student who had packed away a detailed knowledge of natural history and the mechanical arts before he left home. They too have gone the way of the glyptodonts, gomphotheres and giant ground sloths.

Instead, we live in the age of diversiphile students, diversidact professors and diversicrat college administrators. In the new campus ecology, the ideal of liberal education is frequently mentioned, but we shouldn't be fooled. *Diversity* only preserves some of the outward appearance of liberal education, while substituting its own antiliberal agenda on every crucial point.

Overview

Diversity is probably the most powerful concept on American college campuses today; it is certainly the most pervasive. After the *Bakke* decision in 1978, college and university administrations rallied to *diversity* as the secure legal rationale for racial and ethnic preferences in admissions. But as administrators got their minds around the concept and as it was taken up by politically committed faculty members, *diversity* became more than a legalistic dodge. It dawned on some that *diversity* might be an immensely useful idea: a positive-sounding and potentially popular rubric for advancing a political agenda that had so far proven highly unpopular with the American people as a whole.

Justice Powell's idea of *diversity* in the *Bakke* decision seemed little more than a sketchy notion that education would be enhanced (automatically? magically?) by recruiting people of different races and ethnicities to the same campus. Powell gave no particular thought to what was to happen next and no occasion to consider how else the principle of *diversity* might be applied. The academy slowly took up both challenges.

The pursuit of *diversity*, as Powell envisioned it, did indeed become the main rationale for student recruitment and admissions policies that placed strong favorable emphasis on African-American, Hispanic and Native American identity. But *diversity* also became the explicit rationale for many other identity-conscious policies. Let's consider a few.

(1) ***Diversity* entered into faculty recruitment.** Attempts to increase the numbers of faculty members from "underrepresented" groups had been established in the early 1970s, without the promptings of *diversity* per se. Harvard University's 1971 affirmative action program, for example, aimed to increase the number of faculty members who were women or members of minority groups. Williams College adopted a similar policy in 1972. But *diversity* brought much more aggressive steps. In 1987, the University of Michigan announced the "Michigan Mandate," which included a commitment to increase substantially the number of minority faculty members. Then in February 1988, Donna Shalala, chancellor of the University of Wisconsin (and President Clinton's future secretary of health and human services) announced a plan to hire seventy new minority faculty members within three years. Chancellor Shalala ignited a competition of sorts. Within months, Duke University had promised to add at least one black faculty member to every one of its fifty-six academic departments by 1993; Penn State announced a new goal of having a faculty that was 8 percent black; Smith College said it would hire three new minority faculty members; and the University of Vermont declared that it would add from four to eleven minority faculty members by 1992.

The proponents of such plans didn't even bother to try to reconcile the use of racial and group-identity categories with the principle of hiring the best-qualified scholars and teachers. Nor did they pay much attention to the question of where they would find ready-to-hire minority scholars in fields where there were few minority Ph.D.s. As *The Economist* pointed out:

> In 1986 no blacks earned PhDs in geometry, astronomy, astrophysics, acoustics, theoretical chemistry, geology, aerospace engineering or computer engineering. That same year more than 8,000 doctorates were awarded in the physical sciences and engineering; just 39 went to blacks. Moreover, no blacks received doctorates in European history, classics or Russian languages and literature, among other fields. Of those who earned PhDs in the humanities, only 70 were black.

Moreover, having a Ph.D. does not necessarily make a candidate qualified for an academic position, let alone the best-qualified person for the job. When the absence or extreme scarcity of qualified candidates is taken into account, the numbers of new minority hires proposed by Chancellor Shalala and her fellow college and university diversicrats can be seen as a kind of wishful thinking. Even after the faculties of other colleges and universities were raided and candidates of dubious merit were hired, some of the goals were just impossible.

So how did these *diversity*-inspired efforts in faculty recruitment turn out? There is a suspicious reticence on the matter at many of the colleges and universities, but in March 1993, the *Chronicle of Higher Education* reported on the most flamboyant of the promisers, Duke University:

> With the deadline approaching, it is clear the university is not going to meet it. It has hired 19 black faculty members since 1987, but 14 others—including a few new recruits—have left, retired, or moved into non-teaching jobs at Duke. The university had 31 black faculty members in 1987. It now has 36, or 2.2 per cent of the total faculty of 1,467.
>
> Mr. Wesley, a junior at Duke, offers another slogan to illustrate the embarrassing reality: "19 minus 14 doesn't equal 56."

Duke, however, was undeterred and soon announced a new goal of having a total of 76 black faculty members by 2004.

Donna Shalala's plan at the University of Wisconsin fared no better. She had wanted to hire 70 new minority faculty members within three years. By 1995, the net increase was only 14—making a total of 37 black faculty members, up from 23.

(2) *Diversity* also meant gaining the acceptance, or at least the acquiescence, of the existing faculty to the kind of racial quota hiring that so many colleges and universities had embraced. For example, the *Chronicle of Higher Education* reported in 1989 that the University of New Mexico, under pressure from Hispanic legislators, was not only planning to hire more Hispanic faculty members and increase "the proportion of minority and female students," but also to put the existing faculty through *diversity* training. Margaret E. Montoya, a lawyer hired by the university's president to advise him on affirmative action, was then drafting a "New Mexico Plan" that, she explained,

> may include seminars on cultural diversity for current faculty members. "We have to persuade potential faculty that they can come here and thrive," she says, and that will happen only if the campus climate is hospitable.

Making the campus climate "hospitable" became a familiar refrain that translated into self-censorship, speech codes and watered-down standards for tenure and promotion.

(3) *Diversity* also became a factor in establishing new identity-focused courses. For example, the *Chronicle of Higher Education* reported in 1992 on the Ford Foundation's success in getting colleges to add *diversity* classes:

> Ford's Race Relations and Campus Diversity program, now in its second year, has awarded more than $2-million. In the first year, 20 private, residential colleges each received grants ranging from $25,000 to $100,000 for new or revised courses that include multi-cultural topics; artistic activities; and faculty seminars. In the second year, each of five urban, commuter universities received a $150,000 grant for similar purposes.
>
> At Princeton University, the $86,000 Ford grant is supporting seminars on cultural and ethnic diversity that attempt to link the classroom with day-to-day living in a pluralistic society.

Ford Foundation is not alone in this enterprise. The Lilly Foundation and the Phillip Morris Companies also have offered financial incentives for *diversity* programs that many colleges and universities are only too eager to adopt.

(4) In some cases, *diversity* goes beyond particular courses to reshape a broader curriculum. This may be self-evident in the constellation of new "studies" departments—African-American Studies, Chicano Studies and such—but it crops up in unexpected places too, such as mathematics. Eduardo Jesus Arismendi-Pardi, associate professor of mathematics at Orange Coast College in California, for example, is one of the nation's advocates for "ethnomathematics," the effort to incorporate multiple and especially non-European ethnic perspectives into the study of math. The *Chronicle of Higher Education* reported on Professor Arismendi-Pardi's successes as of 2000:

> What started as a talk at a diversity conference last year has quickly made Mr. Arismendi-Pardi, an associate professor of mathematics at Orange Coast College, a big name in California community-college circles. Since April 1999, he has given 31 talks on ethnomathematics at conferences and colleges. Last spring, he won a diversity award from the California Community Colleges system for "his innovative approach to teaching mathematical concepts in a cultural and historical context." And the statewide group representing the faculty of California's 107 community colleges passed a resolution applauding the role of ethnomathematics in making the discipline more accessible to a broader group of students.

Ethnomathematics—*diversity* theory applied to math through the study of Navajo rug designs, African fractals and the Mayan calendar—may seem a long detour on the way to mathematical competence, but it sounds like fun.

Some of the ethnic studies departments, meanwhile, are nurturing ill feelings toward the universities that created them. Evelyn Hu-DeHart, professor of history at the University of Colorado at Boulder, opined in a 1995 essay that universities created such programs "because an ethnic-studies program is the surest way to demonstrate commitment to diversity to get credit for diversity," but they "show disrespect for ethnic studies faculty members and their work" and treat "scholars like unemancipated children of colonial subjects without full citizenship rights." Perhaps the lesson here is that a field born of and premised on resentment has a very difficult time becoming anything more than resentment.

Some might worry, however, that curricular diversions such as ethnic studies programs and ethnomathematics dilute the academic rigor and substance of higher education. They probably do in many cases, but **(5) *diversity* has damaged education in much more far-reaching ways by creating incentives to trim or eliminate academic requirements, standards and expectations.** The most flagrant example of this has been the erosion of the Scholastic Aptitude Tests—an erosion partly indicated by their renaming as the Scholastic Assessment Tests. The SATs were invented precisely to give students from impoverished backgrounds and second-rate schools a chance to show that, despite these limitations, they possessed the intellectual capacity to succeed in college. The SATs were never perfect; in the real world, no test ever is. But the SATs stood the larger test of time. They helped tens of thousands of students who would not otherwise have gotten into college gain admission.

They also proved an embarrassment in America's racial politics. Notoriously, African-Americans and Hispanics on average perform significantly less well than whites and members of other ethnic groups. But after California voters in 1996 passed Proposition 209 outlawing affirmative action and requiring, in principle, that all applicants for admission to a university be evaluated on the same scale, and after the *Hopwood* decision in Texas undermined *diversity* quotas in the Fifth Circuit, the ethnic-group discrepancy on the SATs became an even bigger political issue. In 2001, the *Chronicle of Higher Education* noted that:

> The point differential between white and minority students is also leading to a diminished role for the SAT, simply because it lays bare the use of racial preferences in college admissions. In the 2000–1 academic year, white students scored an average of 1060 on the test, compared with 859 for black students and 925 for Hispanic students.

The discrepancies didn't matter too much when colleges and universities felt free to ignore them in dual-track admissions systems, but with that option disappearing, the diversiphiles began to worry about the possibility of having to take SAT results seriously. As the *Chronicle* reported, "recent court decisions and referendums may lead many colleges seeking a diverse student body to lower the weight they place on the SAT—or to ignore it altogether."

This view became national news in February 2001, when Richard C. Atkinson, president of the University of California system, called upon the nine campuses of the system to drop the requirement that applicants take the SAT. Of course, Atkinson did not *say* that the reason he wished to take the University of California off the SATs was to wish away the ethnic score discrepancies. Rather, he professed to be concerned about all the time that students waste "prepping" for the exams. But the racial issue was on the minds of just about everyone else.

The *diversity* code words for admissions criteria that smuggle race back into consideration are "holistic criteria," "leadership" and "overcoming adversity." The *Chronicle of Higher Education*, noting the unhappiness of admissions directors who can no longer give "black and Hispanic students . . . an explicit bonus," points out that these admissions directors "may be forced to gravitate toward a more holistic set of criteria that recognize a wider range of achievement, such as leadership and overcoming adversity." Such formulations are mere chicanery: ways of engaging in ethnic profiling and discrimination while calling it something else.

The damage that *diversity* does to higher education in this sense is profound. Not only does it bring students to campus who have little possibility of success measured by real standards, but it also prompts the colleges and universities, day in and day out, to lie about their practices.

The College Board, which owns the SAT, has consistently responded to the *diversity* challenge with intellectual cowardice, first by "recentering" the SATs in April 1995 to give higher scores to poor and average performers, and most recently (in 2002) by eliminating the "verbal analogies" section, which demanded the test-taker to reason out and compare sets of relationships. The latter is an especially grievous loss to higher education, for short of literacy itself, few things are more important in liberal learning than the ability to discern the patterns that we perceive through analogical reasoning, whether in poetry, law or science. The verbal analogies section was eliminated to make room for an essay portion that could be evaluated more "holistically."

And to round out this list of *diversity*'s depredations in higher education, I'll add that **(6) *diversity* became an issue in the accreditation of colleges and universities.** In 1990, for example, the Quality Education for Minorities Project—a two-plus-year, $1.2 million study funded by the Carnegie Corporation—recommended "linking accreditation decisions to progress in minority student, staff, and faculty recruitment and retention."

This by no means exhausts the mischief the diversiphiles have perpetrated in academe, but it is enough to start with. *Diversity* on campus can also be seen in the role not of perpetrator but of accomplice, as it gave feminists, gay advocacy groups and individuals with various disabilities a new way of construing moral entitlement to preferential treatment on the model that *diversity* first promised to members of groups defined in terms of ethnicity and race.

Antecedents

But none of this happened overnight, nor did it spring entirely from the imaginings of Justice Powell. I don't take it as my task in this book to trace all the antecedents of *diversity*, but in previous chapters I have glanced at President Johnson's Howard University speech and Executive Order 11246, which created affirmative action; at Reverend William Sloane Coffin Jr.'s passage from radical politics through Esalen and the human potential movement at Big Sur to an involvement in Eastern mysticism; and at the amalgam of Romanticism and modernism that ushered self-heeding *diversity* into the arts. Each of these strands had a strong campus presence. Affirmative action began in a campus speech, and the Civil Rights Movement of course recruited many of its young white supporters from college campuses; Reverend Coffin was the chaplain at Yale (1958–1975) and a Freedom Rider in 1961; and *diversity* in the arts took off from the campus countercultural milieu. But the antecedents to *diversity* in higher education go a little deeper.

In his description of the Free Speech Movement of 1964 at Berkeley, Peter Collier, former editor of the radical magazine *Ramparts*, observed that "As the protest ripened, the FSM proposed that the university was actually an allegory for society at large, where power worked secretly to crush personal freedom just as the chancellor crushed our student rights." *An allegory for society at large*—this notion is indispensable for the aviary- or aquarium-style *diversity* movement that would eventually come to dominate American campuses. For diversiphiles as for the nascent radicals of the sixties, the university is not just an institution with a handful of particular purposes—distilling important knowledge from the infinite welter of facts, fostering love of learning in a few, teaching practical stuff to a few more, extending the research a little further into the unknown. Rather, the university is the world itself, and if by a kind of magical thinking one can arrange this university microcosm exactly as one wishes, the world itself will somehow follow.

The allegorical view of the university that ignited at Berkeley in 1964 and shortly after that on many other campuses was itself inextricably part of the emerging campus Left, the New Left of romantic utopians, which would shortly get its anti-American bearings from radical opposition to the war in Vietnam. Resistance to the war taught a substantial portion of a whole generation to hate America and to view its traditions and its culture with suspicion or, depending on temperament, with disgust. For some, antiwar activism merged with black nationalism, and figures such as Malcolm X and later any number of Black Panthers gained admirers among college students—and some faculty members—who found in their lives an exemplification of alienation from America.

This story has been told often and well by others; I evoke it not as a prelude to a further examination, but by way of stipulating that the concept of *diversity* had an emotional as well as an intellectual context. To find persuasive the ideas that came to be packaged as *diversity*, one has to be predisposed to think that American freedom is hollow and that the promise of equality is phony. The anti-Americanism born at Berkeley and nurtured through a decade of campus antiwar protest created the mass of college-educated people for whom these rejections of root American values were commonplace and commonsense.

By the late 1970s, however, the Big Chill had arrived. Americans—former radicals, domesticated counterculturalists and sixties kids who had grown up and gotten jobs were no longer in awe of the Weathermen and black-bereted thugs in dark sunglasses. The revolutionary ardor had passed, but it had left its permanent sourness toward what most Americans for two hundred years thought valuable. Freedom and equality were, to this important part of a generation, cold and not very believable pieties. But *diversity*—here was something new: an idea that contained an underlying contempt for those stale old pieties, but expressed it in a positive way. *Diversity* was, in a certain sense, sugarcoated anti-Americanism.

Still, even after Powell had offered this confection, it took some time for *diversity* to catch on. The rise of *diversity* as a key concept on campus occurred slowly in the early 1980s and passed largely unnoticed by the general public and even among keen-eyed critics. There was no general hue and cry over the supplanting of academic standards by ideological ones or over admissions policies that disregarded merit in favor of social identity. But public frustration on these matters was quietly building, and it burst into the open in 1987 in a completely unexpected way.

An obscure classicist at the University of Chicago, a gay conservative who was a friend of Saul Bellow's and who enjoyed a small cult following of his own, published a long, pedantic rant about the intellectual banality that had become prevalent on American campuses. The book, *The Closing of the American Mind,* became a sudden and completely unexpected bestseller, and its author, Allan Bloom, a hugely unlikely celebrity.

The Closing of the American Mind was the opening of a major new front on what would soon be called the American culture wars. What had quietly transpired on college campuses for the previous decade or so was suddenly the object of fierce public debate. Bloom attacked the soft-minded tolerance and cultural relativism that set the prevailing tone on campus, poured vitriol on the lies and self-deception by which the campus Left imposed censorship in the name of intellectual freedom, and blasted the moral cowardice of college presidents who failed to defend the principles on which their institutions were founded. He excoriated the lowing herd of consumers of mass culture, grieved over the university's neglect of great writers and its attention to meretricious ones, and caustically dismissed students for the superficiality and trashiness of their taste, especially in music.

Diversity, however, was not even a small part in Bloom's picture of what had gone wrong on campus. Perhaps it was too new to be identified as a central pillar of the anti-intellectual totalitarian ideology he was attacking. Or perhaps *diversity* seemed to Bloom too thin an idea to pose a serious threat. In any case, *The Closing of the American Mind* has no reference to Powell's decision, and when Bloom did turn to race relations, he pondered the situation in terms of affirmative action, desegregation, black militancy and campus self-segregation—and did not mention *diversity*.

The book appeared in January 1987; the *diversity* doctrine had been promulgated by Justice Powell eight and a half years earlier; and *diversity* had since been whole-heartedly adopted by the university establishment as the official justification for racial and ethnic preferences in admissions and hiring. *Diversity* is now so familiar a part of campus chatter that it is difficult to think back to a time, though it was but fifteen years ago, when the idea was still tentative. But Bloom's silence is strong testimony that *diversity* was not yet the buzz word, or even the buzz idea, in 1987.

The Closing of the American Mind does, in fact, provide a searching critique of the idea of "culture" from which the *diversity* doctrine draws, and Bloom was no friend to reducing individuals to the sum of their group affiliations. Yet as much as his criticisms anticipated the *diversity* movement's intellectual ploys, Bloom did not register the gathering force of the movement.

What he missed was that the rationale for affirmative action was about to be supplanted by a new ideal. Affirmative action, as President Johnson had enunciated it, was to be a series of *temporary* steps; and the defenders of affirmative action had preserved that argument. A time would come when, with racial equality an achieved fact, affirmative action would no longer be needed. *Diversity*, by contrast, dispensed with the old notion of equality and in so doing, dispensed with the idea that group preferences would be only a temporary expedient. Affirmative action looked back at a history of injustice that needed to be repaired, and supposed that it, in fact, *could* be repaired. *Diversity*, by contrast, looked back at a history of injustices that must be permanently atoned and forward to a future not of racial equality but of "minority majority" dominance. Affirmative action evoked (however shakily) the moral principle of fairness; *diversity* sometimes shuns moralistic claims in favor of practical appeals (Get ready for the new majority!) and the lure of personal fulfillment. Affirmative action took as its ideal the concept of an *integrated* society; *diversity*, by contrast, focuses on the demand for *inclusion*, and the difference is immense. Integration offered the prospect of institutions and individuals putting aside racial and ethnic differences; inclusion insists that the differences must be accepted on their own terms and that they remain indissoluble. *Diversity* advocates enunciate the dawning of a new age in which bigotry and racialist supremacy will be vanquished, but not at the expense of group identity.

Even though Bloom did not mention *diversity* by name, the success of *The Closing of the American Mind* may itself have helped to propel *diversity* to new prominence, since it underscored the degree to which the campus Left was losing the public relations battle in the late 1980s. The public was now mocking campus "political correctness." Roger Kimball's *Tenured Radicals* (1990) popularized another stinging epithet, and the early nineties saw barrages of books and articles exchanged between defenders of the traditional curriculum and proponents of the new order. A whole sub-genre emerged in which rigidly orthodox campus ideologues portrayed themselves as open-minded and venturesome there-is-no-such-thing-as-political-correctness free spirits. This is the context in which *diversity* finally flowered.

In the preface to *Tenured Radicals*, Kimball cites an event at the University of Pennsylvania first reported by historian Alan Charles Kors in an op-ed in the *Wall Street Journal*. A student serving on a "diversity education" panel wrote to her colleagues expressing "her deep regard for the individual." But this did not sit well with a university administrator who

> responded by circling the passage ... underlining the word *individual*, and commenting "This is a 'RED FLAG' phrase today, which is considered by many to be RACIST. Arguments that champion the individual over the group ultimately privileges [*sic*] the 'individuals' belonging to the largest or dominant group."

Kimball and Kors both cite this story as evidence of a threat to free speech on campus, but it is also a revealing episode in the emergence of *diversity*. The year is 1989, and the student has clearly not absorbed the new code, since the administrator has to spell it out for her.

Diversity required its adherents to find new phrasings that tip-toed around ideas of individual responsibility. Just as the unnamed University of Pennsylvania administrator said, formerly innocuous words began to be treated as red flags. I recall an incident that occurred circa 1990, when I chaired a committee that was charged with developing grant proposals for funding to attract additional minority students to Boston University. We had reached a point where we needed to discuss how to judge the qualifications of some transfer applicants, when one of the faculty members on the committee—a scientist and medical researcher—vehemently objected to the word "qualifications." He said it was "a code word for policies of racial exclusion."

Thus *diversity* emerged on campus during a period of inner turmoil. As we have seen in previous chapters, the U.S. Supreme Court's decisions in *Stotts* (1984), *Wygant* (1986) and *Croson* (1989) began to limit the scope of affirmative action. The 1991 Civil Rights Act outlawed "race norming." The corporate world had begun to embrace *diversity* and "diversity training" as substitutes for affirmative action soon after the 1987 Hudson Institute report *Workforce 2000* introduced a widely distorted picture of the ethnic composition of American labor. And the *Miss Saigon* controversy—an accurate reading of the temper of the time in popular culture—unfolded in 1990. Older forms of identity preferences were clearly in trouble both with the law and in the court of public opinion. *Diversity*, however, had so far sailed along unchallenged and it was at last coming into focus. *Diversity*, its proponents saw, need not be just a makeshift euphemism for affirmative action. It could be a new principle that, in the right circumstances, could checkmate traditional ideas of fairness and liberty.

The University of Pennsylvania administrator cited by Kimball and Kors and the Boston University faculty member I encountered were harbingers of what would soon become orthodoxy.

Diversity's Annus Mirabilis

In other chapters of this book, I have aimed to provide an approximate chronological account of the development of the idea of *diversity* in American life. This seems to be a less profitable approach for *diversity* in higher education, for after the early 1990s, *diversity* underwent something like a spontaneous generation and was suddenly everywhere. It continued in the mission to which it was appointed by Justice Powell—providing a legal pretext for ethnic and racial preferences in college admissions—but it diffused outward into virtually every aspect of university life. *Diversity* became something like *wholesomeness*. Only someone acting waggish would say a word against it, and even the wag would take care that his audience understood he meant that word in jest.

No one remarked how odd this situation was. A few years earlier—say, 1987—*diversity* was a novelty item for law reviews and ethnic studies programs. By 1993, it was a principle of such presumed transcendent clarity that none could even imagine an argument against it. Or at least those who did imagined quietly. "Inclusion" in the sense of group entitlements had become such an obviously good thing that no one ever paused to wonder what happened to the older ideal of integration. "Multiculturalism," *diversity*'s more rambunctious form, could be debated, but *diversity* was exempt—for a while. In *Tenured Radicals*, for example, Kimball fires a glancing shot at multiculturalism, while *diversity* sits at the edge of the frame:

> Part of the rhetoric of "pluralism" and "diversity," the elevation of multicultural experience cloaks the abandonment of traditional humanistic culture. It belongs with prattle about the humanities instilling dissatisfaction and the desirability of undermining the traditional canon.

If it was not yet established as the concept that encompassed all the other components of the new anti-Western ideology, *diversity* was by 1988 well more than another name for affirmative action. At the first conference of the National Association of Scholars (an organization of conservative scholars) in November 1988, for example, *diversity* achieved mention as a source of anti-intellectual pressure on the curriculum. The *Washington Post* reporter who covered the conference observed:

> The scholars also cited the "tendentious" use of the classroom by some professors to pursue political ends, as in the case of "peace studies" and the move toward "diversity" in course reading lists, necessitating the judgment of works based not solely on merit but also on the gender or ethnic background of the author.

And earlier in 1988, the press had begun to register a change on college campuses. In August, the *New York Times* had taken note of the University of Vermont's new *diversity* initiatives and added:

But after the racial flareups at several colleges in the last two years, expanding cultural diversity is one of the hottest topics on campus as the 1988–89 school year gets under way.

In recent years students at many colleges have protested campus incidents that had racial overtones and their schools' lack of commitment to cultural diversity. The demonstrations prompted wide discussions about recognizing racism on campus, recruiting and keeping students and teachers who are members of minority groups and making curriculums more culturally diverse.

Lattie F. Coor, the University of Vermont's president, explained, "Diversity is increasingly important as the country becomes more multicultural and ties with foreign countries expand."

Diversity in its new and expanded sense thus appears to have crystallized some time between the January 1987 publication of Bloom's *The Closing of the American Mind* and the start of the fall 1988 semester. I will leave it to the writers of more fine-grained cultural histories to discover by what rude bridge *diversity* first marched into the groves of academe and began its long occupation. Perhaps some clues will be found in the debates at Berkeley in the spring of 1988 over whether to adopt an "ethnic diversity" requirement in the curriculum, or in the student clubs at UCLA, which in early 1988 included the "Asian-Pacific Students for Sexual Diversity" and the "Helen Keller / Anne Sullivan Lesbian and Gay Disability Diversity Club." The idea was on the march.

Institutionalizing *Diversity*

And by 1990 it had marched pretty far. The Ford Foundation that summer awarded $1.6 million in grants to faculty members working on how to expand *diversity* in the curriculum—where it was already undergoing a growth spurt. Many colleges and universities had adopted new *diversity* requirements. Some, such as the University of Vermont and the University of Cincinnati, required a single *diversity* course; others, such as Williams College, the University of Wisconsin and UC Berkeley, required students to select from a menu of approved *diversity* courses. The *Chronicle of Higher Education* considered the matter fairly novel and covered the debate over which approach—one-size-fits-all or the *à la carte* menu—was the best way to deliver the medicine.

Two of the six regional accrediting agencies for higher educa-tion—the Middle States Association of Colleges and Schools and the Western Association of Schools and Colleges—had adopted across-the-board "diversity standards" in 1988 that went into effect in 1990. The standards made the pursuit of *diversity* an obligatory part of every aspect of higher education that came under review. Because colleges need accreditation in order to qualify for federal funds, including fed-erally guaranteed student loans, these "diversity standards" had the effect of drastic compulsion.

In the spring of 1990, the Middle States Association delayed the reaccreditation of Baruch College on the grounds that it had a "paucity of minority representation on the faculty and in the administration," and because its attrition rate for blacks and Hispanics was judged too high. This was the opening shot in a war that continues to this day. Both Middle States and the Western Association eventually retreated from their explicit *diversity* litmus tests, but *sub rosa* versions of them are widespread.

In 2001, I served on a New England Association of Schools and Colleges accreditation site team and found myself alone in refusing to apply a *diversity* standard to the college we were reviewing. Although the New England Association does not have a *diversity* stan-dard, the college we were reviewing claimed to be committed to *diver-sity*—and that was enough, in the eyes of the other members of the team, to justify putting an assessment of the college's *diversity* efforts into the accreditation report. Official standards are one thing; actual practices are something else.

Diversity Uplifts

Part of the oddity of the situation is that *diversity* seemed to gain its lofty perch without the help of any great mind, any prestigious philoso-pher or social theorist, or any major book. There is no Machiavelli, no *Leviathan*, no *Critique of Pure Reason*, no Adam Smith, no *Communist Manifesto*, no John Stuart Mill, no Weber, no Durkheim, no Madison, no Jefferson, no Darwin, no *Souls of Black Folks*, no *Feminine Mystique*, nor even a *Port Huron Statement*, a *Wiccan Rede* or a Martha Stewart of the *diversity* movement. It arrived unparented, as a kind of collective emanation of ponderous academic silliness.

The most explicit discussions of *diversity* turn up in books of minor note. Ruth Sidel's *Battling Bias: The Struggle for Identity and Community on College Campuses* (1994), for example, was a weepy little defense of multiculturalism, which included an account of how *diversity* enlightens the ordinary, undiverse student. Sidel is a Hunter College professor of sociology who felt her students' pain as they encountered bias all around them. The chapter titled "Facing Diversity" commences with a testimonial from a student named Rebecca Taub who has been morally uplifted by *diversity:*

> I have met so many people here; I have so many more ideas. I am much more open-minded and less judgmental than if I had gone to a more homogeneous school. I always knew who I was, but my experience of living with other kinds of people opens your eyes to different ways of life.

The quotation is more telling than Professor Sidel intended. It teases us with the mystery of how Ms. Taub could have known that a "more homogeneous school" would have made her less "open-minded" and "more judgmental." And we can ponder the pronoun shift in the last sentence, in which Ms. Taub says that *her* experience opens *our* eyes. The mid-sentence shift in grammar suggests the arc of her thought: she begins speaking of her *individual* experience but catches herself. Her inner University of Pennsylvania dean says "RED FLAG," and she promptly shifts to the pseudo-empathetic second-person voice: "Living with other people opens *your* eyes, everybody's eyes—I'm just like everybody else in this regard—to different ways of life."

But if this seems too strained a reading, we can find solace in Professor Sidel's more anodyne conclusion:

> Moreover, entering a relatively closed, intense environment in which issues of race, religion, gender, sexual orientation, and class have high visibility has forced many of these students to face some of the conflicts and contradictions in American society. In certain instances, merely interacting with a variety of people,

often for the first time, has stimulated a somewhat different
world-view, and even a different view of oneself.

Diversity, in other words, is liberating. In the rest of Sidel's chapter we
learn about Angela from Staten Island, Leslie from a small Wisconsin
community, more about Rebecca Taub who grew up in an Orthodox
Jewish family in suburban New Jersey, Steven from Long Island, and
Jeff from the Upper West Side. They all encountered *diversity* in college and benefited from it, although Steven shows some doubtful ten-
dencies:

> "Vassar is looking for a new dean of student life. There is talk of a
> black, a Hispanic, a homosexual." He wonders, "How about the
> best person?" The previous June, he felt there was no need for the
> Black Commencement Committee to break away and form their
> own group.

But Sidel is not deterred by such doubts from reaching the optimistic
conclusion with which she actually began:

> Each of these students, when faced with diversity and the mixed
> messages that are transmitted within a complex, heterogeneous
> environment, has been challenged by the experience and has,
> over the course of their undergraduate years, found meaningful
> ways to interact with the larger community and to feel positive
> about her/himself and her/his educational experience.

Play *diversity*—everybody wins. Sidel's criteria for judging success in
"facing diversity" on campus, however, seem very broad. As long as
a student can make some "meaning" of the experience and find something to "feel positive" about, well then, *diversity* has proven its worth,
no matter the cost.

Whether *diversity* has really contributed anything significant to
the student's education, however, remains obscure. We do now, of
course, have the tortured efforts of Patricia Gurin, the University of
Michigan professor of psychology and women's studies who served
as an expert witness in *Gratz et al. v. Bollinger,* and a little industry
focused on proving this doubtful proposition has sprung up at Harvard University—the Harvard Civil Rights Project—under the stewardship of education professor Gary Orfield and with the generous

support of the MacArthur Foundation, the Mellon Foundation, the Charles Stewart Mott Foundation and the Rockefeller Foundation. (*Diversity* has never lacked well-heeled friends.)

Somewhat higher up than Professor Gurin on the academic food chain is Martha Nussbaum, who attempted a more strenuous defense of *diversity* in her 1997 volume, *Cultivating Humanity: A Classical Defense of Reform in Liberal Education.* A University of Chicago professor of law and ethics, Nussbaum saw classical precedent for focusing higher education on the arts of citizenship. Her up-to-date version of cultivating humanity involves teaching "critical examination of oneself and one's traditions," cultivating "knowledge of non-Western cultures, of minorities within their own, [and] of differences of gender and sexuality," and developing "narrative imagination," which is "the ability to think what it might be like to be in the shoes of a person different from oneself." As it happens, the existing race, gender and class studies in the contemporary university almost exactly meet this collection of philosophical desiderata.

Professor Nussbaum is the most prominent American intellectual to attempt a justification of the *diversity* doctrine. *Cultivating Humanity* is thick with discussion of the topic, but it is a deeply disingenuous book. Professor Nussbaum gets started with her strange falsifications on the second page with a depiction of "today's campuses" as places where "faculty and students *grapple* with issues of human diversity" (emphasis added). The "grappling" is her ennobling conceit for the festering discontents, censorship and fear; the gloating privilege; the rotting intellectual insecurity; and the regnant falsehoods that *diversity* has brought to most campuses.

But even if we imagine that Professor Nussbaum and I have never visited the same campuses and are describing parallel universes, her book leaves the strange impression of *argued* complacency. In effect, she says that what we are already doing is precisely what we should be doing. By her account, *diversity* is the central issue of our time, and colleges and universities are going about the discussion of it in a splendidly constructive fashion. It is a consoling message for worried diversiphiles, I suppose, but not intended for grownups.

I do not mean to exaggerate. The tone of Professor Nussbaum's book is generally triumphant to rhapsodic:

> We are now trying to build an academy in which women, and
> members of religious and ethnic minorities, and lesbian and gay
> people, and people living in non-Western cultures can be seen
> and also heard, with respect and love, both as knower and as
> objects of study ... an academy in which the world will be seen to
> have many types of citizens and in which we can all learn to
> function as citizens of that entire world.

Still, she acknowledges a few excesses:

> Inevitably there is pain and turmoil in these attempts to bring
> about change, and not all proposals for change are healthy ones.
> Some faculty pursue the diversification of the curriculum in a
> way that ultimately subverts the aims of citizenship, focusing on
> interest-group identity politics rather than the need of all citizens
> for knowledge and understanding. Some, too, have been unjustly
> skeptical of rational argument, thinking of its abuses as if they
> were part of the essence of rationality itself. These errors and
> excesses, however, are neither ubiquitous nor uncontroverted.

The little cloud, once acknowledged, is whisked away and we are
restored to Professor Nussbaum's vision of *diversity* on campus as a
movement of "resourcefulness, intelligence and good faith."

Cultivating Humanity was met with considerable approbation
when it was published and, though I think it is a dishonest book, I
recommend it to anyone interested in reading a literate defense of
what the *diversity* movement has accomplished in higher education.
Professor Nussbaum offers an appealing vision of students learning
to be tolerant, inquisitive and knowledgeable about the ways of the
world beyond the parochial barriers of their own lives. The trouble is
that she pretends this sweet, idyllic view of *diversity* more or less
matches the actual facts of contemporary university life.

But the real world of *diversity* is no idyll. Rather, it brims with
tribal vanities, assertions of entitlement, sour anti-Americanism, disdain for freedom and equality, and prideful ignorance. Nussbaum,
however, notices only a handful of excesses committed by some overly
enthusiastic diversiphiles, and claims that these rare missteps have
been seized by bad-faith critics of multiculturalism to discredit the
whole movement. Ultimately, this is a question of selective reading
of the evidence. One of us, Professor Nussbaum or I, is drastically mis-
interpreting both the historical record and the contemporary scene.

Guile

Recently, I read an essay by a student applying to the Boston University School of Law. The school is mindful that racial and ethnic preferences are frowned on by the university and have been ruled illegal in several federal jurisdictions. But like a moth to a flame, it can't help being drawn to the effort to find a way around these restrictions. So it invites students to submit a "diversity essay" if they choose. This is an opportunity to say anything one wishes about *diversity,* but it is usually and correctly understood as a chance to show you are what one of the pro-*diversity* companies we looked at earlier called "a diversity supplier."

The essay I read was from a Law School applicant who wanted to express how important her Native American heritage is to her. She recalled the piece of tribal lore that had affected her most deeply: a Cherokee story about a race between a tortoise and a hare. She carefully noted this was not the story about a race between a tortoise and a hare attributed to Aesop, some 2,600 years ago. The Cherokee, she said, have their own similar story that is just as inspiring. But she stopped short of going into details, and it is not entirely clear from her essay whether she knew how different Aesop's and the Cherokee versions really are.

One of my interests as an anthropologist is Native American cultures, and it happened that I knew the story in question. It was recorded between 1887 and 1890 by the pioneering ethnographer James Mooney, who studied the Cherokee and who later published his monumental *Myths of the Cherokee* in the Annual Report of the U.S. Bureau of Ethnology for 1900. The Aesop version used to be familiar to every American child: the tortoise beats the hare by slow, steady persistence; the hare can run faster, but is arrogant, takes a nap, and misses his opportunity.

In the Cherokee version recorded by Mooney, a terrapin challenges a boastful rabbit to a race. The rabbit accepts and offers the terrapin a head start. The race is to be held at dawn the next day, and the terrapin will be allowed to start from the brow of the first of four ridges they will have to cross. The next day the race begins with the terrapin in position on the first ridge and the rabbit far behind. By the time the rabbit reaches the first ridge, he is surprised to see the terrapin cresting the second ridge. And so it goes. At each ridge, the terrapin is still one ridge ahead. The rabbit races unrelentingly in an effort to catch up, but collapses short of the finish line, screaming in agony, "*mi, mi, mi, mi.*" The terrapin wins.

What has happened? This is no story of patience and persistence beating an arrogant braggart. It is rather a story of artful cheating. The terrapin had simply lined up his look-alike friends on successive ridges and posed himself on the last one, with a short stroll to the finish line. The moral of the story, if it can be said to have one, is "Win by guile." Mooney's informant told him that because the rabbit lost, Cherokee magicians had since boiled rabbit hamstrings in a soup before a ball game and then poured the concoction across the path the other players were expected to take, "so that they may become tired in the same way [as the rabbit] and lose the game." But take note: "It is not always easy to do this, because the other party is expecting it and has watchers ahead to prevent it." Sometimes the concoction works; sometimes it doesn't.

The student who invoked the Cherokee story correctly observed that the rabbit "is defeated not by the plodding determination of the turtle, but rather by means of guile," and she added that the turtle wins by "his ability to out-think the Rabbit." The story taught her, she said, "to focus on the talents and abilities one has" rather than "what is missing."

This young woman's selection of family lore for her "diversity essay" was, nonetheless, a little odd. It is, after all, a story about cheating. Moreover, it is a story in which the terrapin wins by taking advantage of group identity: all the terrapins look alike, and thus their collusion goes undetected.

Presumably it doesn't work to tell the law school to which you hope to be admitted that you have been deeply inspired by the ideal of winning the hard competitions by using any means you can get away with, including falsifying your identity. And yet there is something charming in the young woman's saying this without actually saying it. She takes up the Boston University Law School's own subterfuge of inviting her to submit a "diversity essay" and answers it with a subterfuge of her own. Deceit builds on deceit. Maybe she *is* qualified to study law.

Colleges and universities, including graduate and professional schools, routinely invite students to play the *diversity* game. They insinuate that the applicant gains an advantage by agreeing both to label himself and to emphasize the importance of ethnicity (or some other *diversity* variable) in his life. The invitation is hard to refuse. On the other hand, the answers are virtually impossible to question. Is this young woman from the West Coast really, as she says, "a Cherokee"? Enrolled in the tribe? Raised in the culture? Who knows.

Diversity in higher education invites exaggeration and dishonesty. Few would be surprised to find that *some* students who say they are African-American, Native American, Latino, multiracial or otherwise a member of a "diverse" group have little personal investment in or experience with their claimed identities. Indeed, some students seem to have no antecedent connection nor any current involvement in the group to which they self-reported an affiliation. But colleges and universities take this in stride. They clearly have no better means of determining a student's identity than to take the student's word for it.

Diversity may not make deceivers of us all, but it plainly announces to students before they have even been admitted that a little bit of guile about one's identity won't hurt.

Diversity Illustrated

Diallo Shabazz received some unexpected attention in September 2000 when the *Daily Cardinal*, the student newspaper at the University of Wisconsin at Madison, discovered his face in a crowd. Well, at least in the photograph of a crowd. Anna Gould, an alert reporter at the *Daily Cardinal*, noticed that in a picture of fans at a football game that adorned a University of Wisconsin brochure, the sun was shining brightly on the face of the one black student in the crowd. The white fans around him were sunless.

It soon came out that University of Wisconsin admissions officials had digitally lifted Mr. Shabazz's face from a 1994 photograph and inserted it into the picture of an all-white crowd at the football game, which in turn went into one hundred thousand copies of the admissions brochure. Shabazz was chosen for no reason other than skin color and the fact that the admissions office had his photograph on file. Caught in their sunny-faced lie, admissions director Rob Seltzer and publications director Al Friedman apologized, and Paul Barrows, vice chancellor for student affairs, said it was "an error in judgment."

Shabazz himself said the incident was "a symptom of a much larger problem," and added, "Diversity on this campus is not really being dealt with." A college senior at the time and a member of the Multicultural Student Coalition, Shabazz seemed to struggle with the incident. The *Milwaukee Journal Sentinel* described him standing before a crowd of 250 students, most white, holding up:

> a copy of an admissions booklet with a new cover featuring a building—and no people.
>
> "I refuse to believe this is the best we can do to create diversity on this campus," he said. "Institutions don't apologize verbally. Institutions apologize with policy changes and budget changes."

The image of Diallo Shabazz holding up the depopulated brochure and haranguing a little crowd about the need for more and better *diversity* is the perfect coda to this story. He seems, at last, in accord with Directors Seltzer and Friedman and Vice Chancellor Barrows, who are also on the side of more *diversity*, and who realize indeed it is not about apologizing "verbally." It is about manipulating identity. And it is about pictures.

Diversity pictures are in fact a well-defined college genre. Most colleges and universities produce viewbooks—infomercials—aimed at high school students, and most of these viewbooks (and many other college publications) include photographs intended to show off the racial and ethnic *diversity* of the colleges. The University of Wisconsin merely went one step further when it teleported Diallo Shabazz into a crowd of white people.

In January 2002, Mark Hixxon and Kirsten Hubbard, two students at the University of California, San Diego, contributed a three-part feature on "the issue of diversity" to their student newspaper, the *UCSD Guardian*. Their hook for the second part of this report was an analysis of the cover photo for the viewbook, *Discover UCSD:* "Clockwise from the top, there is an Asian female, a South Asian-looking male, a female of undetermined mixed heritage, a Hispanic female, a Caucasian male, a Caucasian female, and an African-American male." Hixxon and Hubbard then point out that the proportions of groups in the photo approximate the Asian, Caucasian and "other" proportions of the actual student body, but the single African-American student misrepresents the reality. Only "1 percent of UCSD's undergraduate body is African-American."

The *Discover UCSD* photo is not exactly a lie, but it captures the dubious position of college administrators who are committed to selling *diversity* to prospective students even if the campus demographics don't match rhetoric. Hixxon and Hubbard focus on this disparity. UCSD, it seems, succeeds in attracting students who like the idea of *diversity,* but those students are at some risk of being disappointed. Freshman Leila Dingding (her actual name), for example, was attracted to UCSD because "they represented themselves as so diverse." But Miss Dingding has grown skeptical: "Now that I'm actually here, I feel kind of like I was deceived." She adds, "I would feel more comfortable if our school were more diverse," and complains that the summer program before college was more diverse than the actual university.

She is not alone. American grade schools and high schools put enormous effort into instilling in children the doctrine of *diversity.* In many schools, *diversity* is unabashedly taught as a higher and better value than equality, freedom, justice and liberty. According to some critics, the focus on *diversity* in American schools has reached the extreme of undermining instruction in reading and writing. Be that as it may, students like Miss Dingding absorb the main point: Few matters are more important than *diversity,* and college is where one goes to find it.

College officials are fully aware of this market reality and they respond to it by packaging what they have to offer in the language and the images that they calculate will appeal to seventeen-year-olds. I do not mean to suggest that *diversity* is merely a marketing tactic for colleges and universities. To the contrary, higher education has many true believers in the doctrine of *diversity,* and a large penumbra of people who regard *diversity* as benign and possibly beneficial. Their support, whether strenuous or passive, makes *diversity* a powerful force on campus.

But in addition to that, *diversity* is also a come-on to America's miseducated and uneducated youth, who generally arrive at college believing two or three of *diversity*'s simplifications and falsehoods. The typical college applicant generally accepts, for example, that someone's "perspective" is not gained by study and effort but is rather determined by his or her group membership. The typical college applicant finds nothing amiss in the idea that education is what happens when two or more such "perspectives" are in the same vicinity, and remains convinced that an important reason to attend college is to experience being with people who are "different" from oneself.

Even if the admissions office at a university were under the stewardship of people wise enough to doubt these bits of dogma, it would be risky to publish a viewbook that called into question what the large majority of applicants believe. Some students might be inspired by the idea that we go to college to overcome the merely local and particular in our social backgrounds and thereby seek a place in a universal culture. A few might catch fire at the idea that differences in perspective are mostly trivial and that education requires the hard effort of examining argument and evidence to decide, as best we can, which account of all we are offered is more nearly *true*. And some might rise to the idea that they have already learned how to tolerate differences, and that college is a place to pursue more advanced lessons in democratic self-government. But chances are that most high school students, indoctrinated for twelve years in the tenets of *diversity*, would be repelled by such ideas.

In this sense, *diversity* has closed its circle. Colleges and universities incessantly proclaim their commitment to *diversity*. Many prospective college students weigh that commitment as a positive factor in deciding where to seek admission and where to enroll. Once enrolled, the students begin to recognize that actual college *diversity* does not perform according to the theory or the hype. Many students self-segregate into racial and ethnic enclaves in which they acquire a new vocabulary of group rights and generalized resentment. Campus *diversity*, in practice, seldom turns out to be "inclusive." Rather it is accusatory and divisive. The "differences" that come to the fore are those of students who are aggressive in pushing their agendas aimed at gaining power and privilege, not those of the mostly imaginary ideal of cultural exchange. After being exposed to this for a semester or two, students grow disenchanted. But instead of questioning the premises of *diversity* itself, the students typically blame the college for not providing enough or the right kinds of *diversity*. Leila Dingding of UC San Diego concludes: "I would be more comfortable if our school

were more diverse. That way, I would experience more cultural awareness and understanding of our diverse society." Like Diallo Shabazz,
she does not doubt the theory of *diversity*, only the practices of her
own college.

In a subtle way, the feeling that the institution has failed to deliver
is really part of the theory. *Diversity* is, after all, an ideology based on
rejection of America's oldest and most enduring ideals. It frames American history as a story of callously dominant groups and the groups
they dominated, victimizers and victims. As an ideology, it thrives on
people feeling shortchanged. Despite the upbeat brochures of different skin tones, *diversity* can be sustained only to the extent that large
numbers of people continue to feel a sense of grievance. And to that
end, it supplies its own grievance in the form of making students feel
that their colleges perpetually fall short of the goal.

The psychology of *diversity* thus resembles any number of other
movements that cycle their own disappointments back into the original
myth. The failures of the Soviet system proved the need for more communism; the sinfulness of the brethren proved the need for more Puri-
tanism; the grumbling of the volcano required another human sacrifice.

Diversity can be understood historically as a way of transforming the supposedly temporary preferences of affirmative action into
permanent rights. But as the era in which conspicuous barriers were
erected to members of various groups slips further and further into
the past, it becomes more and more difficult to justify those privileges.
Diversity advocates respond to this difficulty in part by promoting the
idea that profound—if mostly invisible—barriers remain. Invoking
invisible and often undetectable barriers, however, is a weak way of
attempting to persuade others. Building frustration and resentment
works better, at least for a while. And it produces profound—if mostly
invisible—benefits.

In this sense, the widespread feeling among college students that
they have not been rewarded with liberating "cultural awareness"—
that their colleges have fallen short—fits with the *diversity* movement's
deeper emotional currents. The promise of personal fulfillment through
diversity usually gleams in the distance. *Diversity* in higher education
is a lesson in disappointment.

Yesterday, Today, Tomorrow

Higher education is by far the institution in American society most affected by the ideology of *diversity*. But if I have seemed to imply that colleges and universities have been completely transformed by *diversity*, I have implied too much. Higher education has absorbed the ideology and made it dominant for the moment. But the undergraduate college and the research university are much older and more substantial than the *diversity* movement, and much of what they are and what they do reflects that deeper history. *Diversity* is a somewhat destructive flippancy that diverts many students from a real education. It is a cost—a tax—on intellectual seriousness and has demoralized many thoughtful scholars who are dedicated teachers, just as it has inflated many lightweight academics.

Diversity's proponents see the movement as easing the university into a constructive relation with social and demographic changes in our society. In fact, we would be better able to accommodate those changes if we held firmly to the principles of universal intellectual inquiry. The descent into cultural relativism for a generation or more will one day have to be made up, for in the end, people will need to know real history, not just fashion; and they will want to pursue rigorous inquiry, not merely record identity group perspectives. The larger numbers of students who are not of European-Caucasian background will in time, I suspect, bitterly resent that they are heirs to a university that lowered its standards and discarded part of its precious heritage in a condescending attempt to cater to people it assumed would otherwise not be able to make the mark.

But I leave that prediction as hostage to a future generation. In our time, the university lives in a world of *diversity*—the ideology, not the demographic fact, and certainly not the intellectual condition. Ideological *diversity*, however, is not congenial to the basic nature of the intellectual enterprise on which the university is founded. We struggle on in an environment radically different from the one in which we evolved—a bit like the osage orange, with which I began this chapter.

I am grateful that the osage orange has survived in some out-of-the-way places. The university today is only too eager to change with the times, and campuses are much more likely these days to plant the new, dwarf, guaranteed-fruitless apple trees. But if one goes looking, perhaps off between the library and the old physics building, an osage orange may still be found.

Likewise, we continue to teach English, history and all the liberal arts—the ghosts of our evolution—dreaming that *our* glyptodonts, gomphotheres and ground sloths will someday return.

TEN

CONSUMING *DIVERSITY*

According to the city directory for 1900, Boston then had about 550 restaurants, including several that are still around: Union Oyster House (established 1714) and Durgin Park (established 1826). At the high end of eating out were the hotel restaurants, such as the Parker House and Young's Hotel. Boston in 1900 was a good place to find seafood and hearty New England fare, but seemingly not a place to indulge an appetite for exotic flavors. A typical restaurant meal cost about fifteen cents.

By 1950, Boston had approximately 1,375 restaurants, and certain kinds of ethnic cuisine were easy to find. The discriminating diner could go to the Napolu Café or to the Pompeii Restaurant, or any of about two dozen Chinese restaurants, from Chop Stick Joe's and China Doll to King Fong's and Hong Far Low's. Fahey's Diner and Sullivan's Restaurant promised something more like corned beef and cabbage. The Terminal Lunch at 838 Summer Street, however, sounds a bit ominous.

By 2002, there were 2,430 restaurants in Boston, catering to a great many tastes. The single largest category consists of Chinese restaurants (127 separate establishments), followed by: Italian (91), Japanese (32), Thai (23), Mexican (19), Spanish (18), Vietnamese (15), Irish (11), French (11), Indian (8), Middle Eastern (7), Caribbean (6), West Indian (5), Korean (5), Persian (2), Greek (2), Sicilian (1) and Jamaican (1). The search engine that offered these results missed a Brazilian and an Ethiopian restaurant I know of, but the proportion of explicitly ethnic restaurants—16 percent of the total—seems about right. The only category in which Boston zeroed out was Cajun; the search engine somehow missed the Dixie Kitchen on Massachusetts Avenue. Don't come to Boston looking for jambalaya, but if only jambalaya will do, Dixie Kitchen is where you'll find it.

What happened in Boston also happened in varying degrees across America. In the last three decades, the American palate changed more than it had in the previous three hundred years. Walk into a suburban supermarket today in the United States and you may encounter heaps of vegetables and fruits (black sapote, carambola or "star fruit," cherimoya, canistel, Surinam amaranth, Peruvian Ají chillies, boniato, cassava and jícama) that a generation ago would have been found, if at all, only in specialty ethnic stores. Indeed, some of these foods could have been found only in jungle markets two weeks up a tributary of the Amazon River, or in the index of a specialized ethnology book.

The American palate has clearly expanded, but that does not mean Americans of times past had no taste for foreign cuisines. Fannie Farmer's *Boston Cooking School Cook Book* (1896), which sold more than 4.1 million copies in successive editions (the sixth most popular cookbook in human history), includes recipes for dishes such as Chicken Curry and Macédoine Salad—and Russian sandwiches and Eggs à la Caracas.

The *Better Homes and Gardens Cookbook* (1930), in its red-and-white checkered picnic-tablecloth cover, sold more than 18.6 million copies over its lifetime—by a long margin, the most popular cookbook of all time. Although it is best remembered as a codification of suburban blandness, it too pays tribute in a fashion to the broader world. In my 1965 edition, I find "Puree Mongole," which evokes the heartiness of the steppes and sounds as though it might contain fermented mare's milk. It can be found in the section "Canned-soup Combinations," and is actually more domestic: "Combine 1 can tomato soup, 1 can green pea soup, 1 can milk. Heat." The Native American sounding "Porcupine Meat Balls" turn out to be only ground beef, but the recipe does pay tribute of a sort to the remote Asiatic origins of American Indians by including the Mongol ingredient, "1 can condensed tomato soup." Then there are Squaw Corn (1 can cream-style corn, 3 slightly beaten eggs, 12 ounces of "luncheon meat in julienne strips"), Chow Mein, and Hungarian Goulash.

Even at its culinary nadir, American cooking expressed a worldview, and incorporated at least by metaphor tastes of faraway places. In longer perspective, of course, most of the ingredients in midcentury American cooking were adoptees from non-Western traditions: corn, potatoes, tomatoes, pumpkins, sweet potatoes, lima beans, peanuts and chocolate from the New World; chickens (and eggs), rice, tea, sugarcane and lemons from Southeast Asia; peaches and apricots from China; bananas originally from the Malay Peninsula; coconut and pineapple from Polynesia; watermelons from sub-Saharan Africa, coffee from Yemen and southern Ethiopia; buckwheat from Manchuria; and wheat, fava beans, spinach, olives, beef, lamb and pork from the Middle East—to mention only a few. Europeans, of course, contributed Brussels sprouts.

In the last few decades, Americans have come, more than ever before, to savor the world's differences. This is literally so when it comes to food, but also in the more extended sense. A great many Americans consume *diversity* by seeking out comestibles and other goods that are marked in some manner with the stamp of *diversity.*

Or, perhaps more accurately, with one of the two stamps of *diversity.* Stamp E identifies a product as authentically Ethnic. It belongs on the food, garment, tool or trifle that the authentic native would eat, wear, brandish or dandle. Stamp H, by contrast, identifies a product as an expression of self-conscious "hybridity." It belongs on anything that crosses over old cultural boundaries to create an exciting new experience. Americans consume both kinds of *diversity,* and *diversity* itself is a large enough idea to contain, without discomfort, both a notion of the ancient purity of folk traditions and the zing of unprecedented combinations.

Who Buys Diversity and Why

The consumerist dimension of *diversity*—the fact that it is an acquired taste as well as a political agenda—has attracted the attention of two very good cultural observers. In 2000, the sociologist Marilyn Halter published *Shopping for Identity: The Marketing of Ethnicity,* and David Brooks published *Bobos in Paradise: The New Upper Class and How They Got There.* On the whole, Halter deals with Stamp E *diversity* and Brooks with Stamp H. Each also gives some attention to the other's topic.

Halter primarily focuses on the behavior of people as members of ethnic groups. She argues that "Through the consumption of ethnic goods and services, immigrants and their descendants modify and signal ethnic identities in social settings no longer sharply organized around ethnic group boundaries and the migration experience." The individual can eat and wear ethnicity without living, working or otherwise confining his activities to an ethnic conclave. "Ethnicity is increasingly manifest through self-conscious consumption of goods and services and, at the same time, these commodities assist in negotiating and enforcing identity differences." In Halter's view, Americans buy ethnically themed goods both to assure themselves of their continuing commitment to a particular heritage and to tell others, in effect, "I belong to this ethnic culture, and you don't."

Halter is also alert to a possible contradiction in this kind of consumption, between wanting to "recreate an old-fashioned and bygone world" and "craving for novelty." But, she observes, "most consumers see absolutely no discrepancy." We simply enjoy the novelty of freely putting on and taking off the accouterments of bygone worlds. We understand that purchasing goods that remind one of a heritage is not the same as living in a time and place where the heritage was a stark fact, rather than a consumer choice. So what? Why shouldn't we gratify ourselves by paying some homage to the past while living fully in the freedom of the present?

Halter has several good terms for this new kind of ethnicity: voluntary ethnicity, convenience ethnicity and portable ethnicity. All of them point to the individual's control over his identity. Ethnicity in this view ceases to be an imposition of stereotypes by others, or even the strongly asserted ties of a particular community. Instead, it becomes a pattern of choices, and it may include such choices as "relearning one's ancestral tongue, eating ethnic cuisine, displaying ethnic artifacts, fostering a hyphenated identity, and even reverse name-changes (back to the old-country original)."

This is perhaps enough to suggest the trajectory of *Shopping for Identity*. Halter's book is a richly detailed examination of the subject, and she is especially keen on the work of marketing experts who specialize in either creating products for niche ethnic markets or figuring out how to interest ethnically minded consumers in buying major brands.

David Brooks' widely noted book examines a different part of our self-absorption. He aims to provide a portrait of America's "new upper class," the educated elite of the '60s, '70s and '80s generations who originally defined themselves as a counterculture and who seemed somewhat surprised when they became the proprietors of the culture itself. Brooks proceeds from the idea that "in the information age at least, classes define themselves by their means of consumption." This points to the clever term in his book's title, the asterisked *BOBOS* in Paradise* are "bourgeois bohemians," a professional upper class that cultivates bohemian tastes. And as it happens, those bohemian tastes often run toward consuming *diversity.*

But let us glance back at Halter for a moment. Although she keeps her eye mainly on the ethnic identity ball, she takes note from time to time of the "tourists" and others who have a taste for ethnic goods other than their own. Tourists, she notes, created the market for the revival of the hula dance in Hawaii, and Anglo-Americans between 1900 and 1936 created the market for handmade Navaho silver jewelry. But one of Halter's most interesting examples is a line of Hallmark greeting cards called the "Common Threads Collection," which was designed "for consumers who appreciate cultural diversity" and who want to bring "multiculturalism into their daily lives." The cards are not targeted at any one ethnic group, but offer "shared truths" from "a variety of the world's cultures." Halter quotes a Hallmark design manager who described the cards as "eth-mix, not ethnic."

Hallmark calculated that "African Americans, Hispanics, or Asians" would be a small part of the market for Common Threads. Instead, "focus group data revealed that the primary interest came from the white or Caucasian market. These were the same buyers who reported ownership of ethnic jewelry, or decorative items for the home and who sought out goods they considered unique, inspiring, meaningful, or creative." Common Threads turned out to be a major success for Hallmark. The cards are a nearly perfect Stamp H product: traditional folk wisdom from an exotic culture hybridized with a quintessentially American product, the mass-marketed greeting card.

Brooks comes to this territory, however, in a less celebratory mood. Rather, "the Bobos are enslaved by their insatiable desire for freedom and diversity." They are pluralistic and tolerant, but they can never climb out of their consumerist appetite: "The more you get, the more you hunger for. The life of perpetual choice is a life of perpetual longing as you are prodded by the inextinguishable desire to try the next new thing." Part of what afflicts Brooks' Bobos is that the lust for *diversity* has no logical or psychologically compelling end. They may go to 838 Summer Street, but the Terminal Lunch is no longer being served. Having let go of the moorings of their own cultural heritages in order to float through the authenticity of other traditions, they can never quite find their way back to any fixed point.

A Taste for the New

The expansion of American markets for ethnic foods and other ethnic goods reflects the confluence of several factors: the rising number of new immigrants, the emergence of consumption patterns associated with Halter's "convenience" ethnicity, the taste among some American whites for "Common Threads" style reminders, and the Bobos' longing for the authentic experience of authentic otherness. But the current diversification of American taste must also be understood as another step in a much older pattern of consumption. Americans, like many other peoples, are intrigued by new tastes and welcome novelty.

In 1900, Hills Brothers in San Francisco began packing roasted, ground coffee in vacuum tins, a marketing step that eventually brought the demise of America's ubiquitous coffee roasting shops. Milton Hershey introduced his first Hershey chocolate bars, both plain and almond. The Mead Johnson Company began making Pablum, one of the most popular baby foods in America, before it became the standard undergraduate curriculum. The Southern Oil Company introduced Wesson Oil; and up in Battle Creek, Michigan, forty-two breakfast cereal plants were rolling, toasting and flaking their way to a new market. Louis Lassen in New Haven, Connecticut, may have invented the hamburger sandwich, although there are rival claimants. And the first honeydew melons were imported to the United States.

I am indebted for these facts to James Trager, who gathered many more like them in his fine book *The Food Chronology* (1995). Let us note that America's diet was changing in 1900. New foods, new forms of preparation and new kinds of marketing were on the scene.

So too in midcentury. In 1950, the federal government lifted all restrictions on food coloring in margarine; a more toast-friendly yellow variety was soon cooling next to the butter in grocery stores. Park-Hines of cake-mix fame was founded in Ithaca, New York. The Minnesota Valley Canning Company adopted its new name, Green Giant Company. And *Betty Crocker's Picture Cookbook* was a bestseller.

At midcentury, America was conflicted about its diet in ways that are still familiar. *Prevention* magazine, with its implausible claims about unpalatable foods, began publication. Food faddist Gayelord Hauser struck a chord with his book *Look Younger, Live Longer,* and spurred a huge boost in sales for Dannon Yogurt. And the U.S. Department of Agriculture issued a report titled "Composition of Foods—Raw, Processed, and Prepared," which listed the nutritional contents of 751 items, including many frozen foods. On the other hand, Kellogg's introduced Sugar Pops cereal that year, and General Foods brought out Minute Rice, which accomplished the task of retaining the taste while eliminating much of the nutritional benefit of old-fashioned rice. And Robert Rosenberg founded The Open Kettle in Quincy, Massachusetts, a coffee and donut shop that he soon renamed "Dunkin Donuts."

The themes of innovation in 1900 and 1950—mass marketing, health and convenience—continue today, but it is not hard to find some benchmarks that represent the era in which *diversity* became a major cultural ideal. For example, in March 1989, the Food and Drug Administration approved the first shipment into the United States of *tora fugu*—blowfish—the potentially deadly Japanese specialty. Nobuyoshi Kuraoka, the owner of Restaurant Nippon, organized twenty-four other Japanese restaurateurs to petition the government. *Fugu* is a food with existential edge. It is culturally exotic for Americans and authentic enough to satisfy the most adventuresome Bobo taste.

In 1990, U.S. tortilla sales reached $1.54 billion, up from $300 million in 1980. That same year, Campbell Soup Company produced its 20 billionth can of tomato soup, only a small fraction of which went toward making Puree Mongole. In 1991, U.S. salsa sales outstripped ketchup sales by $40 million—an event that caught Halter's eye, too.

The spirit of *diversity* is especially visible in the restaurants that opened during this time. In 1989, Olives opened in Charlestown, Massachusetts, and for a while the most celebrated cuisine in Boston was a bistro-style combination of Italian, Spanish and Portuguese dishes.

In 1990, the Eureka Restaurant opened in Los Angeles, offering chef Jeff Olen "Jody" Denton's specialties such as wild mushroom quesadilla, tomato and jícama salsa, roast salmon with black bean sauce and goat cheese, Chinese-style roast duck, miyagi oysters and falafel. Jody was not much constrained by cultural boundaries.

In 1991, Kenthai de Monteiro, the former Cambodian ambassador to Taiwan who had fled to France to escape the Khmer Rouge, relocated to Boston and opened a fusion Cambodian-French restaurant, the Elephant Walk. Earlier this year I sketched out my plans for the chapter on religion to a colleague from the Boston University School of Theology over "S'ngao Mouan" and "Poulet Dhomrei" at the Elephant Walk. In the same year that Ambassador de Monteiro brought Cambodian cuisine to Boston, Ember Martin, who is of Brazilian extraction, and Fernando Moreno from Ecuador opened Sol y Luna in San Francisco, offering a kind of pan–South American cuisine.

In 1994, Sheila Lukins' *All Around the World Cookbook* came out with an initial printing of 350,000 copies—the largest initial printing ever for a cookbook. The mixed success of this particular book is a good barometer of the growing taste for diversity.

Lukins and her partner Julee Rosso were the proprietors of an acclaimed food shop in New York, The Silver Palate, and co-authors of the best-selling *The Silver Palate Cookbook* (1982), an early venture into the eclectic gourmet market. *The Silver Palate* drew on ingredients and recipes from around the world, but it made no *diversity* claims. Rather, the cookbook was written for young professionals with unabashed American tastes, and included sections such as "All-American Salads" and "American As Apple. . . ." Lukins and Rosso hit the right note for the time, but when Lukins turned a decade later to *All Around the World,* based on her trips to thirty-three countries, her adaptations of foreign recipes to American tastes proved less successful. Readers often criticized the recipes as pallid imitations of the originals. One of the volunteer reviewers on Amazon.com captures the general tone of disappointment:

> Many of the recipes are pretty anemic, watered down versions of the real McCoys. I would have liked to see more intense spices and flavors, and less "Americanized" versions of what should have been intriguing international cuisine.

What changed between *The Silver Palate Cookbook* and the *All Around the World Cookbook* was not Lukins. Her talent had always been translating the world's culinary variety into flavors that matched American tastes. But by the 1990s, many Americans longed for the *authentically* different, and mere adaptation was not good enough.

The *All Around the World Cookbook* was halfway *diversity*, promising connection to other cultures without demanding deep immersion in them. The book sold reasonably well. But it irritated—and continues to irritate—those who hungered for a stronger dose of *diversity*, and who didn't want food "tailored for American tastes," as another reader put it. Besides, wrote yet another, "There is not a single recipe from Sub-Saharan Africa in this *All Around the World Cookbook.*" *Diversity* is a hard taskmaster, demanding both purity and breadth.

Diversity was certainly not the only fashion affecting American taste in the 1990s, but it may have been the most significant. It carried forward the ever-present American drive for expanding the cultural frontier by introducing new fruits and vegetables, new recipes, and new points of reference, but added a vigorous component of identity politics. Eating the right foods in the right restaurants, *knowing* the right way to order in half a dozen exotic traditions, and appreciating subtleties that only cultural insiders would normally notice became badges of sophistication. The worlds described by Halter and Brooks converge on the dinner table. Culinary *diversity* is where status seeking among the affluent employs some of the same symbols as the new forms of ethnic consciousness.

Babette's Big *Chocolat*

The consumerist impulse for *diversity* in food extends to watching people in other cultures eat. The *diversity* era has created a niche for a particular kind of entertainment: the ethnic feast flick. The genre is best defined by *Babette's Feast*. This movie, based on a story by Isak Dinesen in the *Ladies' Home Journal* in the 1950s, won the Academy Award for Best Foreign Film in 1986. In Dinesen's story, Babette is an expert cook who was also a refugee communard from the Paris uprising of 1871. She has spent years working for two ascetic sisters living in a small town by a fjord in Norway. When Babette wins a lottery, she decides to spend all her money preparing a grand feast. Her gift somehow liberates the other characters from their bland tastes and stultifying lives.

The movie translated the action to Denmark, but otherwise kept to Dinesen's story. Caught in their stodgy ways, the sisters had never realized what culinary wonders Babette could perform or how rich and, well, *diverse* the world is.

Just before *Babette* feasted American audiences, a Japanese food flick arrived, *Tampopo* (1986). But the genre soon had many other entries. Some highlights, with plot summaries from the *Internet Movie Database* (IMDb.com):

Tampopo. 1986.
> In this humorous paean to the joys of food, the main story is about trucker Goro who rides into town like a modern Shane to help Tampopo set up the perfect fast-food noodle restaurant.

Como agua para chocolate (Like Water for Chocolate). 1992.
> This picture set a new epoch in Mexican movies all over the world.... When Tita is forced to make the wedding cake, the guests at the wedding are overcome with sadness.... Tita has discovered she can do strange things with her cooking.

Yin shi nan nu (Eat Drink Man Woman). 1994.
> Retired Master Chef Chu lives in a large house in Taipei with his three unmarried daughters.... Life in the house revolves around the ritual of an elaborate dinner each Sunday....

Big Night. 1996.
> Primo and Secondo are two brothers who have emigrated from Italy to open an Italian restaurant in America. Primo is the irascible and gifted chef, brilliant in his culinary genius, but determined not to squander his talent on making the routine dishes that customers expect.... Primo begins to prepare his masterpiece, a feast of a lifetime, for the brothers' big night....

Pain au Chocolat. 1999.
> A man, a beautiful woman working in a cake shop, meringues, fig tartlets, sweet glances and ...

Chocolat. 2000.
> A woman and her daughter open a chocolate shop in a small French village that shakes up the rigid morality of the community.

Tortilla Soup. 2001. (Hispanic remake of *Yin shi nan nu*)
   A Mexican-American master chef and father to three daughters
   has lost his taste for food but not for life.

I am not quite sure that *Chocolat* belongs on this list, as it is more concerned with nibbling than feasting, but in a book on *diversity*, I prefer to err by inclusion. What makes these movies attractive to *diversity*-minded Americans, I think, is that they take us beyond the authentic recipe or the authentic restaurant to images of authentic meals in authentic cultural contexts. The ethnics in these films are not just waiters (although some of them are waiters, too), but whole people, and the viewer of the movie gets to see the *diverse* food in a rounded human context.

   Why food flicks instead of, say, movies about truck driving in diverse cultures, or movies about funeral customs in faraway places? There is no shortage of common human experiences on which to develop a genre of peeking into foreign lives, but only a handful of these experiences—love, romance, revenge, food—make for successful films in the United States. Perhaps food flicks succeed because they offer such an intimate view of other people. Commensality—eating together—is the basic human ritual, and everywhere it has similar variations: food as seduction, food as friendship, food as family, eating together as the reassuring bond of everyday life, and feasting as an activity that helps define some of the extraordinary moments.

   For the price of a movie ticket, the ethnic feast flick provides a way to consume the richness and sensuality of *diverse* cultures that just can't be had in the pages of the *All Around the World Cookbook.*

ALT-Cntrl-Dlt

Food is the most popular and accessible medium through which *diversity* becomes a consumer good, but clothing runs a close second. One of the best ways to manipulate identity is to dress up.

   Hot Topic is a popular chain of retail stores usually found in suburban malls. The chain was founded in 1988 by Orv Madden, who, according to Hot Topic's website, realized, "No other retailers were taking timely advantage of the direct correlation between music videos, alternative artists, and teenage fashions." The company went public in 1996, and recorded sales of $336.1 million in fiscal 2001, as reported by the *Wall Street Journal*. The store dominates its particular market segment of teens who classify themselves as "alternative," and, as the *Journal* points out, "Roughly 17% of American high school students consider themselves 'alternative,' while only 11% view themselves as 'popular.'" Hot Topic says its merchandise "reflects a variety of music related lifestyles, which include streetwear, retro influenced lounge, punk, club, and gothic."

Hot Topic is, of course, scorned by purists. The best way to outfit oneself for a "music related lifestyle" is to shop with discrimination at AmVets, Goodwill Industries, Salvation Army and Haddassah thrift shops; prowl yard sales with a discerning eye; or go to specialty shops that cater to bikers or other "affinity groups," as the marketers gently call them. And some fashions are best cobbled together at home. The *Wall Street Journal* mentioned Sasha Lee who spent six hours sewing a pair of pink fur pants and was unhappy when Hot Topic started selling them a few months later.

Hot Topic may be the alternative fashion equivalent of the *All Around the World Cookbook*. It captures the idea of a certain kind of *diversity*, makes it accessible, but in the process dilutes its authenticity. If you are looking for pure punk or goth fashion, you must journey into the demimonde rather than shop the local mall. But can anyone at the Adolf and the Piss Artists or the Alien Sex Fiend concert tell the difference?

Teenage "music related lifestyle" fashions take us some distance from the kinds of *diversity* that captured the imagination of Justice Powell, Reverend Coffin and Professor Sidel. But *diversity* is indeed a broad and encompassing concept, and it applies as well to the make-believe identity politics of adolescence—and the segment of the population that extends "music related lifestyles" beyond adolescence. The young men and women who classify themselves as "alternative" illustrate another of the ways in which the cultural principles of *diversity* in American life find expression in consumerism.

While the ethnic and Bobo versions of consuming *diversity* pay particular attention to food, Alternative Lifestyle Teenagers (ALTs) focus, just as Hot Topic says, on music and clothes. ALTs are Stamp H diversiphiles: they often have a conception of a *pure* version of their lifestyle exemplified by defunct bands, but the emphasis is on hybrid improvisation—putting together a personal synthesis of elements out of the repertoire of "streetwear, retro influenced lounge, punk, club, and gothic," or other subcults. Halter's idea of *portable* or *convenience* ethnicity also applies to the ALTs. The identities they put on are easily and frequently taken off, accentuated in one context, played down in another.

ALTs who move too fluidly among identities, however, are at risk of losing status. ALT message boards are full of vitriol aimed at fellow ALTs, accused of being poseurs or fickle in their ALT commitments. ALTs are also drenched in self-pity, convinced that their lives are tough because of their identities. ("Samantha" declares, "I get it hard cuz im goth/bi." "Ewok" replies in pitch-perfect *divers*-ese, "That's sad, no one should be judged.")

The world of the ALTs has a certain resemblance to a phenomenon noticed by the British anthropologist Gregory Bateson in the 1930s. Bateson studied the Iatmul, a large tribe of headhunters who lived along the Sepik River in northern New Guinea. He was struck by the lengths to which the various clans would go to assert their dissimilarity. In practical terms, each clan was virtually indistinguishable from the next. They all possessed the same kinds of property, recited similar myths and pursued parallel activities. But what looked almost interchangeable to a neutral outsider appeared to the clans themselves as a set of profoundly important distinctions. Each Iatmul clan vigorously boasted of its own superiority, mocked the absurdity of the other clans' myths, and aggressively defended its own slightly different cosmological account of the universe. No Iatmul would have acknowledged that the differences were feigned; they were, to the contrary, felt to be real. Yet they were mostly mere imaginings.

The ALTs likewise live in a world of pseudo-diversity, each "music related lifestyle" being little more than a slightly different assortment of music preferences, clothes and hairstyles, sometimes supplemented with tattoos and piercings. But in an environment in which real similarity overwhelms real difference, feigned difference often becomes a major currency.

The feigned differences among the ALTs, however, are a mirror to the whole *diversity* movement. The teenage shoppers at Hop Topic are, after all, simply practicing the identity masquerade that adults carry on in the slightly different idioms of ethnicity and world culture. ALT *diversity* is not exactly a tryout for the identity masquerades of college students and women and men in their twenties, but it is an introduction to the idea that we can "reinvent" ourselves as easily as we can purchase a new look or a fake ID. Perhaps some of the appeal of *diversity* to those over age eighteen is that it offers a kind of permanent adolescence without the ALT recklessness. While ALTs may risk permanent damage or death in their use of drugs and frenzied pursuit of difference, grownup *diversity* is channeled into safer patterns of consumption. Or a rare nibble of *tora fugu*.

Diversity Consumed

Consumerism is an aspect of American culture that long predates the current *diversity* movement. Our attitudes toward what we can "own," our understanding of how to gratify our material longings, and our sense of personal fulfillment through experiences that can be purchased or objects that can be possessed lie deep in the American character. These psychological qualities are matched by our society's success in building economic structures that foster innovation, material abundance and effective marketing.

The *diversity* movement, in its insistence on the primacy of *group identity* over the transactional give-and-take of social life, stands slightly athwart the cultural premises of American consumerism. *Diversity* arose as a countercultural critique of American society that depicted social relations as based on hierarchy and oppression of disprivileged groups. Consumerism, by contrast, is utterly egalitarian in spirit and tied to a vision of American society that emphasizes economic freedom and individual pursuit of happiness. *Diversity* denies that the individual in American life was ever much more than a destructive illusion, but consumerism affirms what *diversity* denies. And *diversity* offers a vision of the future in which the freedom of individuals to aspire to lives of their own choosing would be tightly constrained by their group identities.

The *diversity* movement rolled across American religion, the arts, business and education encountering few significant impediments. It prevailed as a matter of law and as a set of practices. But the cultural domain of American consumerism has proven a more stubborn target. *Diversity* invaded the marketplace for goods and services, but quickly found itself co-opted. Our economy, rather than dividing into myriad sub-economies matched to the racial, ethnic and other groupings emphasized by the *diversity* movement, simply swallowed the movement and turned it to its own purposes. *Diversity* turned into upscale menus, cookbooks, vacation packages, knickknacks, greeting cards and fashions.

As Marilyn Halter amply demonstrates, the marketing departments of many American businesses looked at *diversity* and saw fresh opportunities for "market segmentation." *Diversity* offered a new way to sort through the multitude of Americans to discover those who had particular tastes, yearnings, disappointed hopes, boredom, ennui or vacuums to be filled. Markets could be segmented by a more finely tuned account of the tastes of members of ethnic groups; products could be packaged in light of the increased self-consciousness of demographic slices that *diversity* had promoted to the status of actual "groups"; and the Common Threads market of guilty (or idealistic) or curious (or lazy) Caucasians also beckoned. At the high end of consumerism, the Bobo thirst for expensive cultural authenticity could be catered to.

The transformation of *diversity* into a consumer good has been a generally benign event for American culture. It has genuinely expanded consumer choices and brought worthwhile products to market that otherwise had little chance to catch on. We are richer in every sense for being able to purchase African textiles, Central American vegetables and Balinese jewelry. And we should be grateful to the marketplace as well for drawing some of the venom out of the *diversity* movement. By emphasizing the make-believe and put-on qualities of *diversity*, by defining *diversity* as a taste for exotic food, unusual clothes and offbeat tourist destinations, our consumerist impulses steer us away from the non-negotiable demands and seething ethnic resentments that the *diversity* movement encourages in political contexts. Better *diversity* as a lifestyle choice than a would-be antidemocratic regime. The marketplace has served us well by domesticating *diversity*.

But this is not to say that the marketplace has relieved us of all the ills wrought by *diversity*. In at least one important way, it has made some of those ills worse: American business has found profits in the fragmentation of American identity. The constant search for statistically measurable differences in consumer preference among demographic slices reinforces group identity and probably helps to turn minor subcultural differentiation into more substantial social and political realities. American business is definitely developing a reliance on the market segments that *diversity* helped to define, and such reliance can easily turn into a vested economic interest in reinforcing social division.

Our appetite for consuming *diversity* is thus not *wholly* benign. Business is business; it rarely looks out for the common good and has little motive to challenge profitable illusions. As it happens, the spirit of American consumerism has blunted and demoralized part of the *diversity* movement by undermining its radical critique of American social relations. People who shop for identity, after all, are acting more like autonomous individuals than like mere members of fixed groups, even if they are fantasizing about their connections to such groups. *Diversity* radicals sense that consumerism undermines their "authenticity" and they rail against it, but it is a hopeless cause. Their discouragement is good news for those of us who favor the continuation of our robust common culture—but good news with an ominous edge.

ELEVEN

SELECTIVE *DIVERSITY*

On my walk to work each morning in Boston, I pass a nineteenth-century mansion that has, behind a spiky wrought iron fence, a half-acre of green grass, lilacs, yews and oaks. Squirrels bound through the clutter of tan leaves; colonies of house sparrows raise a racket inside the bushes; and blue jays sometimes mob the local red-tail hawk high up in the oak. Walled on one side by an MIT residence hall and cornering on a busy intersection, the yard is an unkempt little preserve in the midst of the city. When I head home at the end of the day, the squirrels have retired and a night crew of gray rats are rustling through the dry leaves.

The house and yard belong to the Ramakrishna Vedanta Society. At the corner of the yard is a sign that from time to time promises:

Peace

Peace

Peace

And mentions "Meditation and Vivekachudamani, Crest Jewel of Discrimination."

For years I wondered whether the Crest Jewel of Discrimination was a person, an honorific (like "World Chess Champion") or an activity. In fact, it is the title of a book. The Hindu word that the Ramakrishna Vedanta Society translates as the "Crest Jewel of Discrimination" ought to remind us that "discrimination" is an ambiguous idea. It can refer to a capacity to draw important and valid distinctions as well as to the practice of making invidious and unfair ones.

Diversity, as we have seen, frequently serves as an intellectual justification for discrimination, and thus spends much of its effort insisting that the invidious and unfair distinctions on which it is built are really discriminations of the other type: necessary, valid, and for the greater good. Diversiphiles aim, in effect, to turn the slag of old stereotypes into the new crest jewel of social justice.

Although this alchemy is practiced in many venues where diversiphiles have won power, it is especially prominent at elite women's colleges, such as Wellesley, Mount Holyoke, Smith and Bryn Mawr. These colleges afford a special lens on *diversity* because of an odd combination of historical circumstances. They were founded, as were historically black colleges and universities, to overcome a particular kind of discrimination. In that sense, they embodied a version of the "separate but equal" approach to education. But the discrimination that the elite women's campuses attempted to compensate for—the exclusion of women from the nation's best colleges and universities—disappeared entirely by the mid-1970s. The historically black colleges and universities faced a similar crisis when laws and social attitudes opened doors to African-Americans at formerly all-white institutions.

If that were all that happened, elite women's colleges would not have a place in this book about *diversity*. They would simply be an instance of an American institution that, as an accident of history, exists today without the diversity of sexes among enrolled students. But in fact, the elite women's colleges offer themselves as a much more interesting social experiment. For while they have chosen to remain single-sex in enrollment, they have also become among the most ardent exponents of *diversity* in many other social categories: race, ethnicity, national origin, gender preference. The historically black colleges and universities, by contrast, have shown little interest in the *diversity* movement.

Thus the elite women's colleges offer the example of institutions that have embraced *diversity*, but have done so selectively. Perhaps in the great wide world of possibilities for dividing humans into categories and groups, this is not so strange. *Diversity*, at one level, is always selective. It always is a matter of advancing the claims of some groups and neglecting or suppressing the claims of others. The *diversity* doctrine has never been harnessed to a call for preferential admission to colleges, for example, of Europeans who came to this country as indentured laborers or of Americans who have diagnosed learning disabilities.

Still, there is something a little strange about a college that embraces the *diversity* doctrine but persists in excluding male students. *Diversity,* after all, is almost always construed as one of the reasons why women should have access to formerly all-male enclaves. The apparent double standard in admissions at women's colleges, therefore, invites a closer look. Perhaps it can teach us something about how to tell the difference between good and bad discrimination.

The discrimination of these colleges against men has few if any practical consequences, since the sorts of male students who would be qualified to attend elite women's colleges have numerous other opportunities. But the bifurcation in the admissions policies of elite women's colleges does seem to put on display the opportunistic side of *diversity:* its readiness to justify discrimination in *favor* of one category (e.g. African-Americans) and *against* another (e.g. males) to suit the convenience of the moment.

That element of opportunism is important because it vitiates the colleges' claims to be interested in the *real* diversity of humanity. Rather, the elite women's colleges as a group pursue a tailored and managed *diversity* (Smith College calls it "Diverse by Design"), an artificial assembly of some kinds of social differences in carefully adjusted proportions. Faced with a flat-out contradiction between their simultaneous commitments to *diversity* as a general principle and to single-sex education, such colleges usually practice a kind of emphatic obliviousness. Wellesley College, for example, trumpets its commitment to *diversity* and its commitment to excluding male students on the same page of its viewbook for prospective applicants:

> Wellesley is one of the most diverse colleges in the nation. U.S. News & World Report has ranked us number one on the East Coast and number three in the nation for student diversity.... here we encourage you to explore your multicultural heritage....
>
> Wellesley prepares women who truly want to make a difference in the world. We strive to create a model of global awareness that will enable women to be leaders in this new millennium, and we seek women who can advance this goal.
>
> Diversity at Wellesley encompasses not only ethnic origins, but also cultural, religious, political, economic, and social backgrounds.

Smith College is slightly more circumspect. In its viewbook, Smith attempts to dampen the contradiction by limiting its commitment to *cultural* diversity:

> You've probably noticed that many colleges are talking about multiculturalism. We want you to know that Smith College, a recognized leader in liberal arts education for women, has made a strong commitment to cultural diversity in its community.

Bryn Mawr College, more circumspect still, puts a page in its viewbook between its *diversity* statement and its justification for single-sex education.

None of these or any other women's colleges that I have found seem to feel any need to reconcile the two positions. Perhaps they take it as self-evident that "diversity" is a code word for *ethnic and cultural diversity,* and that prospective students will go along with the idea that they can reap the rich benefits of exposure to *diversity* in general without having to deal with the particular *diversity* of having opposite-sex classmates.

To avow the ideal of admitting *diverse* classes of students and simultaneously to reject, for purposes of admission, one of the most basic forms of actual human diversity is, on its face, hypocritical. No doubt there are other ways to frame the matter, but I take the hypocrisy as central. Even if they didn't avow the *diversity* doctrine, single-sex colleges in America today would be in an ethically doubtful position. But to espouse *diversity* and still exclude students on the basis of sex reveals a kind of deep confusion of guiding principles.

Discrimination

The word "discrimination," as we have noted, has an oddly double character. Earnestly denouncing an unjust act of favoritism or prejudice, one person decries *discrimination,* while across the room someone else coolly praises a colleague for good taste, informed judgment and connoisseurship as evidence of—what else?—her fine sense of *discrimination.* In one word, we epitomize the worst of ignorance and moral obtuseness, and the best of acute perception and disciplined understanding. We discriminate, in either sense, by drawing distinctions. The real questions are whether the distinctions are well founded, fair, and applied to good purpose.

Women's colleges plainly discriminate against men, but in which sense of the word? Is the exclusion of men ethically justified? Or is it, despite layers of rationalization, really founded on nothing better than prejudice?

These are not merely rhetorical questions. I can well imagine that the exclusion of men (or women) from a particular college could be ethically, as well as educationally, justifiable. As it happens, the elite women's colleges I have cited do not offer much in the way of credible ethical explanations for their exclusion of men. Moreover, their current infatuation with *diversity* would probably make them recoil from the best justification for single-sex education.

The strongest argument for single-sex colleges is that some forms of diversity can impede learning for some students. Education generally gains an important benefit not from the social diversity of the students who study together, but from their homogeneity. Perhaps by the sheer act of eliminating one dimension of human variability, a women's college fosters a sense of group identity that promotes intellectual development. The idea has at least some anthropological warrant in the vast number of human societies in which, after childhood, boys and girls are trained and initiated in single-sex groups.

Be that as it may, all colleges tend to wear down the initial differences among students so that something like college-specific intellectual habits and social attitudes begin to emerge. Different colleges even seem to foster their own distinct senses of humor. Alumni of a college not infrequently recognize each other even if they never did while students, and even if they are of different generations. The homogeneity that *results* from a shared undergraduate education might be a clue that homogeneity itself helps the members of a community focus on the task at hand.

I hasten to add that were this speculation borne out, it would not justify policies of excluding students on the basis of *arbitrary* social characteristics. Nor would it warrant the de facto segregation that exists within many colleges. The moral imperative of inclusion ought to override such shortcuts. But again, the differences between the sexes are not, or not entirely, arbitrary, and this might be the ethical ledge on which women's colleges could take a stand.

Marketing Diversity

The Wellesley, Smith and Bryn Mawr College viewbooks I refer to above are sales brochures aimed primarily at a market of seventeen-year-olds. A viewbook by no means represents a college's deepest ruminations about its purposes and such publications seldom notice, let alone attempt to reconcile, the inner conflicts of a college. They are best read as an evocation of the romance of attending a college. Wellesley, Smith and Bryn Mawr are in no way exceptional in presenting *diversity* as part of their romance. The marketing of diversity in college brochures is usually aimed more at white students than at non-whites. The word "diversity" may show up in college appeals to "students of color" too, but nearly always in a manner that peculiarly inverts its meaning, emphasizing not the romance of mingling with those who are genuinely different from oneself, but the security of finding oneself in the company of one's own kind.

When *diversity* is sold to primarily white American teenagers, it is presented in language that evokes an escape from the social narrowness of their high school years. To these students, *diversity* promises an encounter with the larger world in its unprogrammed and nonconforming variety. It is a horizon beyond the typically enormous pressures on the majority of students in American high schools to "fit in" and the typical cultural obtuseness of most of their teachers. To students raised on multiculturalism's peculiarly flattened view of human difference, the chance to encounter genuine difference is thrilling.

The *diversity* pitch aimed at "students of color"—primarily African-American teenagers—is very different. Typically it is longer and far more detailed, and seems to assume that a student of color is insecure about his or her intellectual abilities and skeptical at the prospect of committing him- or herself to a community with a dominant white majority and a reputation for fierce academic competition.

The *diversity* message to these students is one of reassurance. It says, in effect, "You will be welcome; your cultural background will be respected; and the college will provide lots of opportunities for you to participate in the mainstream of campus life—or, if you wish, you may opt out of participation in majority-dominated activities. That's OK with us too. In fact, we have arranged a whole separate curriculum of ethnic studies, should you prefer to minimize intellectual involvement with the larger community." A prominent aspect of these appeals is the patronizing promise to provide *extra* assistance to the minority student to meet the standards and expectations of the college.

In its viewbook, Smith College, for example, assures prospective students that:

> Tremendous importance is placed on the interests and needs of all students of color—African American, Asian Pacific American, Latina, Native American, and multiracial—beginning with their orientation as first-year students.

What exactly are these special "needs" of students of color? The brochure does not say, but it does offer somewhat illuminating comments from alumnae and students:

> "It's not always easy" said alumna Monique King in her senior year at Smith. "For every battle you face at Smith, whether it's because you are from a low income background, or your high school education was different or you are in the minority as a women [*sic*] of color on campus, I say, 'You will get through it. And you'll realize the resource.' Smith is what you make it. You make it work for you."

Another alumna, Christine Hanna, praises the student leaders who helped her adjust to Smith: "We were women of color on a fairly white campus and they told us, 'We are here for you.'" And a third, Aisha Domingue, explains that she was "a really quiet shy person," who blossomed at Smith to lead "protests against the World Bank/International Monetary Fund," and to become "a member of the Lesbian Gay Bisexual Transgender Alliance and Smith's rugby team (until she broke her wrist)."

These are not random statements from Ms. King, Ms. Hanna and Ms. Domingue, but quotations that have been carefully culled and selected by Smith College's professional admissions staff with the hope of making a positive impression on a particular audience. They seem entirely aimed at assuaging the prospective student's fears, and entirely silent on the benefits of studying in a *diverse* community. Diversity thus turns out to have a double life in these brochures. On the one hand, it offers to majority white students an enriching encounter with the Other, and on the other hand, it offers a guarantee of sanctuary and special treatment to (some) "students of color."

Smith College, like many other colleges and universities, is pitching the idea that students will encounter real diversity in their college community. That pitch is essentially a con. Like most cons, it has just enough reality to draw people in. Most American colleges and universities *do* have more human variety than most high schools, which, after all, possess no more diversity than the local communities they serve. But the *diversity* promised by colleges and universities is the managed and artificial variety of the aviary or the aquarium, not the diversity of the world as such. The students are lured with the promise of transforming encounters with the steep diversity outside their previous experience, but what the college actually offers is a pleasant and not very challenging simulacrum of diversity.

The students who attend, in response to the sly promise that the college places "tremendous importance" on "the interests and needs of all students of color," face a different con: the choice between accepting the comforts of the "we-are-here-for-you" multicultural niche, or the far more arduous task of attending college to acquire an education and not just an identity.

Colleges are complex institutions that serve multiple purposes, but beneath every legitimate purpose in higher education ought to be a profound commitment to the pursuit of truth. Colleges and universities that wed themselves to the self-serving lie of promising real but delivering fake diversity deserve to be excoriated. That lie breeds other lies. It tempts colleges and universities to betray their admissions standards and to lie and insist they haven't. It gives the public relations staff a rationale for publishing staged or phony pictures of racial and ethnic harmony. It underlies corrupt choices about grades, courses, faculty appointments and whole academic programs, which, in turn, perpetuate a deeper dishonesty throughout society.

This large hypocrisy eats away at the foundations of American higher education. Clearly one answer would be to hold colleges and universities to the spirit of *real* diversity. If diversity is such a good thing, why not, as at least part of the effort to create a diverse institution, eliminate artificial barriers that exclude some categories of intellectually able and otherwise qualified people? In that light, why shouldn't Smith and the other women's colleges that extol diversity go coed?

Shaker Villages

I have already offered what I think is the single best reason for allowing some single-sex colleges to remain. The pursuit of diversity has been turned into an idol, the worship of which has blinded many to the advantages for some students of studying in a socially homogeneous setting. A small number of single-sex colleges can provide that sort of education without meaningful harm to those they exclude.

But I can also think of some other reasons why it might be better public policy to leave these quaint institutions alone. Like Shaker Villages, they are museums to an odd cultural flowering that will not come again; and there is some benefit to maintaining a kind of diversity among the 3,800 and some colleges in the United States. As one former teacher at a women's college put it, "I think maximizing the educational options that students have is far more valuable than pushing all institutions to be equally diverse."

What other circumstances might call forth a need for women's colleges? Perhaps neuro-anatomists will one day discover brain-specific differences between the sexes that can be best accommodated by teaching men and women in separate classrooms. I am skeptical about this possibility. There are indeed some real differences between women's and men's brains, but none that would prompt a pedagogy of sexual separation. Still, one doesn't know. We are a rich enough society to maintain Wellesley College just in case.

A stronger argument is that private colleges should be allowed, within limits, to experiment even to the extent of practicing certain kinds of systematic unfairness. I would not extend this principle of tolerating discrimination to race or ethnicity, but exclusions based on sex have a marginally better warrant. Intellectual differences attributed to "race" or "ethnicity" (as distinct from culture) are spurious; but differences between men and women are written deeply into our biology. In any case, we are better off as a society tolerating the incidental harm of discrimination at women's colleges than inviting the greater harm of further government edicts interfering with academic autonomy.

These defenses of women's colleges probably will not please their presidents. Their own rationalizations for excluding men take a rather different form.

Relics

Until fairly recently, the United States had hundreds of single-sex colleges and universities. Now almost all of the exclusively male colleges and universities have either voluntarily or by legal intervention admitted women. One of the last all-male colleges, Virginia Military Institute, was forced by legal duress to begin admitting women in 1997. To my knowledge, the only remaining male college of any prominence is historically black Morehouse College in Atlanta, which is closely tied to its all-female sister college, Spellman.

Large numbers of colleges and universities that formerly admitted only females have also gone coed or closed their doors, but some single-sex women's colleges such as Bryn Mawr, Wellesley, Smith and Mount Holyoke are thriving. If we ask why these colleges exist, we have to consider two kinds of answer: their actual historical origins and their current justifications.

We can make short work of the former. All of the major women's colleges were founded at a time when women had limited educational opportunities elsewhere. The Ivy League universities were exclusively male, as were most good liberal arts colleges. The women's colleges opened up possibilities for a top-notch education to an underprivileged category of student.

By the mid-1970s, women had a broad range of educational opportunities. Every Ivy League university and elite liberal arts college had become coeducational. The idea that smart, ambitious, qualified women could not get access to the best colleges and universities ceased to have any validity. The women's colleges then faced a choice. Some, like Vassar College, chose to redefine themselves as coeducational. Others sought a new rationale for remaining single-sex and found it by dusting off an old idea that women get a better education and a better start in adult life in a women's college.

Lisa Unico, professor of chemistry at Edinboro University of Pennsylvania, writes that "Women's colleges are like horseshoe crabs, relics of the past that have yet to go extinct." She notes that their survival thus far seems unrelated to any "valuable adaptation," but that, more likely, "the environment has changed from favoring them to tolerating them."

That assessment may be too gentle. In a recent article, James O'Neill observes: "In 1960, there were close to 300 women's colleges. Today, there are fewer than 65." O'Neill also notes that fewer than "5 percent of college-bound high school women even consider a women's college," and that every few months,

> another women's college drops out of the business, as Vermont's Trinity College did in 2000; or merges with a larger coed school, as New York's Marymount College did with Fordham University [in 2001]; or decides to admit men—which Chestnut Hill [College, near Philadelphia] will do, starting in 2003.

As the original reason for women's colleges vanished, they developed new claims, the most common of which is that (some?) young women are better able to develop intellectually in an environment in which they do not need to compete with males for the attention of their teachers. The expressions of this rationale, however, can be surprisingly coy.

Wellesley College's viewbook, for example, offers this:

> **An Education for Women**
> Wellesley provides its students with a first-rate education—one of the best in the country. What does it mean to attend a women's college? It means that our graduates go out into their communities, their professions, and their ongoing academic careers with the inspiration to succeed. At Wellesley, you'll feel uninhibited in the classroom, supported and encouraged by both professors and peers, and challenged to always achieve more than you thought possible.

Bryn Mawr College, by contrast, is long and argumentative:

> **Why Choose a Women's College?**
> Studies have repeatedly found that women who attend women's colleges

- Have more opportunities on campus to hold leadership positions and are able to see women functioning in top jobs.

- Report greater satisfaction than their coed counterparts with their college experience by almost all measures—academically, developmentally and personally.

- Participate more fully in and out of class.

- Develop measurably higher levels of self-esteem than other achieving women at coed institutions.

Imagine yourself surrounded by hundreds of intelligent women—fascinating, curious, diverse, intellectually passionate, independent, engaged, supportive and admirable women. It's a rare experience, and it can change your life to be one of them.

That's why Bryn Mawr College has steadfastly maintained its primary commitment to women's education and reserves its undergraduate program for women, although it welcomes the contributions of men to its life inside and outside the classroom.

And it goes on. Bryn Mawr College also cites successful graduates and percentages of degrees awarded in the sciences:

- Compared to women nationwide, a Bryn Mawr graduate is twice as likely to earn a degree in biology, eight times as likely to earn a degree in mathematics, 10 times as likely to earn a degree in chemistry and 30 times as likely to earn a degree in physics. In fact, the sheer number of women majoring in physics at Bryn Mawr is surpassed only by the number at MIT.

And it concludes: "Women's colleges believe in women, and their graduates, grounded in that confidence, have achieved greatness in every field of endeavor."

Smith College takes a more hard-sell approach, asking prospective freshmen, "Why Choose a Women's College?" and then answering:

A women's college is a special place. It's a place where young women like you can get the most from a college that puts your intellectual development first.

At a women's college, you'll see what it's like for women to be strong, smart, bold and talented thinkers and leaders. If you want to attend a college where women get all the attention they need as well as academic challenge and bountiful feedback, then Smith College may be the place for you.

The case for a superior women's college like Smith is really amazingly simple: it's where women come first and do best.

In these statements, Wellesley, Bryn Mawr and Smith do not assert a view of men as inferior or unworthy. The official rationales for women's-only education are, in that sense, not prejudicial. But are the official rationales all there is to it?

In the case of formerly all-male colleges, when it has come to litigation, the courts proved highly unsympathetic to accepting the colleges' own explanations of why they preferred to remain single-sex. The claim that some men, like some women, are better able to develop in a single-sex environment was rejected as mere camouflage for an ultimately unjustifiable exclusion of women. How is the women's college case any different?

The presence on the campuses of many women's colleges of students and faculty members who are deeply misandric complicates the problem. Hostility toward and even hatred of men in general is openly expressed and accepted as a legitimate *political* position. Thus the official line (Wellesley's "You'll feel uninhibited"; Bryn Mawr's "It can change your life"; Smith's "Women get all the attention they need") masks a social system that tolerates and perhaps even fosters prejudice.

This adds up to a weak case for elite women's colleges. They unfairly discriminate against men; offer muddled rationalizations for that discrimination; entangle themselves in the destructive ideology of multiculturalism; and exaggerate their benefits to women.

One reply might be: so what? The unfairness of excluding men isn't much compared with the unfairness of excluding someone on the basis of race. Racial exclusions are deservedly in a category of odiousness all their own. Exclusions on the basis of sex deserve skeptical scrutiny, not moral opprobrium. A college probably commits folly in choosing to remain single-sex without a morally and educationally compelling reason, but it is the sort of folly that we should allow, the way we allow people to praise the literary merits of Maya Angelou.

Another sort of answer comes to mind if we look beyond Smith, Wellesley, Bryn Mawr and the other elite women's colleges to the more academically modest versions of this phenomenon. Professor Unico, whom I cited above, taught for several years at Notre Dame College (NDC) of Ohio when it admitted only women students. She paints a portrait of an institution that probably could pass ethical muster for its exclusion of men. NDC was a small Catholic college that served students of modest intellectual talent and often even more modest financial means. Not only were there no male students, but there were few male faculty or staff members. This Catholic college interestingly attracted Arab and Persian Muslim students "who attended, knowing they would be required to take nine credits of theology, because they and their families were comfortable with the almost exclusively female environment."

As Professor Unico recalls it, NDC also attracted "ultra-Orthodox Jewish students" who "probably made up five percent of the student body." The Muslim and Jewish students met on some common ground: "The young Jewish women would compare notes with the young Muslims about the heroic efforts their families were making to find them 'suitable' husbands." NDC was diverse in other ways too. About 35 percent of the students were African-American, "most of whom were Baptist or AME." Unico adds, "There were lots of Hispanic women too." A third of the students came from "wealthy suburbs," and a third from families who lived "below the poverty line."

Professor Unico, who is skeptical about the probity of college viewbooks, says that NDC didn't much resemble its official image as "a hip and tony place." Instead, it was a place where

> young women who were morbidly obese could fight their demons without having to face young men ... a place where my yearly goal was placing one BS-chemist and welfare mom in a job that moved her kid(s) squarely into the middle class; a place that turned out more female, black and Hispanic chemists than any other school in the state—including the historically black ones ... a safe place to do the growing up that had to be done before they had any prayer of making it in the real world; a place where no matter how darling you were, or how coyly you could bat your eyes, you still had to pick up a wrench and adjust the high pressure liquid chromograph yourself.

And it was a place that began admitting male students in January 2001.

Jewelry

I attended a single-sex college and took advantage of the dorm exchange policy to live for two semesters at Bryn Mawr College. I lamented when Haverford College decided to go coed, and have long had a quiet regard for the attractions of single-sex colleges, if not single-sex education. Increasingly, I find it difficult to hold the thread of these convictions and affections together. The purposive *exclusion* of women or men from a college must have a strong justification to overcome the force of the principle that students should be admitted to college on the basis of individual merit, achievement, promise and aspiration. But the strongest case in favor of single-sex education arises from the apparent educational advantages of having a socially homogenous cohort of students—a premise impossible for the women's colleges to embrace as long as they are yoked to *diversity* as the greatest academic good. A single-sex college pursues the *principle* of diversity at the cost of its own coherence.

The *Crest Jewel of Discrimination* turns out to be a sacred Sanskrit text in Advita Vedanta Hinduism that teaches that liberation (*moksha*) can be achieved only through a series of steps beginning with "the discrimination between the eternal and the transient." Passing by the leaf-cluttered lawn and sanctuary for local *Rodentia* on my way to and from the office each day, I am without doubt on the transient side of the equation. So, I suspect, are women's colleges.

TWELVE

MULTITUDES

Parentheses

One of the most quoted bits of Walt Whitman's *Song of Myself* is his parenthetical dismissal of small-mindedness:

> Do I contradict myself?
> Very well then I contradict myself,
> (I am large, I contain multitudes).

The vision of America as large enough to contain robust disagreement, contradictory aspirations and multitudes of ideas as well as multitudes of people still speaks to us today, although perhaps not as loudly and clearly as it once did.

The exhilarating sense of unboundedness to which Whitman gave voice (between the coasts of left and right parentheses) now strikes many as arrogant, and our collective feeling for our political liberties is beset with doubts. We now frequently wonder whether it is proper to be proud of our freedom when so many of our countrymen labored so long in slavery. We now look with some misgiving on the great expanse of the American landscape, mindful of the native peoples who were killed, uprooted or dispossessed.

Where once we told stories of heroic conquest, we now listen with respect to those who castigate our nation's builders for their harsh treatment of the people already here. And where once we saw the history of the nation as an ascent to a "more perfect union," today we are more likely to tell ourselves a story of powerful groups who continually preyed on the weaker. Many Americans have come to think of their nation as ceding rights to the disprivileged only under duress. America according to this new vision is a place where the multitudes were poor, weak and oppressed, and where their best and sometimes only hope of improving their circumstances was through acts of collective resistance.

These doubts are not a random collection of thoughts that have coincidentally arrived in the national consciousness at the same moment. They are rather a reflection of an ideology that has been brewing for generations. The historical account of America as a system of oppression is rooted in the work of Marxist historians and social scientists and their political supporters on the Left, who first began to assemble it toward the end of the nineteenth century. The fortunes of radical politics in the United States waxed and waned over the decades, but never achieved a grip on the popular imagination. Or, never until the 1980s.

For it was then that the Left at last found a combination of political leverage, economic opportunity and cultural advantage to institutionalize much of its anti-American program. *Diversity* was the key to that three-part success.

Politics and Economics

Over the course of this book, I've presented my account of how this happened, but let me compress it to two paragraphs. President Johnson inaugurated legalized racial preferences in 1965, but "affirmative action" met increasing popular resistance and legal challenges, culminating in the Supreme Court's split decision in the 1978 *Bakke* case. The outcome of that case included a one-man opinion drafted by Justice Powell in which he declared that race preferences in college admissions are unconstitutional under most circumstances, but that the minority racial status of an applicant could be considered as "a plus factor" if the college was seeking to increase its intellectual "diversity." Powell's *diversity* argument, though eccentric, connected to some cultural currents in leftist politics, in American churches and among education theorists. (Perhaps it connected as well with the strain of American pragmatism extending back through John Dewey to William James, in which "pluralism" was rated as among the highest educational values.) In any case, within a few years of the *Bakke* case, most colleges and universities relabeled their racial preferences in admissions as programs intended to enhance *diversity.*

The *diversity* movement grew quietly until it burst into prominence in 1987. That year, the Hudson Institute issued its *Workforce 2000* report, which provided the business world with a demographic excuse to switch from affirmative action rationales for ethnic preferences in hiring and promotion, to *diversity* preferences—said to be prudent planning for the future. Higher education and the business sector thus discovered common cause: in order to have the ethnically diverse workers that business would need, universities would have to admit and graduate more minority students, even at the cost of lowering admission standards. The Business–Higher Education Forum's January 2002 report, *Investing in People,* is a late reverberation of the alliance that has made *diversity* a pivotal idea in American life. In the meantime, the ideology of *diversity* has continued to shape much of American culture, including religion, the arts and personal consumption.

Culture

The cultural advantage that the Left acquired in the 1980s was initially driven by the Left's success in staffing the nation's schools and colleges. Roger Kimball's image of "tenured radicals" ascending to power is overstated, but not by much. Among the ranks of teachers and faculty members there were relatively few self-styled radicals, but there were and are large numbers of people who accept the spirit and much of the letter of the radical critique of American society. With schools and colleges taught by people who saw American history mainly in terms of injustice succeeding injustice, interrupted only by popular struggles for rights, the common vision of American society among students, and eventually the nation at large, was bound to shift. It did.

But the *diversity* movement was far more than disaffected teachers and faculty members successfully selling to their students what Ambassador Jeane Kirkpatrick once called the "Blame America First" doctrine. It was also a message of spiritual goodness and artistic liberation. *Diversity* connected with the wooly relativism—the Church of I-Tolerate-Differences—that had been evolving in the mainline Christian denominations since the late sixties. Figures such as Reverend Coffin had bridged Christianity, Eastern mysticism and the self-help movement, and a large body of church-shopping spiritual consumers had grown up negligent of religious authority but hungry to sample many different forms of "authenticity."

In the arts, diversity was a call to recognize that each person could be an authentic interpreter of his own people, and that a people could *only* be interpreted by one of its own. Modernism had left art with a paucity of subjects, and the theme of my-life-as-an-exemplar-of-my-oppressed-group beckoned to many as an improvement over my-life-as-an-existential-cipher. And the art world, already attuned to narcissistic individualism, proved ready to embrace the new forms of identity politics.

Cultural change is sometimes a matter of simply overwhelming the opposition. By the late 1980s, advocates of *diversity* dominated virtually all the key cultural institutions: colleges and universities, churches, arts organizations, museums, large foundations, the press, book publishers and popular entertainment. The coordinated resistance was confined to a few small organizations such as the National Association of Scholars, some conservative churches and a handful of journals.

With the election of Bill Clinton in 1992, *diversity* had the potential to become the undisputed cultural framework for American society. But it didn't happen. Instead, we face a more perplexing situation, in which *diversity* is clearly a dominating ideology but not a completely dominant one. Powerful institutions promote it, but large numbers of people resist, and because the *diversity* ideology built its mansion on the shaky sand of Powell's *Bakke* opinion, the whole edifice shakes at the prospect that the U.S. Supreme Court will overrule the *diversity* rationale. That might happen soon, and if it does happen, we will be a nation that will have to reconsider many seemingly settled ideas.

Demography and Choice

This book, which offers a biography of sorts of the concept of *diversity,* might rightly end with a description of the funeral. I wish I could oblige, but diversity is still among the quick. *Diversity* may not pass away at all. History has no settled script; we can make guesses and offer our views of what we would like to happen. But we live now, as we do in every historical moment, with choices.

We can indeed foresee some of the demographic realities ahead, because they literally have already been born. The proportion of the adult working population made up of members of "minority" groups will continue to grow in a fairly predictable way. But is "demography" destiny? The assertion "Demography is destiny," I think, mistakes the power of social science. Demography supplies some important facts, but it is up to us what to do with those facts. The ethnic composition of America will indeed change, but that need not mean that we govern ourselves from here on out as a collection of ethnic-based and other factions engaged in identity politics.

If such is our fate, it will be because we choose it over alternatives. In particular, it will mean that we choose to elevate the principle of *diversity* over the much older principles of *equality* and *liberty.* I hope that will not happen, but it is a distinct possibility. Should it happen, we should not expect it to take the form of the absolute supremacy of *diversity* over *equality* and *liberty.* We are, as Walt Whitman said, large, and we contain our contradictions as well as our multitudes. *Diversity* itself can pose as a form of equality, at least in imagining an ideal of equalized groups.

The historian John Higham observed in 1992 that despite the fresh triumph of the multicultural movement in America, "the heritage of equality lives on amid the contradictions of the multicultural movement." Higham was optimistic:

> Although truncated and fragmented, this heritage awaits a wider understanding and employment. If multiculturalism can shake off a fixation on diversity, autonomy, and otherness, the vision that American universalism sustained and enlarged through two centuries can be renewed.

Today, there are some tentative indications that Higham may have been partially right. The heritage of equality and the vision of American universalism are showing signs of life.

Diversity After 9-11

One issue is the change in national mood following the September 11 terrorist attacks. That mood may shift and shift again before this page sits open before a single reader, and I aim therefore to register only the passing moment in April 2002, not the deeper shifts, if any, in American attitudes toward national identity. At the moment, however, *diversity* appears to have tumbled in national esteem.

Those who were already critical of the *diversity* movement have sensed the weakness and seized their moment. Terry Eastland, for example, writing in *Commentary*, March 2002, quotes from Steven Emerson's new book, *American Jihad: The Terrorists Living Among Us:*

> "We discovered," he writes, that "international terrorist organizations of all sorts had set up shop here in America. They often took advantage of religious, civic, or charitable organizations"—fooling the public, police, and "naïve leaders of religious or educational institutions," who sponsored such groups in the name of "multiculturalism" or "diversity."

The idea that the *diversity* movement contributed to the vulnerability of the United States to terrorist attack is widely discussed among American conservatives. Stanley Kurtz recently offered one of the most cogent formulations:

> The problem for the Left is that Sept. 11 really may have changed everything—that a near-constant state of mobilization against terror may permanently cripple the politics of multiculturalism at home and anti-globalization abroad.

And the theme is propagating. Even as I sat down to write this, I received a message from a prominent conservative friend who mentions that she is currently working on a piece about "multicultural higher education's negative impact on national security."

Diversity's advocates were quick to sense the danger. As early as September 23, Gregory Rodriguez, senior fellow at the liberal New America Foundation, published an opinion essay in the *New York Times* in which he referred to the "hyphenated identities" of members of ethnic groups and worried that

> after the attacks, not only is the drive for unity bound to tilt the nation's ethnic balance back in favor of the American side of the hyphen, it could permanently undermine the more extreme forms of multiculturalism. In the worst-case scenario, it could also dampen the nation's recent appreciation of diversity.

In fact, it is hard to detect any real dampening of that appreciation. The flood of pro-diversity propaganda continued unabated and was perhaps even swelled by the many writers who feared that "racial profiling" aimed at Arabs and Muslims would undo America's multiculturalist spirit.

In November 2001, the Nellie Mae Education Foundation issued *Diversity Among Equals: The State of Affirmative Admissions in New England,* a study purporting to show "there is no significant evidence that New England colleges and universities have reduced standards to admit greater numbers of minority students." The same month also brought a note from Vartan Gregorian, president of the Carnegie Corporation of New York, enclosing a copy of *Muslims in America: Identity, Diversity and the Challenge of Understanding.* Dr. Gregorian, former president of Brown University and one of the leading figures in American higher education, hoped the "Carnegie Challenge Paper" would contribute to "a balanced and informed understanding" of American Muslims and "provide the spark for ongoing conversation." The author of the report, Sam Afridi, a former speechwriter for President Clinton, speaks of "the terror of September 11 and its aftermath" presenting "unique challenges and opportunities for Islam in America." But the opportunity he seizes is to recite the standard *diversity* credo:

> The United States offers a unique laboratory for [cross-cultural] understanding. The quest for greater awareness and knowledge can also help our country advance its mission to set an example for the rest of the world by moving beyond tolerance towards accepting and even celebrating racial, ethnic or religious differences.

On December 7, 2001, I heard Professor Gordon Light from Harvard University address the New England Association of Schools and Colleges, speaking, in part, on the constructive way Harvard had responded to students who felt that mere proximity to *diverse* students wasn't fulfilling the promise of diversity. Harvard's solution: a little booklet titled *Reflections on the Individual, Freedom, Diversity, and Community of Harvard College,* which is required reading for entering freshmen and the basis for discussions between students and faculty members. The booklet is an anthology introduced by Afro-American studies professor K. A. Appiah (who subsequently announced his departure for Princeton, as Cornel West did a little later) and includes thoughts by Professor Appiah himself; former Harvard president Neil Rudenstine ("the real fruits of diversity can be harvested if those of us in our universities—and in our larger society—can make the essential imaginative leaps that alone will enable us to 'connect' "); and Professor Martha Nussbaum.

Then January 2002 brought the publication of *Investing in People* by the Business–Higher Education Forum, which formed the subject of part of Chapter 8.

No, *diversity* was not shaken—at least not immediately—by 9-11. If anything, it tempted some of the critics of the campus Left to jump prematurely into the fray. On November 13, 2001, the American Council of Trustees and Alumni (ACTA), founded by Lynne Cheney, issued a thirty-eight-page report, *Defending Civilization: How Our Universities Are Failing America and What Can Be Done About It,* identifying by name some of the Leftist ideologues who since the 9-11 attacks had been engaged in what polite people call "antiwar activism." ACTA was roundly condemned both in the American press and abroad. "Defend Academic Freedom" ran the headline of a paid advertisement in the *London Review of Books,* with the names of a couple of dozen leftist luminaries standing in for "3,000 signatories as of 12/13/01." The multiculturalists relished the opportunity to pose as victims, and ACTA, feeling the absence of public support, beat a hasty retreat.

The Right thus did not seem to gain much purchase against *diversity,* but that was not the whole story. For while groups like ACTA were unable to rouse public anger against the multicultural Left, the Left itself began to split. Figures such as Noam Chomsky, Howard Zinn, Susan Sontag and Edward Said, who were known for their hard-line anti-Americanism, were increasingly isolated from more main-stream liberals who found themselves drawn back to more positive views of America.

Christopher Hitchens, the acerbic British journalist, man of the Left, longtime basher of most things American, and columnist for *Vanity Fair* and the *Nation* (from which he resigned in September 2001), for example, declared that in the aftermath of 9-11, "the ordinary people" of the United States "behaved with distinction." He supported the war against the Taliban, surprised even himself by expressing (very grudging) respect for President Bush's conduct, and heaped scorn on the antiwar, anti-American Left:

> Looking at some of the mind-rotting tripe that comes my way from much of today's left, I get the impression that they go to bed saying: what have I done for Saddam Hussein or good old Slobodan or the Taliban today?
> ... if, as the peaceniks like to moan, more Bin Ladens will spring up to take his place, I can offer this assurance: should that be the case, there are many many more who will also spring up to kill him all over again. And there are more of us and we are both smarter and nicer, as well as surprisingly insistent that our culture demands respect, too.

Moreover, Hitchens came to this defense of America immediately after the 9-11 attack. On September 16, he wrote:

> The single most impressive fact about the past few days has been the general refusal to adopt an ugly or chauvinistic attitude towards America's most recent and most conspicuous immigrants: the Middle Eastern ones. The response of public opinion has been uniformly grown-up and considerate. As if by unspoken agreement, everyone seems to know that any outrage to multiculturalism and community would be an act of complicity with the assassins.

Thus while some on the Left fretted that the American people would respond to the attack with assaults on Arab-Americans and a surge of prejudice, Hitchens correctly observed that Americans simply were not headed in that direction.

The split between the Chomsky-Zinn-Sontag-Said Left and liberals who rediscovered their admiration for America reverberated in the academy. David Graham, the Du Bois Professor of Afro-American

Studies at the University of Massachusetts, for example, published a screed in November 2001 that begins:

> This "war against terrorism" is in fact an open declaration of war against the peoples of the developing world; initially the peoples of the Middle East and Africa, and ultimately the peoples of South and Central America and the Caribbean, all Asia, the South Pacific and the islands of the Seas—some four-fifths of humanity.
>
> It is a desperate attempt to meet and overcome this developing world's growing challenge to the continuation of four centuries of European and American hegemonic domination, exploitation, suppression, insult and injury by its executors in America and Europe.

But while some faculty members and students fantasized about the West's global hegemony, rehearsed blame-America-first clichés, marched against the war, and expressed nightmarish certainty that American Arabs and Muslims would be attacked, many others reassessed their positions. For example, Elizabeth Cobbs Hoffman, a professor of foreign relations at San Diego State University, exemplified the new tone in a January 13 article:

> The fall of the twin towers shook the twin assumptions of a generation of scholarship: that America's relations with the Third World are essentially wicked and that our country's domestic history can only be understood as a continuing battle over race, class and gender.

Professor Hoffman knows she risks "censure" for stepping out of the mold, but she nonetheless sets out to rebuild "an intellectual bridge between love of country and a sophisticated understanding of the nation's place in the world." And she is careful to make clear that she is no conservative: "I grew up with Che Guevara, Bob Dylan and the Vietnam War. I come from the activist left, and I am proud of that heritage. I remain a liberal." She doesn't want to do anything to "whitewash America's character flaws," but she is concerned that "this generation of historians ... has yet to deliver to students, and to the public, a usable and balanced interpretation of the past." Such a balanced interpretation would include, she says, "an open-minded examination of America's historical willingness to defend freedom."

If scholars like Professor Hoffman prevail in the universities, then perhaps the single-threaded, close-minded, historically false and ideologically driven epoch of *diversity* on campus will indeed begin to fade.

Jihad Johnny

On December 1, 2001, Northern Alliance forces in Afghanistan putting down a rebellion in a prison at Mazar-e-Sharif captured an American citizen who had been fighting for the Taliban. John Walker Lindh was soon a familiar name in the United States: a twenty-year-old from Marin County, California, who had converted to Islam, moved to Yemen, then Pakistan, and then volunteered to serve in Ansar, a group of mostly Arab recruits to Osama bin Laden's pro-Taliban forces. Lindh, as we later learned, had e-mailed his father to defend the Islamic terrorists who attacked the USS *Cole* in Yemen, killing seventeen American servicemen. After his capture, he remained an unrepentant supporter of the Taliban.

Lindh's case touched a nerve among Americans, many of whom looked to the circumstances in which the young man had been raised for an explanation of his decision to turn against his country and assist its enemy. Lindh grew up in a permissive family in a "progressive" California community, and it is in this connection that he comes into the story of *diversity*. Within weeks of his capture, conservative commentators were drawing the connections between the two poles of John Walker Lindh's life: the anomie of a do-your-own-thing upbringing in California and the fanatic commitment of a Taliban fighter at Mazar-e-Sharif.

Shelby Steele, writing in the *Wall Street Journal*, was the first to draw the elements together into a consistent whole. He noted that Lindh's parents had encouraged him to "choose his own spiritual path." But he had to find that path in

> a world where learning is self-referential, where adults are only broadly tolerant. There are no external yes's and no's, or rights and wrongs here, just fashionable relativism.... Traditional American history, culture and religion are without any special authority. Worse, historic racism and sexism may leave these American offerings with less moral authority than foreign options.

Steele went on to examine the loathing of American culture that these views inspire in some young people. The long American hunger for authenticity is, in this context, bent toward the idea that "it would be inauthentic and corrupt for you to embrace your own culture first."

Steele labels this set of attitudes "post '6os cultural liberalism," and says that it gave "every step [of Lindh's journey] toward treason a feel of authenticity and authority." He writes that such cultural liberalism "thrives as subversive, winking, countercultural hipness," and that, within that context, the "myth of the victim-sage" was the guiding light of Lindh's life. Steele does not use the word "diversity," but no matter. What he describes is the *diversity ideology* in its full-blown, white upper-middle-class, suburban incarnation.

A few days after Steele's op-ed article, *Boston Globe* columnist Jeff Jacoby offered an analysis focused less on the Marin County context and more on Lindh's permissive parents:

> Devout practitioners of the self-obsessed nonjudgmentalism for which the Bay Area is renowned, Lindh [the father] and Walker [the mother] appear never to have rebuked their son or criticized his choices. In their world, there were no absolutes, no fixed truths, no mandatory behavior, no thou-shalt-nots.

Jacoby mentions their placid reaction to Lindh's dropping out of his alternative high school and their pride when, after reading the *Autobiography of Malcolm X*, he left the Catholic Church, declared himself a Muslim at age sixteen, and began to wear white robes and a skullcap. Jacoby concludes:

> If [his mother] and Frank Lindh had been less concerned with flaunting their open-mindedness and more concerned with developing their son's moral judgment, he wouldn't be where he is today. His road to treason and jihad didn't begin in Afghanistan. It began in Marin County, with parents who never said "no."

The connection between Marin County and the parents' permissiveness here seems left to the reader to discern, but we can discern it clearly enough. The Lindhs were nominally Catholic, but they actually belonged to the Church of Diversity.

A few days later, a third conservative commentator weighed in on the cultural antecedents to John Walker Lindh's treason. Andrew

Sullivan, writing in the *Sunday Times* (London), presented a powerful essay contrasting the lives of Lindh and Mike Spann, the CIA officer who had interrogated Lindh and had been killed by Lindh's comrades. Sullivan picks up Steele's theme of Lindh's destructive search for "authenticity":

> Named after John Lennon, he had to "imagine his own faith." He dabbled in Buddhism and became enamoured of hip-hop. Like many a liberal white American adolescent, black culture seemed an authentic way to rebel against the society that spawned him.
>
> He tried on many guises, chatting on the internet under a variety of screen names ranging from John Lindh, John Doe and Disciple of the Englober to Hine ECraque, Professor J, Brother Suleyman Al-Mujahid and Mr. Mujahid, among others.

Sometimes Lindh pretended to be black. In Sullivan's analysis, "Radical Islam squared [Lindh's] adolescent circle." He adds, "In liberal enclaves in California, there is no actual right and wrong. There is only judgment (abhorrent) and tolerance (admirable)." The capture of his son by the Northern Alliance didn't seem to change this picture for the father, Frank Lindh, who, as Sullivan notes, said on television, "I don't think John was doing anything wrong," and on another program, "We want to give him a big hug and then a little kick in the butt for not telling us what he was up to."

Frank Lindh's words breathe the human reality into Steele's, Jacoby's and Sullivan's characterizations of John Walker Lindh's upbringing. "Big hug" and "little kick" are the language of an indulgent parent faced with a mischievous child caught in a prank. The complete absence of moral seriousness in the man is astonishing. In another interview, the father, a San Francisco energy lawyer, said of his son, "He is a very sweet person and very devout in a religious sense." On February 14, when John Walker Lindh was in court in Virginia to plead "not guilty" to charges of terrorism, Frank Lindh approached John Spann, the father of murdered CIA officer Mike Spann, and said, "I'm sorry about your son; my son had nothing to do with it. I am sure you understand." John Spann spurned the offered handshake and walked away.

President Bush referred to Lindh in mid-February 2002 as "some misguided Marin County hot-tubber." For Martin County liberals, this was too much. Having endured the condescension of conservative columnists for their moral relativism and the derision of many other Americans for their superficiality, Marin County liberals were at last ready to say that something was not right. To imply a connection between Lindh's alternative lifestyle choice and their household amenities was unfair, and many apparently said so. The *Houston Chronicle* reported that "Residents of the wealthy, liberal enclave north of San Francisco scolded him for smearing their reputation." Steve Kinsey, a Marin County supervisor, opined to the *New York Times* that the president's remark had created "a great sense of pain and bewilderment, a deep prejudice against a progressive community." Bush sent a wry letter to the *Marin Independent Journal,* saying he was "chastened and will never use 'hot tub' and 'Marin County' in the same sentence again."

Some exponents of what might be called the Marin County worldview have defended their position more vigorously. Linda Hirshman, a professor of philosophy and women's studies at Brandeis University, for example, wrote that "right wingers" were trying to blame Lindh's parents and Marin County, "that Sodom and Gomorrah around San Francisco in the pro-Gore state of California," where "people change religions like suits of clothing, and nothing is condemned except judgment and standards." In Hirshman's view, this reveals a double standard among conservatives, who, she said, did not generally blame the parents of Oklahoma City bomber Timothy McVeigh or the Columbine High School killers, Eric Harris and Dylan Klebold. She wrote:

> In fairness, if Democratic-leaning communities like Marin County are responsible for John Walker Lindh, Republican Colorado and patriotic Catholic upstate New York should have a piece of the deaths in Oklahoma City and Littleton.

It is a peculiar conclusion. Indeed, Colorado and upstate New York might deserve a share of the blame for their failure to instill better character in McVeigh, Harris and Klebold, but to reach that conclusion we would have to find a plausible connection between the broader cultural context of their upbringings and their subsequent actions. With John Walker Lindh, the connection seems inescapable; with McVeigh, Harris and Klebold, it seems nebulous. In that sense, Hirshman's call for "fairness" is just a rhetorical flight.

Others, however, have attempted a different kind of defense of Lindh, by attempting to bring his case back to his highly particular circumstances. At sixteen, when Lindh converted to Islam, his parents' marriage broke up and his father moved in with a friend named Bill Jones. Some commentators have suggested that his father's relationship to Jones spurred John Walker Lindh's ardent embrace of Islam. And indeed, in some of the younger Lindh's rantings, he emphasizes Islam's opposition to homosexuality. Sullivan quotes Lindh writing, "It seems quite unusual to have a Muslim convention at a theme park owned by Disney.... Isn't this the same theme park that sponsored 'gay day' this year?" But the particularities of Lindh's life, including his parents' divorce, do not push against the culture of Marin County. Rather, the events seem to flow with the larger narrative.

We are left, I think, with an extreme instance of what can go wrong with *diversity* when it is allowed to become the governing principle of peoples' lives. It is freedom without a sense of purpose; an invitation to set out on a quest for identity without meaningful boundaries. To some, of a serious cast of mind but without serious counsel, it leads to dark extremes. Tolerance without moral clarity is a kind of torpor. *Diversity* creates the problem and then prescribes its own solution: more *diversity*. It leads some to a kind of ethnic fundamentalism, others to the make-believe of "music related lifestyles," and a few to the "authenticity" of religious beliefs to which they have no cultural connection. John Walker Lindh's flight out of torpor was to the other imaginary pole, of fiery commitment. It was his misguided attempt to awake.

Well, perhaps. We really don't know what this young man thought he was doing. I offer this interpretation on a venture. The story of *diversity* has a multitude of characters. Lindh has his place beside Reverend Coffin.

Sweetness

"He is a very sweet person and very devout in a religious sense." Frank Lindh's belief in his son's *sweetness* may be unfathomable. Yet I don't think we quite complete this account of *diversity* without recognizing its unfathomable qualities. One is that *diversity* possesses a kind of sweetness—a sweetness that extends over the hard and often mean things that people do in the name of diversity.

Americans recognize that racism is not sweet, even when racists are acting solicitously. We also recognize that cutting into line isn't sweet; nor bumping people as we pass; nor a thousand other acts of petty rudeness. We are not a society of elaborate manners, but we sense courtesy and its lack. And Americans are alert to what is not sweet in our economic relations: we know when we encounter the hardhearted company or the opportunistic dealer.

Diversity manages somehow to defy all these rules. It can be, by turns, racist, line-jumping, people-bumping, rude, exploitative and conniving—and yet it retains a certain sweetness.

Because of its sweetness, even if the political movement fades, *diversity* will linger a long time in our attitudes and tastes. But where does this sense of diversity as something intrinsically nice come from? In one sense, it is rooted in the teaching of *diversity*'s key ideas and images to young children. The magical images of rainbows, crayon boxes and quilts are part of the emotional cathexis that warms us to the ideas that we derive our basic identity from the groups into which we were born; that we should celebrate group differences; and, eventually, that American history is a story of dominant whites oppressing other groups. In any case, the schooling in these views begins with very young children, and it has been kept up for a generation. It seems unlikely that people raised on this diet will lose the taste, although they may, like the punks and goths we glanced at in Chapter 10, invert it, or, like John Walker Lindh, attempt to starve it into submission.

Diversity advocates have also developed a large repertoire of symbols, catchphrases, images and cute consumer goods that reinforce its niceness. It would take a considerable reserve of bile to find anything offensive, for example, in the Pleasant Company's multiethnic American Girl doll collection, and an almost pathological meanness to turn against the cheerful goodwill evident in many other *diversity* appeals to children.

An eighth grader, a girl who lives in the Roxbury section of Boston, recently sent a thank-you note to the president of Boston University for his donation to a school charity. The note was neatly typed on a piece of stationery with an eye-catching border of thirty smiling people of diverse ages, sexes, colors and shapes—and a tiny yellow picnic basket, soccer ball and dog. The child's stationery, I suppose, is a bit of identity politics framing another bit of identity politics. College presidents choose their charities carefully, and eighth graders get some help and encouragement in writing replies. But the sweetness is real, and it does not end with children's gestures.

At a deeper level, the sweetness of *diversity* may be rooted in the sense of liberty it affords—not liberty in the sense of freedom to strive, but liberty from the toils of some kinds of complexity and adult cares. *Diversity* invites us to let ourselves be. Nonjudgment is sweet. In a stroke it liberates us from the hard work of judging moral and political perplexities and assures us that, in avoiding that work, we are really living up to a higher principle. Imagining a world in which oppression has been banished is sweet, and to realize that such a world can be brought about by the essentially passive acceptance of quotas and preferences makes it sweeter still. *Diversity* offers a sweeter utopian dream than the old visions of worker struggles. The divers-utopia can be achieved seemingly in smiling relaxation; it can come without conflict; it can come without force.

Of course, this sweet dream of life without conflict is not *diversity*'s only image of the world. In some contexts, *diversity* can be pugnacious, assertive, eager for conflict. But these realities do not intrude on the dream or sour it.

And *diversity*'s sweetness extends into personal satisfactions. It invites us to take pleasure in mere identity, as though a race, an ethnicity, a gender, a sexual preference or a disability were in itself a source of contentment. To find contentment merely in labeling oneself is to set the bar low—perhaps to lay it flat on the ground. But those who feel a sense of achievement in declaring their identities can savor the sweetness of a self who has banished personal inadequacy and ethnic shame for the delights of "authenticity." And the sweetness of diversity lies at last in the idea that no matter what work you do, or don't do, the world owes you respect for who you are.

Caliban

The sweetness of *diversity* may lie in its power to regress us to the state of infants, but it is best to remember that *diversity*'s *enfants* are sometimes of the *terrible* variety. Licensed to do whatever feels authentic, they can act as destructively as Caliban, the character Shakespeare invented in *The Tempest* to represent the wild man of the New World. Caliban's freedom has been curtailed by Prospero, who has made him obey. (Prospero speaks of Caliban: "This thing of darkness I / Acknowledge mine.") But when opportunity arises to escape, Caliban joins with the "drunken butler," Stephano, to plot the overthrow of Prospero. Caliban is delighted:

> Caliban: 'Ban, 'Ban, Ca-Caliban
> Has a new master. Get a new man!
> Freedom, high day! High day, Freedom!
> Stephano: O brave monster! Lead the way.

Caliban comes to mind partly because the name was cleverly attached to John Walker Lindh (the "California Taliban") soon after his capture. The appellation seems more and more apt as Mr. Lindh continues to win supporters among diversiphiles who are impressed with his raw conviction and sweet (if murderous) sincerity. Shakespeare's Caliban is also an idol of sorts these days in multicultural academe, the new "underdog" hero of *The Tempest*.

In 1976, the literary critic Stephen Greenblatt published an essay, "Learning to Curse," that began Caliban's rehabilitation as a figure of native resistance to European imperialism. Since then, the conceit has grown and it is now difficult to find a college Shakespeare course in which *The Tempest* is taught that does not attempt to salvage Prospero's "poisonous slave" who "never / yields us kind answer." Caliban is multiracial, "got by the devil himself / upon [his] wicked dam," the black witch Sycorax. He is the indigenous human population of the island where Prospero and his daughter, Miranda, were cast up years earlier. Prospero at first treated Caliban kindly ("Strok'st me and made much of me" recalls Caliban), gave him flavored water and taught him how to talk. In turn, Caliban welcomed the newcomers and showed them "the fresh springs, brine-pits, barren place and fertile." But Prospero at length subjects Caliban to servitude and limits his movement ("here you sty me / in this hard rock").

Or maybe not. Prospero remembers a different history. He responds to Caliban's account by calling him a "lying slave," and declaring that he treated Caliban with "human care" and exiled him from Prospero's own house only when Caliban "didst seek to violate / The honor of my child."

Caliban, the indigene—dispossessed of his land by a white European male, who subjects him to harsh labor and stereotypes him as a sexual predator—is cultural *diversity* in all its oppressed innocence and authenticity. We can overlook his plots to have Stephano murder Prospero by knocking "a nail into his head," or battering him with a log, "paunching" him with a stake, or cutting his throat; his wish to burn Prospero's books; and his lascivious eye for Miranda. Caliban is shameless ("Let me lick thy shoe."), craven ("I'll fall flat. / Perchance he will not mind me."), and murderous, but he is also a victim of hierarchy and therefore the man/child for our own time.

His plans having come to nothing, Caliban accepts Prospero's pardon and declares, "I will be wise hereafter, / And seek for grace." But it seems unlikely. All Caliban has really gained from his subjection to Western culture is the ability to speak, a gift which he uses, as Professor Greenblatt noted, to curse his oppressor.

Today, of course, Caliban would be on a different footing altogether. Admitted to an elite college on a full scholarship (mixed-race, single-parent family; great *diversity* essay), he would find a whole Caliban curriculum to choose from.

Vague Diversity

A good friend of mine objects every time I characterize *diversity* as a principle, an idea or a concept. He says, "No, it is just a word." I understand his point. *Diversity* is a word used by so many people in so many vague and contradictory ways that it may be a stretch to raise it to so august a status as principle, idea or concept. Have I dressed a mere rumor in an Attic toga?

Perhaps, but in fact *diversity* **is** a principle, in the same manner that Americans commonly understand freedom and equality as principles. They stretch across almost all the contexts of social life, inhabit our thinking about who we are as individuals, and give us grounds for what we can and cannot expect of others. *Diversity* is that sort of thing too, albeit it is much younger and has not had the benefit of great statesmen, far-thinking philosophers and centuries of common use to develop intellectual depth or practical ruggedness. A principle need not be sublime; it may even be ludicrous.

Likewise, to speak of *diversity* as a concept is to suggest that it has an intellectual shape and history. Is *diversity* so vague as to prevent us from understanding what people mean by it? Is its history so shadowy that it is futile to trace it? *Diversity*, as I've pointed out several times, has no great authors, no profound books, and no body of clearcut analysis that we can turn to in hope of exact definitions. Yet this whole book is testament that the concept of diversity can be teased out and that many of the events in its history can be recovered. In the end, however, I leave the case to be decided by others. Is *diversity* a concept? I say it is misguided, illegitimate and unfortunate, but a concept nonetheless.

And is *diversity* an idea? Why quibble? People have ideas about *diversity*, and though their ideas may not withstand scrutiny in the light of day, it seems a small concession to try to understand their ideas as ideas.

The other word that I have used over and over to characterize *diversity* is ideology. The word is not neutral; rather, it registers my judgment that *diversity* offers a closed loop of thought and experience. Once one enters this loop and accepts the main propositions of *diversity*, it is difficult to see out of it. Like other ideologies, *diversity* seeks to *explain away* rather than to explain inconvenient facts. It invests its positions with emotional commitments and usually attacks the critic rather than answer his criticism. It sets itself up as a way of *viewing* the world in predetermined categories rather than *exploring* the world with the possibility of finding new understanding. *Diversity* is, deep down, static, comfortable and complacently convinced of its own superiority.

Ideologies are always in opposition to something, and *diversity*, despite being by far the dominant worldview within much of American society, persists in seeing itself as an underdog, fighting for the oppressed against the oppressors. That *diversity* itself could be the oppressor is, within that worldview, unthinkable.

Disappearing, Indelible *Diversity*

Diversity is both disappearing and indelible. It is close enough to mere fashion that it might go out of fashion, but it is now so indispensable to American party politics, so rooted in the marketing practices of American business, so overwritten into government regulations, and so tenderly looked after by higher education that it cannot simply vanish.

As I finish this book—July 24, 2002—the *diversity* movement looks wobblier than it has at any time since Justice Powell's opinion elevated it from a countercultural conceit to a Supreme Court dictum. The mood of national unity in the wake of 9-11 lingers; John Walker Lindh's Caliban trial has ended in his pleading guilty to reduced charges; Ward Connerly's ballot measure, the Racial Privacy Initiative (which would ban the state from collecting racial information), has won the signatures needed to get it on the California ballot in March 2004. The Supreme Court has yet to take the University of Michigan case in which it might refine or overrule *Bakke,* but the odds are strong that it will. Cornel West is decamping in high dudgeon from Harvard for Princeton, but the broader message seems to be that Harvard is finally drawing some limits on how much intellectual silliness it will overlook in the name of Caliban.

But even if all these misfortunes rain on *diversity* at once, *diversity* will be with us for a while. Its legacy is a strange combination of cheerful debauch, aching resentment, fretful demand and cloying sweetness—a great rhetorical swipe at our subjection to old hierarchies that delivers us, unashamed, into a new and more durable bondage.

Even should we as a nation choose to put it behind us, *diversity* will linger in the lives already mortgaged to the notion that we are but members of identity groups, not free people who chart our own lives. *Diversity*'s false promise of authenticity will leave many playing out a large portion of their lives inside its masquerades. We will be left, for a long while still, with the reign of *diversity*'s pasteboard stereotypes.

ACKNOWLEDGMENTS

I am grateful to my editor, Peter Collier, for proposing this book and for his willingness to indulge my departures from the straight and narrow expository path.

I am also grateful to my colleagues in the President's Office at Boston University, Ms. Tammy Egan, Mr. Ivan Bernier, Dr. Chandler Rosenberger, Dr. Craig Klafter, Dr. Nancy Baker, Ms. Joanne Evans and Mrs. Christine Carr, for their thoughtful counsel and generous assistance. I am indebted to Jon Westling, president of Boston University from 1996 to 2002, for his inspiring combination of intellectual courage and curiosity. This book was written while I served as his chief of staff and associate provost.

My thanks to Dr. Stanley Kurtz, Dr. Keith Whitaker and Dr. Edwin Delattre, who generously read and critiqued each chapter of this book as it was drafted. I am deeply appreciative as well for the advice of Dean John Bertherong on "Diverse Gods"; Professor Frederick Lynch on "Identity Business"; and Professor Lisa Unico on "Selective Diversity."

The original manuscript for this book included several other chapters, and I am grateful to Professor Victor Kestenbaum for his help on the philosophical background to diversity; Professor Kosta Steliou for assistance on genetic studies of human diversity; and Mr. William Lukas for his help on current evolutionary theory. Though these topics are not in the index, working through them was an indispensable step in writing this book.

I owe a special debt of gratitude to Chancellor John Silber of Boston University for his critique of an early draft of "Imagined

Diversity." Boston University is one of the few places in American higher education where a book that challenges one of the entrenched academic orthodoxies could be thought through, openly discussed, and written in confidence that it would be judged on the quality of its arguments, evidence and exposition.

The germ of this book was an essay I published on *National Review Online* in May 2001. I am grateful to NRO editor Kathryn Lopez for her encouragement and for her editorial daring.

Notes and References

Chapter 1: Diversity in America

page

3   Martin Luther King Jr., *Letter from Birmingham Jail,* April 16, 1963.

3   Martin Luther King Jr., Nobel Peace Prize Lecture, Oslo, Norway, December 11, 1964.

3   Martin Luther King Jr., *Address at the University of Pittsburgh,* November 2, 1966. I found the attribution in a temporary website, http://www.clpgh.org/exhibit/neighborhoods/oakland/oak_n261 .html, connected to an exhibit mounted by the Carnegie Public Library in Pittsburgh.

3   Martin Luther King Jr., Sermon at Washington National Cathedral, Palm Sunday, 1968.

4   Martin Luther King Jr., quoted in *The Cathedral School,* January 18, 2002, supposedly transcribing the text of a sermon at St. John the Divine Cathedral, May 17, 1965.

4   "Clinton Honors Little Rock Nine: President Recalls Their Sacrifice, Seeks Rededication to Racial Progress," http://www.cnn.com/ ALLPOLITICS/1997/09/25/clinton.littlerock/, September 25, 1977.

5   (Rohit Ananth's prize essay): Danielle Grote, "Local Students Attend March," *The Digital Collegian,* State College, published independently by "students at Penn State." http://www.collegian. psu.edu/archive/2002/01/01-18-02tdc/01-18-02dnews-06.asp.

6   Christopher Columbus, *Four Voyages to the New World: Letters and Selected Document,* ed. R. Major (New York: Corinth Books, 1961).

7   Bartolemé de Las Casas, *In Defense of the Indian.* (1552; DeKalb: Northern Illinois University Press, 1974).

7   Matthew T. Mellon, "Benjamin Franklin's Views on Negro Slavery,"
         Early American View on Negro Slavery (1934; New York: The New
         American Library, 1969), pp. 5–28.

8   James Wilson, "Address on the Slave Trade Clause, December 3,
         1787," Debates in the State Ratifying Conventions: Pennsylvania,
         November 20–December 15, 1787, *The Debate on the Constitution,*
         vol. 1 (New York: The Library of America, 1993), pp. 829–830.

9   Henry Davenport Northrop, ed., *Marvelous Wonders of the Whole
         World: Being an Account of Thrilling Adventures, Famous Sights, Cele-
         brated Voyages, and Renowned Explorations and Discoveries in All Parts
         of the Globe* (Philadelphia: Henry L. Warren & Co., 1886).

9–10   Henry Davenport Northrop, *Indian Horrors or Massacres by the Red
         Men, Being a Thrilling Narrative of Bloody Wars with Merciless and
         Revengeful Savages, Including a Full Account of the Daring Deed and
         Tragic Death of the World-Renowned Chief, Sitting Bull, with Startling
         Descriptions of Fantastic Ghost Dances; Mysterious Medicine Men;
         Desperate Indian Braves; Scalping of Helpless Settlers; Burning Their
         Homes, Etc., Etc. The Whole Comprising a Fascinating History of the
         Indians from the Discovery of America to the Present Time; Their Man-
         ners, Customs, Modes of Warfare, Legends, Etc.* (Oakland, San Fran-
         cisco and New York: Pacific Press Publishing Co., 1891).

12–13   (Prof. Willie): Curtis J. Sitomer, "Racism and Law: A Vote for Fixing
         What the Founding Fathers Forgot," *Christian Science Monitor,* June
         10, 1987, p. 1.

15   Bryant Rollins, "A New Vision for America," *Boston Globe,* October
         12, 1997, p. D7.

15–16   James Madison, "The Federalist No. 10," November 22, 1787, *The
         Federalist,* ed. Javcob E. Cooke (Middletown, Connecticut: Wesleyan
         University Press, 1961, 1967), pp. 58–59, 64.

17–18   Northeast Public Radio, "Destiny Threads: Adventure in Hand-
         made Home and Personal Fashion." The description of Destiny
         Threads came from the website of WAMC, a Northeast Public
         Radio station in Albany, New York, that includes a section titled
         "Spotlight on Our Underwriters." The spotlight has now moved
         beyond Destiny Threads, but it was to be found at: http://www.
         wamc.org/destiny.html.

Chapter 2: Imagined Diversity

19   Alfred Russel Wallace, *The Malay Archipelago* (1869; New York: Dover Publications, 1962), pp. 340–341.

22   (California test data): Jacques Steinberg, "Increase in Test Scores Counters Dire Forecasts for Bilingual Ban," *New York Times*, August 20, 2000, p. 1.

25–26 Gregory Clay, "Tiger's Love Life Creates Storm," *Sunday Telegraph (Sydney)*, March 31, 2002, p. 67.

26   (Harrison): Solomon Moore, "Milestone for Those of Mixed Race," *Los Angeles Times*, March 16, 2000, p. A1.

27   (Columbus, Ohio): Lornet Turnbull, "Mixed–Race Individuals Identifying Themselves," *Columbus Dispatch*, April 18, 2001, p. A1.

27   ("mood"): Solomon Moore, "Census' Multiracial Option Overturns Traditional Views," *Los Angeles Times*, March 5, 2000, p. A1.

29   (Finding William Harris): Captain James Wilson, cited in T. Walter Herbert Jr., *Marquesan Encounters: Melville and the Meaning of Civilization* (Cambridge: Harvard University Press, 1980), p. 133.

30–31 David Denby, "Jungle Fever," *New Yorker*, November 6, 1995, pp. 118–129.

34   California State University, San Bernardino, "CSUSB Vision for Diversity," *Strategic Plan for Diversity*, http://diversity.csusb.edu/vision.htm.

34–35 University of Michigan, "Preamble," *Understanding the Difference That Diversity Makes: Assessing Diversity and Tolerance Initiatives on College and University Campuses*, 1995, http://www.personal.umich.edu/~nettlesm/dif/pre.html.

35–36 Deborah Burke, "Interview with John Sykes," *Diversity at OSU*, 2002, http://diversity.orst.edu/expressions/interview7_full.html.

36–37 Angel Wilson, "Perspectives on Diversity," *College Prep 101*, Oklahoma State University, http://home.okstate.edu/homepages.nsf/toc/diversity3, updated February 14, 2002.

37   Sarah Gonzales, "Perspectives on Diversity," *College Prep 101*, Oklahoma State University, http://home.okstate.edu/homepages.nsf/toc/diversity2, updated February 14, 2002.

37   (Michigan State): Stephanie A. Casola, "'U' Recognizes Diversity Efforts," Statenews.com, April 4, 1997, http://www.statenews.com/editionsspring97/040497/nw_diversity.html.

38   William A Shack and Elliott P. Skinner, eds., *Strangers in African Societies* (Berkeley: University of California Press, 1979).

38   Igor Kopytoff, ed., *The African Frontier: The Reproduction of Traditional African Societies* (Bloomington: Indiana University Press, 1987).

38   (Chamba): Richard Fardon, *Raiders and Refugees: Trends in Chamba Political Development, 1750 to 1950* (Washington, D.C.: Smithsonian Institution Press, 1988).

41   Clarence Page, "Supply–Side Affirmative Action," *In Showing My Color: Impolite Essays on Race and Identity* (New York: HarperCollins, 1996), p. 217.

42   (Quebec): "List of Constitution Reform Proposals," *Ottawa Citizen*, September 25, 1991, p. A5.

43   Jeffrey Rosen, "Without Merit," *New Republic*, May 14, 2001.

44   (G. Pritchy Smith): Robert Holland, "New Teachers Face NCATE Litmus Test on Diversity: Educators Must Exhibit 'Correct' Attitudes toward Race and Lifestyles," *School Reform News*, January 2002.

44   Jonathan R. Alger, "The Educational Value of Diversity," *Academe: Bulletin of the AAUP*, vol. 83, no. 1 (January–February 1997).

46   (first Mineta quotation): Walter Shapiro, "Afghan 'Nasty Characters' Trigger Vietnam Déjà Vu," *USA Today*, October 5, 2001, p. A9.

46   (second Mineta quotation): Rich Lowry, "Mineta's Folly," *National Review Online*, January 10, 2002.

47   Paul Cunningham, Statement at the 1994 Multicultural Ministries Quadrennial Conference, Nashville First Church of the Nazarene, quoted on: http://www.multiculturalministries.org, June 2002.

48   Wallace, *The Malay Archipelago*, p. 340.

Chapter 3: Diversity Before *Diversity*

49–51   Rev. John George Wood, *The Uncivilized Races or Natural History of Mankind, Being a Complete Account of the Manners and Customs, and the Physical, Social and Religious Condition and Characteristics, of the Uncivilized Races of Men Throughout the Entire World*, 2 vols. (London, 1869; Hartford: American Publishing Co., 1870).

52   Mark Twain, *Roughing It*, edited with an introduction by Hamlin Hill (1872; New York: Penguin Books, 1981, 1985), p. 166.

52   (Goshoots): David Hurst Thames, Lorann S. A. Pendleton and Stephan C. Cappannari, "Western Shoshone," in *Handbook of North American Indian*,. vol 11, *Great Basin*, ed. Warren L. D'Azevedo (1986), pp. 262–283.

55–60   Charles Goodrich, *The Universal Traveller; Designed to Introduce Readers at Home to an Acquaintance with the Arts, Customs, and Manners, of the Principal Modern Nations on the Globe, Embracing a View of Their*

Persons—Character—Employments—Amusements—Religion—Dress—
Habitations—Modes of Warfare—Food—Arts—Agriculture—Manufac-
tures—Superstitions—Government—Literature, &c. &c. Derived from
the Researches of Recent Travellers of Acknowledged Enterprise, Intelli-
gence, and Fidelity and Embodying a Great Amount of Entertaining and
Instructive Information (Hartford: Philemon Canfield, 1838), pp. 229,
482, 469, 476–478, 11.

61 Richard Hakluyt, *Voyages and Discoveries*, edited and abridged by
Jack Beeching (New York: Penguin Books, 1972, 1982).

61 Beeching, "Introduction" to Hakluyt, *Voyages and Discoveries*, p. 25.

61 Samuel Purchas, *Purchas His Pilgrimage, Or Relations of the world and*
the religions obserued in all ages and places discouered, from the creation
vnto this present: Contayning a theologicall and geographicall historie of
Asia, Africa, and America, 4th ed. (London: William Stansby for Hen-
rie Fetherstone, 1626).

61 Francis Bacon, *Bacon's Essays and Colours of Good and Evil*, ed. W.
Aldis Wright (1625; London: MacMillans and Co., 1926).

62 Georgius Candidius, Evert Ysbrant Ides and Sir Thomas Roe, *An*
Entertaining Account of All the Countries of the Known World Describ-
ing the Different Religions, Habits, Tempers, Customs, Traffick, and Man-
ufactures, of Their Inhabitants, 4th ed. (1752).

62 Henry Rowe Schoolcraft, *Algic Researches: North American Indian*
Folktales and Legends (1839; New York: Dover Publications, 1999).

62–63 Henry Rowe Schoolcraft, *Information Respecting the History, Condi-*
tion and Prospects of the Indian Tribes of the United States, 1851–1857.

63 Lewis Henry Morgan, *League of the Ho-De'-No-Sau-Nee, Iroquois*
(Secaucus, New Jersey: The Citadel Press, 1972). The book was first
published in 1851 by Sage & Brother, in Rochester, New York, where
Morgan lived.

63 Henry Wadsworth Longfellow, *The Song of Hiawatha* (New York:
Rand, McNally & Co., 1900). Longfellow first published the poem
in 1855. The quoted lines are from the beginning of chapter 22
(p. 180 in the cited edition).

64 George Catlin, *Letters and Notes on the Manners, Customs, and Condi-*
tions of North American Indians, 2 vols. (1844; New York: Dover Publications, 1973).

64 George Catlin, *O-Kee-Pa: A Religious Ceremony and Other Customs of*
the Mandan, edited with an introduction by John C. Ewers (1867,
1967; Lincoln: University of Nebraska Press, 1976).

64 Charles Pickering in *The Races of Man and Their Geographical Distri-*
bution (New York: Leavitt & Allen, 1850). pp. 226–227.

64   Barry Alan Joyce, *The Shaping of American Ethnography: The Wilkes Exploring Expedition, 1838–1842* (Lincoln: University of Nebraska Press, 2001), p. 22.

66   J. L. Blake, *The World As Exhibited in the Manners, Customs, and Characteristics of All Nation.* (New York: Leavitt & Allen, 1853).

66   John Clark Ridpath, *History of the World. Being an Account of the Ethnic Origin, Primitive Estate, Early Migrations, Social Conditions and Present Promise of the Principal Families of Men, Together with a Preliminary Inquiry on the Time, Place and Manner of the Beginning Comprising the Evolution of Mankind and the Story of All Races; Complete in Four Volumes* (1894; New York: Merrill & Baker Publishers, 1897).

66   R. Talbot Kelly, *Peeps at Many Lands: Burma* (London: Adam and Charles Black, 1908).

66   Charles F. Horne, *The World and Its People or A Comprehensive Tour of All Lands,* 7 vols. (New York: Ira R. Hiller, 1924, 1925).

66   Holland Thompson, ed., *Lands and Peoples: The World in Color,* 30 vols. (New York: The Grolier Society, 1929–1932).

67   Roswell C. Smith, *Smith's Geography: Geography on the Productive System for Schools, Academies, and Families* (New York: Daniel Burgess & Co., 1854).

67   James Greenwood, *Savage Habits and Customs,* Beeton's Boy's Own Library, 3rd ed. (London: S. O. Beeton, 1865), p. 111.

67   Jane Andrews, *The Seven Little Sisters Who Live on the Round Ball That Floats in the Air,* Introduction by Louisa Parsons Hopkins (Boston: Ginn & Co., 1896).

67–68   Milton Hadley, *Little Men and Women; Or Boys and Girls of Many Lands, Containing Full Descriptions of the Children and Youth of France, Norway, Italy, Sicily, India, Africa, Arabia, China, Egypt, Mexico, Canada, Kaffit Tribes, Hawaii, Cuba, Greenland and Other Countries. Little Folks of All Countries with Captivating Accounts of the Manners, Dress, Amusements, Social Customs, Education, Employments, Etc. Etc., Including Charming Stories of the Little Indian Boys and Girls in Our Western States and Territories, Etc.* (Philadelphia: National Publishing Co., 1903), pp. 114, 130.

68   Grace Duffie Boyan and Ike Morgan, *Kids of Many Colors* (Chicago: Jamieson Higgins Co., 1901), p. 5.

68   Robert Louis Stevenson, *A Child's Garden of Verses* (New York: Peter Fenelon Collier, Publisher).

69   J. Glen McSparran, ed., *Uncle Ben in Africa,* 10-Cent Books, Inc. (Columbus, Ohio: The Educational Publishing House, 1933).

69   Martha Fulton Sager, ed., *Uncle Ben in India and Egypt*, 10-Cent
        Books, Inc. (Columbus, Ohio: The Educational Publishing House,
        1933).

72   Jacobus X, *L'Amour aux Colonies: Singularities, Physiologiques et Pas-
        sionnelles* (Paris: Isidorf Liseux, 1893).

72   Jacobus X, *Untrodden Fields of Anthropology: Observations on the Eso-
        teric Manners and Customs of Semi-Civilized Peoples; Being a Record of
        Thirty Years Experience in Asia, Africa, America and Oceania, by a
        French Army-Surgeon*, 2 vols. [bound as one], ed. Charles Carring-
        ton, privately reissued by the American Anthropological Society,
        New York. No date on title page. 1898 or 1900 according to several
        conflicting library catalog records. Translation of *L'Amour aux
        Colonies*. This translation first appeared in 1896, published in Paris.
        Another edition with 21 photographs by A. Vignola appeared in
        1900.

72   Jacobus X, *Crossways of Sex: A Study in Eroto Pathology*, privately
        reissued by the American Anthropological Society, New York. No
        date. Probably a 1930s reprint.

72   (Dr. X): *An Anthropological Tour in Authentic Photographs of Strange
        and Primitive Lands; Their People and Customs, many of which were
        personally investigated by Dr. Jacobus, World Famous French Army
        Surgeon in his Field-studies and Explorations in the Untrodden Fields of
        Anthropology in the Sex Life of the Strange Peoples of Four Continents*
        (New York: Falstaff Press, 1937).

72–73   Anoymous, *The Secret Museum of Mankind* (New York: Manhattan
        House, 1935).

73   Anonymous, *The Secret Museum of Mankind* (Salt Lake City: Gibbs
        Smith, Publisher, 1999). No original publication date, but many
        19th-century photographs. Paper.

77   Elizabeth Hays, "Boaters Fear Curb; Gerritsen Beach Owners Sound
        Off," *Daily News* (New York), February 13, 2002, p. 1.

77   Neera Mehta Miller, Letter to the Editor, *Atlanta Constitution*, March
        20, 2002, p. 2E.

78–79   Warren L. D'Azevedo, "Introduction," *Handbook of North American
        Indians*, vol. 11, *Great Basin* (1986), pp. 2–3.

79–80   Effie M. Mack, *Mark Twain in Nevada* (New York: Charles Scribner's
        Sons, 1947), pp. 49–50, 166–167.

Chapter 4: The Language of Diversity

82–84   The definitions in this section and the examples from Disraeli,
Chaucer, Caxton, Henry Bradshaw, Jehan Palsgrave, John Ray and
the others, except Sir Thomas Browne, are quoted from the *Oxford
English Dictionary*.

Sir Thomas Browne, *Religio Medici,* ed. Robin Robbins (New York:
Oxford University Press, 1972), p. 66.

The word "diversity" or its cognates occurs in a positive sense in
the description of colors and ornaments quite early. The *Oxford
English Dictionary* cites Wyclif (1382): "Forgid of gold, and of siluer
... and dyuerste [1388 dyuersite] of trees," and "The doter of the
King ... in goldene hemmes, aboute wrappid with diuersitees [cir-
cumamicta varietatibus]." In *The Faerie Queene,* Spenser describes
King Arthur's helmet:

Vpon the top of all his loftie crest,
A bunch of haires discolourd diuersly,
With sprincled pearle, and gold full richly drest,
Did shake, and seem'd to daunce for jollity ...

The *Oxford English Dictionary,* again, cites Pope (1731):

A waving Glow the bloomy beds display, Blushing in bright
diversities of day.

But diversity of the physical world was not always positive. In *The
Tempest,* Shakespeare alludes to:

Roring, shreeking ... And mo diuersitie of sounds, all horrible.

84   James R. Mellon, *Nathaniel Hawthorne in His Times* (Boston:
Houghton Mifflin, 1980), pp. 243–244.

84–85   Charles Darwin, *The Origin of Species by Means of Natural Selection or
The Preservation of Favoured Races in the Struggle for Life* (1859; New
York: Avenel Books, 1979), pp. 125–126, 156, 107.

94   Adelle M. Banks, " 'Jabez' Publisher Tells Gay-Friendly Web Site to
Back Off," *Washington Post,* February 2, 2002, p. B9.

95   Robert M. McIntyre and Judith L. Johnson, "Personality and Leadership in Diverse DoD Workgroups and Teams," in *Managing Diversity in the Military: Research Perspectives from the Defense Equal
Opportunity Management Institute,* ed. Mickey R. Dansby, James B.
Sewart and Schuyler C. Webb (New Brunswick: Transaction Publishers, 2001), pp. 97, 98. The reference to K. L. Larkey is to an article,
"Toward a Theory of Communicative Interactions in Culturally
Diverse Work Groups," *Academy of Management Review,* vol. 21
(1996), pp. 462ff.

95 Gary L. Whaley, "Three Levels of Diversity," in *Managing Diversity in the Military*, ed. Dansby et al., p. 63.

97–98 John Hope Franklin et al., *One America in the Twenty-first Century: Forging a New Future*, Report of the President's Advisory Board on Race (Washington, D.C.: U.S. Government Printing Office, September 1998).

Chapter 5: *Bakke* and Beyond

99ff. *Regents of the University of California v. Bakke*, 438 U.S. 265 (1978).

99ff. Howard Ball, *The Bakke Case: Race, Education and Affirmative Action* (Lawrence, Kansas: University Press of Kansas, 2000), pp. 122–124, 114, 127, 130, 125.

103–4 *Allan Bakke v. The Regents of the University of California, Supreme Court of California Decision, September 16, 1976*, 18 Cal. 3d 34 at 39, 44, 52, 61, 66 and 85 (1976).

104–6 The Regents of the University of California, *Petition for a Writ of Certiorari to the Supreme Court of the State of California*, December 14, 1976, in *Landmark Briefs and Arguments of the Supreme Court of the United States: Constitutional Law*, ed. Philip Kurland and Gerhard Casper, 1977 Term Supplement, vol. 99, *Regents of the University of California v. Bakke* (Washington, D.C.: University Publications of America), pp. 3–23.

105 Allan Bakke, *Brief for Respondent in Opposition*, in *Landmark Briefs and Arguments*, ed. Kurland and Casper, pp. 25–62.

106–7 The Regents of the University of California, *Brief for the Petitioner*, in *Landmark Briefs and Arguments*, ed. Kurland and Casper, pp. 97–196. Quotations from pages 122, 135, 140, 141, 142, 160 and 172.

108 Archibald Cox, Oral Argument before the Supreme Court in *Regents of the University of California v. Bakke*, October 12, 1977. My transcription from the audio recording available at: http://oyez.org/cases/cases.cgi?command=show&case_id=324.

109 Gene I. Maeroff, "Carnegie Education Study Bids Universities Be Bold," *New York Times*, October 10, 1973, p. 32.

109 Gene I. Maeroff, "City U Out of-City Hiring Held Biased against Jews," *New York Times*, March 10, 1975, p. 23.

109–10 (Wynne): Bill Peterson, "Sociologist's Study Says That Suburbs Isolate Children from Reality, Diversity," *Washington Post*, November 23, 1977, p. A2.

111 *DeFunis v. Odegaard*, 416 U.S. 312 (1974).

111 *Swann v. Charlotte-Mecklenburg*, 334 F. Supp. 623, at 1227 (1971).

111 *Bradley v. Richmond*, 338 F. Supp. 67 at 117 (1972).

111 *Bradley v. Milliken*, 345 F. Supp. 914 at 919 (1972).

111–12 *Lora et al. v. Board of Education of the City of New York*, 456 F. Supp. 1211 at 1266 (1978).

112 Russell Baker, "Nobody Sues about a Fullback," *New York Times*, October 15, 1977, p. 23.

112 Editorial, "Diversity and the Schools," *Washington Post*, March 13, 1978, p. A20.

112 Michael Knight, "Harvard Admissions Plan Held a Model of Flexibility," *New York Times*, June 29, 1978, p. 23.

113 (Silver Springs): Carol Krucoff, "Montgomery School Integration: Finding Advantages in Diversity," *Washington Post*, September 7, 1978, p. Md 1.

113 "Law School at Penn Abolishes Minority Admissions Committee," *New York Times*, December 17, 1978, p. 52.
   "However, Dr. Phyllis W. Beck, the law school's vice dean, said the law school would continue to seek 'diversity' in its student body and that an applicant's race would continue to be a factor in the admission procedure." Dean Beck explained that the change was intended to make the school's procedures consistent with the standard described in the *Bakke* decision.

113 (Lubicks): "Diversity—and Problems," *Washington Post*, June 13, 1979, p. A1.

115 Lyndon B. Johnson, "To Fulfill These Rights: Commencement Address at Howard University," June 4, 1965, http://score.rims.k12.ca.us/activity/lbj/lbjspeech.html.

116 Nicholas Lemann, "Taking Affirmative Action Apart," *New York Times*, June 11, 1995, section 6, p. 36.

118n Columbia University, Harvard University, Stanford University and the University of Pennsylvania, Brief of *Amici Curiae*, June 7, 1977, in *Landmark Briefs and Arguments*, ed. Kurland and Casper, pp. 689–738.

119n Werner Sollors, Caldwell Titcomb and Thomas A. Underwood, eds., *Blacks at Harvard: A Documentary History of African-American Experience at Harvard and Radcliffe* (New York: New York University Press, 1993).

119n Neil L. Rudenstine, "Student Diversity and Higher Learning," in *Diversity Challenged: Evidence on the Impact of Affirmative Action*, ed. Gary Orfield and Michal Kurlaender (Cambridge, Massachusetts: The Civil Rights Project, Harvard University, Harvard Publishing Group, 2001), pp. 31–48.

122 *Hopwood v. Texas*, 236 F.3d . 256 (5th Cir. 2000).

122   Gary Orfield, "Introduction," in *Landmark Briefs and Arguments*, ed. Gary Orfield and Michal Kurlaender, p. 5.

122   *Grutter v. Bollinger*, 288 F.3d 732 (6th Cir. 2002).

122   *Gratz v. Bollinger*, 122 F. Supp. 2d 811 (E.D. Mich. 2000).

123–25 William G. Bowen and Derek Bok, *The Shape of the River: Long-Term Consequences of Considering Race in College and University Admissions* (Princeton: Princeton University Press, 1998), pp. 253–254. My review, "Delta Blues," *Partisan Review*, vol. 66, no. 3 (1999), answers their central points.

125   Patricia Gurin, "Expert Report of Patricia Gurin," *Gratz et al. v. Bollinger*, No. 97-75321 (E.D. Mich.), copyright: The University of Michigan, 1977–2002.

125f.   See Ball, *The Bakke Case*, pp. 83, 145–206. I am indebted to Ball for much of the factual material in this section, although I strongly disagree with his opinions.

126   Robert Bork, *The Tempting of America: The Political Seduction of the Law* (New York: The Free Press, 1990), p. 106.

     "It makes little sense, or justice, to sacrifice a white or a male who did not inflict discrimination to advance the interests of a black or a female who did not suffer discrimination. No old injustice is undone, but a new injustice is inflicted."

127f.   *Smith v. University of Washington*, 233 F.3d 1188 at 1200 (9th Cir. 2000).

128   *Gratz v. Bollinger*, 122 F. Supp. 2d 811 (E.D. Mich. 2000).

128ff   *Hopwood v. Texas*, 236 F.3d . 256 at 274-275 (5th Cir. 2000).

128   *Johnson v. The University of Georgia*, 263 F.3d at 1245 (11th Cir. 2001).

131   Stuart Taylor Jr., "A Racial Quota That Will Be DOA at the High Court," *National Journal*, May 21, 2002, http://www.theatlantic.com/ politics/nj/taylor2002-05-21.htm.

131–34 *Grutter v. Bollinger*, 288 F.3d 732 at 796-797 (6th Cir. 2002).

135–36 Eugene Volokh. "Diversity, Race as Proxy, and Religion as Proxy," 43 *UCLA Law Review*, 2059 (1996).

137ff.   Two articles describing the effects of diversity-inspired admissions policies on academic standards at the University of Michigan:

     "Color It Wrong: Universities Shouldn't Be in Bias Business," *Columbus Dispatch*, December 18, 2001, p. 14A.

     A University of Minnesota statistician calculated that "a minority applicant's chances of being admitted to Michigan's law school were 234.5 times greater than those of a white student with the same grade point average and law-school admission test scores."

     Stephan Thernstrom, "Alamo in Ann Arbor: A Test Case for Racial Preferences," *National Review*, vol. 51, no. 8 (September 13, 1999).

137–40 Gurin, "Expert Report of Patricia Gurin."

140   Thomas Wood and Malcolm Sherman, *Race and Higher Education: Why Justice Powell's Diversity Rationale for Racial Preferences in Higher Education Must Be Rejected* (Princeton: National Association of Scholars, 2001).

141   (July 2001 survey): Richard Morin, "Misperceptions Cloud Whites' Views of Blacks," *Washington Post*, July 11, 2001, p. A1.

141   Gary Orfield, Michal Kurlaender, eds., *Diversity Challenged: Evidence on the Impact of Affirmative Action* (Cambridge, Massachusetts: The Civil Rights Project, Harvard University, Harvard Publishing Group, 2001).

141   (Civil Rights Project): Mary Leonard, "Diversity Benefits Whites, Project Finds; Research Called 'Long Overdue,'" *Boston Globe*, May 18, 2001, p. A8.

142–43 R. C. Davidson and E. L. Lewis, "Affirmative Action and Other Special Consideration Admissions at the University of California, Davis, School of Medicine," *JAMA: Journal of the American Medical Association*, vol. 278 (1997), pp. 1153–1158.

144–45 The Chavis case is described in more detail by William McGowan in *Coloring the News: How Crusading for Diversity Has Corrupted American Journalism* (San Francisco: Encounter Books. 2001), pp. 1–5.

144–45 Jeff Jacoby, "Affirmative Action Can Sometimes Be Fatal," *Boston Globe*, August 14, 1997, p. A19.

144   Lemann, "Taking Affirmative Action Apart," pp. 36–37.

144–45 Julie Marquis, "Doctor's Possible Suspension Fought," *Los Angeles Times*, June 8, 1997, p. A 3.

144–45 Mark Lasswell, "The Rise and Fall of an Affirmative Action Hero," *Wall Street Journal*, October 13, 1997, p. A 17.

Chapter 6: Diverse Gods

152   Herodotus, *The History*, trans. David Grene (Chicago: University of Chicago Press, 1987), pp. 132, 223–224.

154   Visions Inc. Mission Statement, http://www.visions-inc.com.

155   (Rev. Dan Finn): Chris Berdik, "United State of Boston," *Boston Sunday Globe*, March 10, 2002, pp. CL 1, 6.

156   (Neo-Pagan writer): Letter received by e-mail, September 6, 2001.

156   (Neo-Pagan): Letter received by e-mail, September 7, 2001.

157   Ronald Hutton, *The Triumph of the Moon: A History of Modern Pagan Witchcraft* (New York: Oxford University Press, 1999), p. 206.

157   M. Rose Bohusch, Letter received by e-mail, September 24, 2001.

157–58 Cecylyna Dewr, *You Have a Pagan Student in Your School: A Guide for Educators* (Indianapolis: Pagan Pride Project, 1998).

158   "Nemeton Statement of Beliefs," Boston, December 2001.

158   John C. Mayer, "Dispelling the Nazi Curse on Germanic Paganism," *Connections Journal: Online Journal of Community, Philosophy, and Magick*, Spring 1996, http://connectionsjournal.com/files/archives/highlights/nazicurse.html.

159   (Neo-Pagan): Letter received by e-mail, September 7, 2001.

160   (Church trends): William M. Newman and Peter L. Halvarsen, *Atlas of American Religion: The Denominational Era, 1776–1990* (New York: Alta Mira Press, 2000), p. 49.

160   (Largest churches): Eileen W. Lindner, ed., *Yearbook of American and Canadian Churches*, New York: National Council of Churches (Nashville: Abington Press, 2002).

161   Dean M. Kelley, *Why Conservative Churches Are Growing* (New York: Harper and Row, 1972).

161–62 William Sloan Coffin Jr., *Once to Every Man: A Memoir* (New York: Atheneum, 1978), pp. 335–339.

163   William Sloan Coffin Jr., "Civility, Democracy, and Multicultural-ism," *The Heart Is a Little to the Left: Essays on Public Morality* (Hanover, New Hampshire: Dartmouth College, 1999), p. 69.

164–65 Wade Clark Roof, *A Generation of Seekers: The Spiritual Journeys of the Baby Boom Generation* (New York: HarperCollins, 1993), pp. 244–245.

166   E. Allen Richardson, *Strangers in This Land: Pluralism and the Response to Diversity in the United States* (New York: The Pilgrim Press, 1988), p. 219.

166   Walter H. Consur Jr. and Sumner B. Twiss, eds., *Religious Diversity and American Religious History* (Athens, Georgia: University of Georgia Press, 1997), pp. xiii–xiv, xvi, xvii.

167   Matthew W. Backes, "Lyman Beecher and the Problem of Religious Pluralism in the Early American Republic," *The American Religious Experience*, paper presented at a meeting of the Society for Historians of the Early American Republic, July 2000, http://are.as.wvu.edu/backes.htm.

170   Barry Kosmin and Seymour Lachman, *One National Under God: Religion in Contemporary American Society* (New York: Harmony Books, 1993), pp. 216, 239.

170   (National Council of Churches): Lindner, ed., *Yearbook of American and Canadian Churches*.

170   (Mennonites): Newman and Halvarsen, *Atlas of American Religion*, pp. 49, 50.

171   J. Howard Kauffman and Leo Driedger, *The Mennonite Mosaic: Identity and Modernization* (Scottdale, Pennsylvania: Herald Press, 1991). Data available at http://www.TheARDA.com.

172–73 Thomas Jefferson, "A Bill for Establishing Religious Freedom," *Thomas Jefferson: Writings* (New York: The Library of America, 1984).

Chapter 7: *Diversity* Afflicts the Arts

175   Joe Williams, "Oscars Make History," *St. Louis Post-Dispatch*, March 25, 2002, p. D1.

177   Holland Cotter, "Beyond Multiculturalism, Freedom?" *New York Times*, July 29, 2001, section 2, p. 1.

178   Felix Hoover, "Diversity Fosters Beauty, Gospel Singers Learn," *Columbus Dispatch*, March 1, 2002, p. 1E.

179   Neva Chonin, "The Healing Sound of Music," *San Francisco Chronicle*, December 3, 2001, p. D1.

179   Alex Witchel, "Union Weighs 'Miss Saigon' Casting," *New York Times*, July 25, 1990, p. C12.

179–80 Mervyn Rothstein, "Union Bars White in Asian Role; Broadway May Lose 'Miss Saigon,'" *New York Times*, August 8, 1990, p. A1.

180   (Editorial): "This Is Equity?" *Washington Post*, August 15, 1990, p. A20.

180   (Patterson): Mervyn Rothstein, "Equity Panel Head Criticizes 'Saigon' Producer," *New York Times*, August 16, 1990, p. C15.

180   Stephanie Gutmann and Phil West, "Casting Call Still a Whisper; Hiring: The 'Miss Saigon' Controversy Has Bared the Bitterness among Actors and Actresses of Color over Inequities They See in Film, Theatre and Television Casting," *Los Angeles Times*, August 16, 1990, p. F1.

181   Robin Bartlett, Victor Garber, Craig Lucas, Terrence McNally, Ellen Parker and Larry Kramer, "We Still Need Affirmative Action," *New York Times*, September 2, 1990, section 2, p. 9.

181–82 (Wilson speech): Jack Kroll, "And in This Corner," *Newsweek*, February 17, 1997, p. 54.

182   Robert Brustein, "Subsidized Separatism," *New Republic*, August 19–August 26, 1996, p. 39.

182   Robert Brustein, "On Cultural Power," *New Republic*, March 3, 1997, p. 31.

182   ("Bravo"): "Theater's Fences," *Boston Globe*, January 31, 1997, p. A14.

183   (Wilson): Matt Wolf, "Poet of Broadway," *The Guardian (London)*, January 24, 1996, p. T10.

183 (New York State Council on the Arts report): "Diversity in the Wings," *Wall Street Journal*, March 20, 2002, p. A20.

183 *(Sesame Street):* Elaine Dutka, "Elmo, Big Bird and the Terrorist Attacks," *Los Angeles Times*, January 5, 2002, part 6, p. 2.

183–84 (Heintz-Knowles): Eric Deggans, "Getting Race Right: The Shows," *St. Petersburg Times*, December 27, 2001, p. 1D.

184 ("Nonviolence Project"): Marlys Duran, "Students Paint Their Visions of Nonviolence; Diversity Club behind Littleton High Project," *Rocky Mountain News*, February 8, 2002, p. 32A.

184 Anne Marie Welsh, "From Diversionary, a 'wider range of voices and themes,'" *San Diego Union-Tribune*, March 24, 2002, p. F3.

185 *(Hamartia Blues):* Quoted from Theatre Offensive's website: http://thetheateroffensive.org/now_playing.html. I am grateful to Dr. Keith Whitaker for pointing out this instance.

185 (Hellerer): Brian Meyer, "Adult Club Proposed in Building near Hyatt," *Buffalo News*, March 17, 2002, p. B1.

185 Richard Bernstein, "The Arts Catch Up with a Society in Disarray," *New York Times*, September 2, 1990, section 2, p. 1.

185–86 Cotter, "Beyond Multiculturalism, Freedom?"

187 James Auer, "Talent Not Limited by Race," *Milwaukee Journal Sentinel*, September 12, 2001, p. 2E.

187–88 Glenn McNatt, "School 33 Shows Works from Historically Black Colleges," *Baltimore Sun*, February 12, 2002, p. 8E.

188 Ellen Pfeifer, "Banal PC Blather Passes for Inspiration at Pops," *Boston Herald*, May 6, 1999, p. 64.

189 Peggy Cooper Cafritz, "Culture in Black and White: Why Don't Washington's Arts Institutions Reflect Our Diversity?" *Washington Post*, January 20, 1991, p. B5.

190 (California Arts Council): Zan Dubin, "Why Arts Councils Must Attract Ethnic Minorities," *Los Angeles Times*, October 13, 1989, p. F1.

190 (Seattle): Melinda Bargreen, "Museum, Opera Get Arts Grants," *Seattle Times*, September 27, 2000, p. B3.

190 (American Symphony): Edward Rothstein, "Orchestras Still Preserve the Myths, but Who Cares Now?" *New York Times*, February 10, 2001, p. B9.

191 (Portraits): Helen Dewar. "Senate Takes Step toward Artistic Diversity," *Washington Post*, May 14, 2001, p. A19.

191 (Barron). Robert Polner, "Diversity Is First on His To-Do List," *Newsday*, December 10, 2001, p. A13.

191   (Firefighters' memorial): Greg Freeman, "Objections to Statue
      Reflect Lack of Diversity in NY Fire Department," *St. Louis Post-
      Dispatch*, January 20, 2002, p F3.

192   Jacqueline Hall, "Making Things: Davis Devotes Art to Building
      Tradition, Respect in Young African-Americans," *Columbus Dispatch*,
      December 9, 2001, p. 5F.

193   Eugene L. Meyer, "In Pr. George's, a Happy Diversity Party," *Wash-
      ington Post*, April 24, 1996, p. A1.

194   ("Music America"): Roberta Hershenson, "A Music Tradition That
      Plays On in the Key of D, for Diversity," *New York Times*, December
      30, 2001, section 14WC, p. 8.

194–95 Paul Farhi, "T.V.'s Skin-Deep Take on Race: False Harmony, Not
      Black Shows, Called Problem," *Washington Post*, February 13, 2000,
      p. G1.

197   (Heiner): Stephen Romei, "Protester Defaces Infamous Portrait," *The
      Australian*, December 20, 1999, p. 9.

197   Mike Claffey, "No Jail for Prof in Art Defacing," *Daily News (New
      York)*, November 15, 2000, p. 36.

197f. Vanessa E. Jones, "Two Black Artists Get Their Chance to Define
      Themselves: Critics May Not Approve, but Naturalism Is the Lan-
      guage They've Chosen," *Boston Globe*, June 23, 2002, pp. L1, 6.

197   Natalie Hopkinson, "Art Viewed at Arm's Length; Harlem Exhibit
      Acknowledges Popularity of 'Black Romantics,'" *Washington Post*,
      June 19, 2002, p. C1.

198   Michael Kimmelman, "A Black World of Ins and Outs," *New York
      Times*, April 26, 2002, p. E2.

Chapter 8: Identity Business

201   Hermann Melville, *The Confidence-Man, His Masquerade* (1857; New
      York: Oxford University Press, 1989), pp. 1–2, 8.

202–4 Frederick R. Lynch, *The Diversity Machine: The Drive to Change the
      "White Male Workplace"* (New York: The Free Press, 1997).
            BaFa, Diversophy, pp. 165–169.
            Name Five, xi, xiii.
            Lewis Griggs, 48.
            R. Roosevelt Thomas Jr., 58.
            Lillian Roybal Rose, 66–70.
            Annual National Diversity Conferences, 13, 71–80.
            Los Angeles Sheriff's Department, 204–237.
            California Community College system, 238–273.
            University of Michigan, 274–323.

Reagan White House, 30–32.

Proportional representation, 35.

Destructive course, 325.

203–4 (James Woods): Matthew Brelis and Michael Kranish, "Fighting Terrorism: Impact on U.S.; Hijackers Reportedly Made Trial Air Trips," *Boston Globe*, October 11, 2001, p. A1.

204 Andrew Ferguson, "Chasing Rainbows," *Washington Magazine*, April 1994.

204 *Lynch*, The Diversity Machine, p. 9.

204 ("The study estimates"): Leonard Silk, "Economic Scene: Changes in Labor by the Year 2000," *New York Times*, January 6, 1988, p. D2.

204 Lynch, *The Diversity Machine*, p 60.

204 Arnold Packer, personal communication, March 25, 2002.

206 (*Times* repeated): Alex S. Jones, "Publishers Are Urged to Spur Minority Hiring," *New York Times*, April 27, 1988, p. D20.

207 Robin Pogrebin, "What's New in Women in Business," *New York Times*, August 14, 1988, section 3, p. 11.

207 C. Emily Feistritzer, "Will American Workers Be Ready for the 21st Century?" *Washington Post*, August 7, 1988.

207 "What Boston's Business Leadership Is Saying," *Boston Globe*, December 27, 1988, p. 38.

207 "Demographics Breeding Changes and Challenges," *St. Louis Post-Dispatch*, May 14, 1989, p. 6E.

207 "Caterpillar Wants to Attract Women, Minorities," *St. Louis Post-Dispatch*, November 20, 1989, p. 61.

207 Leslie J. Allen, "Challenge of '90s Demographics of Workforce Facing Dramatic Change," *St. Louis Post-Dispatch*, January 22, 1990, p. 18.

207 Clarence Page, "Fairness, Not Quotas, Is the Relevant Issue," *St. Louis Post-Dispatch*, July 30, 1990, p. 3B.

207 Forrest S. Gossett, "U.S. Employers Facing Boggling Demographics," *Toronto Star*, August 28, 1989, p. B2.

207 Clarence Page, "Progressive Firms Plan for Diverse Work Force," *Toronto Star*, August 7, 1990, p. A13.

207 Paula Todd, "Fighting Job Discrimination, Province Considers Many Options for Promised Employment Equity Law," *Toronto Star*, December 28, 1990, p. A21.

207 "Workplace Diversity," *Seattle Times*, March 20, 1991, p. G1.

208 Sherry Stripling, "Seeing the Light: Seattle City Light Puts Mistakes in the Past as It Strengthens the Diversity of Its Work Force," *Seattle Times*, September 19, 1983, p. L1.

208   (BLS report): Joel Dreyfuss, "Get Ready for the New Work Force," *Fortune,* vol. 121, no. 9 (April 23, 1990), p. 165.

208   Bureau of Labor Statistics, U.S. Department of Labor, "Employed Persons by Occupation, Race, and Sex," p. 175.

208   Bureau of Labor Statistics, U.S. Department of Labor, "Labor Force Status of 2000 High School Graduates and 1999–2000 High School Dropouts by School Enrollment, Sex, Race, and Hispanic Origin, October 2000," April 13, 2001.

210   (CEO survey): Alan Farnham, "Holding Firm on Affirmative Action," *Fortune,* vol. 119, no. 6 (March 13, 1989), pp. 87–88.

210   (Decision in *Griggs v. Duke Power*): *New York Times,* March 9, 1971, p. 1.

211   *(Weber):* Mike Causey, "Women, Minorities Get Weber Case Aid," *Washington Post,* June 29, 1979, p. B2.

211   *(Fullilove)*: Linda Greenhouse, "Congress's Power to Give Benefits Based on Race Is Supported by 6 to 3," *New York Times,* July 3, 1980, p. A1.

211   (Boston police and firefighters): Fred Barbash, "Court Backs Down, Won't Decide Case on Affirmative Action," *Washington Post,* May 17, 1983, p. A2.

211   (Justice White's opinion): "Excerpts from Supreme Court Decision in the Seniority Case," *New York Times,* June 13, 1984, p. B12.

211–12 Aric Press with Ann McDaniel, "A Right Turn on Race?" *Newsweek,* June 25, 1984, p. 29.

212   (Bankers): William A. Carmell and Dale E. Callender, "Supreme Court Didn't Kill Affirmative Action," *ABA Banking Journal,* September 1984, p. 56.

212   (Labor Dept. study): Robert Pear, "Study Says Affirmative Rule Expands Hiring of Minorities," *New York Times,* June 19, 1983), p. 16.

212   Robert A. Pitts, "Diversification Strategies and Organizational Policies of Large Diversified Firms," *Journal of Economics and Business,* vol. 28, no. 3 (Spring-Summer 1976), p. 181.

213   Anonymous, "John Hancock: Competing through Diversity," *Trusts & Estates,* vol. 124, no. 7 (1985), p. 12.

213   "Diversity Helps Risk Managers Move Up," *Business Insurance,* May 9, 1983.

213   Dillard B. Tinsley and Jose Angel Rodriguez, "Mexican American Employees—Stereotypes or Individuals?" *Business and Society,* vol. 20, 21, no. 2, 1 (Winter 1981-Spring 1982), p. 40.

213   Regis McKenna, "Marketing in an Age of Diversity," *Harvard Business Review,* September-October 1988, pp. 88–93.

214   Gretchen Haight, "Managing Diversity (Minorities in the Work-
        force)," *Across the Board* (New York.), vol. 27, no. 3 (March 1990),
        p. 22.

214   "Managing Diversity: Companies Must Be Prepared for a 'Rainbow'
        of Cultures in the Work Force," *Business Journal* (Milwaukee), vol. 7,
        no. 29 (April 30, 1990), p. 12.

215   See Lynch, *The Diversity Machine*, p. 26.

215–16 "Diversity During the Downturn," *U.S. Black Engineer and Informa-
        tion Technology*, vol. 25, no. 4 (January-February 2002), pp. 34–49.

216–21 Business–Higher Education Forum, *Investing in People: Developing
        All of America's Talent on Campus and in the Workplace* (Washington,
        D.C.: American Council on Education, January 2001).

223   (top 10 percent): Jeffrey Selingo, "What States Aren't Saying about
        the 'X-Percent Solution': New college-admissions plans rely on
        segregation and may produce a new set of inequities," *Chronicle of
        Higher Education*, June 2, 2000.

223–24 Jeffrey Selingo, "U. of California's 4-Percent Plan Helps Hispanic
        and Rural Applicants Most," *Chronicle of Higher Education*, May 14,
        2002.

223–24 Larry R. Faulkner, "The 'Top 10 Percent Law' Is Working for Texas,"
        news release from the Office of Public Affairs, University of Texas at
        Austin, October 19, 2000, http://www.utexas.edu/admin/opa/
        news/00newsreleases/nr_200010/nr_10percent001019.html.

224–25 Ron Nissimov, "UT's Leader Offers Bid to Ease Growth," *Houston
        Chronicle*, October 3, 2000, p. A15.

Chapter 9: *Diversity* on Campus

226–27 Connie Barlow, *The Ghosts of Evolution: Nonsensical Fruit, Missing
        Partners, and Other Ecological Anachronisms* (New York: Basic Books,
        2000), pp. 14, 1, 5.

227–28 Edward Tylor, *Researches into the Early History of Mankind*, ed. Paul
        Bohannan (1865; Chicago: University of Chicago Press, 1964), p. 141.

229   "Affirmative Action on the Line: Key Events Affecting Minority
        Enrollment," *Chronicle of Higher Education*, April 28, 1995.

229   Isabel Wilkerson, "Campus Blacks Feel Racism's Nuances," *New
        York Times*, April 17, 1988, p. 1.

229   Luix Overbea, "How Some Universities Are Working to Establish
        Racial Harmony," *Christian Science Monitor*, June 16, 1988, p. 19.

230   "Universities: Racism, Cynicism, Musical Chairs," *The Economist*,
        June 25, 1988, p. 30.

230   Denise K. Magner, "Duke University's Struggle to Recruit Black Scholars," *Chronicle of Higher Education*, March 24, 1993.

230–31 Robin Wilson, "Hiring of Black Professor Stalls at Some Major Universities," *Chronicle of Higher Education*, June 2, 1995.

231   Mary Crystal Cage, "Hispanic Political Leaders in New Mexico Subject Higher Education to New Scrutiny," *Chronicle of Higher Education*, September 13, 1989.

231   Liz McMillen, "Grant Makers Seek to Promote Racial Tolerance," *Chronicle of Higher Education*, February 26, 1992.

232   Elizabeth Greene, "Good-Bye Pythagoras? 'Ethnomathematics' Embraces Non-European Methods of Math; Critics Fear a Decline in Rigor," *Chronicle of Higher Education*, October 6, 2000.

232   Evelyn Hu-DeHart, "The Undermining of Ethnic Studies," *Chronicle of Higher Education*, October 20, 1995.

233   Ben Gose and Jeffrey Selingo, "The SAT's Greatest Test: Social, Legal, and Demographic Forces Threaten to Dethrone the Most Widely Used College-Entrance Exam," *Chronicle of Higher Education*, October 26, 2001.

233   Murial Cohen, "Plans Offered for Minority Student Aid," *Boston Globe*, January 10, 1990, p. 8.

234   "Excerpts from 'Education That Works: An Action Plan for the Education of Minorities,'" *Chronicle of Higher Education*, January 10, 1990.

235–36 Peter Collier, "Something Happened to Me Yesterday," in Peter Collier and David Horowitz, *Destructive Generation: Second Thoughts about the Sixties* (New York: Summit Books, 1990), p. 282. Other writers have also emphasized the origin in the radical Left politics of 1960s of the idea of the university as a microcosm of society. Yale English professor David Bromwich, for example, in commenting on Russell Jacoby's *The Last Intellectuals*, notes, "a single article of faith from the sixties has passed unchallenged into the eighties— namely, the idea that the university is a microcosm of society. That is why what one does at a university will suffice as a complete account of what one does in society." David Bromwich, *Politics by Other Means: Higher Education and Group Thinking* (New Haven: Yale University Press, 1992), p. 119.

237–39 Allan Bloom, *The Closing of the American Mind: How Higher Education Has Failed Democracy and Impoverished the Souls of Today's Students* (New York: Simon & Schuster, 1987).

239   Roger Kimball, *Tenured Radicals: How Politics Has Corrupted Our Higher Education* (New York: Harper & Row, 1990), p. xvi.

239   Alan Charles Kors, "It's Speech, Not Sex, the Deans Ban Now," *Wall Street Journal*, October 12, 1989.

241   Kimball, *Tenured Radicals*, p. 63.

241   Barbara Vobejda, " 'New Orthodoxy' on Campus Assailed," *Washington Post*, November 14, 1988, p. A3.

242   Allan R. Gold, "U. of Vermont Promoting Diversity," *New York Times*, August 31, 1988, p. B8.

242   Robert Marquand, "Berkeley Campus Ponders Ethnic-Issues Proposal," *Christian Science Monitor*, April 22, 1988, p. B4.

242   Philipp Gollner, "Student Groups on Rise at UCLA," *Los Angeles Times*, February 2, 1988, p. 3.

242   Denise K. Magner, "Racial Tensions Continue to Erupt on Campuses Despite Efforts to Promote Cultural Diversity," *Chronicle of Higher Education*, June 6, 1990.

242   Denise K. Magner, "Difficult Questions in Courses That Explore Race Issues," *Chronicle of Higher Education*, March 28, 1990.

243   Courtney Leatherman, "Regional Accrediting Agencies Prod Colleges on Diversity," *Chronicle of Higher Education*, August 15, 1990.

244–45 Ruth Sidel, *Battling Bias: The Struggle for Identity and Community on College Campuses* (New York: Penguin Books, 1994), pp. 203–223.

246–47 Martha C. Nussbaum, *Cultivating Humanity: A Classical Defense of Reform in Liberal Education* (Cambridge: Harvard University Press, 1997).

248–49 James Mooney, *Myths of the Cherokees*, Bureau of American Ethnology, Annual Report 19, 1897–1898, part 1 (1900), pp. 270–271.

250–51 William Claiborne, "Black-White Issue Leaves University Red-Faced; Brochure Photo Altered to Illustrate Diversity," *Washington Post*, September 21, 2000, p. A2.

251   Sharif Durhams, "Answer to UW Photo Scandal Is More Diversity, Students Say," *Milwaukee Journal Sentinel*, October 25, 2000, p. 2B.

251–52 Mark Hixxon and Kirsten Hubbard, "Faces in the Crowd," *UCSD Guardian*, January 22, 2002.

252   (Reading and writing): Sandra Stotsky, *Losing Our Language: How Multicultural Classroom Instruction Is Undermining Our Children's Ability to Read, Write, and Reason* (New York: The Free Press, 1999).

Chapter 10: Consuming *Diversity*

257   *Boston Directory* (Boston: George Adams, 1900).

257   *Polk's Boston (Suffolk County, Massachusetts) Directory* (Boston: R. L. Polk, 1950).

258f.   Kenneth F. Kiple and Kriemhild Coneè Ornelas, eds., *The Cambridge World History of Food*, 2 vols. (New York: Cambridge University Press, 2000).

258   The rankings in cookbook sales are from Alice Payne Hackett and James Henry Burke, *Eighty Years of Best Sellers: 1895–1975* (New York: Bowker, 1977), pp. 47–49. The complete list of the top six best-selling cookbooks is:

> *Better Homes and Gardens Cook Book* (1930): 18,684,976 copies sold
> *Betty Crocker's Cookbook* (1950): 13,000,000
> *The Joy of Cooking* (1931): 8,992,700
> *The Good Housekeeping Cookbook* (1942): 5,250,000
> *The Pocket Cook Book* (1942): 4,900,000
> *The Boston Cooking School Cook Book* (1896): 4,100,000

259–60 Marilyn Halter, *Shopping for Identity: The Marketing of Ethnicity* (New York: Schocken Books, 2000), pp. 7–9, 64–66.

260–62 David Brooks, *Bobos in Paradise: The New Upper Class and How They Got There* (New York: Simon & Schuster, 2000), pp. 61, 237.

262–64 James Trager, *The Food Chronology: A Food Lover's Compendia of Events and Anecdotes from Prehistory to the Present* (New York: Henry Holt & Co., 1995), pp. 364–367, 534–536.

264   Julee Rosso and Shelia Lukins, *The Silver Palate Cookbook* (New York: Workman Publishing, 1982).

264   Shelia Lukins, *All Around the World Cookbook* (New York: Workman Publishing, 1994).

266–67 http://www.imdb.com.

267–68 (Hot Topic): Maureen Tkacik, "Hey Dude, This Sure Isn't the Gap," *Wall Street Journal*, February 12, 2002.

269   (ALTs): http://www.hottopic.com/underground/faqs-underleft.html.

269   Gregory Bateson, *Naven: A Survey of the Problems Suggested by a Composite Picture of the Culture of a New Guinea Tribe Drawn from Three Points of View*, 2nd ed. (1936; Stanford: Stanford University Press, 1958).

Chapter 11: Selective *Diversity*

The quotations in this chapter from the Smith College, Wellesley College and Bryn Mawr College viewbooks were copied from these colleges' web-pages in February 2002.

> Smith College, "Multicultural Affairs,"
> http://www.smith.edu/oma/

Wellesley College, "Multicultural Students,"
> http://www.wellesley.edu/Admission/viewbooks.html.
Bryn Mawr College, "Diversity,"
> http://www.brynmawr.edu/about/diversity.shtml.
Smith College, "Campus Climate: 'Smith Is What You Make It,'"
> http://www.smith.edu/oma/climate.html.

283   Lisa Unico, personal correspondence, March 13, 2002.

283   James M. O'Neill, "How to Get the Girls? That's the Dilemma at the Nation's Women's Colleges, Where the Attributes Are Often Viewed As Shortcomings," *Philadelphia Inquirer,* March 24, 2002, magazine section, pp. 12 16.

The audacious claims made on behalf of single-sex education for women rest on rather shaky empirical studies. A favorite authority for many women's colleges is a study published in 1973 by M. Elizabeth Tidbell, who searched through *Who's Who* and found that graduates of women's colleges were disproportionately numerous. As Wendy Kaminer and other critics have pointed out, Ms. Tidbell ignored all other variables (e.g. family wealth) and her data represented a period before most Ivy League and other elite colleges went co-ed. Tidbell's analysis has been refuted by subsequent work, including that of Faye Crosby. See Wendy Kaminer, "The Trouble with Single-Sex Schools," *Atlantic Monthly,* vol. 281, no. 4 (April 1998), pp. 22–36.

Tidbell, however, is still widely cited. Mayra and David Sadker defend women's colleges as contributing to their students' "positive self-esteem and high academic and career achievement," and emphasize the importance of women "role models and mentors" in such settings. The Sadkers provide a useful list of ten supporting studies—six of them by Tidbell. See Mayra and David Sadker, *Failing at Fairness: How Our Schools Cheat Girls* (New York: Simon & Schuster, 1994), pp. 233, 321–322.

286   Lisa Unico, personal correspondence, March 4, 2002.

287   I found my explanation of the "Crest Jewel of Discrimination" at http://www.advaita-vedanta.org.

Chapter 12: Multitudes

292   John Higham, "Multiculturalism and Universalism: A History and Critique," in *Hanging Together: Unity and Diversity in American Culture,* ed. Carl J. Guarneri (New Haven: Yale University Press, 2001), p. 239.

293   Terry Eastland, "Islamism, Inc." (review of Steven Emerson, *American Jihad: The Terrorists Living Among Us*), *Commentary*, vol. 113, no. 3 (March 2002), p. 78.

293   Stanley Kurtz, "Left Plays Survivor," *NRO*, March 7, 2002, http://www.nationalreview.com/kurtz/kurtz03072.asp.

294   Gregory Rodriguez, "Aftermath: Melting Pot, Identify Yourself," *New York Times*, September 23, 2001, section 4, p. 1.

295   Sam Afridi, *Muslims in America: Identity, Diversity and the Challenge of Understanding*, New York: Carnegie Corporation of New York, November 2001.

295   K. A. Appiah, ed., *Reflections on the Individual, Freedom, Diversity, and Community of Harvard College*, Cambridge, Massachusetts: Harvard College, August 2001.

295   *Defending Civilization: How Our Universities Are Failing America and What Can Be Done About It*, American Council of Trustees and Alumni, November 13, 2001.

295   "Defend Academic Freedom," advertisement, *London Review of Books*, January 24, 2002.

296   Christopher Hitchens, "Comment: Hey, I'm doing my best: President George W. Bush is a year old today. Surprisingly, our low expectations of him have been confounded by his strong leadership, says Christopher Hitchens," *The Observer*, January 20, 2002, p. 25.

296   Christopher Hitchens, "Ha Ha Ha to the Pacifists," *The Guardian (London)*, November 14, 2001, p. 5.

296   Christopher Hitchens, "America at War: The Clash of Two Worlds; American Society Can Outlast or Absorb Practically Anything," *Independent on Sunday (London)*, September 16, 2001, p. 28.

297   David Graham, "A War Like No Other? You Bet!" November 27, 2001, copyright Black Electorate Communications, http://www/blackelectorate.com/articles.asp?ID=492.

297   Elizabeth Cobbs Hoffman, "Nothing Wrong with Teaching What's Right about U.S.," *Los Angeles Times*, December 30, 2001, part M, p. 3.

298–99 Shelby Steele, "Radical Sheik," *Wall Street Journal*, December 10, 2001.

299   Jeff Jacoby, "American Taliban: Blame Lindh's Permissive Parents," *Boston Globe*, December 13, 2001. p. A19.

300   Andrew Sullivan, "Parallel Lives," *Sunday Times (London)*, December 16, 2001.

300   ("a very sweet person"): Ricardo Alonso-Zaldivar and John M. Glionna, "American Taliban Took Odd Route," *Los Angles Times*, December 4, 2001, part A, p. 1.

300   (Frank Lindh addresses John Spann): Damon Johnston, "Family Feud over Taliban Fighter," *Courier Mail*, February 15, 2002, p. 11.

300   "Bush Gets Himself in Hot Water in California," *Houston Chronicle*, February 28, 2002, p. A2.

301   (Bush's hot tub remark): Julie Dunn, "Getting Himself out of Hot Water," *New York Times*, March 3, 2002, section 3, p. 5.

301   Linda Hirshman, "Selective Blame Game Played by Conservatives," *Boston Globe*, December 27, 2001, p. A15.

302   (Lindh's parents' divorce): Rene Sanchez, "John Walker's Restless Quest Is Strange Odyssey," *Washington Post*, January 14, 2002, p. A1.

305   The earliest reference I have found to Lindh as "Caliban" is: Stephen Schwartz, "Innocent of Treason; Everything You've Heard about 'Tokyo Rose' Is Wrong," *Weekly Standard*, January 14, 2002, p. 9. But Schwartz uses the term in quotation marks and in a manner suggesting that he expects his readers to be familiar with it already.

305   Stephen J. Greenblatt, "Learning to Curse: Aspects of Linguistic Colonialism in the Sixteenth Century," in *First Images of America: The Impact of the New World on the Old*, ed. Fredi Chiappelli, Michael J. B. Allen, Robert I. Benson and Robert S. Lopez. (Berkeley: University of California Press, 1976), p. 957.

INDEX